The Inequality
of Pay

The Inequality of Pay

BY
HENRY PHELPS BROWN

UNIVERSITY OF CALIFORNIA PRESS
1977

Published in the United States by
University of California Press
Berkeley and Los Angeles

© Oxford University Press 1977

ISBN 0–520–03380–9
Library of Congress Catalog Card Number: 76–50253

Printed in Great Britain by The Pitman Press, Bath

To

EVELYN

whose compassionate understanding of
the 'under 5s' and unceasing work
for them is helping to remove a major
source of needless inequality

Preface

This work has received invaluable stimulus and support from two foundations. In the United Kingdom, the Nuffield Foundation made me a grant that provided me with essential research assistance. I am grateful to Nuffield College, Oxford, for undertaking the administration of this grant. In the United States, the University of California at Berkeley, in honouring me with an invitation to deliver its Hitchcock Lectures in 1974, led me to develop for the first time as a connected argument the thoughts that have since been expanded into the present book. My visit to Berkeley, moreover, enabled me to strengthen my association with the Director of its Institute of Industrial Relations, Lloyd Ulman, and to draw upon his wide knowledge of the world of labour and lively insights into its workings.

It was my good fortune to engage as my research associate Imogen (Lisa) King, whose imaginative yet rigorous mind, eye for essentials, and lively interest in the issues we discussed made our collaboration highly productive: the handling of sociological and psychological materials in Chapters 4, 6, and 7 benefited from it in particular.

Especially also am I grateful to those who gave freely of their time to read my script in part or whole, and comment upon it with a care that has enabled me to improve it at many points—Jan Adam, Anthony Heath, Richard Layard, James Meade, Jim Pemberton, and Paul Taubman—to all of whom I pay tribute while absolving them of all responsibility for any remaining errors.

In a wide-ranging inquiry the guidance of specialists is indispensable. It has been given to me with a helpfulness that makes my present acknowledgement quite inadequate, but I ask the reader who finds interest in the materials of this book to bear in mind the scholars who have contributed to them. I also beg those scholars themselves to forgive a merely summary statement as I now record my indebtedness to Jan Adam, W. Brus, and J. M. Nichol, for data and discussion concerning the Soviet-type economies; Phoebe Allen of the Oxford University Press, for many corrections and helpful suggestions; John Bowlby, for guidance in ethology; Janet Chapman, for her analysis of the Russian pay structure; John Creedy, for his studies of lifetime earnings; Pieter de Wolff, for his analysis of the variance of individual earnings; H. M. Douty, for guidance in the statistics of the U.S. labour market, and discussion of its workings; John Goldthorpe and Keith Hope, for patient explanation of their scale of social standing and the method of their inquiry into social mobility; Emile Primorac, for Yugoslav data; R. J. H. Russell, for critique of the Weber–Fechner law; J. E. Shatil and Zvi Sussman, for information about the Kibbutzim and egalitarianism in Israel; and A. R. Thatcher, for discussion of the form of the distribution of earnings. I also remember gratefully the work of Gloria Clark in a research assistantship that circumstances terminated all too soon.

Throughout the five years and more during which this work has been in the making, Rita Leimer as my secretary has advanced it with unfailing helpfulness.

As I think of all I owe to these I have named, and more besides, I take comfort in Milton's thought, albeit he puts it in the mouth of Satan—

> that a grateful mind
> By owing owes not, but still pays, at once
> Indebted and discharged.

Contents

List of Figures   xiii

List of Tables   xiv

1. THE PROBLEM
   1.1. The growth of interest in the inequality of pay   1
   1.2. The economist's approach to pay determination   10
   1.3. The sociologist's approach to pay determination   17
   1.4. The practical issue   21
   1.5. The plan of this work   25

2. A SURVEY OF THE PAY STRUCTURE BY OCCUPATION
   2.1. Grouping by occupation   28
   2.2. The comparability of figures of pay by occupation   29
   2.3. A conspectus of the pay structure by occupation in Western countries   31
   2.4. The pay structure by occupation in the Soviet-type economies   38
   2.5. Material and moral incentives in China and Cuba   51
   2.6. Egalitarianism in Israel   54
   2.7. Yugoslavia: a special case   56
   2.8. The relative pay of particular occupations   58
   2.9. Review and discussion   65

3. THE COURSE OF CHANGE IN THE PAY STRUCTURE
   3.1. Changes in the differential for manual skill   68
   3.2. Changes in the relations between the pay for white-collar and for manual occupations   81
   3.3. Changes in the relative pay of occupations linked with particular industries   89
   3.4. The influence of trade unions on occupational differentials   94
   3.5. Review and discussion   98

4. PAY STRUCTURE AND STATUS
   4.1. The ordering of occupations by average earnings   101
   4.2. The ordering of occupations by status   104
   4.3. Pay differentials and the scale of status   107
   4.4 The nature of status   111
   4.5. Station in life as a basis of assigned income   118
   4.6. Is status prior to pay?   122
   4.7. Evidence for status moulding pay in modern societies   128

4.8.   The influence of custom   134
4.9.   Divergences between the rank orders of status and pay
       4.9.1.   Instances of pay and status offsetting one another   136
       4.9.2.   Stratification by status differing from ranking by pay   137
4.10. Review and discussion   141

5. DISCRIMINATION
   5.1. Forms of discrimination   145
   5.2. Discrimination against women
         5.2.1.   Discrimination against women before the market   148
         5.2.2.   Discrimination against women within the market   153
   5.3. Discrimination against minorities   160
         5.3.1.   Discrimination against blacks before the market   160
         5.3.2.   Discrimination against blacks within the market   166
   5.4. The effects of raising minimum wages, as a test for the presence
         of discrimination   174
   5.5. Review and discussion   177

6. SOCIAL CLASS AND INTERGENERATIONAL MOBILITY
   6.1. The assignment of occupations to social classes   181
   6.2. Intergenerational mobility between occupations   185
   6.3. Changes in intergenerational mobility over time   198
   6.4. The extent of intergenerational movement into and out of the top
         grade   199
   6.5. Review and discussion   206

7. SOCIAL CLASS, MENTAL ABILITY, AND EDUCATION
   7.1. The association between occupation and I.Q.   208
   7.2. Evidence for the genetic determination of I.Q. potential   214
   7.3. The effects of differences between classes in the upbringing of children
         on the development of I.Q.   220
   7.4. The relation between parents' class and their children's I.Q.   223
   7.5. Class differences in the use made of education   229
   7.6. Class differences in extent of education   232
   7.7. Education as investment: human capital theory   236
   7.8. Entry into employment   245
   7.9. Review and discussion   251

8. DIFFERENCES OF INDIVIDUAL EARNINGS
   WITHIN AN OCCUPATION
   8.1. The extent of the variance of earnings within particular occupations   256
   8.2. Short-period fluctuations of earnings   260
   8.3. The variation of earnings with age   263
   8.4. Differences in individual performance   269
   8.5. Differences within local labour markets   272
   8.6. Differences of region and of unionization   276
   8.7. Review and discussion   283

9. THE DISTRIBUTION OF INDIVIDUAL EARNINGS
   9.1. The form of the distribution of individual earnings   285
   9.2. Processes by which distributions are formed   290
   9.3. An index of ability to work   294
   9.4. The generation of the distribution of ability to work by factors imping-
       ing in successive stages of personal development   298
   9.5. The link between ATW and pay   306
   9.6. The influence of particular factors upon individual earnings 310
   9.7. Review and discussion   317

10. CONCLUSIONS CONCERNING THE SOURCES AND
   THE MALLEABILITY OF THE INEQUALITY OF PAY
   10.1. The sources of the inequality of pay   322
   10.2. The possibilities of reducing the inequality pay   328

   References   333

   General Index   349

   Index of Authors   357

List of Figures

2.1 The relation between pay differentials and university enrolment in different countries   37

2.2 Earnings of 28 occupations, relative to unweighted average of all, in Yugoslavia 1969 and Great Britain 1970   58

3.1 Wages of building craftsman and labourer in Southern England, 1264–1954   68

3.2 Ratio of skilled to unskilled wage rate in six countries, 1900–60   74

3.3 Occupational differentials at the McCormick Works, Chicago, 1858–1959   75

3.4 Great Britain, 1780–1938, wages of certain occupations linked with particular industries   90

3.5 Changes in Dutch inter-industrial wage structure   93

4.1 Weekly earnings in Great Britain, 1970   102

4.2 British weekly earnings in occupational groups   103

4.3 The relation between status and relative pay   108

5.1 Median earnings by level of qualification and sex in England and Wales, 1966–67   149

6.1 Indexes of affinity in England and Wales, 1949   187

6.2 Indexes of affinity in U.S.A. 1962   191

6.3 Indexes of affinity for daughters in France 1964   192

7.1 Test scores by occupation   210

7.2 Parent's occupation and child's test score   223

7.3 Scores in intelligence tests by children of different social class   225

8.1 Distribution of earnings within occupations   257

8.2 Changes between April 1970 and April 1971 in earnings of a matched sample of British employees   261

8.3 Annual earnings of French employees at different ages   263

8.4 Age–earnings profiles   264

8.5 Cross-sections and cohorts   265

8.6 Age–earnings profiles for different educational qualifications   268

8.7 Age–earnings profiles in various professions   268

8.8 Variance of professional earnings by age   270

8.9 Variance of individual earnings within occupations   272

8.10 Inter-regional differences of earnings in different industries in U.S.A.   278

8.11 Effect of differences in unionization   282

9.1 Distribution of wage-earnings on normal and logarithmic scales   286

9.2 Paretan tail of earnings distribution in U.K.   287

9.3 Distribution of earnings of groups of employees   288

9.4 The generation of a normal distribution   291

9.5   The generation of a skew distribution   292
9.6   A type of 5-stage generation of distributions of ATW   301
9.7   Generation of distribution of ATW when value of index is changed proportionally
      stage by stage   302
9.8   Generation of distribution of ATW when value of index is changed proportionally
      stage by stage, and changes at successive stages are positively correlated   304

List of Tables

1.1   The social and economic structure of England in 1688   2
2.1   The structure of earnings in European economies and U.S.A.   32
2.2   Salary structures in pairs of French and German firms   33
2.3   Salary for a post of given managerial responsibility as a ratio to product per head 36
2.4   Relative professional earnings, in Europe and N. America   38
2.5   Comparison of pay structures in Hungary and Great Britain   39
2.6   Comparison of pay structures in engineering in Leningrad and in Great Britain   40
2.7   The pay structure of engineering in Soviet-type economies and in Great Britain   41
2.8   Non-manual earnings relative to manual in Soviet-type economies and Great
      Britain   42
2.9   Relative white-collar pay in different industries in U.S.S.R.   42
2.10 Relative wage-earnings by industry in U.S.S.R.   43
2.11 Wage differentials in steel plants in U.S.S.R. and in some Western countries   45
2.12 Relative earnings of occupations in Czechoslovakia   47
2.13 Range of pay within Chinese enterprises   52
2.14 Relative pay of certain occupations in Yugoslavia 1969 and Great Britain 1970   57
2.15 Relative earnings of professions, in five countries   59
2.16 Comparison of white-collar salary structures in U.S.A. and Great Britain   60
2.17 Rank order of wages of manual workers in different countries   61
2.18 Variation of rank order of fitter's pay from country to country   62
2.19 The margin for skill among manual workers   63
2.20 Relative earnings of coal-miners, in different countries   64
3.1   The differential for manual skill, 1860–1910   71
3.2   The differential for manual skill, 1900–1961   73
3.3   The pay structure of the British Civil Service, 1876–1950   82
3.4   Relative earnings of professions in the twentieth century   84
3.5   Salaries relative to wages in the U.S.A., 1890–1952   85
3.6   Salaries relative to wages in Great Britain, 1913–1960   85
3.7   Relative levels of wages in some British industries since 1780   90
3.8   The raising of wages by trade unionism in the U.S.A.   95

4.1 'Social groups' and earnings in Russian industry 104

4.2 Ranking of occupations by status in Warsaw and in England and Wales 106

4.3 Job attributes that indicate status 113

5.1 Cost of schooling and training for non-white and for all males in U.S.A. 163

5.2 Earnings and representation of non-whites in various groups of occupations in U.S.A. 164

5.3 Analysis of difference in pay between black and white workers in U.S.A. 168

6.1 Index of affinity—numerical example of intergenerational mobility 182

6.2 Index of affinity—calculation of indexes from numerical example 183

6.3 Indexes of cohesion formed from numerical example 184

6.4 Indexes of affinity in England and Wales 1949 188

6.5 Length of stay of a family line in a status category 189

6.6 Occupations in U.S. study of intergenerational mobility 190

6.7 Indexes of affinity in U.S.S.R. 193

6.8 International comparison of intergenerational mobility 194

6.9 International comparison of adjusted intergenerational mobility 198

6.10 International comparison of intergenerational mobility into the élite 200

6.11 Comparative mobility into élite, by father's grade 201

6.12 Comparative intergenerational mobility into upper non-manual occupations 202

6.13 Socio-economic origins of French men and women in high-grade occupations 204

6.14 Socio-economic origins of British managers 205

7.1 Test scores of entrants to U.S. and U.K. armed forces 209

7.2 Distribution of mental ability by occupation 211

7.3 Correlation between characteristics of twins 215

7.4 Correlations between the test scores of unrelated and related persons 217

7.5 Environment and I.Q. of identical twins 219

7.6 Child's I.Q. and family income 224

7.7 The intergenerational transmission of genotype I.Q. 227

7.8 Father's occupation and extent of child's education 234

7.9 Extent of education and lifetime earnings 235

7.10 Private and social rates of return on extensions of education 237

7.11 Lifetime earnings offered by different extents of education and different occupations 240

7.12 Effect of greater education of the labour force on jobs obtained 244

7.13 Training for entrants to employment 251

8.1 Dispersion of earnings within an occupation in U.S.A. and G.B. 258

8.2 Regional differences in wage rates in U.S.A. 278

8.3 Regional differences in wages in G.B., 1886 and 1967 280

9.1 Distribution of earnings of male manual workers in Great Britain from 1886 319

1

The Problem

1.1. The growth of interest in the inequality of pay

In the agelong outcry against the contrast of poverty and riches, the rich man used to be seen as essentially the man of property. High incomes came from great possessions. The landowners stood over against the landless labouring people. As time went on, the forms of property that yielded income came ever more conspicuously to include commercial and industrial capital, but in the mind's eye of the social analyst, reformer and revolutionary alike, labour remained undifferentiated. Only in more recent years has attention begun to be directed to differences in the earnings of different kinds of labour as a major source of inequalities of income.

The traditional perception of society was natural in eras when most high incomes were drawn from landed estates, and the lawyers and merchants who gained high incomes by their own activity were relatively few, and likely in any case to put their money into land. In 1696 Gregory King drew up his *Natural and Political observations and Conclusions upon the State and Conditions of England* (Chalmers 1801; Clark 1937, c. X), in which he tabulated the economic and social structure of the England of his day. Some elements of his table, arranged under anachronistic subheadings drawn from the usage of our own times, are set out in Table 1.1. What stands out here is the broad division and contrast between the landed families and the mass of the labourers. The families who did not own or get their living on the land made up less than half of all families. It is true that some of them like the merchants and lawyers were earning relatively high incomes, but they would have been seen as mingling with the landed families. The artisans and craftsmen who were credited with some $2\frac{1}{2}$ times the labourers' earnings were relatively few in number. It was the labourers—a third of all families—who made up the great bulk of the population, over against the men of property. They formed a body undifferentiated in the extent of the contrast between their incomes and those of the propertied families; and close beside them, almost as numerous and with even lower money incomes, were the cottagers. So the scene set for a study of the distribution of the product was one in which the share of labour was remitted as wages to a body of labourers among whom differences between one man and another were so relatively small that they could be disregarded.

This disregard was at once qualified and supported by the ready adoption of a convention that took the extent of one man's earnings in excess of another's as the measure of how far an hour of his work contained more of the common stuff of labour than did an hour of the other's. Adam Smith was keenly interested in differences of earnings, and made some shrewd observations about

Table 1.1
The Social and Economic Structure of England in 1688

Elements drawn from Gregory King's 'Scheme of the income and expense, of the several families of England calculated for the year 1688', grouped under modern subheadings.

	No. of families	Annual income per family
Living on the land		£s
Temporal and spiritual Lords	186	2,600
Baronets and Knights	1,400	780
Esquires and Gentlemen	15,000	314
Freeholder	180,000	66
Farmers	150,000	44
Cottagers and paupers	400,000	6·5
	746,586	
Self-employed		
Merchants and traders	10,000	240
Persons in the law	10,000	140
Persons in sciences and liberal arts	16,000	60
Shopkeepers and tradesmen	40,000	45
Artisans and handicrafts	60,000	40
	136,000	
Salaried		
Persons in offices	10,000	180
Clergymen	10,000	48
	20,000	
Wage-earners		
Common seamen, common soldiers, labouring people and out-servants	449,000	15·5
Total number of families	1,361,000	

Source: Clark (1937), c.x.

their causes. But he also held in effect that in arriving at the payments to be made for different kinds of labour the market reduced them to different quantities of a common stuff.

There may be more labour in an hour's hard work than in two hours' easy business; or in an hour's application to a trade which it cost ten years' labour to learn, than in a month's industry at an ordinary and obvious employment. But it is not easy to find any accurate measure either of hardship or ingenuity. In exchanging indeed the different productions of different sorts of labour for one another, some allowance is commonly made for both, it is adjusted, however, not by any accurate measure, but by the higgling and the bargaining of the market, according to that sort of rough equality which, though not exact, is yet sufficient for carrying on the business of common life. (1776, Bk. I, c. v.)

This way of reducing differences of quality to those of quantity is arbitrary—it begs the question of whether there is in fact any common stuff of labour to be measured; but it commended itself to the economists who followed Smith in applying the labour theory of value to the distribution of income—especially, for our present purpose, Ricardo and Marx. Ricardo virtually repeated Smith's words. Marx (1930, p. 13) defined the common stuff as 'simple labour power, such as, on the average, the ordinary man, without any special development of faculty, is equipped with in his bodily organism. ... Skilled labour counts only as intensified, or rather multiplied, simple labour, so that a smaller quantity of skilled labour is equal to a larger quantity of simple labour'. So it came about that those who perceived inequalities of income through Ricardian and Marxian spectacles saw the community as made up of three classes, described by Ricardo in the Preface to his *Principles* (1817)—'the proprietor of the land, the owner of the stock or capital necessary for its cultivation, and the labourers by whose industry it is cultivated'. The inequalities that mattered were those that arose out of the division of the national product between land and capital on the one hand, and labour on the other. Inequalities between one worker and another escaped attention.

It followed that the egalitarian drive in socialism was directed against wealth, against private property in land and capital, and not against high salaries or high earnings of the self-employed. The consummation of Marxian and other forms of revolutionary socialism was the expropriation of the capitalists, that of evolutionary or democratic socialism the nationalization of the means of production, distribution, and exchange. But when the inequalities of income arising from property had been swept away, what would be done about those that arose from work? Extraordinarily little seems to have been thought or said about that. Marx's precept for pay under socialism was that it should be proportionate to the quality and quantity of the work performed. This precept is followed in the Soviet-type economies today, and (as we shall see) means in practice paying according to much the same considerations as govern the pay for jobs involving different degrees of skill, experience, and responsibility in the Western economies, even if the differentials are not always the same as in the West. Perhaps most democratic socialists have shared Tawney's view that when much greater equality of opportunity had been achieved by abolishing privileges of wealth and extending the social services, especially education, the remaining inequalities would be not only much smaller but much more acceptable.

'The career open to talent', which today is a sham, would become a reality [he wrote in his widely influential *Equality* (1938, p. 185)]. ... While diversities of income, corresponding to varieties of function and capacity, would survive, they would neither be heightened by capricious inequalities of circumstances and opportunity, nor perpetuated from generation to generation by the institution of inheritance. Differences of remuneration between different individuals might remain; contrasts between the civilization of different classes would vanish.

That in recent years these 'differences of remuneration between different individuals' have attracted much more attention may be attributed to a number of developments.

(i) One is that income from property has increased much less in the aggregate than has income from work: its share in the national product has fallen. This has come about in a number of western countries in the course of economic growth. In a wide survey, with particular reference to the recorded distribution of the national income in Canada, France, Germany, Switzerland, the U.K., and the U.S.A., Kuznets (1966, p. 218) has observed that

the proportion of property income in national income (excluding the equity of individual entrepreneurs), which ranged between 20 and 40 per cent in the mid-nineteenth century, has, after a long period of stability or slight rise, declined—in some countries beginning with the post-World War I period, in others beginning with World War II—and is now at or below 20 per cent. Even more clearly discernible is the decline in the share of income from capital, including that on equity of individual entrepreneurs, from almost a half to about 20 per cent—although the allocation of the income of entrepreneurs between service and property components has many elements of arbitrariness.

In part, this decline in the share of property income may be attributed to the form that technical advances have taken: on balance they may have economized in capital, in that they have enabled a given contribution to output to be made by equipment the construction of which absorbs less current resources than did the equipment it supersedes (Phelps Brown & Browne 1968, pp. 283–6). Thus the equipment of a modern mechanized farm is conspicuous, but the amount of such equipment used to help produce a given output may well represent a smaller capital at the values of the day than the horses and wagons did that it supersedes. Evidently, in so far as less capital is used to produce a given output, the return to capital will absorb a smaller part of the product, and the share of labour will rise. Quite apart from capital-saving changes in the form of the equipment, the amount of capital used per unit of output is reduced when a given equipment is operated by two or more shifts in the day. It is probably also reduced by the general contraction of self-employment that was noted by Kuznets in the passage just quoted: the 'individual entrepreneurs' of whom he speaks were typically artisans each working with his own equipment, and their supersession by manufacture on the larger scale would have economized in the use of equipment by eliminating duplication.

But these possibilities apart, a general rise in the share of labour income would still have been expected because of the increased personal productivity of the labour force. Men and women are healthier, better educated, and more highly trained than they used to be. Over a certain range, at least, a rise in the standard of living 'feeds back' to raise the capability of the workers who have the benefit of it. Later in this book (Sec. 7.7) we shall discuss the concept of 'human capital', by which the embodying of education and training in a human being is treated as being like the construction of a machine. The users of this concept might say that the last hundred years have seen a great extension of human capital relatively to physical capital, and ascribe to this shift in the form and *situs* of capital much of what appears as a rise in the share of labour incomes.

(ii) At the same time, in the U.K. at least, the ownership of property has ceased to be concentrated in the hands of distinct and conspicuous groups of wealthy landowners, industrialists, and financiers, though there are still some of each. About 45 per cent of the total net wealth of persons consists of houses, household equipment, and cars, the ownership of which is spread fairly widely. Land accounts for only 8 per cent. The remainder takes a financial form—stocks and shares, deposits with savings banks and building societies, life insurance. Of the shares in U.K. companies, a little more than half are held by persons, directly or through investment trusts; more than a quarter are held by insurance companies and pension funds. The dividends accrue in much the same way—rather more than half to persons, rather more than a third to the members of occupational pension schemes and the holders of life assurance policies. Almost half the recipients of dividends had incomes of less than £2,000 in 1972–73, when the median income was £1,700; 57·5 per cent of all dividends went to pensioners and aged persons at all levels of income. Of all personal wealth in 1960, some 42 per cent is estimated to have been owned by women. (Royal Commission 1975a, Tables 10, 33, 42; Royal Commission 1975b, Table 10, paras 70, 83, 88, 313.) The extension of state and occupational pension schemes has diffused what may be regarded as a form of property even though it is not transferable: the accrued value of pension rights has been reckoned to amount to as much as three-quarters of the value of all transferable personal assets (Royal Commission 1975a, Table 37).

(iii) While in these ways the relative significance of property incomes has diminished, earned incomes, and in particular the spread between the higher earnings and the lower, have come to figure more prominently. One reason for this is the diversification of occupations, and the expansion in the relative numbers in the generally more highly paid white-collar occupations. In Great Britain the professions, management, and administration together contained less than 7½ per cent of the whole working population in 1911, but more than 12 per cent in 1951; meanwhile the proportion of clerical workers—though by no means all of these were still earning more than manual workers—had more than doubled (Routh 1965, Table I). These developments again represent a pattern of change common to many countries in the course of economic growth: the more advanced the stage of development, the greater the proportion of the labour force in white-collar occupations. In the U.K. by 1973 income from employment was amounting to nearly 70 per cent of all personal income; income from self-employment made up another 10 per cent, and so did receipts from national insurance and other cash benefits; only 10 per cent of all personal income came from rent, dividends, and interest (Royal Commission 1975a, Table 9). The very biggest incomes were still derived mainly from property, but it can be estimated that more than a third of the top 10 per cent of all incomes were incomes from employment.[1] In addition, there were some high incomes from self-employment.

It is possible to make an estimate of how far the inequality of incomes in the aggregate would be reduced if everyone had the same income from property, and how far if all labour incomes were the same. Pen (1971, p. 64) cites an estimate that in the Netherlands in the 1950s one-quarter of the variance of incomes was attributable to inequalities of property-holding, and three-quarters to inequalities of earnings.

That high earnings have thus come to bulk large relatively to property incomes, provides the setting for the observation sometimes made that recent years have seen a transition on the political left from socialism to egalitarianism. The attention of socialism is focused upon the ownership of wealth, and its policy is directed towards collectivizing or diffusing that ownership. Egalitarianism is concerned with *all* inequalities of income, and its policy is directed towards reducing those inequalities no less when the incomes are derived from work than when they derive from property.

(iv) At the same time, political attitudes apart, the question of what the rate of pay for this or that job ought to be has become at once a more open and a more insistent one. It used not to be raised so much because there seemed no point in raising it: wages were what they were in the nature of things, or by reason of impersonal and ineluctable forces. In Great Britain, at least, down to 1914, differentials were largely ruled by custom, while the movements of particular groups of rates up or down was largely governed by the state of the market. A conspicuous instance of the stability of differentials has been traced in the building trade: from about 1410 until 1914 one and the same differential between the craftsman and the labourer persisted in the south of England. 'In the fifteenth century the craftsman got half as much again as the labourer, 6d. a day to his 4d; in the 1890's he got half as much again, 7½d. an hour to his 5d.; he got half as much again, or within a halfpenny of it, in every settled period in between' (Phelps Brown & Hopkins 1955). What has obtained from time immemorial carries the authority of the generations by which it has been accepted: so many people would not have accepted it for so long if it had not been right and proper. Even where the market fluctuated, and rates in particular trades and regions moved up and down from time to time, there was still an understanding that these were only variations about long-term norms of relativity. Looking back over British wage bargaining on the eve of the First World War, Clay (1929, pp. 12–13) observed that

the parties to the negotiations never had to face the problem as it presents itself to analytical study; all they had to do was to make slight modifications and adjustments in a system of rates and conditions, which was generally accepted . . . If we seek an explanation of these

---

[1] In 1972/73 the top 1 per cent of all personal incomes (including income from all sources) numbered about 200,000 and lay above £7,233 per annum (Royal Commission 1975a, Table 10). From the Survey of Personal incomes (Board of Inland Revenue 1975) it has been estimated that about 62,000 incomes from employment were above £8,000; the number above £7,233 may have exceeded this by some 20,000.

wage standards, we can find it only by a historical investigation; but, however and whenever established, they were stable compared with the prices of commodities, they tended to move together and to preserve stable ratios between them and they may fairly be said to have constituted a system.

Indeed, collective bargaining as it arose in the nineteenth century, though in one sense its purpose and effect were 'to take wages out of competition', did not purport to override the forces of the market. The gains made in the rising phase of the trade cycle, and the cuts accepted in the falling phase, were alike governed by what contemporaries called 'commercial considerations' – aptly so, for the coercive factor was the price the employer was getting for the product, and this was recognized as being generally beyond his own power to control. Alfred Marshall, a singularly well-informed and perceptive observer of the performance of British trade unions down to 1890, held 'that the direct influence of Unions on wages is small relatively to the great economic forces of the age'; his assessment of that influence came down to little more than a justification of the unions' claim that they could 'make economic friction act for the workman instead of against him' (1892, VI. xiii. 5, 18).

But with the First World War came changes of a kind that would break up the rule of custom and that of market forces alike. The doubling of money wages in five years carried men away from old landmarks, especially in so far as the rise in the general level was brought about by flat-rate cost-of-living allowances that narrowed differentials. At the same time wages were under effective regulation by a governmental agency which promoted the extension of collective bargaining as a means of regulation; and this showed that wages were not always and inevitably governed by the forces of competitive markets. Cataclysmic events in 1921–6 seemed for a time to have brought the old order back, but the Second World War and the years of full employment that followed renewed and intensified the influences of 1914–20. By degrees the collective bargainers, on both sides of the table, found that they could push wages and salaries up, almost at will, without bringing down on their heads the troubles for their industry and the loss of jobs that used to be feared. The compulsive factor in negotiations became not 'what the market would bear' but the rise someone else had obtained. Incomes policy was developed to check this, but the very conception of that policy implied that wages and salaries were not fixed by impersonal forces but could and should be adjusted in accordance with certain guidelines; moderating the general rise was found to depend on arriving at acceptable relativities. But meanwhile, in the scramble for rises and the race to keep up, each group was stimulated, if it had not already a customary relativity that it could uphold, to make good its claims by an assessment of its own job requirements in comparison with those of others. Incomes policy, moreover, has meant restraint and control, which themselves change the employee's attitude towards his pay. 'As long as people feel free to negotiate individually or collectively the highest level of earnings their employers are prepared to concede, or as long as the distribution of incomes is seen as the result of some mysterious economic or historic forces, then differences in earnings may be endured that become quite unacceptable when they are seen to be determined by a democratically accountable agency' (PEP 1974, p. 34). As soon, moreover, as incomes policy moves on from the temporary freezing of all rates of pay, or the raising of them by a common margin, to the regulation of particular rises, it finds itself confronted with reasoned claims for bigger rises in some sectors than can possibly be allowed in all, or with the resentment of the lower-paid at being held down to modest rises when others are already getting more, and some vastly more. Incomes policy then becomes distribution policy.

(v) As the pay structure became more labile, the question of what shape should be given it became more debatable, because for an increasing proportion of jobs the market did not set clearly defined limits within which pay would have to lie. In the traditionally predominant industries it had done this. In coal-mining, for instance, the tonnage raised per worker could be and was measured, while the price per ton obtained in a competitive market was outwith the control of any one company. How that price, net of oncosts, should be divided between wages and profits was a matter for debate and negotiation; but when from a given starting-point the market price went up, there was a case for a rise in wages, and when it came down so as to wipe out most or all of the existing profit margin, there was a case for a cut. The product was physical, and relatively homogeneous: that it was physical meant that the miner's work could be traced directly into particular units of output, that it was relatively homogeneous meant that it was likely to be sold in a competitive market that set a uniform price on it day by day. These conditions did not remove all the debatable margin in the miners' pay, but they greatly narrowed it.

So it was very widely in industries employing most manual workers down to 1914; but in the occupations that have increased in relative numbers since then it has been otherwise. Even where the product of the firm as a whole is physical, the work of administrative, clerical, and technical employees cannot be traced directly into units of output; and within the typical firm the number of such employees has been growing steadily, relatively to that of manual workers. Many white-collar workers are in the service trades where there is no physical product. A great part of the expansion of white-collar employment has taken place in public administration, where the product has no selling price. In all these ways jobs have multiplied in which it is hard to see what valuation the buyer or consumer sets upon the work, and the market for the product imposes no close constraints upon decisions about the pay in those jobs.

(vi) Meanwhile attitudes too have changed. Acceptance of the existing pay structure was promoted by fatalism and deference: fatalism that reduced the stings of hardship by regarding them as inescapable, and deference, by which those who were worse off 'knew their place' and looked up with respect, not resentment, to 'their betters'. Both attitudes have receded under the impact of rising standards of living, changed styles of upbringing in the home and at school, and a new view of the formation of personal quality. The experience of a rise in standards of living more rapid and sustained than has ever been recorded before has instilled and heightened expectations of its continuance. In itself this need not affect differentials, but it makes existing rates of pay appear more transient and mutable than they did in a slower-moving world. Changed styles of upbringing, laying less stress on discipline, conformity, and deference, and more on freedom, self-realization, and parity of esteem, have brought all forms of subordination and inequality under suspicion. A social hierarchy is no longer accepted unquestioningly, still less with reverence. People are more ready to ask for more. Meanwhile psychology and sociology have brought out the extent to which the qualities that command high incomes are the outcome of genetic inheritance and of upbringing in the home and at school. So far as they are genetically determined, they confer advantages but not deserts—why should a man be highly paid, it has been asked, for being born with a high genotype I.Q., any more than for having big ears? Equally, a high income cannot be seen simply as the just recompense of achievements, if a man's capacity to achieve depends greatly on the family into which he has happened to be born. Increased awareness of these respects in which the ability to meet job requirements—or the lack of that ability—depends on factors other than a person's own energies and self-discipline, has sapped the view that how people get on depends mostly on their own efforts, and that high earnings are morally justified as the reward for high endeavour.

(vii) When the national products and the standards of living of the Western economies were growing rapidly in the 1950s and 1960s, it was possible to show how the greatest transfer that could conceivably be made from the higher incomes in order to raise the lower would bring to the recipients a once-for-all benefit smaller than the gain they could expect to make cumulatively each five years or so, without any redistribution, as long as economic growth continued. Meanwhile the experience of annual improvement was a source both of satisfaction and of heightened expectations to employees generally. But the check to growth in the early 1970s meant that any one group could satisfy these expectations only by improving its position relatively to other groups. When in the U.K. some cuts in real income had to be accepted, the question of who should bear them raised still more acutely the issue of equity between different levels of pay.

Such are some of the reasons which can be advanced for the growth of concern with the inequality of pay. The discussion that it has stimulated has ranged between two poles. On the one hand rates of pay have been seen as fixed, occupation by occupation, through the impersonal working of the market forces of supply and demand: in this process differentials are of no significance in themselves, and they emerge only—if anyone cares to calculate them—as an arithmetic by-product of the rates after they have been fixed. On the other hand the differences between rates of pay are treated as the objects in themselves of concern and action. They are seen as bound up with, and often as the product of, other forms of inequality between man and man: they are set by a consensus about what is right and proper for persons of given standing, or they result from class differences, or are deliberately manipulated to maintain the privileges of the powerful. Probably none of the discussants has identified himself with either view to the total exclusion of the other. There is indeed not a little common ground within which the two views can be seen, in point of analysis if not of practical policy, as simply supplementing one another. But for the most part they do conflict; and there is substantial justification as well as expository convenience in contrasting the approaches which for brevity may be typified as those of the economist and of the sociologist.

To give a full account of either would require a treatise on economics or sociology, but that is beyond not only our scope but our purpose here. We are making our own attack on the problem of why pay differs as it does from one person to another, and we shall work from the evidence. But though there is talk sometimes of letting evidence speak for itself, much always depends on the ear of the listener. In approaching the evidence on pay determination, the economist and the sociologist will be on the alert for different points; they will bring to bear different conceptual systems and frameworks of connection and causality. It is these approaches, and not the principles of economics and of sociology as a whole, that concern us here. At the outset of our inquiry we need to enter far enough into the paradigms and perceptions of the economist and the sociologist to appreciate the selective attention to factors and relations with which each will approach our particular problem. Let us then sketch their approaches in turn. We shall do so by contrasting them as ideal types, more single-minded, more blinkered in their vision, than are economists and sociologists in flesh and blood.

1.2. The economist's approach to pay determination

Economic theory abstracts certain propensities of human behaviour, together with some of the circumstances of production and of markets, and uses these elements to build models in the mind's eye. It then sets these models in motion and, always in the mind's eye, observes what comes about.

In his account of pay determination, the economist generally builds his model around the employer who combines natural resources, capital and labour to produce an output, and pays each of these factors of production according to what it is worth to him, that is, according to its own contribution to output. But such a model is complicated: it has to solve the problems of how the employer separates the specific productivities of factors whose productivity depends on their working together, and of whether, supposing those specific productivities measured, remunerating the factors in accordance with them will use up the whole value of the output, neither more nor less. We shall gain a clearer initial view of the economist's approach to pay if we bypass these problems by using a model in which the workers are all independent small-holders and craftsmen. True, any such worker uses land and capital which make their contribution to output even though it does not have to be remunerated separately; but let us neglect this for the present, and treat each self-employed man's output as if it were wholly the product of his labour.

Let us imagine, then, an island community where every man works on his own account. The workers meet to exchange their produce, the fisherman brings his fish to market, the weaver his cloth, the farmer his meat or grain. How much each earns depends on how much he produces and on the rates at which he can exchange his product for the products of others that he wants to consume. If the island uses money, then the money income of the weavers depends on the size of their output and the price that cloth is fetching. If more people take up weaving, the output will go up, and in the absence of any rise in other workers' incomes and/or the intensity of their desire for cloth, the price of a yard of cloth will have to go down if the extra output is to be cleared; the individual incomes of weavers will thereby be lowered. Thus the community as buyers of cloth establish a demand curve for weavers' work: at any one time, the greater the number of people who are to be occupied as weavers, the lower must be the income of the individual weaver.

Over against this demand curve we can see the likelihood of a supply curve, recording a prevailing relation between the income offered by weaving and the number of persons who will be attracted to and retained in that occupation. There are reasons to believe that the greater the number that is to be attracted and retained in the long run, the higher must be the income per person. A certain number of persons may be willing to work at weaving for a relatively low income: they may be specially attracted by that kind of work, or follow their fathers into it, or have poor access to other occupations that would yield them a higher income. It is among persons who are less attracted by weaving than these, or who have more effective access to other occupations, that additional weavers must be found, and they will not take up weaving unless a higher income is in prospect. And so on: corresponding to each higher number of weavers will be a higher income per weaver, at which alone that number will be attracted and retained. We assume here, it will be noticed, that the income which has to be paid to the man it is hardest to attract will have to be paid to all.

Here, then, we have a supply curve showing that the greater the number of persons to be retained as weavers, the higher will have to be the income per weaver. This supply curve must be set over against the demand curve we have already met, which shows that the greater the number of persons to be found work as weavers, the lower the income per weaver will have to be. If initially the number at work were small, the community as buyers would set a higher valuation on the output of any one weaver, and so confer a higher income on him, than would be required to attract that small number of weavers into the occupation. As the number at work rises, the demand price for the man-year of weaving comes down, but the supply price goes up. There will be some number at which demand price and supply price are equal; or, putting it the other way about, some income for the weaver such that the number of weavers required to make the cloth that can be sold at the price which will yield that income, is matched by the number of persons whom that income will attract to and retain in weaving.

Traditional economic analysis now goes on to envisage processes ensuring that the income of weavers will always be tending towards this level. Suppose the income were above the level: then more people would be attracted to take up weaving than there was work for, more cloth would be made than could be sold at the price, and the price of cloth and the income of weavers would fall. Conversely if the income were below the level: what was now from the consumers' point of view a shortage of cloth would raise its price, and with it the income of weavers. To take lasting effect both sorts of adjustment of income must be accompanied by an adjustment of the number in the occupation, the first by some in it quitting for lack of work, the second by some outside it being drawn in by the higher income it now affords.

On the assumptions that the conditions of demand and supply, and the adjustment of disparities between them, are such as have been depicted here, we can call the level of weavers' income at which the demand for and supply of weavers' work are balanced, the equilibrium level. The economist who takes these assumptions to represent basic tendencies in the actual world regards the different incomes obtainable in different occupations as each set by the equilibrium of demand and supply for the kind of work in question – set in the sense, not that each income will be held precisely to an equilibrium level, but that it cannot move far away from that level in either direction without setting up reactions that will tend to bring it back.

So far we have shown how the demand curve expresses the valuation that consumers set upon the weaver's work through their willingness to buy cloth, according as more or less of that work is being performed and more or less cloth is being brought to market. In doing this we have ignored the part played by the yarn and the loom in the making of the cloth, but these as well as the weaver's work have to be paid for out of the proceeds of sale of the cloth. In the usual case the employer has to arrange for this, and the demand curve for weavers' work will express the rate at which he will pay for given amounts of it when he also has to pay for the yarn and the loom that he uses together with it. This is the problem which we put aside at the outset but which we must now take up: how is the valuation that the market sets upon the joint product of a number of factors of production divided so as to set a separate valuation on the contribution of each of them?

One approach to this problem begins by taking as given what has to be determined, namely the prices of the factors of production: at any one time the employer is hiring these factors at the going rates for them, and is combining them in proportions prescribed by the current method of manufacturing his particular product. Thereby he incurs a certain cost per unit of product, and he will maintain output at his present level only if the price he gets for the product covers that cost. Other employers in other trades will be proceeding similarly, except that they will be combining the factors of production in different proportions, according to the technique of each trade. Suppose now, that for some reason the general level of pay for labour rises relatively to what is being paid for the other factors: then the cost of production of the products that use much labour per unit, say, of equipment will rise relatively to the cost of products in which less labour is used per unit of equipment. There will have to follow a corresponding change in the relative prices of the products. The economist will expect consumers to react to this by buying less of the products of the labour-intensive trades and more of those of the capital-intensive trades. The labour-intensive trades will contract—even though, in a growing economy, this contraction may be only relative; and the capital-intensive trades will expand. Taking the two kinds of trade together, we find a reduction in the amount of labour used per unit of equipment. A rise in the general level of pay for labour has thus brought about a fall in the amount of labour demanded to work together with a given amount of equipment.

In this way we can see how a valuation will be set upon the contribution of a factor of production even though this contribution can be made only with the collaboration of other factors. It makes no sense to ask how much of a given bale of cloth was made by the weaver and how much by the loom, but from the consumers' valuation of the cloth we can derive a demand curve showing, in given circumstances, how many weavers there will be jobs for at each of a number of alternative rates of pay for weaving. We can rest, then, on our model of the island community, as finding the pay for any kind of work to be determined ultimately by the interplay between consumers' willingness to buy the product and workers' willingness to do the work.

But the economist has still to explain why the pay for any one kind of work should be higher than that for any other. If initially some occupations offer higher pay than others, why do not workers move away from the lower-paid occupations and into the higher-paid, so raising rates of pay in the one and bringing them down in the other, until all occupations pay much the same? The answer is found in a number of obstacles to movement. They can be grouped under two heads, according as they affect the number of jobs available in a particular occupation or the number of potential takers of those jobs.

The number of available jobs is evidently restricted by obstacles to entry. Some obstacles are erected deliberately, in order to keep the number of entrants down and the pay of the incumbents up: such at least is the effect, even where the ostensible or genuine motive is to protect the public by maintaining standards. Jobs of a certain kind may be reserved to those who are already members of an association, and entry to this is restricted by entrance fee or quota. Legislation may provide for licensing, by which entrants are admitted only within certain quotas, or on proof of unsatisfied demand, or on attainment of certain standards. Even where there is no overt restriction of numbers, the enforcement of standards of proficiency at the threshold of entry can be used to keep numbers down—the standards may be set unnecessarily high, or the number of places in schools providing the required training may be limited. The effect is the same where there is no overt restriction of total numbers but certain types of potential entrants are debarred. Work that women could do may be reserved for men, by custom or trade union pressure. Members of particular ethnic or religious groups may be similarly excluded, or, like women in some cases, be admitted only under quota. Here, then, in various ways is the possibility of *restriction of entry*.

The number of available jobs can also be kept down by keeping up the rate of pay. In a given state of demand, the higher the rate of pay the smaller will be the number of employed. The economist recognizes that there are particular groups of employees so placed that a rise in their relative pay will have little effect on the numbers employed (Marshall 1892, VI. xiii. 3). But this cannot hold of all groups, and the demand for labour in a given employment will generally be elastic in the longer run: a higher rate of relative pay will mean fewer jobs, because the consequent rise in the price of the product reduces sales, or because employers change their methods of production so as to use less of the dearer labour per unit of output, or for both reasons. A rise in the relative rate of pay restricts employment when it keeps the number of jobs offered below the number of workers who would be willing to take those jobs at that rate of pay. Such a rise in pay may be brought about by trade union pressure, or it may come about inadvertently, through the maintenance of a customary differential. The rate of pay may also be raised, in effect, relatively to the demand, when the demand falls, but custom, or unwillingness to inflict or accept a cut, keeps the rate of pay up. These possibilities may be summarized as those of *the fixing of disequilibrating rates of pay*.

Over against these two ways in which the number of jobs may be restricted, we may note five factors affecting the number of potential entrants.

(1) One is the extent to which differences of pay only offset differences in the amenities of the work and the working life of an occupation. Men differ in their likes and dislikes, but a majority may find the amenities of one occupation less attractive than others, or its drawbacks as a job or way of life more repellent. In so far as they have a choice between occupations they will therefore avoid entering the less agreeable or more disagreeable occupation unless its disadvantages are offset by higher pay. If this were the only factor affecting the number of entrants, the economist would expect to find the less agreeable occupations the more highly paid. More generally, the pay of different occupations would differ by amounts which in the judgement of the recruits to those occupations offset equal and opposite differences in their amenity. This factor may be called *differential amenity*.

(2) Some occupations are regionally concentrated in the nature of things, as in mining, or as a matter of history. Because of the costs of moving, and the uncertainties and deprivations attendant on migration, those born or settled in one region may not move into an occupation carried on elsewhere, even though they would prefer to work in it if they could. The other side of the same penny is that larger numbers may enter an occupation in one region than would do so if movement to other regions were easier. The objective costs of migration, and the subjective resistances to it, can thus cause pay differentials between occupations to persist in so far as occupations are regionally concentrated. We may call this factor *regional immobility*.

(3) Some people may fail to enter jobs that they would be able to move into and would prefer to work in, simply because they do not know that they are available, or, though they know of their existence in a general way, have never

envisaged them as within their own reach. This obstacle appears both in the search for jobs by adults and—perhaps even more—in young people's choice of employment and courses in preparation for employment. We may call it *lack of knowledge*, if this term may cover lack of orientation as well as of information.

(4) Entry to most occupations requires training, and not all with the ability to complete a training course successfully have access to it. Regional immobility may make itself felt again here. A prerequisite for most training courses is a certain level of general education, and entry is closed to those whose schooling has stopped short of that. Where these obstacles are absent, there is still a major and general obstacle in the form of cost. There may be fees to be paid, and the pupil must be maintained while he is training. Even where these costs are borne by the employers or the state, the pupil or his family have generally still to bear the cost of forgoing the larger income he could earn there and then if he was not training. There is also an effort involved in learning, and taking examinations, that some find deterrent. The factor of *training costs*, then, as we may call it if we use 'costs' in a broad sense, is another source of persistent occupational differentials.

(5) Were the provision of free education and training courses together with student maintenance grants so full that everyone had effective access to every sort of course, there would still be many who could not complete particular courses because they lacked the prerequisite physique, temperament, or mental ability. This is the obstacle of the *limitation of personal qualities*. The high income attained by some who possess outstanding—and that means rare—qualities, has been considered as a 'rent of ability'.

Such are the factors which, on the economist's view, prevent rates of pay fixed by the interplay of supply and demand tending to equality throughout all occupations: that is, they are the causes of the inequality of pay. In taking account of them the economist is taking a realistic view of the imperfections of 'the labour market', but this analysis still relies on the market forces of supply and demand. It is implicit in this analysis that differentials have no bearing on the setting of rates of pay, and appear only as a matter of arithmetic after the rates have been set: the difference between the hourly rate of pay of the carpenter and the labourer has only the same significance as that between the prices of a ton of copper and a ton of steel. Here are objects that are different in kind, with only a nominal similarity of the units in which they are quoted, the hour or the ton; and the price of each is set by the supply of and demand for each.

Thus the economist's analysis does not lead him to see different rates of pay as constituting a structure. If someone chose to arrange occupations in a rank order, according to the average rates of pay prevailing in them, the economist would see little more sense in that than in ranking raw materials according to their prices per ton. In neither case, to his mind, would there be a structure, in the sense that the relations between the elements were both constituents of a unitary system and part of the nature of the elements themselves.

Yet economists have related their account of differences in pay to the social structure. We said above that if the agreeableness or disagreeableness of occupations were the only factor affecting the number of entrants, the economist would expect to find the less agreeable occupations the more highly paid. The observation that the facts were very much the other way about led John Stuart Mill to insert in the 3rd edition of his *Principles* (1852, II. xiv 1) the following paragraph:

These inequalities of remuneration, which are supposed to compensate for the disagreeable circumstances of particular employments, would, under certain conditions, be natural consequences of perfectly free competition: and as between employments of about the same grade, and filled by nearly the same description of people, they are, no doubt, for the most part, realized in practice. But it is altogether a false view of the state of facts, to present this as the relation which generally exists between agreeable and disagreeable employments. The really exhausting and the really repulsive labours, instead of being better paid than others, are almost invariably paid the worst of all, because performed by those who have no choice.

The last words—'performed by those who have no choice'—were the germ of the concept of *non-competing groups* (Cairnes 1874, I. iii. 5; Taussig 1929, cs. 47, 48). According to this concept, there were two kinds of differentials, those between occupations all of which were commonly entered by persons from households in the same socio-economic grade, and those between occupations that drew their labour from different grades. The differentials of the first kind were seen as being due mainly to differences in the amenity of the occupations and, especially, differences in the cost of training for them—factors (1) and (4) above. When the elements of compensation for deterrent aspects of the work and for the investment of time and money in training had been deducted, the net pay of all occupations manned from the same socio-economic grade would tend to equality: for if in one occupation it were higher than elsewhere, the attraction of labour to that occupation would bring pay down there, and raise it elsewhere, until a common level was restored. But there could be no such movement between occupations manned from different socio-economic grades, and pay differentials between those occupations were therefore of a very different kind. If the general level of pay in the occupations manned from one grade rose relatively to that in other grades, there could be little corrective reaction through the movement of labour – if the grades really were noncompeting, no reaction at all. Movement was prevented by lack of knowledge, lack of means to meet the costs of migration and training, and lack of ability—factors (2) – (5) above, including (4) in so far as it acts as a barrier.

In this way the economists have absorbed some features of the social structure into their account of differences in pay. But having accepted that those features affect the supply of labour to different occupations, they have not doubted that it is by the interplay of that supply with the demand that the normal rate of pay in each occupation is determined. In the same way they have not shut their eyes to all that goes on in the labour market to make it at particular times and places not so much a market as an arena for contests of power; but they have seen these episodes as the source only of abberrations about trends and relationships that are independently and more powerfully determined. Thus Marshall remarked of the development of combinations in his day that

> they present a succession of picturesque incidents and romantic transformations, which arrest public attention and seem to indicate a coming change in our social arrangements now in one direction and now in another; and their importance is certainly great and grows rapidly. But it is apt to be exaggerated; for indeed many of them are little more than eddies, such as have always fluttered over the surface of progress. And though they are on a larger and more imposing scale in this modern age than ever before; yet now, as ever, the main body of movement depends on the deep silent strong stream of the tendencies of normal distribution and exchange; which 'are not seen', but which control the cousrse of those episodes which 'are seen'. (1890, VI. vii. 10).

But the sociologist sees the main body of movement as dependent on quite other streams than those of market forces.

1.3. The sociologist's approach to pay determination

The sociologist lacks one great advantage or enticement of the economist: he cannot build a model whose components are quantitative variables, and when he sets it in motion use mathematics to record its processes neatly and demonstrate the outcome with rigour. But these distinctive properties of economic theory are, in a sense, accidental. The starting-points of economic and sociological theory are alike—the abstraction of certain human propensities, so that their outcome when they are allowed to operate in isolation may be observed in the mind's eye.

The difference between them lies in the propensities they abstract. The economist is concerned with man as a maximizer, making a rational adjustment of means to ends. These ends are not necessarily material or selfish – they may as well be spiritual or aesthetic or altruistic; but whatever they are, economic man takes them as given, and the calculations by which he adjusts the available means to them are self-contained—his relations with other people form part of his data, not of himself. The propensities abstracted by the sociologist differ in two salient respects. People are seen as engaging in other forms of activity besides the taking of means to ends: they act in certain ways because to do so is customary, or an obligation, or 'the natural thing to do', or right and proper, or just and fair. This they do in great part—and this is the second salient point of difference—because their affections, needs, and concerns, indeed their very selves, are engaged with other people: there is not so well defined a boundary as for the economic man between self and others.

These differences appear clearly in the approaches of economist and sociologist to the act of exchange. For the economist each party to an exchange is concerned only to maximize his own benefit from it. In a particular case, it is true, this benefit may include the satisfaction of doing good to the other party. A person, for example, may willingly pay a higher price for an article made by the blind than he need pay for it elsewhere. But the economist would see what is being paid in this way as including a donation. His own professional concern is with the payment net of any such altruistic element, and what net payment each party to an exchange is willing to make is arrived at by a calculation into which his personal relation with the other does not enter. For the sociologist, on the contrary, following the social anthropologist, an act of exchange is essentially the manifestation of a personal relation. As such, it may have a many-sided significance: it may discharge an obligation or impose one; it may confer prestige; it may signalize the ties that bind the parties to one another as members of a society. Exchange theory in sociology shows us how people become in some way entitled to or assured of a certain receipt. There is a near-economic form of it, in which highly valued services are seen to be given high status, with the implication that they will be assured reciprocally of high remuneration. There is a near-legal or contractual form: in a traditional society, a 'station in life' has certain rights.

What distinguishes the sociological from the economic approach in this is that the sociologist is concerned with exchanges as establishing or arising out of relations between members of a society—members in the sense that the personality and activity of each cannot be understood, cannot indeed exist, apart from his relations with the others; whereas the economist considers persons in so far as they can be isolated, dealing with each other only impersonally, 'at arm's length'. In the modern economy, it is true, most of the transactions with which the economist is concerned are of that kind, but not all, and in particular not those by which rates of pay are fixed. Here, the sociologist will say, even though the legal employer is not always in a face-to-face relation with the employee, the pay forms an organic part of the relations between members of society.

Sociologists have not generally attacked the problem of how particular rates of pay are determined. The reader will see shortly that when we want to report the views of those who see social rather than economic factors as predominant in the determination of particular rates of pay, it is the words not of sociologists but of economists who are sensitive to those factors that we cite. But sociologists have seen the inequality of pay as one of, and one with, the various manifestations of social inequality. The conclusions they have reached about the nature and origin of social inequality therefore provide them with their own approach to the inequality of pay, and lead some of them at least, as we shall see, to views about the possibility of changing it very different from those typical of the economist.

One way in which the inequality of pay appears as one of the several facets of social inequality is manifest in the agreement between the ranking order of occupations by pay and by social standing or *status*. Status is a matter of attitudes: people generally see others as above or below themselves, or at the same level, in a hierarchy of esteem, and they express this perception by an attitude of deference to those they see as above them, acceptance of those they see as equals, and derogation (such is the term of the sociologist) towards those they see as beneath them. It is found that a principal indicator of the level to which a given person is assigned is his occupation; indeed people are generally ready to assign status to any occupation as such, without needing to know who it is that in a particular case is following it. If the attention of the economist is drawn to the general agreement between the rank orders of occupations by status and pay, he is likely to regard it as an interesting observation, no doubt, but no concern of his; or else he may hazard the suggestion that the same capabilities as command a higher rate of pay as a fact of the market also command higher esteem. That would explain why certain occupations were generally found in the same regions of the two ranking orders, but hardly why the two orders should generally agree so closely in their ranking as the sociologist finds they do. Then can it be that the rate of pay, determined as the economist believes it to be, is in turn the principal determinant of the status assigned to the occupation concerned? The sociologist raises the opposite possibility, that it is the status that determines the pay: people generally feel it is only 'right and proper' that an occupation of higher status should have higher pay, and this consensus brought to bear through custom or negotiation or award puts and keeps the relative pay where it is.

Thus Talcott Parsons (1954, p. 84) in his 'analytical approach to the theory of social stratification', having observed how 'within the broad framework of the direct differential valuation of occupations and achievements as managerial, professional, skilled, unskilled, etc., there is an income hierarchy which, on the whole, conforms to that of direct valuation', went on to remark in a footnote, 'How this correspondence comes about is an interesting sociological problem. The one thing which can be said here with certainty is that an ordinary economic explanation, though true within certain limits, is quite inadequate to the general problem. The explanation is to a large extent institutional.'

It is significant that two clear-cut statements of the priority of status to market forces can be cited from economists, but economists who have been much concerned with wage-fixing in practice. The British economist Barbara Wootton has said (1946, p. 144),

All wages are to be explained more in terms of conventions than as the result of strictly economic factors. This is not, of course, a final explanation, since it is necessary to enquire how these conventions came to be established, and how in course of time they change. Emphasis upon the conventional element in wages does, however, direct attention to the secondary place to be assigned to such economic influences as movements of supply and demand. The conventions which make the pattern of wages whatever it happens to be at any given time are sociological in a broad sense, rather than economic. Further, a convention, once established, has very great powers of self-preservation. In so far as wages are governed by economic forces, they may reflect the economic conditions of earlier generations.

Here market forces are not dismissed altogether, but they are given a secondary place. Similarly the Dutch economist Jan Pen (1971, p. 17), after asserting that a secondary school teacher can hardly be said to earn more than a primary school teacher by reason of a greater contribution to production, goes on: 'In my opinion what counts is that society feels that a secondary school teacher *ought* to earn more. He is further up the ladder, and the number of rungs can be measured by the difference in income. This is a social evaluation. . . . The interplay of the market and social convention is not an easy thing to disentangle, but one thing is certain, namely that the latter has a considerable effect on income distribution.'

Beside this belief that relative pay is assigned to occupations according to a 'social evaluation' is the belief that whether or not a consensus exists about what it is right and proper for them to receive, some people are assured of higher incomes than others by reason of difference in *class*. The class of a family is apparent from its life-style but rests upon its position in the economic system. In the original Marxian analysis people were divided into two classes according as they did or did not own capital. More recent analysts see access to education and technology as conferring the same economic advantage as the ownership of capital used to do. The children who are born into well-to-do homes, it is said, receive more expensive education, and are helped forward both in their entry into employment and their subsequent advancement by their parents' knowledge and connections, and the personal associations they themselves form through their education. The differential advantages they thus enjoy may be enhanced by the transfer of capital to them by their parents; but for our present purpose the essential contention is that they have privileged access to the higher-paid employments. These employments are substantially reserved to them, because the required qualifications can be attained by few who have to start life with less education and fewer resources, or because of a tacit agreement to admit only those of 'the right type'. In the Western economies, certainly, there is no outright hereditary system in which the occupations one can enter are delimited by the caste of one's parents: there have always been some who made their way up from 'humble origins', and educational opportunities have been much extended of late. But despite this element of social mobility, the chances of a child of given potential entering a highly paid occupation vary with the social class of his parents.

The contention that relative pay depends more on social structure than on market forces has had its impact upon economists. Looking back on the analysis of the distribution of income that he developed in the 1930s, Champernowne (1973, pp. 14–15) noted that he had embodied in it 'the idea . . . that a man's income depended on his qualifications for obtaining it, and that its growth or decline would depend on his trading in qualifications and on changes in the effectiveness of individual qualifications for obtaining income'; but now, he says, he would 'give much more importance to a point which then only got a bare mention in the introduction, namely that the values of these various qualifications are not primarily determined by marginal productivity and the price-mechanism, but "depend upon the social structure of the community under study, and upon the economic conditions of the times" '.

The view that differences of pay depend on those of class is consistent in part with the economist's view of the determination of the pay of each occupation by market forces. Class acts to restrict the supply of labour to some occupations, and increases the number who have little choice but to offer themselves in others; but with the supply curves once fixed and shaped in this way, pay might still be determined by the interplay of supply and demand. We have seen how economists themselves have incorporated these effects of class in their account of the labour market, through the concept of non-competing groups. But in another way, the sociologist has seen class differences as overriding the impersonal working of the market, because class privilege is linked with the exertion of *power*.

Power has been defined by Goldthorpe (1974, p. 218) as 'the capacity to mobilise resources (human and non-human) in order to bring about a desired state of affairs'. He associates power with advantage—'the possession of, or control over, whatever in society is valued and scarce', so that classes are evidently differentiated with respect to advantage. He then sees social inequality as by no means entirely in the nature of things, nor the outcome of impersonal processes, but as being in part deliberately created or maintained by those who have the power so to do, for their own benefit. 'In spite of frequent attempts, it has not proved possible to give a satisfactory explanation of the persisting degree and form of inequality in Britain or in any advanced society, by reference primarily to "external" constraints'—such, we may say, as those exerted by market forces—'and without reference to the purposive exercise of their power and advantage by more privileged groups and strata. In other words, it has not proved possible to explain social inequality otherwise than as a structure with important self-maintaining properties' (ibid., p. 229).

Those who believe that it is power that determines the distribution of income have generally had the Western economies in view; but the Soviet-type economies have been analysed in the same way. Thus a Polish economist has remarked how certain of the New Left have stigmatized the 'marketization' of those economies, with the widening of pay differentials that they believe it to have caused, as reflecting 'the wish of the ruling élite (and the managerial class closely linked to this élite) to widen income differentials as a means of securing and enhancing their privileged position' (Brus 1974, p. 7).

1.4. The practical issue

From the account just given of the two approaches, we might well think that their perceptions were complementary rather than conflicting. We have typified 'the economist' and 'the sociologist', but the economists who have studied labour questions have never doubted the influence of custom and notions of fairness, or the power of combinations, and sociologists likewise have been well aware of the effects of scarcity on the relative pay of different groups. Most actual situations, we might conclude, present a mixture of the forces and processes on whch the two types of investigator focus their attention; the inequality of pay in particular seems to be brought about and maintained by both economic and sociological factors.

But this agreement extends only over the size of particular differentials and the position of particular groups in the pay structure: about the main lines of that structure there is opposition outright. The practical issue is, can prevailing differences of pay be reduced substantially and generally, on conditions not in themselves unacceptable? Some sociologists at least hold that there is nothing in the nature of things to prevent this. Most economists would rejoin that the imposition of an equalization of pay would be bound to bring disruptive consequences that could be contained only by measures such as forced labour that would be even more repugnant to the egalitarian than are our present inequalities.

We have seen how sociologists are apt to ascribe the inequality of pay to those differences of status, class, and power to which they trace so much in the stratification of society and the setting of man apart from man. On this view, did people cease to believe that differences in pay were right and proper, and were the class and power structure of society levelled, then there would be no remaining obstacle to the equalization of pay throughout all occupations, for the widely different rates of pay that actually prevail are what they are not because they are the values that solve the equation of supply and demand, but because people generally believe that they *ought* to be what they are, or because particular people have the power to fix them and do so to suit themselves. The sociologists who take this view feel it their duty to proclaim that the inequality of pay is not an economic necessity, but is the outcome of particular attitudes and choices, and can be changed if those attitudes and choices change. We may cite two Oxford sociologists.

... When concerned with problems arising out of competition and conflict, such as those found in economic life [Goldthorpe (1974, p. 230) has written] applied social scientists must seriously ask themselves whether they do not have an obligation to state, clearly and insistently, that the context of inequality in which these problems typically exist is neither unalterable nor indisputably desirable, and need not, therefore, be taken as a 'given'. In other words, they must consider whether they are not obliged to emphasize what they know about the nature of social inequality, including its self-perpetuating but 'man-made' characteristics.

In similar terms Fox (1973, pp. 223–4) has written that

... for much of the time men do not perceive the conventional and arbitrary nature of many of the arrangements under which they live and suppose them to be part of an inevitable and unchangeable order. It is one important aspect of the social scientist's professional obligation, therefore, to make himself and others aware that this is not so. It is part of his responsibility to make clear that the the existing order is in no way determined by laws inherent in the universal nature of things; that its most hallowed features are conventional in the strictest sense and thus subject to change originating from man's deliberate choice. ...

These views are not visionary, but are based upon an analysis of contemporary society that the writers believe to show where and how society is capable of being changed. The change they envisage is not to a Utopia, but to a society in which those elements of the social order that are 'man-made' have been refashioned by the now conscious choice of those concerned.

But whatever may be possible with other forms of inequality, most economists will contend that the inequality of pay could not be generally and considerably reduced without consequences following no less unacceptable than those that would follow the attempt to make wheat, copper, cotton, and coal sell at the same price per ton. For they see the rate of pay in any occupation as having the same two functions as the price of a material product. First, it must be such as to balance demand and supply, that is, to equalize the number of persons whom ultimately the consumers are willing to employ at the given rate, with the number who are willing to work in the occupation at that rate. Set a rate other than this, and then either there must be direction of labour, with compulsion to work in the jobs assigned, or else the prices of the products must be set, below or above the cost of production, so as to induce the customers to take more of the products of the employments the workers choose to enter in greater numbers at the new rate of pay, and less of the products where labour is now in short supply; or something of both sorts of measure. Setting the rate of pay so as to induce a certain number of persons to work in a particular employment is a matter not merely of attracting a quota of the already qualified labour force, but also of inducing enough entrants to qualify themselves, and the longer and more exacting the required training, the higher as a general rule must be the attainable pay. Wherever, moreover, there is a promotion ladder, the differences of pay between the rungs provide an incentive to work hard and acquire qualifications in order to gain promotion, and a compensation for the added strain and responsibility that the higher posts may carry. But in balancing supply and demand employment by employment, rates of pay are also performing a second function, namely that of allocating productive resources between different lines of output so that output in the aggregate shall meet the needs of consumers, weighted by their expenditures, as fully as possible.

Thus the economist sees intervention to reduce differences of pay as bound to vitiate the functions of pay as part of the pricing system, functions that must be provided for in a collectivist no less than in an individualist economy. There is a choice between equality and freedom. There is a choice between equality and prosperity.

But the sociologist may riposte by asking whether the economist's conclusions do not hold more of his model than of the real world. That model consists of a set of simultaneous equations—those, for instance, which impose the condition that the aggregate costs of each undertaking, including the return to capital, shall equal the aggregate receipts, or that factors of production shall be remunerated in proportion to their marginal value products; and many other conditions, as well as the one most directly concerning us here, namely that the number of persons prepared to work in an employment at a certain rate of pay shall be equal to the number whom at that rate of pay the consumers as the ultimate paymasters are willing to employ. In this system of equations the rates of pay are among the dependent variables which must be free to take and change their values if all the conditions of the system are to be satisfied. The model can claim mathematical rigour, and yet, it may well be held, there is nothing rigorous about its application to the practical issue of whether the inequality of pay can be reduced, unless we can be assured that it embodies the truth and the whole truth about the real world; and this we cannot be.

There is the question first of whether the adjustments of the real world are carried out so exactly as the equations imply. Instead of the point of intersection of two textbook curves, the real world shows us a zone of inertia formed by the overlap of two fairly broad bands. In particular it is doubtful whether managers' decisions about how much of a given factor of production to employ and in what proportions to combine the products are governed closely by estimates of marginal value products or by the imperatives of technique: the amounts employed and the techniques used may be adapted to physical availabilities, and the proportions in which factors are combined may not be varied in response to changes in the relative prices of the factors within a certain range. Many different occupational structures have in fact been found in firms making similar products in the same industry (Layard et al. 1971). Because the reactions of human agents are not precisely calculated, there are tolerances in many parts of the system that can take up some at least of the pressures that spread out when the variables on which they directly impinge are not free to move so as to absorb them.

But much more than this, it may be contended, the economist's model leaves out the many ways in which people can be, and today already often are, drawn into particular employments other than by the relative pay offered. There are the attractions of a particular kind of work and way of life. For those already in the labour force, there are administrative guidance on a change of job and assistance with retraining and resettlement. For entrants to the labour force there are the representation of the public interest in the choice of career, and the appeal to the motive of public service, together with the subsidization of training for occupations in which more workers are needed or for which the high cost of training would otherwise prove a deterrent in the absence of the prospect of attaining high pay. Above all, there is the sheer need to find a job of one kind or another, almost irrespective, for entrants at least, of the pay. At the present time, if more people than can be used would like to enter certain occupations, the relative pay in these occupations is not always reduced, even in the longer run, but those who cannot find a place in them have to go elsewhere, and the knowledge that places are not easy to get diverts potential applicants; while a known shortage of labour in an employment of itself directs entrants towards it. In all, it may be argued, there would be no need to resort to forced labour. Under these alternative arrangements, people would not feel their freedom of choice to be less than the effective freedom they enjoy under the constraints of the present system.

A collectivist society, it might be added, can bear even the disequilibrium of an excess of costs over sales receipts that may be the outcome of fixing rates of pay without regard to market forces. For the total outflow of pay to workers will return as payment for their produce: if in one line of output sales receipts fall below costs, in another they will exceed them, and the books can be balanced by subsidies in the first case paid out of levies on the surplus in the second. Market economies can and do make some use of the same possibility, by way of subsidies and indirect taxes. It may well be pointed out that this balancing of the books still leaves the consumers with an allocation of resources less satisfying to them than the one that would be realized by a contraction of the loss-making industries and a transfer of resources to the surplus-making; but to this it could be replied that the economist's model leaves out of account the satisfaction of workers in being able to follow their familiar occupations despite an insufficient demand, as well as the social benefits to be expected from a nearer approach to equality.

The debate between economist and sociologist on whether the inequality of pay could be much reduced without disruptive consequences thus turns upon the questions of how closely existing differences of pay are determined by market forces; what provision can be made to motivate the exertions and guide the deployment of labour in the absence of such differences; and whether these alternative arrangements would result in a lower level of satisfaction or standard of living, when we take account of the welfare of people as workers as well as consumers.

We shall take these questions up not directly in the first instance, but by inquiring how pay is in fact determined in the world about us. The findings of this inquiry should show how far inequality of pay is imposed by market forces and how far by custom and convention, by status, class, and power. These findings in turn should enable us to consider on what conditions it would be possible to reduce existing inequalities.

1.5. The plan of this work

To learn why pay differs from one person to another, we have to find out how the pay of any one person gets fixed. The question this work sets out to answer is, therefore, in what ways are particular rates of pay determined?

Our inquiry will not take the form, usual in economic theory, of a chain of deductive reasoning on assumptions taken to be representative of the dominant tendencies of human behaviour and of the relevant circumstances of the real world. Our seeking the reasons for what is so often taken for granted requires us at the outset, not to pluck tendencies deemed dominant and circumstances supposed relevant out of our everyday knowledge, but to look for what shows itself to be dominant and relevant on a survey of actual societies. To study differences of pay, moreover, is to study social structure, with all in it that concerns the sociologist as well as the economist. Our inquiry will therefore proceed by way of a survey of the evidence in as much detail as is compatible with a synoptic view of a variety of societies and aspects of their structure. Our aim will be to draw such inferences as the evidence allows, point by point, concerning the determinants of pay. These inferences will commonly take the form of a heightening or lowering of the probability that a particular factor or process is influential. Here the comparative method will do something to fill the gap left by our inability to experiment.

Much of our evidence will consist in statistics of pay, and we have to con-

sider how pay is defined and measured. Today we are increasingly conscious of
how complex are the terms of contracts of employment. The problems that this
complexity raises for any comparative study of pay over a wide range in space
and time are considered in Sec. 2.2.

It is an additional limitation of our survey that it pays only partial attention
to the ways in which rates of pay are arrived at. These ways are
various—unilateral announcement; individual bargaining; collective bargaining;
regulation by statute or by statutory bodies; arbitration. We shall discuss the
working of unilateral announcement in the Soviet-type economies, and the
effect of trade unions on differentials in the Western economies, but we shall
not examine procedures generally. Evidently a study of the actual processes and
transactions by which particular rates of pay get fixed is likely to throw light on
the immediate pressures on the parties and the considerations that are upper-
most in their minds: but there is a distinction between the how and the why.
The procedure does not itself determine the outcome: different procedures may
only provide alternative channels for the same currents. While, therefore, a
study of processes should yield us insights that we shall miss here, the outcomes themselves are still the best evidence for their own determination.

Inequality of pay presents itself in two main aspects, differences between the
average pay in different occupations, and the distribution of individual earnings. The first of these aspects occupies Chapter 2–7, the second Chapters
8–9.

The study of the occupational pay structure begins in Chapters 2 and 3 with
surveys of that structure in various types of economy, and of the changes that
have come about in it in the course of time. These surveys bring out the inter-
connection between pay structure and social structure as that is formed by
status and class. The study of status that follows in Chapter 4 centres upon the
question that the economist and sociologist approach so differently, why there
is generally so close an agreement between the rank orders of occupations by
status and by pay. What has been held to be an outstanding instance of
differences of pay being dependent upon differences of status is examined in
Chapter 5 on discrimination. Of the various aspects of class, we take as most
pertinent to our present inquiry the grouping of occupations by class according
to the tendency of the children of those engaged in a given occupation
themselves to enter occupations in the same class. Chapter 6 is much concerned
accordingly with intergenerational mobility between occupations, and this is
developed in Chapter 7 by a study of the connection between class, mental
ability, education, and entry into employment.

So far we shall have been working only with the average pay in each occupation, but there is generally a wide dispersion of individual pay about that
average. The examination of these differences in Chapter 8 throws light on the
factors affecting individual pay, in the presence of a given structure of pay by
occupation. These factors we explore by another approach in Chapter 9, which
tries to account for some of the remarkable properties of the statistical form of
the distribution of individual earnings, and thereby to contribute to a

philosophy of the inequality of pay between one person and another.

That philosophy as a whole must be derived from a study of the differences of pay between occupations that is attempted in Chapters 2–7, and the account of the process by which individuals acquire the means of entry into particular employments that is offered in Chapters 8–9. A final chapter, 10, brings together the main findings that have been reached in these two ways.

2
A Survey of the
Pay Structure by Occupation

2.1. Grouping by occupation

The pay of any two persons may differ for many reasons—because, it may be, they work in different industries or firms or localities; or because of differences in their personal capability, or age, or sex. But the most conspicuous reason lies in differences of occupation. It is these that come first to mind as the source of systematic differences in pay. It seems part of the natural order of the societies we know that occupations requiring greater skill, experience, and effort should be paid more highly. If asked to account for the level of a person's earned income, the first thing we look to is that person's occupation.

This does not mean that pay always differs more between occupations than it does on other accounts. As we shall see later, the spread of industrial earnings among manual workers in any one occupation in Great Britain is usually nearly as wide as that between the lowest average earnings in any manual occupation and the highest—that is, nearly 2 to 1. But the biggest differences in earnings, where we find one person earning four, five, or twenty times as much as another, are almost all linked with differences of occupation.

There is a hierarchy of occupations, moreover, in respect not only of pay but of social standing. It is by reference mainly to occupation that the British Office of Population Censuses and Surveys (1970, pp. x–xi) allots each person to one of a small number of 'socio-economic groups', although those who belong to these groups are described not as those with similar work and incomes but as those with similar 'social, cultural and recreational standards and behaviour'. Our occupations, and the pay that goes with them, are bound up with the structure and stratification of our societies.

It is really this linkage that makes the grouping of occupations possible. If occupations are distinguished by the kind of work done, then they are very numerous indeed—in the United States they number more than 21,000 (U.S. Dept. of Labor 1965). But when we group those whose pay falls within the same band, we find we are also bringing together occupations which, in the general judgement, resemble one another also in the degree of skill and the extent of education and training they call for, and the weight of responsibility they impose, or at least they resemble one another in the aggregate effect of some combination of these factors; and so they also share in the social status that these factors carry with them. In practice, when 'type of work' does not enable us to assign an occupation to a group readily, we call in the linked characteristics to decide.

2.2. The comparability of figures of pay by occupation

We speak of 'the rate for the job', 'equal pay for equal work', 'fair relativities', and the like implying that pay can be cited in a compact form, readily comparable in its different instances; but in fact a single figure can give only an imperfect account of the pay obtaining in a given occupation. The difficulty is partly that the pay of different persons in the same occupation usually differs widely—how widely we shall see later, when we come to consider the distribution of individual earnings. But even for any one person, earnings are often made up of a number of elements that can hardly be reduced to a single figure.

There are first the components of what is paid out in respect of the work done in any one pay period. There is commonly a basic time-rate, but this may account for only a minor part of total earnings, for these may also contain forms of payment by results or bonus on performance; payment for overtime; premiums for shift, night, or weekend work; other allowances for work in special conditions; allowances for tools, clothing, or travelling time; and allowances for seniority or age.

Other components of the pay to which the employee is entitled under his agreement with the employer accrue to him at longer intervals, or occasionally. Such are periodic bonuses and profit-sharing distributions; sick pay; holiday pay; and severance or redundancy pay.

Beyond these are the fringe benefits which equally form part of the employee's entitlement but which are not remitted to him currently. Such are the employer's contributions to pension and life assurance.

In some employments the pay also includes benefits in kind, such as accommodation at reduced rents or rent-free; board and lodging—as for seamen and members of the armed forces; or the provision of a car, even though the employee must make some payment for his private use of it.

There remain amenities that are made available to employees generally, but are not provided in specified amounts to any one employee as part of his agreed and enforceable terms of employment. These amenities include subsidized canteens and recreational and educational facilities; medical services; contributory pension or life insurance schemes in which the participation of the employee is voluntary; and sale of the firm's own product to employees at concessionary rates.

Only in a detailed inquiry into particular employments can all the above elements be taken into account. In any broad survey the need to represent the earnings prevailing in each occupation by a single figure, and to take such figures from available sources, obliges us generally to work only with the payments that are made in money, account being generally taken, when these payments are cited by the week or month, of what may also be paid out at longer intervals—such as payment for 'the thirteenth month'—and, where this is substantial, of the cash equivalent of payments in kind. For the purposes of the present inquiry this measure of pay is not so inadequate as might at first appear. We are concerned with the pay structure, that is, with comparisons of the pay in different occupations at a given time and in a given region, and in each such setting some of the elements that our measure of pay leaves out of account will attach to a number of occupations in much the same degree, according to the prevailing practice there. It seems likely, however, that in Western countries, at least until quite recently, fringe benefits have attached to the monetary pay of white-collar and especially of professional and managerial employees in higher degree than to that of manual workers, so that the ratio of the higher salaries to manual wages in money somewhat understates the difference in their total remuneration. But this distortion appearing in some measure in most economies, including the Soviet-type, is less liable to vitiate the comparisons between economies that it is a main purpose of this chapter to set out.

In another way the figures we shall present for professional and managerial earnings tend rather to overstate their size relatively to the earnings of manual workers. Our figures for all occupations are representative or average rates for all those engaged at a given time, whatever their ages. But generally those who follow the professions undergo relatively lengthy courses of education and training, and, when they begin to practise, their earnings often remain low for some time; and among managers it is rare for anyone to rise above middle management under the age of 40. Manual workers, even those who serve an apprenticeship, generally begin to earn earlier, and reach their highest earnings in their middle or later 20s; after 40 their earnings tend rather to fall off. In Sec. 8.3 we shall examine the very different patterns of lifetime earnings, or 'age–earnings profiles', to which these circumstances give rise. Here we may note that if lifetime earnings are reduced to a single total, the ratio of this total for the professional and managerial occupations to that for the manual is lower than the ratio, of the kind we shall be citing, between the average earnings in the two groups as they stand composed at any one time. Here again, since the difference may be expected to be present in most of the economies we compare, it is unlikely to vitiate the comparisons; but it needs to be borne in mind when we consider the pay structure of any one economy.

It will be seen that of the two aspects of pay, as a cost to the employer and an income to the employee, the measures we shall be using here lie nearer to the former. We omit the contributions that the employer may make to certain funds on the employee's behalf, and the overhead costs of certain services he maintains for the benefit of employees generally; but we do take much the greater part of the charges he has to bear in respect of any one additional employee. It might be said that we are also taking much the greater part of the employees's monetary income, but if we sought to penetrate the veil of money, and consider his real income, or the net advantages of the job for him we should have much more to take into account. In particular, we should have to assess the balance of amenity or deterrence in his working conditions. These conditions vary greatly. Until recent years at least they have generally been harder where pay has been lower, and they continue to make a difference of kind between manual and other occupations (Wedderburn & Craig 1974). A major part is played by the hours of work (Bienefeld 1972), which have often increased the disparities flowing from pay. But here perforce we attempt no summation of net advantage, and consider only the pay.

Similarly, we take pay before deduction of tax, and without addition of publicly provided supplementation to income, now sometimes termed 'the social wage'. It is true that progressive direct taxation makes the differentials in pay after tax smaller, and in some countries much smaller, than those in the same pay before tax. It is also true that the degree of progression varies considerably from country to country, and this affects international comparisons—the salaries of top management, for example, relatively to average manual earnings, appear higher in the U.K. than in France before tax, but the other way about after tax. There are increasing signs, moreover, of negotiations being conducted with an eye to the gain that will be realized by a representative employee after deduction of tax at the marginal rate he pays (Lindbeck 1975, pp. 148–50). Certainly any full comparison of particular differentials will need to look at the differentials in what employees are left with on the average after tax, as well as in what the employer pays out. But though it may be the 'take-home' that figures foremost in the employee's assessment of his own earnings, and in the comparisons he makes with pay at adjacent levels, we can hardly confine our attention to direct taxation. There are also indirect taxes, while income may be augmented by benefits in cash and kind (Royal Commission 1976b, Table 12). For a survey of the breadth we are now attempting, moreover, the available materials leave us no choice but to take pay before tax.

We shall be working, then, with a small-scale map, which omits many significant particulars, partly because some of the local features have not yet been mapped, but also because detail is in any case incompatible with breadth of coverage. The justification of this procedure will be found in the interest of the conspectus it affords.

2.3. A conspectus of the pay structure by occupation in Western countries

A view of some of the main proportions of the pay structure in seven Western countries is afforded by Table 2.1. A first finding is that the rank order is the same throughout, except that the technicians earn less than the lower administrative occupations in some countries and more in others. This uniformity of rank order is not unexpected: many people would say that it is in the natural order of things that the professionals should earn more than the clerks, and the skilled manual workers more than the unskilled. The figures we see here only establish the interprenetration of the pay structure and the stratification of society that we have already mentioned as a general condition of the Western countries. But we have yet to see whether the same rank order will appear in economies so different as those of the Soviet type. In any case what we take for granted needs explanation as much as the unexpected: in particular we have to ask ourselves whether the rank orders of pay and status agree as they do because pay confers status, or status decides the pay, or both are set together by some other factor. This is a question to which we shall return.

The Inequality of Pay

Table 2.1

The Structure of Earnings in European Economies and U.S.A.

Six European economies and U.S.A. at dates 1958–65: average earnings of men in certain groups of occupations, expressed in each country as relative to a rough average of all earnings.

Average of all earnings formed by combining groups 1 and 2; 6 and 7; 8; 9; with weights 3, 5, 9, 3; and set = 1·0.

Group of occupations	Denmark 1965	France 1964	West Germany 1965	Italy 1959	Norway 1964	U.K. 1960	U.S.A. 1958
1. Higher administrative	2·6	2·9	1·45		1·9		1·4
				3·3		2·1	
2. Engineers, professional	2·4	2·4	1·55		1·9		1·4
3. Lower administrative	1·3	1·55	1·05	0·95	1·0		
						0·95	
4. Technicians	0·9	1·2	1·2	1·4	1·15		
5. Foremen	1·1	1·15				1·15	1·15
6. Clerks, trade	0·7	0·85			0·8		1·0
			0·8	0·7			
7. Clerks, office[1]	0·8	0·8				0·8	1·05
8. Manual workers, skilled	0·75	0·7	1·0	0·6	0·9	0·9	
							0·9
9. Manual workers, semi-skilled		0·6	0·9	0·5	0·85	0·65	
10. Manual workers, unskilled	0·6	0·5	0·8	0·45	0·8	0·6	0·6

[1] Including shop assistants, except in the U.K. where they are included with semi-skilled manual workers.

Source: U.N., E.C.E. (1967), Table 5.16.

In the meantime a second feature of Table 2.1 demands attention: the rank order may be much the same throughout, but the distances between the ranks are not at all the same. Allowance must be made for the boundaries between the groups of occupations having been drawn differently in the various countries, but this will hardly account for differences as great as we find when we run our eyes along the bottom row and the top. The unskilled workers in West Germany and Norway, for instance, were paid 60 or 70 per cent more, relatively to the rough average we have taken for their countries, than those in France and Italy. At the other end of the scale, the relative pay of the higher administrative group in France was double that in West Germany; that of the two top grades in Italy exceeded that in Norway by nearly 70 per cent, and that in West Germany by 120 per cent. Evidently the West German and Norwegian structures and also that of the U.S.A. are much more compact than those of France and Italy.

Especially striking is the difference between France and West Germany in the relative remunerations of top management. A remarkable study by a team of French social scientists enables us to explore this (Daubigny & Silvestre 1972; Silvestre 1974). These inquirers took seven pairs of industrial firms, each made up of a French firm and a German counterpart—a firm of about the same size, using similar methods to produce the same kind of product, and situated in a region providing similar local supplies of labour. Taking three groups – higher management; the administrative, technical, and clerical (A.T.C.); and manual workers—the inquirers found that in six pairs out of the seven the average pay of the A.T.C. bore a substantially higher ratio to that of the manual workers in the French firm than in the German, and—again in six pairs, and even more markedly—the pay of higher management bore a higher ratio to the pay of the A.T.C. in the French than in the German firm. The effect on the whole span from higher management to manual worker is shown in Table 2.2: the six German ratios range from 1·88 to 2·34, the six French from 2·86 to 3·57.

Table 2.2

Salary Structures in Pairs of French and German Firms

Seven pairs of closely comparable industrial firms, one French and one German in each pair, 1971–72: (1) Average pay of higher managers as relative to that of administrative, technical, and clerical grades (ATC); (2) Average pay of ATC as relative to that of manual workers; (3) Average pay of higher managers as relative to that of manual workers, viz. (1) × (2).

	Pair 1		Pair 2		Pair 3		Pair 4		Pair 5		Pair 6		Pair 7	
	Fr.	G.	Fr.	G.	Fr.	G.	Fr.	G.	Fr.	G.	Fr.	G.	Fr.	G.
(1) Higher Managers/ATC	2·18	1·79	2·40	1·68	1·92	1·53	2·39	1·69	2·32	1·33	1·91	1·77	2·09	—
(2) ATC/Manual	1·52	1·13	1·47	1·21	1·49	1·37	1·32	1·28	1·54	1·41	1·58	1·32	1·28	1·28
(3) Higher managers/ Manual,(1) × (2)	3·31	2·02	3·53	2·03	2·86	2·10	3·15	2·16	3·57	1·88	3·02	2·34	2·68	—

Source: Daubigny and Silvestre (1972), Tables 5 and 6.

The economist is not surprised to find one factor of production costing more relatively to another in country A than in Country B. He expects that country A will arrange its production so that it uses less of the relatively dear factor together with each unit of the cheap one. In the present instance, therefore, he will expect to find the French firms using fewer A.T.C. and managers than the German firms do in collaboration with each hundred manual workers. But in fact it was the other way about. In six of the seven pairs the ratio of non-manual to manual employees was substantially higher in the French firm. The relative numbers in higher management were much the same, over all the pairs, but the French firms employed much greater relative numbers in middle management, and in the technical services such as inspection and setting-up that help to direct manual labour. If this was the outcome of market forces we should infer that the Frenchmen in these grades were individually so much more efficient than their German counterparts that even at their higher relative rate of pay their labour cost relatively less. We should also have to infer that some inherent or contrived limitation prevented other Frenchmen from attaining the same capability and so reducing its scarcity.

In the absence of evidence agreeing with these inferences we have to look for alternative explanations. The possibilities entertained by those who carried out the inquiry, and their colleagues who reflected on the findings (Sellier, Maurice, Silvestre 1972), arise from the consistent differences found in what can only be termed national styles of organizing production and ordering human relations within the firm. The differences in relative pay are only part of other systematic differences between the French and German firms, and seem to be bound up with them. The German firms have virtually a single pay structure comprehending all those they employ, who find their places in it largely according to their personal capability; the French firms come nearer to having three separate structures—one each for manual workers, middle management, and upper management, with gaps between them; and each person's place depends on the status of his post as well as on his own capability. The importance of status in the French firms appears in a greater formalization of the hierarchy of grades and appointments, with more ranks distinguished as well as wider pay differentials between them: immediately above the manual workers, for instance, a French machine tool firm had four ranks—charge hands, foremen, assistant superintendents, and superintendents, whereas its German counterpart had only foremen. It appeared that the French firms relied for direction on bureaucratic authority, the German on functional relations between collaborating specialists. A further difference in national style lay in training for the higher qualifications: in France this was mostly carried on outside the firm, and provided the student with a diploma, whereas in Germany it was mostly carried on within the firm, and the qualifications acquired were valid only within the firm, and not formalized.

Only the last of these contrasts admits of a properly economic analysis. Those who hold a generally recognized certificate of qualification can move from one firm to another, and take advantage of any competition there may be between firms for their kind of qualification. Those whose attainments are established only to the knowledge of their present employers cannot: they tend to be confined to an internal labour market (Doeringer & Piore 1971), where the employer has some discretion in shaping the pay structure, and is likely to be able to retain persons of given qualifications on lower differentials than they could command if those qualifications were more marketable.

But the other systematic differences between the French and German firms are to be accounted for only as each type of organization is seen to be embedded in the social structure of its own country, following its usages and adopting its customary practices. A particular instance noted by the French economists is that the French collective agreements on the wages of manual workers generally embody the 'Parodi scale', a standard pay structure with a fixed number of grades and fixed differentials between them, drawn up for use in the reconstruction at the end of the Second World War (Daubigny 1969); and this is contrasted with the flexibility and simplicty with which the basic terms of the German collective agreement at the industry-wide or regional level can be applied to the domestic circumstances of each firm. But much more generally, the hierarchies of pay and authority may differ between French and German firms because the structure of status and the prevailing attitudes to authority differ in the two societies. Is it the case, for instance, that a greater reliance on bureaucratic authority in French society leads to the need to maintain 'social distance' and support authority within the firm by discontinuities of gradation, and wide differentials? Is the German firm relieved of some of this need to strengthen the chain of command through the working of its legally instituted Works Council, which makes possible a nearer approach to administration by consensus? The trade union possesses a greater authority over its members in Germany than in France with its tradition of anarcho-syndicalism, and this makes possible the conclusion of central agreements that are binding on the member within the firm: does this help the German firm to maintain discipline and output among its manual workers without setting middle management so far above them in status and pay as in the French firm, or is the decisive factor here the greater deference to authority and the greater willingness to integrate with the group that German culture inculcates? How far, again, can the difference in the pay structures of the two countries be traced back in time, how far are they simply customary?

It has seemed worth examining this study in some detail, because it suggests the existence of a systematic difference of national style between the pay structures of two countries of comparable industrial development, a difference, that is to say, due to social structure, institutions, culture, and tradition rather than or as well as to current market forces. Do we find similarly suggestive differences between other countries? The comparison of six countries in Table 2.3 can provide only a qualified answer. Here the managerial salary is in all the countries that of a post having the same responsibility according to the method of evaluation used by a firm of international consultants; in each country this salary has been expressed as a ratio to the gross domestic product per economically active person. We notice at once that though the French ratio is higher than the German, it is not nearly so much so as in Silvestre's paired comparisons. A number of considerations may account for this: probably the chief are that Silvestre takes an average salary for higher managers whereas Table 2.3 takes a single post defined by its evaluated content; and that in Silvestre the denominator is the pay of other workers in the same firm, whereas in Table 2.3 it is the product per person throughout the economy. But the main interest of Table 2.3 is in its conspectus of six countries on a common basis. That the ratio is lower in the U.S.A. and Canada than in Europe agrees with the expectation that in the more highly developed countries trained managerial

Table 2.3
Salary for a Post of Given Managerial Responsibility
as a Ratio to Product per Head

Six countries, 1974: in each country, median base salary before tax for job of given evaluated content (in U.K. earning £16,950) expressed as ratio to gross domestic product per economically active person; ratios expressed as relative to U.K. ratio = 100.

	Relative ratio
France	121
W. Germany	112
U.K.	100
U.S.A.	80
Canada	76
Australia	69

Source: Royal Commission (1976a) Table G.7, p. 194.

capability will be relatively plentiful and consequently relatively cheap: but why is the Canadian ratio lower than the U.S. ratio, and why is the Australian ratio lower still? There must be an admixture of factors at work here, social and traditional factors as well as market forces.

But we have also to note two wide-ranging surveys that have found in market forces a generally applicable explanation of differentials being wider in some countries than in others. Fisher (1932) surveyed the skilled manual worker's differential over the labourer in the same industry, throughout the many countries from which the International Labor Organization was gathering statistics. He observed that the differentials of bricklayers and masons over the general building labourer 'are small in the Netherlands, Germany, New Zealand and Australia, where educational standards are relatively high and where illiteracy is practically unknown; they are rather high in Yugoslavia, Poland, Portugal, Latvia and Spain'. An effective elementary educational system, that is to say, reduced the relative number of those who are not schooled enough to be able to acquire a skill, and could offer themselves only as unskilled labourers; and this reduction in the relative supply of that kind of labour raised its relative price. But though this explanation held for a good many countries, there were some where it was evidently overridden by some other factor. In Stockholm the differential was high—could that be, we may ask, because of strong craft unionism? It was high, too, in Canada and the United States, and here the overriding factor might be found in the great number of recent immigrants who could find at least their first employment only as labourers; though here too craft unions were strong.

The second study was of the differential between unskilled labour and the higher administrative and professional occupations. Taking two appointments in the public service whose pay was recorded for some 34 countries, those of head of the meteorological service and office messenger, Scitovsky (1966) found

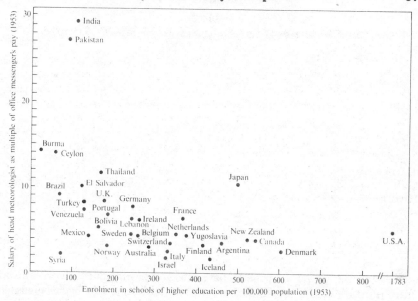

Fig. 2.1. The relation between pay differentials and university enrolment in different countries. *Source*: Scitovsky (1966).

a wide range of variation in the ratio of the one to the other, from about 2 to 1 in Iceland and Israel to 30 to 1 in India. Figure 2.1, reproduced here from his study, shows that the ratio was fairly consistently lower, the bigger the enrolment in higher education as a proportion of the country's population. The implied mechanism is again that of demand and supply: the greater the relative number of those whose education enables them to fill the higher posts, the lower their relative pay. An alternative explanation would not look for a direct connection between the large numbers of students in higher education and the relative pay of the small number of persons in occupations for which a high level of education is a prerequisite: this explanation would rely rather on the expectation that for a number of reasons (to be noted in C.3 below) such relative pay will vary inversely with the level of development of the economy, and would regard the number of students in higher education only as one among a number of possible indicators of that level.

Scitovsky also provides estimates that enable us to compare the salaries of the higher civil servants with the earnings of some leading professions, in a number of countries. These estimates are drawn upon in Table 2.4, where each figure for income is expressed as a relative to the average income per occupied person in the given country at the time. He calls attention to the limited range of the earnings of the professions, as there expressed, in comparison with the wide range of the relative salaries of the civil servants. A historical explanation, he suggests, can be found in de Tocqueville's *De la démocratie en Amérique*:

The Inequality of Pay
Table 2.4
Relative Professional Earnings, in Europe and N. America

Eight countries, at dates in the 1950s: earnings in five professional occupations as multiples of the average income per head of the occupied population in the given country at the time.

Country	Physicians	Dentists	Lawyers	University professors	High civil servants
U.S.A.	3·8	2·6	2·3	1·9	3·5
Canada	2·9	2·1	2·6	2·0	4·1
France	4·8	5·5		2·9	3·7
W. Germany	2·6	1·9	2·9	4·1	6·7
U.K.	4·3	3·3	3·2	3·8	8·9
Denmark	3·0		2·6	2·3	2·6
Norway			2·2	2·1	2·6
Sweden		2·2		2·4	2·6

Source: Scitovsky (1966), Tables 5–9.

aristocrats tend to give the porter a bare subsistence and allot high pay to the offices of state that they themselves or their sons may occupy, whereas a democracy will be generous towards the lowly and parsimonious towards the exalted. Whether the porter's wage was arbitrarily assigned or (as is more likely) was the market rate for unskilled labour, we can certainly see the high salaries as set by political power. We can also see how, once set, they would be perpetuated by custom, even when political power and the channels of recruitment to high office had shifted. Thus in Fig. 2.1 the relative pay of the civil servant in India and Pakistan stands out as far higher, in relation to the extent of higher education in the countries concerned, than is found anywhere else, and this can be explained by the civil servant of the 1950s in India and Pakistan having taken over the expatriate level of pay received by his British predecessor.

A survey of the earnings of general medical practitioners in the 1950s found them to lie between $4\frac{1}{2}$ and $5\frac{1}{2}$ times the average income per occupied person in France, Italy, the Netherlands, Switzerland, the U.K., and the U.S.A. (I.L.O. 1959): in the last two countries the multiples are higher than Scitovsky's, but again we note the narrow range.

2.4. The pay structure by occupation in the Soviet-type economies

We have extensive particulars of basic rates in the Soviet-type economies. For the U.S.S.R., indeed, these particulars are comprehensive: all rates are set centrally, and at least for certain years manuals are available in which they are tabulated (Chapman 1970). But though job descriptions are also published (Kirsch 1972), there are hazards as always in matching occupations in different countries. Particulars of earnings, including the effect of the very widely used methods of payment by results, are much harder to come by. But the available evidence brings out the features of the pay structure that appear in Tables 2.5–2.10.

Table 2.5
Comparison of Pay Structures in Hungary and Great Britain

Average earnings of men in certain occupational grades, reported for Hungary in 1966, and recorded in Great Britain in September 1968, all expressed as relative to the earnings of unskilled manual workers = 100.

Hungary			Great Britain
			Higher managerial and administrative staff—
Higher professionals	186	241	administrative
		188	engineers
			Lower managerial and professional staff—
Average level experts	154	169	administrative
		149	technicians
Office clerks	144	121	Clerks, office
Manual workers, skilled	132	139	Manual workers, skilled
Manual workers, semi-skilled	115	129	Manual workers, semi-skilled
Manual workers, unskilled	100	100	Manual workers, unskilled

Sources: Hungary: S. Ferge, *Volosag,* 1966, Budapest; cited here from Lane (1971), Table 8, p. 78. *Great Britain:* Dept. of Employment and Productivity, *Employment and Productivity Gazette* (H.M.S.O., London), May 1969, pp. 408–9.

(1)   Managers' salaries form a separate structure at some remove from other non-manual occupations. 'The structure of salary rates for non-manual workers', the E.C.E. report on *Income in Post-War Europe* (U.N., E.C.E. 1967) remarked, 'seems to be characterized by relatively small differences between occupations outside the managerial class, but by a distinct interval between the latter and all other categories—the size of the gap being a function of the scale and national importance of the enterprise.' Chapman (1975) cites as other factors helping to determine 'the category an enterprise falls into for purposes of establishing the level of managerial salaries', the variety and quality of output, and the level of growth of the productivity of labour achieved in the enterprise. Big differences in salaries result, between enterprises of the same category in different industries, and enterprises of different categories in the same industry. In the early 1960s, among Category I enterprises the range of the director's salary between industries was 3·5 to 1. In engineering, the director's basic salary ranged from 4·7 times the technician's in Category I enterprises to 2·4 times in Category VII.

It will have been the factors of scale and national importance that account for the top managers in one Russian iron and steel plant in 1956 getting 20 times as much as the lowest-paid manual worker (Gardner Clark 1960). But this will have been exceptional. Generally, as Table 2.7 indicates, the pay of top management in the Soviet-type economies is kept within an upper limit to which there is no counterpart in the private enterprise in the West. As we shall

Table 2.6

Comparison of Pay Structures in Engineering in Leningrad and in Great Britain

Monthly earnings in Leningrad, reported in 1967; weekly earnings in Great Britain in April 1970; expressed as relatives to the unweighted mean of 8 occupational grades = 100.

Leningrad engineering workers			British workers in mechanical engineering
Management (factory directors, shop superintendents)	146	130	Managers; supervisors and foremen
Non-manual workers in highly qualified technical-scientific jobs (designers)	107	117	Engineers, scientists, technologists
Qualified non-manual workers (technologists, bookkeepers)	93	103	Technicians
Highly qualified workers in jobs with mental and manual functions (tool setters)	109	100	Machine tool setter, setter-operator
Qualified workers of superior manual work (fitters, welders)	101	103	Fitter (production); fitter, maintenance; welder, skilled
Qualified manual workers (machine-tool operators, press operators)	91	89	Machine operator (metal) semi-skilled
Non-manual workers of medium qualifications (inspection and office workers)	71	83	Clerk (intermediate), storekeeper, storeman, semi-skilled
Unqualified manual workers	82	76	Unskilled building or engineering worker

Sources: Leningrad: Lane (1971), Table 5, pp. 64–5, adapted from O. I. Shkaratan, 'Sotsial' naya struktura Sovetskogo rabochego klassa', *Voprosy filosofii,* 1, 1967. *Great Britain:* Dept. of Employment, *New Earnings Survey 1970* (H.M.S.O., London, 1971), Table 36, average weekly earnings in April 1970 of full-time men aged 21 and over, paid for a full week.

see (Sec. 9.1), the 'Pareto tail' of Western distributions of earnings does not appear in the Soviet-type distributions.

(2) Among the non-manuals, engineers receive relative pay similar to that obtaining in the West, but techologists and technicians stand somewhat lower, and the clerical and administrative grades very much so. Our Tables show the position of the engineers as similar in Hungary, Leningrad, and Great Britain; Table 2.7 actually shows the chief engineer as standing higher in the Soviet-type economies than in Great Britain, though we must remember that in the Soviet-type economies the title of engineer is given only to university graduates, whereas in the Western economies it can be applied more widely. The technologists and technicians are less differentiated from skilled manual workers than in the West, and Table 2.8 shows a general tendency for the

Table 2.7

The Pay Structure of Engineering in Soviet-type Economies and in Great Britain

Maximum salary rates of occupations in engineering in three Soviet-type economies, about 1962, compared with average pay in similar occupations (not confined to the engineering industry) in Great Britain, in 1971.

Relatives to unweighted mean of six included occupations = 100.

	Czechoslovakia	Eastern Germany	Poland	Great Britain
Director	188	160	166 {	362 Managing director 254 General manager
Chief engineer	167	159	149	138 Chief engineer
Production chief	151	131	142 {	208 several works } Works 160 single works } Mangr.
Chief accountant	131	145	119	175 Chief accountant
Engineer	98·5	88	80	83 Engineer[1]
Foreman	64	84	89·5	69 Foreman[2]
Technician	57·5	72	93	67 Technician
Highest-paid manual worker	60	53·5	70	Fitter toolroom, 68 tool/die maker
Charwoman	30	—	—	23 Charwoman

[1] Average, weighted by numbers in sample of: civil, structural; electronic; mechanical; planning and production; other.

[2] Average, weighted by numbers in sample, of: senior or higher level; other foreman or supervisor.

Sources: For the three Soviet-type economies, U.N., E.C.E. (1967), Table 8.6. *For Great Britain,* top six occupations, A.I.C. Salary Research Unit, annual survey of U.K. executive salaries and fringe benefits, at July 1971, as reported in *The Times* (London) 8 Nov. 1971; bottom five occupations, Dept. of Employment, *New Earnings Survey 1971* (H.M.S.O., London), Table 57, median gross weekly earnings at April 1971.

relative pay of clerks and administrative grades to be conspicuously low by traditional Western standards, even though in Table 2.5 the Hungarian office clerks stand relatively high. The tendency extends to the service occupations generally, not excluding the professions outside industry.

Table 2.9 shows for the U.S.S.R. how low average wages and salaries were in certain of these sectors in 1964, relatively to the average wage in industry, and how much less they had risen than that wage since 1935. Nove (1966, p. 215), from whom Table 2.9 is drawn, also observed that '... until recently a qualified medical doctor earned only about 80 roubles a month, well below the average earnings of an industrial worker' (which in 1965 were about 103 roubles a month). 'Teachers' pay was significantly less than this.' It is the relative pay of the white-collared that provides the most extensive contrast between the Soviet-type pay structures and those of the Western economies.

Table 2.8

Non-manual Earnings Relative to Manual in
Soviet-type Economies and Great Britain

Average monthly earnings of two classes of non-manual workers as per cent of those of manual workers in four Soviet-type economies in 1964 or 1970; relative median weekly earnings of similar classes in Great Britain, 1970.

	Czechoslovakia[1] 1964	Czechoslovakia[1] 1970	Poland[2] 1964	Hungary[3] 1970	Soviet Union 1964	Great Britain 1970
Managerial, engineering and technical	130	133	165	151	144	131
Admin. and clerical	84	84	105	97	84	106

[1] All industry.
[2] Socialist industry.
[3] State and co-operative industry.

Sources: For Czechoslovakia 1970 and Hungary: Michal (1972), Table 4. *For Czechoslovakia 1964, Poland, and the Soviet Union:* U.N., E.C.E. (1967), Table 8.18. *For Great Britain:* Dept. of Employment, *New Earnings Survey 1970* (H.M.S.O., London 1971), Table 30, averages weighted by numbers in sample of Engineers, scientists, technologists, and Technicians; and of Supervisors and foremen and of Office and communications; full-time men throughout.

(3)   Among manual workers the differential for skill is much the same as in the West: Tables 2.5 and 2.6, comparing Hungarian industry as a whole with British, and engineering in Leningrad with that in Great Britain, show the skilled manual worker as receiving between 30 and 40 per cent more than the unskilled throughout; though in engineering it appears that the relative pay of the semi-skilled was lower in Leningrad. But we shall see that in the U.S.S.R. the differentials of the 1960s were lower than those that had prevailed between the First Five Year Plan and the wage reform of 1956.

Table 2.9

Relative White-collar Pay in Different Industries
in U.S.S.R.

U.S.S.R., 1935 and 1964: average wages and salaries of workers in certain sectors of white-collar employment as relatives to the average wage of workers in industry = 100.

	1935	1964
Posts	88	74
Trade etc.	80	74
Health	101	66
Education	105	79
Credit and insurance	121	80
Administration	146	97

Source: Nove (1966).

Table 2.10
Relative Wage-earnings by Industry in U.S.S.R.

U.S.S.R., 1928 and 1966: average wage-earnings in certain industries as relatives to the average in all industries = 100.

	1928	1966
Coal	90	184
Iron and steel	106	121
Electric power	125	98
Machinery and metal working	130	99
Paper	95	100
Shoes	124	82
Garments	114	73

Source: Chapman (1970), p. 47.

The white-collared apart, the most remarkable feature of the comparison between the Soviet-type and Western pay structures is the extent of their similarity. This will surprise those who expected the Soviet-type economies to have achieved a much greater equality. In fact, as we shall see later, the dispersion of individual earned incomes is lower in these economies than in some if not all of the Western economies. But it is no part of the Soviet philosphy of pay under socialism to give equal pay for unequal work: and in the U.S.S.R., at least, egalitarianism is a heresy. Marx made it clear in his *Critique of the Gotha Programme* that only an eventual state of communism could apply the principle of 'from each according to his ability, to each according to his needs'; until that state was reached 'bourgeois equity' must continue to apply, and each be paid according to the quantity and quality of his work. The concept of the quality of a given type of work has subsequently been extended to comprise its social importance, under the title of 'complexity'. Chapman (1975) quotes the Russian economist Kunel'skii, in an article of 1972 on 'the socio-economic problems of wages', as saying that 'complex labour, being more effective from the point of view of the national economy, should be valued more highly than simple labour'. On social importance Michal (1973, p. 425) has observed that if it is

supposed to reflect supply and demand conditions so that labour can be allocated primarily through earnings differentials (which is the present practice in Eastern Europe), it does not reflect much more than an attempt at consistency between the planned technology, planned output, and the resulting demand for various categories of labour on the one hand, and the supply of labour on the other. Some East European studies, while trying to define the 'optimum' inequality of earnings by differentials in social importance of work, measure the latter by the required differences in earnings to satisfy the above-mentioned condition of consistency. This is then a circular reasoning, similar to that in some Western studies which try to explain income distribution by differentials in factor productivity while measuring the latter in terms of factor earnings.'

But there has also been a pragmatic principle at work – the principle that it is by pay differentials that men and women should be induced to acquire the qualifications for different occupations, put up with working conditions where these are deterrent, bear responsibility, move in the required numbers into given industries and localities, and work hard when they are on the job. That they will act in this way in the pursuit of self-interest is accepted. Already in 1921 Lenin made this clear. 'Not directly relying on enthusiasm' he said when he wrote on 'The Fourth Anniversary of the October Revolution', 'but aided by the enthusiasm engendered by the great revolution, and on the basis of personal interest, personal incentive and business principles, we must first set to work in this small-peasant country to build solid roadways to Socialism by way of state capitalism' (Lenin 1921). Looking back on Czechoslovak experience in the 1960s, the economist Ota Šik has written, 'If contradictions arise between the direct material interests of people and their social interests, because of erroneous economic management, especially the system of wage and salary payments, people will generally act according to their immediate interests, and the moral appeals to combat these immediate personal interests will not be very effective' (Šik 1967, pp. 202–3). Soviet-type planners therefore aim at setting 'correct' differentials—those that will just suffice to induce workers in the required numbers to work in Siberia rather than Central Russia, or in heavy industry rather than light; to go through training courses; or to maintain a higher output in a given job. In 1926 the wage structure had been revised with the deliberate purpose of reducing inequalities that were felt to be incongruous under the dictatorship of the proletariat; but when the First Five Year Plan under Stalin intensified the need for skilled manual workers, the differential for skill was widened greatly (Bergson 1964, pp. 111–12).

The Soviet willingness to use wide differentials as incentives is illustrated by Table 2.11, which shows the differentials for manual workers in a Soviet steel plant in 1956 to have been much wider than those in steel plants in five Western countries. Among the manual workers in the Soviet plant, the highest-paid earned twelve times as much as the lowest-paid. We know the reason: 'As a Soviet personnel manager explained to the writer, the big wage-rate differentials are part and parcel of a tremendous effort to raise the qualifications and performance of workers in the Soviet iron and steel industry' (Gardner Clark 1960, p. 287).

But the differentials among manual workers in the U.S.S.R. have been reduced since 1956. The account which follows is drawn from Chapman (1975). As part of the general ordering of the wage structure begun in 1956, a minimum wage was ordained, first for certain industries and then, from 1959 onwards, as a general minimum of 40 roubles a month. At the same time the ratios of the highest to the lowest wage rates were set at smaller figures, industry by industry: in engineering, for instance, where the ratios had ranged from 1·9 to as much as 3·6 to 1, the new scale was kept within 2 to 1. A second programme of wage reform began with the raising of the minimum wage by a half, to 60 roubles a month, in January 1968. Initially this was accompanied by

Table 2.11
Wage Differentials in Steel Plants in U.S.S.R. and in Some Western Countries

Differentials between basic wage rates (weekly earnings for G.B.) for 13 manual jobs in a steel plant in each of U.S.S.R., 1956, and 5 other countries, 1960.

Lowest-paid blast furnace and open-hearth job in each plant = 100.

	Plant					
	U.S.S.R.	U.S.A.	German	Dutch	Italian	British
Production						
1st helper, open hearth	264	179	144	155	142	282
Keeper, blast furnace	243	141	133	130	120	250
Charging machine operator	243	148	127	126	122	220
1st pourer, open hearth	226	148	127	115	125	179
Operator, 125-ton crane	164	138	117	120	122	219
Operator, 10-ton crane	164	114	113	119	110	187
Stocker, open hearth	146	107	105	115	108	179
Repair and maintenance						
Stopper maker	175	110	109	115	110	n.a.
Maintenance fitter, 1st class, open hearth	164	141	127	124	122	172
Maintenance electrician, 1st class	164	141	124	130	122	189
Electric welder	132	141	113	124	122	n.a.
Greaser, open hearth	125	114	109	103	110	n.a.
Bricklayer helper	100	103	107	112	108	155

Source: M. Gardner Clark (1960), Table 7.

some raising of other rates only up to 70 roubles, except for one specially scarce type of labour, the machine tool operators. Later 'middle wages' were also raised, but the ratios from top to bottom were left smaller than they had been after the reform of 1956–60, being set in a number of industries at 1·7 or 1·6 to 1.

The raising of the low paid may well have been politically motivated – the lifting of the minimum to 60 roubles was announced on the eve of the fiftieth anniversary of the Revolution. It may also mark a widely increased concern with poverty, and a wish to reduce the difference between low family incomes and the incomes of the more affluent, such as other countries have experienced as the general standard of living has risen. 'Egalitarianism is still frowned on, but there is a new commitment to equity' (Chapman 1975). But the reduction of differentials has also fitted in with changes in the economy and the labour market. Education and training have raised the general level of capability, and reduced the difference between that of skilled and of unskilled labour. Increased mechanization has eased the pressure of demand for some manual skills, and increased the productivity of the semi-skilled and the labourer. In addition, the raising of the relative earnings of the lower paid may be ascribed to 'efforts to maintain the high rate of participation in the labour force in light of a higher level or real wages; the increased demand for workers in the consumer goods and services industries where pay and prestige have traditionally been low; . . . difficulties in filling the unattractive heavy manual jobs which no one likes, particularly the young, who have developed higher expectations; the greater relative scarcity of labour and the desire to have management economise on redundant labour' (Chapman 1975).

In the light of this survey of the factors governing the pay structure of the Soviet-type economies, how can we account for the much lower relative pay they assign to the white-collared occupations generally? We know that they did not do this originally as part of their calculus of incentives: it was actually a number of doctrinal and political considerations that led to the advancement of manual workers' pay while the pay of the white-collared was held back. There was the Marxian view of work in the 'non-material sphere' as unproductive. To reverse the previous relation between the pay of the more educated who had light work in comfortable conditions and that of the less educated who exerted themselves physically, often in rough conditions, was in accord with the egalitarian impulse of the Revolution, and the white-collared did not feel warranted in standing out against it. To retain the support of the manual workers was essential for the regime. 'In addition, a preference for blue-collar workers fitted in very well with the official propaganda that the working class is the governing class under socialism' (Adam 1972). Can it be, then, that these influences prevailed to the neglect of incentives, and allowed differentials to come about that were incorrect by the planners' own usual standards? Or did these historically operative factors only serve to put the relative pay of the white-collared in its right place in contemporary economies? May it not be the place of white-collar pay in the Western structure that is anomalous, a relic of former days when the prerequisite level of education was so much rarer than it is now, and have not the Soviet-type economies shown that in contemporary societies the supply of qualified white-collar workers, and the willingness with which they apply themselves when in post, can alike be maintained by relative pay much lower than is usual in the West?

We can best take those questions up with reference to Czechoslovakia. Table 2.8 shows the pay of administrative and clerical workers relatively to that of manual workers in Czechoslovakia as being substantially lower than in Hungary and Poland, but the same as in the U.S.S.R. The relative pay of a number of occupations in Czechoslovakia is given in Table 2.12: we notice particularly the registered nurse earning 41 per cent less than the skilled manual workers, the high school teacher 5 per cent less, and the district physician (general practitioner) only 12 per cent more. A recent authority observes that 'the link between earnings, formal education, skill and responsibility seems to be especially weak in Czechoslovakia' (Michal 1973).

When in the mid-1960s the Czech national product ceased to rise, and in part

Table 2.12
Relative Earnings of Occupations in Czechoslovakia

Table 2.12A: Probably in 1965 or 1966: average earnings of certain occupations as relatives to those of a toolmaker or maintenance fitter, 6th grade.[1]

Sales clerk (shop assistant)	52	Foreman, engineering	107
Typist	59	District physician	
Registered nurse	59	(general practitioner)	112
Elementary school teacher	64	Senior designer	126
Turner, 5th grade[1]	88	Senior research worker	150
Bricklayer, 6th grade[1]	93	Associate professor in university	168
High school teacher	95	Head physician in a hospital	168
Toolmaker or maintenance fitter,			
6th grade[1]	100		

[1] Manual workers are classified according to skill in grades 1 to 8, the 8th grade being the highest.

Source: J. Adam (1972), Table 3.

Table 2.12B: From data published in 1967: cumulative earnings over working life, ages 16–60.

	'000 Kr.
Rigger	1,125
Engineer[1]	989
Turner	949
Technician[2]	900
Lawyer	888
Economist[3]	771
Unskilled worker	692

[1] With college education.
[2] With secondary education.
[3] An administrative worker in the dept. of accounts and planning.

Source: Kýn (1975), p. 152.

actually fell, critics of the regime traced the trouble to egalitarianism. One of them, the sociologist Machonin, saw this egalitarianism as having been imposed by the Party when it seized power, as a means of securing acceptance of its bureaucratic rule by appealing to a traditional sentiment of the workers. But by the mid- 1960s, he contended, 'bureaucratic-egalitarian social relations were demonstrably the main brake on further development of industrial culture . . . Czechoslovakia of the early 50's and early 60's was a proof of the futility of considering whether it is possible on the present social foundations to replace material incentives by others, such as moral ones. It also refutes the efforts . . . to prove that the socialist type of society . . . can replace . . . the differentiation of rewards by the force of organisations, administration and power' (Gellner 1971, p. 321). The Communist Party accepted the criticism. 'The party', its Action Programme of 1968 declared, 'has several times criticised egalitarian views, but in practice wage levelling spread to an unusual extent and became one of the main obstacles to intensive economic growth and to an increase in the standard of living. ... The application of the principle of remuneration according to quantity, quality and social importance of work presupposes differentiation ("de-levelling") of incomes' (Adam 1972, p. 162 fn. 25). There was propaganda to gain acceptance of higher pay for the white-collared. A television programme, for instance, showed an ambulance going out on an emergency call, with a doctor seated beside the driver. 'And who earns more,' the commentator asked, 'the doctor or the driver? The driver. Does that make sense?' Yet it was found hard to give the white-collared a rise while denying one to the manual workers, and it was easier to resist inflation by holding white-collar salaries down than by restraining manual workers' piece-rate earnings.

There is thus no doubt that the smallness of differentials in Czechoslovakia was held responsible by some observers for a slow rise of productivity. But the differences between the Czechoslovak and the other Soviet-type economies are differences of degree rather than kind. In all of them the pay for education and responsibility, at least in the lower administrative, technical, and clerical grades, stands lower relatively to the pay for manual skill than it does in the Western economies. But if what is to a great extent a common structure proved compatible with sustained economic development in some at least of the other countries, it can hardly be given the major share of the blame for the slowing down of development in Czechoslovakia.

It seems also that in Czechoslovakia at least the low relative pay of the white-collar occupations proved compatible with the maintenance of an adequate supply of labour to them. In part this may have been because the potential supply had long been there without the relative pay having come down so as to extend the demand; in part it certainly was because more women were drawn into the white-collar occupations. A Czech economist has observed in this context:

Where the inflow of women is weak, e.g. in technical professions, wage levelling causes the number of suitable applicants for admission to university studies to lag behind planned targets. Many young people (mainly the sons of wage earners) are discouraged by the prospect of studying five and a half years in order to get a degree, only to then receive a reward which is considerably lower than the income of many people of the same age who have chosen a non-professional occupation. Even after gaining practical experience, only a small percentage have the chance to get a job which is paid considerably better than that of a skilled wage earner. (Adam 1972, p. 169 fn. 45).

On the other hand a Czech sociologist told the present author that the supply of entrants to the medical profession was maintained because sufficient young people preferred staying on at school for the pre-medical course, to going out to work forthwith: the difficulty was rather that when they were qualified and in post they did not exert themselves more than they had to in order to get by.

The two views may be reconciled by Adam's observation (op. cit., pp. 169–70) that 'the effect of wage levelling frequently appears as an influx of women rather than as a shortage of labour in the discriminated occupations. In some professions (primarily elementary and high school education, health care and law) this influx had reached such an extent that there is concern over excessive feminization' – the difficulty being that many of the women having also the cares of housewife and mother are driven too hard, and cannot keep up with the advance of knowledge in their professions or exert themselves enough in their work outside the home. Hence an endeavour since 1968 to reduce the proportion of women admitted to study law and medicine.

There is thus evidence that one major departure from the pay structure of the West has been associated in one at least of the Soviet-type economies with a change in the make-up of the labour force concerned and in the job content. We have also seen the need felt in the U.S.S.R. to reduce the extent of the only other major departure, the limited differentials of top management. But though the Czech critics may have been right in holding that the purpose of raising productivity would have been better served by wider differentials generally, this cannot be established. What is indicated by the experience of the Soviet-type economies and by the preponderant similarity between their pay structures and those of the West is that differentials have certain functions to perform in the economy, and must be kept within certain limits if they are to perform them.

These functions are threefold. First, differentials must be not inconsistent with the required numbers of people deciding to complete training courses and acquire occupational qualifications. Second, given a labour force with certain qualifications, differentials must be not inconsistent with the required numbers of people deciding to move into and remain in particular places of work, industries, and localities. The first two functions can be summed up as the matching of the supply of labour to the demand. The third function appears when the first two have been performed: people with given qualifications being occupied in given jobs, their pay must be so arranged, individually and one with another, as to stimulate them to work hard. This appears directly in the use of methods of payment by results to give the more productive worker higher pay than the less productive in the same job. It also appears indirectly in management and the professions, where it has been found that the consciousness of being paid substantially more than the less qualified is necessary to induce the more highly qualified to exert themselves above what is needed to get by.

The outcome is a pay structure that appears in much the same form throughout the Soviet-type economies. For manual workers there is, or used to be, commonly a structure of eight grades; though here, in the U.S.S.R. at least, market forces impinged farther—enterprises competed for workers by offering them the pay of higher grades, until 'by 1956 there were virtually no workers in the two lowest grades' (Nove 1966, p. 216). The reform carried through in 1958–60 adopted a scale for skill with six grades, and a ratio of 2 to 1 between the pay of the highest and the lowest grades (Kirsch 1972). Administrative, technical, and clerical employees have scales like those of manual workers: these scales are commonly based on the foreman's rate, which 'is most often set at a level some 10–20 per cent above that of a highly skilled worker' (U.N., E.C.E. 1976, c. 8, p. 11). For managers there is a scale of 5 to 7 grades, but the level of pay throughout the scale depends on the size of the undertaking: the top manager of one of the biggest coal-mines will get 70 per cent more than the top manager of one of the smallest, though both are in the same grade.

The pay of workers whose qualifications put them in a certain grade is itself differentiated in four ways (Shkurko 1964):

(1)   There are three (Kirsch says four) grades of conditions of work; according as the work is light or heavy, safe or dangerous, agreeable or disagreeable.

(2)   Because piece-work calls for greater effort, the time-rate for piece-workers is higher—in engineering by as much as 16 per cent. This is distinct from the bonus that the piece-worker may earn by fulfilment or overfulfilment of norms. In practice this bonus rises, as a proportion of the basic rate, with the grade of skill, so that the differentials in earnings for piece-rate workers are wider than those contained within the 2 to 1 span of the 6-grade scale. According to Shkurko two-thirds, and to Kirsch 90 per cent, of Russian manual workers are on piece-work.

(3)   The pay is higher grade by grade in the industries that are deemed to be of 'national importance' and/or have a higher planned rate of growth.

(4)   There are regional differences, to offset the deterrent effect of remoteness and hard climate, and to compensate for higher local cost of living. These regional differentials range from 10 to 100 per cent.

Pronouncements from high quarters make it clear that the Russian administrators regard their ability to vary the various sorts of differential as an effective means of changing the allocation of labour, or of maintaining it as the supply of labour to a particular employment changes. Thus Mikoyan in recommending the new scales to the Party Congress of 1956 said,

During the period when we were carrying out industrialization in a peasant country, this gap [between high and low paid manual workers] was natural, since it stimulated the rapid formation of cadres of highly skilled workers of whom the country was in dire need. Now, when there exists a working class which is highly skilled and has a high cultural level, and which is annually replenished by people graduating from 7- and 10-year schools, the difference, though necessarily preserved, must be reduced. (Conquest 1967, pp. 49–50.)

Again Shkurko, Deputy Director of the Labour Institute in Moscow, has observed:

The introduction of complex mechanization and automation is leading to the disappearance of unskilled labour and narrowing the distinction between skilled workers, engineers and technicians. If the principle of remuneration in accordance with the quantity and quality of work is to be respected, this reduction in the range of levels of skill ought to be followed by a corresponding reduction of wage differentials. However, to avoid undermining the workers' interest in improving their skill, knowledge and experience, any reduction in differentials must be strictly related to changes in the occupational skills of the labour force. (1964, pp. 364–5.)

But pay differentials are not the sole or very possibly even the main means by which the required allocation is sought in practice. There are also administrative incentives and pressures, which in Poland have been described as 'the long-standing policy of planned recruitment, the training of cadres and the planned employment of persons graduating from higher and secondary schools, housing policy, and social policy (especially the building of creches, kindergartens and collective residential centres)' (Morecka 1965). These all operate on the supply of labour to particular occupations and places of work. So far at least as the allocation of labour between industries is concerned, no rise in the relative earnings afforded by an industry has proved necessary in order to bring about a rise in the relative size of its labour force—between 1957 and 1963 even an opposite relation has been found, with the numbers occupied rising less than elsewhere in industries whose earnings rose more, and conversely (Galenson & Fox 1967). The same lack of correlation between changes in relative earnings and relative numbers has been found in a number of Western countries in fifteen years after the Second World War (O.E.C.D. 1965). As to allocation between occupations, again, though Morecka (1965) has seen a possible connection between a relative rise in manual workers' pay in Poland in 1950–3 and the investment drive of those years, she has found none between the relative pay of different types of worker and the phases of economic development over 1950–63. These observations bring out the multiplicity of the forces that bear on the allocation of labour: the relative pay is only one of these. To be consistent with a given allocation, however, it must still lie within certain limits: if it falls below a certain level, for instance, the industry concerned will find itself short of recruits and losing some of its present workers.

This has in fact happened often, and brought about both official and unofficial changes in the Russian structure (Kirsch 1972, pp. 168–70). In 1968 a troublesome shortage of machine tool operators was met by an increase in basic rates that broke up the consistency of the structure. This shortage may have been one of those due to a decrease in the willingness of workers, as the younger folk with their higher level of education enter the labour force, to take monotonous jobs or work in rough conditions: the differentials officially provided for working conditions have been proving too small. At points where shortages of labour arise on these and other grounds, management resorts to raising the bonus that is supposed to be dependent on norm fulfilment. 'By the late 1960s most incentive payments were not utilized for establishing on-the-job incentives' (Kirsch, p. 168).

2.5. Material and moral incentives in China and Cuba

China and Cuba are two Socialist societies in which much more reliance than in the Soviet-type economies has been placed on devotion to the common cause. Here, it has been hoped, would be the great incentive for labour, whereby workers would be motivated to move into and stay in particular jobs and places, and to apply themselves wholeheartedly when on the job. In China, a sustained campaign of education and propaganda has extolled self-sacrificing zeal and inculcated self-subordination to the common purpose; this is one purpose served by the cult of Mao and the study of his thoughts. In Cuba the appeal has been to *conciencia, espíritu comunista,* and *estímulo moral* (Bernardo 1971, p. 54). In both countries this approach has set its mark on differences in pay, but in both it has conflicted with the planners' need to set rates of pay that will stimulate production there and then.

China initially adopted the Soviet-type 8-grade scale for manual labour in industry, and throughout the subsequent upheavals it seems to have retained it. In the 1960s, the scale typically showed a ratio of 3 to 1 from top to bottom, the pay in each grade being about one-sixth higher than that in the grade below. This is a wider range than in the U.S.S.R. where a ratio of 2 to 1 is more usual in basic rates, although that in earnings is higher. But China probably resembles the U.S.S.R. in paying the white-collar worker at a low rate, by Western standards, in comparison with the skilled manual. In his survey of 38 Chinese enterprises in 1966, Richman (1969, p. 799) found that in most of them 'the average pay for administrative cadres was a bit higher than for workers, but there were exceptions'. The relative pay of top management may also not differ widely from the Russian. Richman's survey provides the figures that are set out in Table 2.13. We see that in the largest enterprises (as judged by

Table 2.13
Range of Pay Within Chinese Enterprises

38 Chinese enterprises, 1966: ratio of highest basic monthly pay to minimum and to average basic monthly pay, by size of enterprise.

Total employment in the enterprise	No. of enterprises	Median ratio of maximum basic pay to	
		minimum basic	*average basic*
3,000 and over	13	4·8	2·5
1,200 and less than 3,000	12	4·1	2·1
less than 1,200	13	3·0	1·8

Source: Richman (1969), Tables 9–2, 9–3.

numbers employed) the median ratio of the highest pay in the enterprise to the lowest was 4·8, which may not be far below the Russian average; in four of these enterprises the ratio was 5 or more. But in the smaller plants the ratios were lower, and the median in all the plants was only 3·15. In most of the plants the highest pay went to the director or deputy director, the party secretary or the chief engineer, but in eight of them it went to a skilled worker.

Subsequent indications are that the scales of pay, both for manual workers and management, are one part of the administration of labour that survived the Cultural Revolution of 1966–8. The differentials of the salaried may even have been widened, with certain managers (now called 'responsible comrades') continuing to be paid 5 or more times as much as the unskilled manual worker (Howe 1973, pp. 38, 74).

But the Chinese have departed from the Russian pattern in their treatment of individual piece-rates. In 1942 Mao had advocated the use not only of piece-rates but of *progressive* piece-rates, that is, of scales offering the worker successively higher increments of earnings for equal successive increments of output. This was in accordance with some Russian practice; but it did not agree with the Chinese tradition of group solidarity, or with the renewed drive for selflessness and non-material incentives in the Cultural Revolution. This revolution was in great part a battle between those who wanted to use material and individual incentives in the interests of speedy economic development, and those who were prepared to subordinate economic to social values. The former policy is summed up in the title of an article in a Peking journal in 1963—'Even if pay according to work is bourgeois, it helps socialist construction' (Hoffman 1967, n. 15). It came to be identified with Liu Shao-Chi. In 1971, Mehnert (1972, pp. 80–1) was told in a silk-weaving factory how Liu's people there had 'started offering the workers additional sums for special achievements. Workers who produced more than others would receive extra money over and above the salaries paid to them in accordance with their wage category.' The bonuses were small, but that did not make them any less objectionable in principle. Though 'everyone sees the necessity for various pay categories; the strong workman belongs in a higher category than a weaker woman', quite different and quite wrong are differences in pay for those in the same category: 'this capitalist and revisionist method of payment disturbs the unity of the factory community. . . . The followers of that traitor and scab Liu were encouraging egotism among the workers.'

The story brings out what to Western observers may seem a contradiction in the Chinese pay structure: if it is right and proper to pay a man more than a woman because the man being stronger produces more, why should not a man who exerts himself and produces more than another man likewise be paid more? To the Chinese the answer is simply that the latter differential appeals to self-interest, whereas the former cannot. Strangely but intelligibly, therefore, the Chinese treat payment in proportion to the amount of work done as a self-evident principle of natural justice when differences in that amount are not within the worker's own control, but as mischievous when they are. Hence the survival of the 8-grade scale.

But in the placing of a worker in this scale incentives return, for the grade to which a worker attains depends not only on his capabilities and his length of service, but on his performance, and on the 'political consciousness' he evinces by his study of the thoughts of Mao, his attendance at meetings, and his zeal at work. What is looked for here is not an outstanding personal achievement, but conformity with group norms, and so long as this is so, material incentives are permissible—the worker who does better will get higher pay, or at least the worker who falls short will not get it. But where outstanding achievement is to be rewarded, as in fact it is of set policy, the rewards must be non-material—medals, titles, honourable mentions, ceremonious meetings with national leaders.

Cuban practice has been made up of the same elements as Chinese. Soviet wage scales were adopted in 1962–63. In 1966–67 there was a move from piece-rates to time-rates, and differentials were narrowed. The scale that obtained outside agriculture in 1963 had shown rises of one-sixth in pay from one grade to the next, just like the Chinese, with a consequent ratio of 3 to 1 from top to bottom. A 7-grade scale in agriculture originally overlapped with a little more than the lower half of the non-agricultural scale, but wages in agriculture have since been raised to equality with the non-agricultural. The scale for administrators seems to have differed from that for manual workers outside agriculture only in being expressed in monthly instead of hourly rates. The managers, who were in the top two grades of the administrative scale, would thus be getting no more than the highest-paid manual workers, though there were relatively few of these (Bernardo 1971, pp. 69–71).

The move away from piece-rates brought greater reliance on moral incentives. The *espíritu comunista* is inculcated in the schools and by the media, and preached by the publicity department of the Commission of Revolutionary Orientation. Committees for the Struggle against Bureaucracy organize competitions between brigades, factories, and localities. Awards of many non-pecuniary kinds are made to workers who have done well, in respect of 'over fulfillment of the plan, full attendance and punctuality, voluntary labor' (that is, work done at weekends or during vacations), 'renunciation of overtime pay, and interest in the social life of the work center'. But it has also proved necessary to provide disciplinary sanctions against slackness, absenteeism, and insubordination (Bernardo 1971, pp. 54–68).

2.6 Egalitarianism in Israel

It has been widely believed that an egalitarian policy was pursued by the Histadrut, which is at once the trade union confederation and the organization administering much socialized production in Israel. In the early 1920s, it is true, egalitarian principles did prevail there, but Sussman (1973) has shown how these principles soon gave way to market forces. The attempted equalization of rates throughout the establishments managed by the Histadrut itself came into conflict with the need of management to attract and retain an efficient and willing labour force. The egalitarian drive had been reinforced by the wish to maintain a minimum wage high enough to be no deterrent to potential immigrants from Europe, but this minimum came under pressure from the unemployment of Jewish labour, in the presence of Arab labour that was available at lower rates and was in practice much employed by Jewish employers. This pressure was the more effective because, though policy was laid down centrally, it was in many local negotiations that wages were actually fixed; and the responsibility of the Histadrut for providing employment through its own labour exchanges made it sensitive to pressures in local labour markets. So it came about, in Sussman's words (p. 110) that 'it was not long before egalitarian blueprints became the exclusive domain of minorities within the Histadrut'.

The Kibbutzim present an example, not so much of equal pay for those doing different work, as of a complete separation between work and income, and the application instead of the principle 'from each according to his ability; to each according to his need'. In these producers' co-operatives there is no payment of wages to the individual worker, nor reckoning of his share in the proceeds. Most of the needs of the worker are met by provision in kind: each family handles money, if at all, only to the extent of a lump sum made available annually for the purchase of supplies not provided in kind within the Kibbutz. There are several varieties of Kibbutz, but of one at least of these Rabkin and Spiro (1970) were able to report in 1970, 'Compared with the situation twenty years ago, Kibbutz egalitarianism persists with almost no change, although it is not without its strains. Egalitarianism is maintained in all aspects of the formal social structure—an equal voice in Kibbutz affairs, the rotation of "black work" assignments, equality in housing, in eating, in financial arrangements, and in all other domains.' In a history now of some seventy years, the Kibbutzim have shown their viability as a means of carrying on not only agriculture but, in later years, some branches of light manufacturing. They have demonstrated the possibility in certain special circumstances of extending over a compainionship of as many as 1,500 persons the commensal arrangements that generally prevail only within the family (Tannenbaum et al. 1974, pp. 32–6).

How, then, does the Kibbutz match workers and tasks, and what incentives keep its workers on the job? Generally those who have a special bent for a particular occupation are able to engage in it; but if there is no vacancy there, they must go where there is one, by agreement with the labour manager if possible, and ultimately by the direction of the general assembly. The same arrangements apply to those who have no special bent. Some jobs that members agree in finding distasteful are filled in rotation. Of one Kibbutz it was reported that most members were reluctant to accept managerial responsibilities 'without commensurate rewards'; but the posts did in fact get filled by rotation from among the 12 or 15 members who were recognized as having the required ability (Spiro 1970, pp. 210–11, 268). In the same Kibbutz, it was observed that the members started work punctually and continued to work steadily throughout the scheduled hours, though they had no clock to punch or supervisor set over them. The underlying motivation was not far to seek. The membership was small enough for members to be aware that the well-being of all depended on the work of each, and slacking to be readily noticed, while hard or skilful work would gain prestige—was indeed the outstanding source of prestige. Most members found an intrinsic satisfaction in their work, and the teams working in different departments—the orchard, the dairy, and the like—were stimulated also by the 'socialist competition' between them. These motives for doing a good day's work operated, moreover, in the supportive context of the motives for belonging to the Kibbutz and making a success of it: the complete social security it provided for its members; not only 'the profound sense of belonging' that its members found in it, but also 'freedom from that psychological insecurity which stems from economic competitiveness'; and dedication to the ideals of the movement (Spiro 1970, pp. 83–8).

But Kibbutzim are of different kinds, and in some of them the increased division of labour in recent years has put egalitarianism under strain. The development of manufacturing and the adoption of more advanced technology have called for skills that not all members are able to acquire. The younger members in particular have found it hard to accept that all work faithfully performed is of equal value, and that the unskilled labourer deserves as well of the community as does the technologist (J. E. Shatil, personal communication).

2.7. Yugoslavia: a special case

The pay structure of Yugoslavia might be expected to be of the Soviet type, for this is an economy in which the means of production (other than peasant holdings of land) are owned collectively, and policy is controlled by the Communist Party. From 1947 to 1951, moreover, Yugoslavia used the Russian system of centralized planning, and the average rate of pay for each of nine categories of skill continued to be prescribed by the central administration until 1961. But in applying that framework to their own workers, enterprises had considerable elbow-room in practice, and from 1962 onwards each enterprise was charged with establishing its own pay structure.

In this a basic rate of pay would be assigned to each job according to a job evaluation to be carried out under the supervision of the workers' management council in the enterprise. The resultant scale was subject to agreement by the local trade union council, and confirmation by the 'district people's committee' or local authority (Bićanić 1973, c. 6). In 1956 an ordinance made compulsory the use of a uniform method of job evaluation, of a familiar Western kind, using the three main headings of skill and experience, working conditions, and responsibility. We are told (I.L.O. 1962, pp. 186–9) that the evaluators could also take account of 'the relative shortage of certain qualified workers or the value attached to certain work in a particular local community', and in turning evaluation points into money the enterprise could give effect to 'the more or less egalitarian outlook within the collective'. The outcome might well be a wide diversity of rates and relativities from one enterprise to another, but in one industry seen by the I.L.O. mission whose report has just been quoted the enterprises had set up a committee to secure more uniformity in the pay for a given job throughout the industry.

We do not know whether these procedures have set their own mark on the pay structure, or have only been the means of tidying and ratifying the existing differentials as these had been set by market forces. But that it was the latter is indicated not only by the way in which competition for scarce labour had pulled the actual away from the prescribed rates in the earlier years of centrally prescribed scales, but also by the political reaction against the 'variation of 7:1 between the highest and the lowest group within a single enterprise' that these procedures of later years were codifying; as also by the failure of this reac-

Table 2.14

Relative Pay of Certain Occupations in Yugoslavia 1969 and Great Britain 1970

In each country, pay for each occupation is expressed as relative to the unweighted average of pay of all occupations listed.

Yugoslavia			Great Britain
M.D. in general practice	158		
Dentist, medically qualified	123	158	Medical or dental practitioner
Sales manager	122	156	Marketing, advertising, sales manager
University professor	190		
University reader	145	152	University academic staff
Asst. lecturer—lecturer	110		
Architect	147	134	Architect, planner
Chemist	133	130	Natural scientist
Civil engineer	155	127	Engineer, civil structural or municipal
Enterprise manager	163	126	Works manager, production manager
Mechanical engineer	144	117	Engineer, mechanical
School teacher—			School teacher—
secondary etc. schools	95	114	secondary etc. schools
Docker	71	114	Docker, stevedore
Computer programmer	121	111	Systems analyst, computer programmer
Manager of purchasing dept.	109	101	Purchasing officer, buyer
Construction technician	107		
Mechanical technician	95	99	Technician—design, costing, production
Draughtsman	68	98	Draughtsman
Welder	77	98	Welder—skilled
		88	Welder—semi-skilled
Typesetter	104	98	Compositor, typesetter
Tinsmith	76	90	Sheet metal worker
Crane operator	80	89	Crane operator
Medical laboratory tech.	78	81	Technician, laboratory etc.
Store manager	89	79	Retail shop manager or departmental manager
Bricklayer	62	77	Bricklayer
Baker	74	73	Baker (table hand), confectioner
Cook	63	73	Chef/cook
Postman	61	73	Postman, mail sorter, messenger
Unskilled worker	47	72	Unskilled building or engineering worker
Butcher	66	63	Butcher, meat cutter
Agricultural worker	49	56	Average, farming, forestry, and horticultural

Sources: Yugoslavia: Statistički Godišnjak Jugoslavije 1971, Table 122–8, pp. 271–3, average net monthly earnings in 1969. *Great Britain:* Dept. of Employment, *New Earnings Survey 1970* (H.M.S.O., London, 1971), Table 30, median earnings for full-time men aged 21 and over in a week of April 1970.

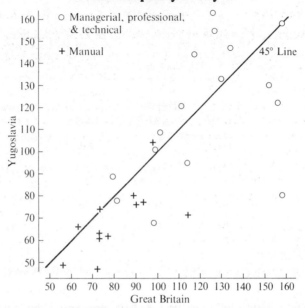

Fig. 2.2. Earnings of 28 occupations, relative to unweighted average of all, in Yugoslavia 1969 and Great Britain 1970. *Source*: as for Table 2.14.

tion—'many of the experts, always in short supply, moved to better-paid jobs, and the tendency was reversed again' (Bićanić 1973, p. 112).

Certainly the pay structure as we find it in 1969 shows a wide variance. Table 2.14 and Fig. 2.2 indicates a wider variance than in the corresponding occupations in Great Britain. We lack data for the position of the administrative and clerical grades that stand lower in the Soviet-type economies than in the West; but Fig. 2.2 shows that a majority of the managerial, professional, and technical occupations cited stand higher above the mean than do their British counterparts, and a majority of the manual stand lower beneath it. It is significant that these wide differentials are found where the workers themselves—in conjunction always, it is true, with the local representatives of the Party—have been given a voice in the codification of the structure.

It agrees with the tenor of these findings that in a comparison of some large industrial plants in Yugoslavia with matched plants in the United States, the rate at which pay rose with level in the internal hierarchy has been found to be not very much lower in the Yugoslav than in the American plants (Tannenbaum *et al.* 1974, p. 107).

2.8. The relative pay of particular occupations

So far we have been looking at the relative pay of broad grades, each containing many occupations. Let us now see how the different occupations stand in relation to one another within any one grade.

Table 2.15
Relative Earnings of Professions, in Five Countries

Median annual earnings of each profession in the year shown, as a relative to the unweighted mean of all the professions shown in the given country.

	U.K.[1] 1955–56	Belgium 1954	Victoria, Australia 1956	Canada 1956	U.S.A. 1950
Doctors	133	154	139	127	137
Dentists	135	111	101	101	110
Engineers	75	—	96	} 95	81
Architects	67	80	88		95
Accountants	92	77	75	82	—

[1] Those aged 30–65 only.

Source: Royal Commission on Doctors' and Dentists' Remuneration, 1957–60 (1960), Table 3 and Appx. F.

We lack the evidence for a conspectus of the professions, but particulars of five professions in five countries appear in Table 2.15. They show that in all five countries the doctors and dentists were earning more on the average than the engineers, architects, and accountants. That in 1955–56 the dentists stood so much higher in the U. K. than in the other countries may be attributed to the still recent and probably unintended effects of the establishment of the National Health Service. But the medicals' differentials differed widely from country to country—in Belgium, for instance, the doctors were earning twice as much as the accountants, in the U.K. less than 1½ times as much.

As against this, it is the extent of agreement that stands out in the comparison of the relative pay of a number of professional, managerial, technical, and clerical occupations in the U.S.A. and Great Britain that appears in Table 2.16. The American range, it is true, is wider, and (as we found more generally in Sec. 2.3) it is so because the higher-paid occupations diverge more from the average than the lower-paid. The accountants stand markedly higher in Great Britain, and one wonders how far this is due to the functions performed under the same title being different in the two countries, or to the British accountants being more 'professional'. The only other salient difference is the higher relative pay of the British technicians and draughtsmen: their greater unionization suggests itself as a possible cause. For the rest, the extent of agreement between the averages of rates of pay collected in each country over a wide range of industries and localities suggest the working of forces that tend to set similar relative valuations on similar work.

Among manual occupations, however, what is remarkable on an international survey is the lack of agreement. The I.L.O. maintains a list of more than 40 manual occupations, for which it gathers particulars of the hourly

Table 2.16
Comparison of White-collar Salary Structures
in U.S.A. and Great Britain

U.S.A. 1968 and G.B. 1970: Comparison of relative pay of employees in certain professional, administrative, technical, and clerical occupations.

Relatives to unweighted mean of median pay in twelve occupations.

U.S.A.			G.B.
Directors of personnel	154	138	Personnel or training managers
Engineers	150	123	Engineers
Chemists	146	138	Natural scientists
Managers, office services	130	129	Office managers
Accountants	114	135	Accountants
Buyers	110	107	Purchasing Officers, buyers
Engineering technicians	90	105	Technicians—design, costing, production
Draftsmen	86	104	Draughtsmen
Secretaries and stenographers	65	58	Secretaries, shorthand typists (female)
Switchboard operators	54	52	Telephonists (female)
Clerks, accounting and file	53	67	Clerks senior, intermediate, and routine (male and female)
Typists	49	48	Copy/audio typists

Sources: U.S.A.: U.S. Dept of Labor (1969a), average of median monthly salaries in a number of grades in each occupation, weighted by the numbers of employees in those grades. *Great Britain:* Dept. of Employment, *New Earnings Survey 1970* (H.M.S.O., 1971), Table 30, median gross weekly earnings; for engineers and clerks, average of earnings in a number of grades, weighted by the numbers of employees in those grades.

wages of adult workers from member countries all the world over. We can take 20 of these occupations, for each of which men's wages in October 1968 were reported by most of 22 countries, so that we have 22 fairly comparable wage structures. They prove to be very dissimilar, in the size of differentials and even in rank order. It is true that these disparities are more marked among the 11 South American, African, and Asian countries than among the 9 European countries with Australia and New Zealand. In the latter, differentials are generally narrower and the range from top to bottom is generally smaller—only in Spain does it exceed more than the two smallest ranges in the other group. But the difference is still only one of degree; and variety of rank order is as conspicuous among the European countries as elsewhere.

We can therefore survey the 22 wage structures as a whole. Table 2.17 gives the median place held by the pay of each occupation in the rank orders country by country: the medians of 16 of the 20 occupations are found to lie within the range from the 4th place down to the 10th. This lack of differentiation appears even more clearly in the right-hand column of Table 2.17, which gives for each occupation the median of its relative rates of pay country by country—the pay of each occupation has been expressed as a relative to the unweighted average of the pay of the same six jobs in all countries. We see that the median relative rates of pay of 14 occupations lie within a range of only 6 percentage points, from 103 down to 97. This might come about simply because in all countries the rates of pay of all those occupations were close to one another and to the average, so that differences in their rank order were largely accidental. But this is not so. There is never a range of less than 32 percentage points between the lowest and the highest relative pay; in half the countries the range is more than 50 points, and the occupations are spread fairly evenly over most of the range.

The concentration of the medians thus arises from our bringing together very different rank orders, in which one and the same occupation is liable to appear high here and low there. Table 2.17 shows that 15 occupations are at

Table 2.17
Rank Order of Wages of Manual Workers
in Different Countries

20 occupations in 22 countries,[1] October 1968: median, highest, and lowest of places in the rank order country by country, and median of the rates of pay expressed as relatives to the unweighted average of pay in occupations 1, 2, 4, 10, 12, 15 in each country.

	Place in rank order			Median relative pay
	Median	Highest	Lowest[2]	
1. Electric fitters (inside wiremen)	4	1	12	103
2. Plumbers	4	1	12	102
3. Carpenters	4	1	12	101
4. Painters	4·5	1	15	102
5. Machine compositors	5	1	10	118
6. Bricklayers	5	1	12	100
7. Tram and bus drivers	5	1	14	99
8. Coal hewers, underground	6	1	16	103
9. Iron and steel melters	6	1	16	97
10. Garage mechanics (general duties)	6·5	1	14	98
11. Patternmakers	7	2	13	101
12. Fitters (assemblers)	7	1	15	98
13. Cement finishers	8	1	16	97
14. Bakers (ovenmen)	9	1	15	97
15. Cabinet-makers	9	1	18	92
16. Tram and bus conductors	10	2	18	86
17. Labourers (unskilled), municipal parks and gardens	13·5	3	17	75
18. Construction labourers, unskilled	14	1	18	81
19. Railway goods porters	14	3	20	75
20. Spinners (male)	14	4	19	74

[1] Algeria, Senegal, Tunisia; Argentina, Mexico, Peru; Hong Kong, Israel, Japan, Pakistan, Singapore; Austria, Belgium, West Germany, Italy, Netherlands, Spain, Sweden, Switzerland, U.K.; Australia, New Zealand.

[2] The number of countries for which quotations were available for any one occupation was between 15 and 21 except for occupations 5 and 8 (both only 7 countries).

Source: I.L.O., *Bulletin of Labour Statistics* 1969, 2nd qr. Copyright © Geneva I.L.O. (1969).

the very top of the rank order in at least one country, and all but one of these also appear in the 12th place or lower still in at least one other country. The variety of places that one occupation can hold is illustrated for the fitter (assembler) in Table 2.18. There is no occupation whose position in the rank order does not vary over at least 11 places.

But the last four occupations in the order of Table 2.17 are set apart from the rest, with median rank orders of 13–14, and median relative pay of only 74–81.

Table 2.18
Variation of Rank Order of Fitter's Pay
from Country to Country

Pay of fitters (assemblers), October 1968; place in rank order of pay of occupations in Table 2.17, in 20 countries.

Place in rank order	Countries
1	Pakistan, Tunisia
2	West Germany, Singapore
3	Senegal
4	Austria, New Zealand
5	Netherlands
6	Spain, Switzerland
7	Argentina, Israel, Sweden
9	Australia
10	Peru
12	Belgium, Hong Kong, Japan
15	Italy, U.K.

Source: I.L.O., *Bulletin of Labour Statistics* 1969, 2nd qr. Copyright © Geneva I.L.O. (1969).

These are the two kinds of unskilled labour, with the railway goods porters, and the male spinners. They suggest a prevailing break in the manual pay structure between a lower bloc and the rest. Despite the presence of the semi-skilled spinners, the separation of this bloc suggests that one form of differential at least is found fairly uniformly, that namely which sets the unskilled apart. But Table 2.19 shows that there is nothing uniform about the size of this differential, either industry by industry or country by country.

Once above the unskilled, moreover, we find no breaks in the ranking, and no consistency in it either. How can we account for this variousness? Perhaps something is due to uncertainties of reporting—inevitably there is much room for disparity in the way the figures are collected, and the same occupational title may cover different levels of skill in different countries. One's mind turns to explanations of this kind when one finds railway goods porters, for instance, earning as much as plumbers in Japan, and more than all the building crafts in Austria; or municipal labourers getting more than machine compositors in Sweden—though in what country are wage statistics collected

Table 2.19
The Margin for Skill Among Manual Workers

Eleven countries, 1938 and 1972: percentage by which hourly wage of a skilled manual worker exceeded that of an unskilled labourer in each of three industries.

	Printing and publishing, machine compositor		Manufacture of machinery, iron moulder		Construction, carpenter	
	1938	*1972*	*1938*	*1972*	*1938*	*1972*
Argentine	194	24	26	18	35	29
Australia, Sydney	40	43	24	38	40	14
New Zealand	35	29	13	16	21	23
Belgium	71	23	24	25	24	22
Ireland	63	22	32	13	35	12
Italy		58	33	16	30	24
Netherlands	36	19	30	26	8	10
Sweden, Stockholm	59	40	14	12	10	27
Switzerland	130	70			27	28
U.K.	35	21	33	30	33	17
U.S.A., New York	24	84			61	28
San Francisco		59				27

Sources: "Changing wage structures; an international review", *International Labour Review*, 73, 1956, 275–83; I.L.O., *Bulletin of Labour Statistics*, 1973, 2nd qr. Copyright © Geneva I.L.O. (1973).

and processed more efficiently? The variousness is too pervasive, moreover, to be accounted for merely as the distortion of what if accurately reported would prove to be a common structure.

The absence of such a structure has therefore to be accounted for. We can do this on various assumptions. We might assume, for instance, that the relative pay of an occupation was determined in each country by the play of supply and demand in its domestic market, and that this worked to different effect in different countries—as well it might. If indeed in one country the market did put a higher price on carpenter's work than on garage mechanic's, and in a second country it was the other way about, there might well be no movement either of labour or of its products between the two countries to reduce the disparity. But we might also assume that market forces tended to put the same relative prices on given kinds of work in different countries, at least in countries at the same stage of development, but that they were not strong enough to offset the influence of other factors that differed from country to country. These other factors might be such as custom, perhaps perpetuating a relativity set by the social structure or market forces of long ago; or the strength of trade union organization in some occupations; or the working of public agencies for the fixing of rates of pay; or the standing, within the industrial structure of an economy, of the industry in which a given occupation is mainly engaged.

This structure appears when the industries of an economy are arranged in the rank order of the average earnings of their employees. When a limited number of broad sectors of activity are distinguished, the structures of some economies at similar stages of economic development have been found to resemble one another fairly closely (Lebergott 1947, for Canada, Switzerland, U.K., U.S.A., and (omitting two industries) U.S.S.R., in 1940s, with less agreement for Sweden; O.E.C.D. 1965, p. 23, for Denmark, Sweden, U.K., and U.S.A. in the 1950s.). But any one industry may hold very different ranks in the structure of comparable economies. Construction is one such. Its craftsmen—the bricklayer, the carpenter, the painter, the plumber—appear fairly close together in the ranking order of the 20 occupations of Table 2.17 in many countries, but at different levels: they stand notably higher in Belgium, Italy, and Sweden, and also in Pakistan, though here the bricklayer is detached from the others and ranks low. In Sweden even the cement finisher and the labourer in construction rank above electric fitters. Road transport is an industry whose representatives among the 20 occupations—the tram and bus

Table 2.20
Relative Earnings of Coal-miners,
in Different Countries

Twelve countries, 1970 or 1971; average earnings in coal-mining relative to average wages (or wages and salaries) in non-agricultural sectors.

	Coal-mining	Non-agricultural	Ratio of (1) to (2)
POLAND, 1970, monthly, zlotys	4,331	2,497[3,4]	1·73
U.S.S.R., 1971, monthly, roubles	206·5[3]	128·0[3]	1·61
HUNGARY, 1971, monthly, forints	3,220[3,4]	2,241	1·44
BULGARIA, 1970, monthly, leva	165·5[5]	123·0[6]	1·35
BELGIUM, 1971, daily, francs	786·1[1]	543[7]	1·45
SPAIN, 1971, hourly, pesetas	65·47[3]	45·74[3]	1·43
U.S.A., 1971, hourly, $	4·85	3·43	1·41
U.K., 1971, weekly, £	31·65[1]	25·25[8]	1·25
NEW ZEALAND, 1970, hourly, $NZ	1·66[3,4]	1·29[3]	1·29
CANADA, 1971, hourly, $Cdn.	3·51	3·28[2]	1·07[2]
YUGOSLAVIA, 1971, monthly, dinars	1,452[3]	1,446[3]	1·00

[1] Males only.
[2] Manufacturing only.
[3] incl. salaried employees.
[4] incl. value of payments in kind.
[5] 'mining'.
[6] incl. agriculture (except co-ops), machine tractor stations, and state farms.
[7] Daily earnings (M frs. 588·8; F frs. 373·8) weighted by relative numbers (36:10) of M and F salaried employees and wage-earners in mining, transport, manufacturing etc., and services.
[8] Weekly earnings (M £30·93; F £15·80) weighted by relative numbers (167:100) of M and F in non-agricultural sectors.

Source: I.L.O., Yearbook of Labour Statistics 1972, Tables 2, 18, 19, 20. Copyright © Geneva I.L.O. (1972).

drivers and conductors—sometimes rank low, sometimes high: in Belgium they lie at the bottom, above only the municipal labourers, in Switzerland they are at the very top. In every country where they are found, coal hewers are distinguished from most other occupations in the same way, by the nature of their work and the conditions in which it is performed, but Table 2.20 shows how widely their relative pay varied in 1970–71 from one country to another. It stood highest in the four Soviet-type economies, lowest in Yugoslavia. We have seen how their high standing in the Soviet-type economies follows from the priority deliberately given to their industry in planned development.

We must conclude that the prevailing agreement between countries in the ranking order of the pay of broad grades of occupations finds no counterpart in the ranking order of the pay of particular manual occupations. We have touched on a number of factors that can account for this. But we do not know whether these and other possible factors determine the relative pay of different occupations in any one economy within narrow limits, or whether their effect is to create zones of indeterminacy, so that quite different alternative ranking orders once established in any one economy could persist.

2.9. Review and discussion

(a) With the partial exception of the lower white-collar occupations, and the notable exception of the Kibbutzim, in every society and period we have surveyed we have found that the grades of work requiring more education, experience, and skill, and carrying more responsibility, have been the more highly paid. This has been found to be so even in Mao's China and Castro's Cuba. It shows that the inequality of pay arises from factors common to societies of very various economic, political, and social complexions; but it does not of itself show whether these factors are market forces, or moral judgements about the relative remuneration that is right and proper for work of a given kind, or both.

It will be both, if the moral judgement about what is only fair or right and proper is a judgement that those who produce more deserve to receive more in return. Of Poland it is reported on good authority that 'the majority of workers, particularly those with longer industrial tenure ("hereditary proletarians"), support the principle of earnings differentials, with limits of course, and strongly endorse the link between income and real contribution' (Brus 1974, p. 26). Market forces and moral judgements are intertwined again if the moral judgement is that those who possess higher qualifications deserve to be more highly rewarded, for qualifications are in practice deemed higher only in so far as they confer a greater ability to produce according to the valuation set upon products by the market. The wide acceptance of Job Evaluation may be attributed to its agreeing with this way of thinking.

(b) We noted the position of the lower white-collar workers as a partial exception to the general uniformity of rank order by grade: in the Soviet-type economies the lower administrative, technical, and clerical workers are paid less than many manual workers. This may have a political origin, through the

Marxian conception of 'the working class' reinforcing the need of revolutionary governments to find a broad base of support in the majority of the working population, especially in the indispensable skilled manual workers. But we must also note how, as far back as the 1840s, John Stuart Mill thought that the spread of literacy would have brought down the relative pay of clerks had it not been for the traditional valuation of their status; and the effective reason for the comparatively low position of clerical pay in the Soviet structure may be that this tradition was destroyed by revolution, so that market forces could take the effect that continued to be denied them by customary attitudes in the West. But we have to consider shifts of demand as well as of supply: that white-collar pay has not fallen more relatively to manual or that salaries as a whole have even risen relatively to wages in the U.K. and the U.S.A. may be attributed to the extension of demand for workers with secondary education, both in public administration and within industry.

(c) The case of the Kibbutzim is instructive. Here are societies small enough, almost all of them, for relations between the members to be personal, face-to-face relations; and these members, many of them migrants from hostile environments, and all of them feeling themselves still ringed about with enemies, have felt an ardent mutual loyalty and responsibility. The smallness of their numbers differentiates them from the members of vastly bigger societies most of whose economic dealings with one another are impersonal, and conducted 'at arm's length'. Their intense collective consciousness has generated a cohesion and dedication largely transcending the pursuit of self-interest and the calculus of individual input and receipts. If these have indeed been the essential conditions for the equality of incomes in the Kibbutz, they indicate by contrast the conditions that lead to the inequality of pay everywhere else —dealings at arm's length, and the consequent predominance of the pursuit and calculation of self-interest over concern for those, most of them personally unknown to one, with whom one is related only through the market. There is probably this further condition for the acceptance of equality of income, or the separation of income from output, that the members of the community shall not differ greatly in the skill required by their tasks. Where industrial development and the division of labour have gone some way, the association of differentiation of skill with equality of income has been felt to be anomalous.

(d) Though the ranking of grades of labour by pay is so widely similar, the differentials between the grades vary considerably. If it is market forces that differentiate pay, evidently they do not do so with uniform outcome. This might be readily accounted for, consistently with those forces being in sole possession of the field, by differences between countries in the supply of and demand for the different grades. But the explanations offered for particular instances suggest that the market forces share the field with others. The instances of the higher pay of civil servants in France and the U.K. and in India, indicate the workings of political power at their origin, and of custom in their perpetuation. The difference in the relative pay of managers between France and Germany, and between China and Cuba, indicates the influence of national style, culture, or tradition; though the part attributed to the marketability of the French manager's diploma directs our attention again to market forces. These forces may also be invoked to account for differentials in Yugoslavia being wider than in the Soviet-type economies, in that Yugoslav enterprises have been freer to compete with one another for scarce skills.

(e) The above considerations concern grades: the ranking order of the particular occupations within at least the manual grades shows no such uniformity, except that the unskilled are generally separated by a distinct interval from the semi-skilled and the skilled. The wide variety of rank order within these last two grades taken together can be attributed to differences between countries in the structure of supply and demand, that is, to differences in the natural abilities, the training, and hence the mobility of labour, in natural resources and technique, in the form of international trade, and in the tastes of domestic consumers. But we have noted the possible influence of other factors—custom, trade unionism, and methods of wage regulation by government.

(f) At many points in the above discussion we have noticed the likely operation of market forces. It is possible, of course, to account for any observed state of or change in differentials by supposing appropriate conditions or shifts of supply and demand, but we have put such conditions forward in explanation only where we have independent evidence for or can rely on general knowledge of their actuality. It remains to add that the Soviet-type economies have made their acceptance of market forces explicit in their adjustment of differentials as a means of allocating and stimulating a labour force which has been left mainly free, except in wartime, to choose and change employments. The planners, we have seen, aim to set 'correct' differentials, which will be not inconsistent with the required numbers of persons acquiring given qualifications, moving into and working in given employments, and, when they are there, working with a will. This adjustment of differentials is supplemented by administrative measures, but it is unlikely that the planners are just the victims of their own preconceptions when they believe that the adjustment takes effect.

(g) Though the pay with which we are concerned here is by definition that of employees, we cannot discuss the operation of market forces without noticing their evident impact on the pay of the self-employed. Those whose earnings are made up of fees, royalties, and payments under contracts for services evidently depend upon the valuation that consumers put upon their performance. Those among them with very high earnings—some actors or authors or boxers, for example—evidently earn highly because what they do is productive of interest and pleasure to many people who are prepared to pay for it. The same principle of payment according to productivity is likely to apply to those whose services reach the public only indirectly, and in the first instance are evaluated and paid for by an employer.

3

The Course of Change in
the Pay Structure

3.1. Changes in the differential for manual skill

Despite the heading for this section, we have to look first at a case of the differential for skill not changing at all from end to end of 500 years, and varying little from time to time in between. The pay of the craftsman and labourer in building can be traced fairly continuously in Southern England from about 1300 to the present day (Phelps Brown & Hopkins 1955). In the fourteenth century the two rates stood in a varying relation with one another, but by 1412, at the end of the doubling of the craftsman's rate that followed the Black Death, they settled in the ratio of 3 to 2 – namely 6d. a day for the craftsman and 4d. for the labourer. In the 1890s the rates in the same series were 7$\frac{1}{2}d$. an hour for the craftsman, 5d. for the labourer; in 1914 in central London they were 10$\frac{1}{2}d$. and 7d: still 3 to 2. Fig. 3.1 is drawn on a ratio scale, so that the vertical distance between its two curves measures the ratio of the one rate of pay to the other, and it shows that in all the settled periods between 1412 and 1914 that ratio was never far from 3 to 2.

At any one time we might see the craftsman's and the labourer's rate as each being set by the supply of and demand for its own kind of labour, and the differential between them would then be only an arithmetic by-product and not an object of policy. But when we see one and the same differential reasserting

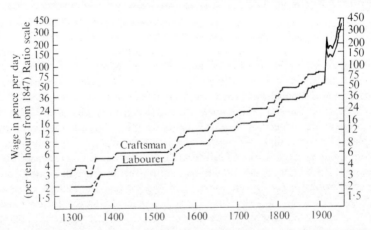

Fig. 3.1. Wages of building craftsman and labourer in Southern England, 1264–1954. *Source*: Phelps Brown & Hopkins (1955).

itself over five centuries and it takes the simple form of 'half as much again', we are bound to suppose that men kept it in their minds as a rule of thumb which they accepted as fair and reasonable if only because it was so customary.

Yet custom could have maintained that rule only in the absence of other pressures, be these from market forces, governments, or combinations of masters and men. We shall see that it ceased to hold in England from 1914 onwards, and from what we know about some other localities in the earlier centuries it was evidently not inherent in the nature of building. In Vienna it did prevail through much of the sixteenth and eighteenth centuries. Augsburg did arrive at it eventually, but only for the mortar-mixer, whose rate seems to have been higher than the labourer's, and rose during the sixteenth century to make the ratio 4 to 3 or less, a ratio maintained for some 140 years until 3 to 2 was attained in 1713. In Valencia likewise the craftsman rose less than the labourer in the sixteenth century, until by 1589 the ratio was only 6 to 5. These relative rises of the rate for the unskilled in Augsburg and Valencia occurred in a century when population in Europe was rising rapidly, and we should have expected increasing numbers to have forced down the relative rate of the unskilled. But the rise in population enforced a general and drastic fall in the standard of living of the manual worker (Phelps Brown & Hopkins 1959), and when standards of living are being reduced, the real wages of workers who are not far above the subsistence minimum to start with can be reduced only in less proportion than those of the higher-paid. That may account for what happened in Augsburg and Valencia, but in Southern England it was different. Here, though by the 1600s the real wages of building workers had been brought down to 40 per cent or less of what they had been a hundred years before (Phelps Brown & Hopkins 1956), the craftsman was still getting half as much again as the labourer—12 pence a day to the labourer's 8 pence. The reason may well be that the standard of living from which the descent had begun was substantially higher in England.

Evidently there was nothing universal in the appeal of the rule of thumb; and that it did prevail in some places for so long may well owe much to the exceptional technical stability of building—down to quite recent times, the workers in 'the industry that capitalism forgot' were performing the same processes with the same tools and materials as their predecessors of many centuries before, and there can have been little change in the relative number of craftsmen and labourers required. Where technical change impinges, it affects the differential for skill along with other differentials. The initial effect of industrialization has been to raise the pay of the skilled manual worker relatively to that of the unskilled. Towards the end of the eighteenth century in Great Britain, 'it would seem that the difference in pay between skilled and unskilled increased. The notion, widely prevalent, that machine production reduced the need for skill, receives no support from the evidence available. . . .' (Ashton 1955, p. 234). Men skilled in the new processes—the fitters, for example, who could build and maintain the new steam engines—were in great demand, and employers sought to entice them away from other firms by the offer of higher pay. At the same time the growth of population, and the movement of rural workers into industry, made it unnecessary to bid up the rate for unskilled labour except where industry was growing in a remote locality; where such remoteness was combined with operations demanding a high proportion of unskilled labour, in canals and railways, it did bring high relative pay to the navvy. In the American mainland colonies in the eighteenth century, rapid growth went with a higher differential for the craftsman than obtained in England at the time: instead of the English differential of 'half as much again', the carpenters and bricklayers in the province of New York were paid more than twice as much as the labourers (Smith 1776, I. viii).

The effect of population growth in widening the differential for skill is apparent on a comparison of that differential in the south and the north of the U.S.A. in recent years. Birth-rates in the south have been high; there has been much migration from the countryside into the towns of the region and much migration to other regions. But a 'relative labour surplus' has remained, 'largely at unskilled and semi-skilled level; it has exerted, despite migration, heavy and continuous pressure on job opportunities within the region'. This, Douty infers (1968, p. 76), explains why the differentials between north and south 'tend to vary inversely by occupational skill level'. He goes on to cite Heer (1930, p. 35) as finding the difference between wages in the South and in the rest of the country in the 1920s to be at its greatest for common labour and 'to become progressively less with each advance in grade of skill. In the case of one or two highly skilled occupations it disappears entirely.' This effect is not marked in 'industries in which differences in grades of skill are slight and in which advancement from one occupation to another is comparatively easy. It is strikingly evident, however, in industries in which there are broad differences in skill between various occupational groups and in which passage from one group to another is difficult.'

In recent years the countries in the early stages of industrialization generally show much wider differentials for manual skills than are found in the developed countries. In eight Latin American countries and three Caribbean countries, for instance, the pay of skilled workers in the metal industries and metal mining in 1965 was from 75 to 100 per cent above the unskilled rate; the corresponding margin in the United States was only about 40 per cent (International Metal Workers Federation 1965).

Yet it has also been observed that the differentials in the developing countries are narrowing rapidly (Gunter 1964; Turner 1965). A major factor is minimum wage legislation. Of the narrowness of the differential for skill in many African countries Taira (1966) observed 'This is because legal minimum wages are relatively high in these countries and are raised from time to time irrespective of the underlying economic conditions.' Brazil shows the effect on differentials of changing policy towards the minimum wage. Of the 1950s Fischlowitz (1959) remarked that despite shortages of skilled workers and a surplus of unskilled, the differential for skill had not been widening. 'Exactly the opposite tendency prevails—towards an extreme uniformity of wage rates which certainly discourages any great effort to acquire higher vocational skills.

... This may be attributed primarily to the levelling effect of public intervention in wage matters and particularly to the minimum wage.' But in 1964–67 the minimum wage was indexed to the projected rate of inflation which the actual rise of prices exceeded, so that its real value was reduced by 20 per cent, and in 1967–70 it was barely constant, whereas by 1970 real salaries in industry stood 10 per cent above their 1964 level (Fishlow 1972).

In the second half of the nineteenth century more figures of the differential for manual skill became available for the first time. A number of them are set out in Table 3.1 These allow of two general statements. First, the ratio of the

Table 3.1
The Differential for Manual Skill, 1860–1910

Germany, U.K., and U.S.A. at dates from 1860 to 1910: ratio of wages of skilled manual worker to those of his helper or of a labourer.

U.S.A. A: Aldrich Report, 1893.
B: Bulletin 18 of the Dept. of Labor, 1898.
M: McCormick Works, Chicago.

		1860	1870	1875	1880	1885	1890	1895	1900	1904	1907	1910
Germany												
Building			144[1]	147	152	165	160	157	156	155	143	137
Cotton spinning			164[1]	159	166	200	189	195	180	184	178	170
Mining, Dortmund					123	127	141	137	156	143	154	138
U.K.												
Building					157	157	153	149	150	153	154	153
Shipbuilding					185	185	196	189	192	189		
Engineering					167	167	170	167	172	167		
Railways[2]						198[3]					196	
U.S.A.												
Building	A	159	171		141		179					
	B[4]		170	168	178	185	189					
Blacksmiths	A	161	187		154		160					
	B		157	163	177	163	167					
Machinists	A	153	194		173		174					
	B		154	153	166	158	162					
Ironmoulders	A	151	165		155		157					
	B		175	155	168	159	163					
Patternmakers	A	119	182		161		189					
	B		176	184	194	182	193					
	M						163	150	156	173	180	173
Boilermakers	B		144	147	166	157	160					
Compositors	B		177	183	199	187	185					

[1] 1871.
[2] Engine drivers/goods porters.
[3] 1886.
[4] Weighted average of 4 building crafts/labourers in manufacturing.

Sources: Germany: Bry (1960), Table A.14. *U.K.:* Knowles and Robertson (1951). *U.S.A.:* A & B, Long (1960), Tables 45 and A.4; M, Ozanne (1968), Chart D-1.

skilled wage to the unskilled generally lay on or between the building trades' typical ratio of 3 to 2 and the ratio of 19 to 10 more typical of the shipwrights, the patternmakers, and the compositors. In fact, nearly half the entries in this particular table lie between 150 and 169, and nearly four-fifths of them between 150 and 189. Only the German miner's ratio lies mostly below 150. The British railway engine driver stands out as receiving virtually twice the wage of the goods porter. Second, no series shows a rising or falling trend. From one date to the next there is a good deal of movement, some of it abrupt, especially in the U.S. series from the Aldrich Report, each of which is drawn from only one or two firms; but from end to end the movement is small.

That differentials in British engineering changed as they did through these years was noted by Rowe (1928, c. V.) as calling for an explanation. He described the revolution in engineering methods that came about at this time, and noted that though it left unchanged the relative skills required of many grades, it did bring about great changes in the two most extensive grades, those of fitter and turner. In the 1890s, he wrote, 'one could speak of a large and fairly homogeneous group of skilled men as fitters, but this grade has now become spread out into a large number of grades of specialists, with marked differences in degrees of skill and craftsmanship. On the average if one can be struck, the modern fitter is undoubtedly far less skilled than his predecessors. The turner also is probably less skilled, and one might expect to find the rate for turners, and the rate, or rates, for fitters falling away during the last thirty years from the rates' for other skilled men. But actually a single rate for the fitter was maintained, and in the 1920s it was still about the same as the smith's rate; the turner's rate did show some tendency to fall relatively to the smith's, but not by any significant amount. Nor was there much change anywhere else in the structure. 'For practical purposes, it may be said that there was no disturbance in the structure of differential rates during this period of nearly thirty years' down to 1914.

Rowe gave two reasons for this. One was the predominance of the fitters and turners in the Amalgamated Society of Engineers, which in turn dominated the trade union side of the industry.

It was not to the interest of the turners that the fitters should disintegrate into a series of groups with varying wage rates, for the example would strike too near home, quite apart from the probable loss of organized bargaining power. Equally it was not to the interest of the fitters that the turners should abandon their equality of status with the other skilled grades, for that would have completely compromised the fitters' position, which was in reality even less tenable than that of the turners.

But trade union policy might not have prevailed against the shifts in the supply of and demand for particular grades that were coming about at the time, had it not had the support of custom. This was the second reason.

One cannot help being struck by a sense of the artificiality of the wage structure within any one industry, if not throughout industry as a whole, and in respect of the engineering industry, it is difficult to suppose that the influence of consciously directed trade union policy would have been at all considerable if it had not been reinforced by the domination of custom, not only in the minds of the wage-earners, but also to some extent in the mental attitude of their employers.

If the fragmentary evidence allows us any generalization about the differential for manual skill down to 1914, then, it is that it did not change much; but since 1914 in a number of occupations and countries it has certainly contracted. In the U.S.A., for instance, skilled workers generally were paid more than twice as much as common labourers in 1907, and less than 40 per cent more in the early 1950s. In the U.K. the fitter in engineering was paid about 70 per cent more than the labourer in 1914, and less than 20 per cent more in the early 1950s. These and other movements are shown for six countries in Table 3.2 and Fig. 3.2. But a glance at Fig. 3.2 is enough to restrict generalization. The

Table 3.2

The Differential for Manual Skill, 1900–61

Five countries at dates from 1900 to 1961: ratio of wage rate of skilled manual labour to that of unskilled.

	U.S.A.		Canada		Australia	U.K.		France		Germany
	(a)	(b)	(c)	(d)	(e)	(f)	(g)	(h)	(j)	(k)
1900						150		145		155
1907	184	205	209[5]	190[5]		154		133[12]		143
1912–14	198		201[6]	188[6]	136[10]	150[11]	171[10]	119[13]		135
1920–2	169	175[1]	229[7]	165[7]	126	127	133	108[14]		104
1928–30	178	180[2]	235[8]	171[8]	124	134	140	103	144	127
1938–40	170	165[3]			128	130	132	107	138	124
1945–7	148	155	207[9]		126[9]	126	125	119	117	143
1951–3	137	137[4]	203	120	116	116	116	128[15]	145	
1959–61	127		161	134	125	113			153[16]	

(a) Building trades journeyman and labourer, union hourly rate.
(b) Skilled worker's and common labourer's rates.
(c) First two entries, bricklayer's and building labourer's rate, average of rates in 7 cities; 1920–2 onwards, bricklayer's and mason's rate, building labourers, Toronto.
(d) First two entries, machinist, car cleaner, railways; 1920–2 onwards, machinists, maintenance, and labourer, in motor vehicles, parts and accessories, Ontario.
(e) 20 skilled, 20 unskilled occupations, Melbourne.
(f) Craftsmen, labourers, building.
(g) Fitters, labourers, engineering.
(h) Masons, navvies, Paris.
(j) Fitters, labourers, time workers in metal industries, Paris.
(k) Building.

[1] 1918–19.   [5] 1906.   [9] 1947.   [13] 1911.
[2] 1930–32.   [6] 1913.   [10] 1914.   [14] 1921.
[3] 1937–40.   [7] 1923–29.   [11] 1913–14.   [15] 1951–52.
[4] 1952–53.   [8] 1930–33.   [12] 1906.   [16] 1960–61.

Sources: Canada, entries for 1907 and 1912–14, Peitchinis (1965), Table 17.3. *Australia*, first 4 entries, Oxnam (1950); last 3 entries, Hancock (1969), Charts II and V. *Germany*, Bry (1960), Table A.14. *All other entries*, O.E.C.D. (1965), Table 6.

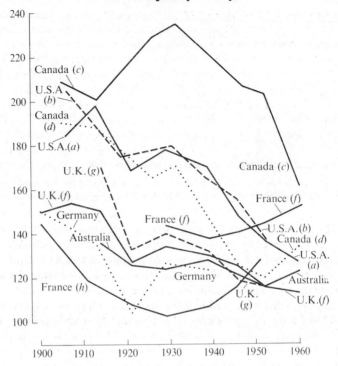

Fig. 3.2. Ratio of skilled to unskilled wage rate in six countries, 1900–60. (Rubrics and detail in Table 3.2.)

differential fell through both World Wars in building in Canada, U.K., and U.S.A., in engineering in the U.K., and in the series already cited for skilled workers and labourers generally in the U.S.A. Building in Germany shows a fall through the First World War. But by 1926 the building craftsman's differential in Canada was much higher than before the war; the change in the general differential in Australia after 1921 was inconsiderable; and in France the building and engineering differentials were both higher after the Second World War than before.

A further warning against assuming a general tendency of the differential for manual skill to narrow since 1914 is provided by the remarkable study by Ozanne (1968) of a century of wages in the McCormick (International Harvester) works in Chicago. Fig 3.3, which is reproduced by permission from Ozanne's work, shows the differential for skill (for most of the time, the ratio of the mean earnings of the pattern shop to those of common labour) as on a falling trend only through the first twenty years, down to 1880. in the 1900s it rose again, sharply; and thereafter, despite steep drops in the First World War and after 1935, it reverted always to a higher level than ever prevailed before 1900. On this evidence, together with that from U.S. Government wage sur-

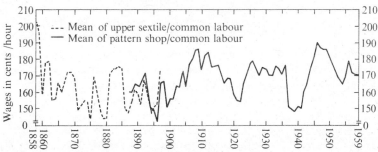

Fig. 3.3 Occupational differentials at the McCormick Works, Chicago, 1858–1959.

Index is skilled rate/common labour rate × 100. From 1858 to 1914 data are based on wage rates as of the first week in April, from 1915 to 1959 on annual average wage rates of a sample of workers. *Source*: Ozanne (1968).

veys cited in Table 3.1, Ozanne concludes (p. 154) 'that there has never been any long-term narrowing trend as this country matured industrially. Ober's 1907 wide occupational differential [this is the figure in U.S.A. col. (*b*) in Table 3.2] may, in the light of the McCormick Works data, have been the top of a wave rather than a half-way point on a long-run decline.'

None the less, what happened in some instances at least during and after the two World Wars stands out as a major and apparently sustained break with the past . Annual series show how during the years of high employment and rising prices the differential narrowed, and at some time after the wars widened again, but not so much as to regain its old extent.

It has been held that this was no more than a strong case of what generally happened in the course of the 8-year business cycle. We can see how, as activity rises, the demand for labour may be expected to extend in greater proportion for the less skilled than for the more skilled (Reder 1955). Firms will supply themselves with more workers in the higher grades by advancing some of their existing employees from lower grades. As the demand for labour subsequently contracts, an opposite process, of 'bumping' downwards, will set in. Fluctuations in demand are thus concentrated upon the lower grades, whose rates of pay will consequently vary more than those of the higher grades. This seems the more likely to have come about where, as was often the case, the pay of the higher grades was more regulated by collective agreements than that of the unskilled, so that it rose less promptly when demand rose, and was more resistant to cuts when demand fell. Silvestre (1971) has found that for purposes of wage movements the French economy since 1945 has had two sectors, one in which wages have been relatively high, output has been concentrated in a small number of firms, and employees have been highly unionized, and another which has been the opposite of the first in all three respects. In the first sector, the level of activity as evidenced inversely by unemployment has had no influence on wage movements, at least in the short run, but in the other sector the two have been closely associated—wage movements have depended on 'the state of competition in the labour market'.

So there are processes or institutions, both in the 'internal labour market' of the firm and in the labour market external to it, that seem likely to have made the differential for skill rise and fall inversely with the level of activity. But have they actually operated widely enough, and have they had sufficient possession of the field to the exclusion of other factors, to bring the supposed effect about? Outside the war years, this effect seems to have been expected rather than observed. We lack annual series of the differential for skill over a sequence of cycles, except in one case where the expected effect certainly did not appear. In the instructive study already referred to of the McCormick works in Chicago, Ozanne (1968, p. 152) reports that so far from widening differentials, 'recessions at McCormick's compressed differentials in 1858, 1873–79, and 1893–1894. In 1884, 1920–1921, and 1929–1933, wage cuts were strictly proportional and thus had no effect on differentials.' When compression occurred it was due to the resistance of common labour to any cut whatever. Thus a cut applied to common labour in 1884 in the same proportion as to the skilled workers led to a violent strike: 'the memory of this was so strong that in the recession beginning in 1893 all cuts of the first three years completely exempted common labour, despite skilled labour cuts in 1893 and 1894' (Ozanne 1968, p. 152). Again, in a wide survey of differentials in U.S. industries through 1914–46, Bell (1951) found that 'the conventional model of the occupational wage structure narrowing and widening during expansion and depression period, respectively, is, at best, a rough approximation, with the period 1929–33 ... an exception to this general tendency'. The furniture, rubber, and leather industries did conform with the model. In agricultural implements, foundries, and railroads differentials remained little changed. Differentials in the other industries surveyed showed no consistant cyclical pattern. In the great recession of 1929–32, '. . . none of the 16 industries surveyed by the Bureau of Labor Statistics experienced a definite widening of occupational differentials', and in a number of them these differentials were contracted—as in McCormick long before, through the low-paid being spared. For the U.K., on a review of the evidence from 1880 to 1950, Knowles and Robertson (1951) found that 'fluctuations in employment (below the level of "full employment") do not seem to have influenced the fluctuations of skill differentials very much.' Brown and Sisson (1975, p. 26) report that the unemployment rate in Coventry, England, rose from 0·8 per cent in 1964 to 4·8 per cent in 1971, then fell back to 2·45 per cent in 1973. In the local engineering industry over the same 9 years there was a progressive reduction in the spread of the earnings of the 14 occupational groups, and a steady rise in the ratio of the labourers' earnings to those of skilled production workers.

Thus what economists have seen as likely to occur in the course of the cycle, through supply and demand, a certain type of managerial policy, and the greater unionization of the skilled workers, does in fact seem to have occurred only exceptionally. For the most part it did not occur because the administration or negotiation of wage changes was directed by other principles or pressures, especially the felt inequity of cuts to the low-paid and their resistance to them even when not unionized.

The contraction of the differential for manual skill through the two World Wars stands out as an effect specific to those periods. The reasons that may be given for it with some confidence only amplify those already suggested as operative in the rising phase of the 8-year cycle. In addition, the enforced reduction of consumption in wartime brought into play the same factor as we have seen narrowing differentials in cyclical depressions: when wartime scarcities manifested themselves in a rising cost of living, the public control of money wages eased the impact on the lower-paid by granting the same absolute cost of living allowance to them as to the higher-paid. If a public agency or private employer felt unable to give less than a certain amount to the low-paid, the total cost would be less if the rise were extended to other employees as an equal absolute and not an equal percentage rise. For a time, at least, the higher-paid might feel that their differential was safeguarded if it was unchanged as a sum of money. Meanwhile the balance of supply and demand was tending to raise the relative pay of the less skilled. The more skilled were drawn on less for military service; in the munitions industries, where the demand for the more skilled workers extended, the supply was raised by upgrading or training persons formerly excluded, or the work was broken down so that parts of it at least could be done by less skilled persons. Generally, resistance to the crossing of occupational boundaries was reduced, and women in particular were admitted to jobs that they used to be kept out of or thought incapable of doing. As vacancies in the more skilled occupations were filled by drawing the less skilled upwards, the extension of the demand for labour of all kinds, and the competition of employers, became concentrated upon the less skilled, at the same time as they were being removed in greater proportion to the armed forces. Thus supply and demand worked in the same way as the sense of equity in wage administration. In the United Kingdom at least, a third factor may have had some effect before the end of the First World War: the number of trade unionists doubled in the course of the war, largely through the recruitment of the less skilled, whose interests might then be expected to do more to shape trade union policy (Turner 1952). Douty (1953) has pointed to the effects in the U.S.A. during the Second World War of the then recent extension of trade unionism: the new industrial unions contained a numerical preponderance of the lower-paid, and were still preoccupied with gaining recognition and negotiating rises 'across the board', to the exclusion of concern for differentials. But that industrial unionism was not a necessary condition for the narrowing of the differential for manual skill appears from this differential also having narrowed in building with its long tradition of craft unionism.

If these were the reasons for the contraction of the differential for manual skill during the two World Wars, how can we account for the three cases displayed in Fig. 3.2. where there was no such contraction? We can suggest answers at least for two of them. The comparative absence of change in the Australian differential from 1921 onwards has been attributed to the working of the system of public regulation of wages by conciliation and arbitration, in the states and the Commonwealth: the arbitrators were explicitly concerned with the differential, and generally accepted the claim that it should be maintained percentagewise (Oxnam 1950; Hancock 1969). That the differential in France was wider after the Second World War than before it may be attributed to the adoption at the end of the war of the Parodi scale, which gave the three grades of skilled worker 40, 55, and 70 per cent more than common labour (Daubigny 1969).

After the wars, when controls were removed, and some of the shifts in supply and demand were reversed, the same processes and pressures as narrowed the skill differential during the war now worked to reopen it. In the cases we are discussing, however, after neither war did it return to its former size. A major change thus seems to have been brought about within the wage structures concerned.

These and other findings have led to a general recognition of a contraction of the differential for skill as a common feature of the developed economies since 1914. A number of reasons have been put forward to show how it arose naturally out of the course of their development. But before we take up these reasons we must pause on the question of fact. Two qualifications are necessary. First, the contraction of the differential was by no means general. If we look back at Table 2.19, we see that though contraction predominated, none of the three differentials there—those of the machine compositor, the iron moulder, and the carpenter—contracted in all eleven countries between 1938 and 1972, and in seven countries at least one differential actually widened. If the reasons given for contraction were a sufficient cause of it in some cases, why were they not in others? The second qualification concerns Great Britain. Here at least it has been found that though the differentials of particular occupations certainly have contracted, those between the broad classes of skilled, semi-skilled, and un-skilled manual workers have changed extraordinarily little. Thus Routh (1965, Table 46) took the median earnings of men in each of three occupational classes—

(a) foremen, inspectors and supervisors, and skilled manual workers;
(b) semi-skilled manual workers;
(c) unskilled manual workers—

in six industries, in 1906 and 1960. On the average of the six, the ratio of (b) and (a) was 75·7 in 1906, and 73·3 in 1960; that of (c) to (a) was 61·9 in both years.

At first sight this looks like a conflict of evidence. In fact there need be no conflict, for where we find contraction we are following one occupation through, but where there is no contraction we are dealing with groups of oc-cupations that are composed variously from time to time. Within the group of skilled occupations, while some of the old-established ones are losing ground new ones arise to command higher pay: in building, for instance, the traditional crafts may now be earning less than the new, non-craft occupations of steel erector, bar bender and fixer, and tower crane operator. Various economic and social forces tend to raise the relative pay of the unskilled, but meanwhile semi-skilled jobs are expanding relatively to the labourers'; and the relative pay of those who remain in the latter does not rise. We are confronted not with a change in the balance of supply and demand for different grades of skill, so much as a switch of demand from old forms of skill to new. Perlman (1969, p. 85) has suggested that switches of this kind have operated in the U.S.A. in recent years to delay or reduce the contraction of differentials that social development has been tending to bring about, in the same way as they operate to raise differentials in the early stages of industrialization. 'It can be argued that mechanization does not require relatively more skilled than unskilled labor than characterized the prior pre industrial labor mix. But because of the difficulty of transferring pre industrial skills into those required by mechanized industry ... temporary shortage of skilled labor appears. This argument suggests that since the 1950's, changing American industrial requirements have created problems in labor supply similar to those facing a developing country.'

We must not build too much on Routh's finding. Differentials did generally narrow within four of his six industries, and that they widened in the other two just enough to offset this may be only coincidental. Ober (1948), working with groups of the skilled, semi-skilled, and unskilled which, like Routh's, were variously composed from time to time, found a reduction of the differential for skill in the U.S.A. from 105 per cent in 1907 to 55 per cent in 1945–7. But evidently we have to allow for the presence, alongside the forces tending to narrow differentials, of others tending to widen them or set up new ones. The former are partly economic, but largely social, and affect the supply of labour to different occupations; the latter are technical, and create a demand for labour in new specializations.

The economic and social forces in the U.S.A. have been discussed by Muntz (1955) and Keat (1960). The sharp reduction from the First World War onwards of the immigration of predominantly unskilled and often illiterate workers reduced the rate of growth of the unqualified labour force. This opened job opportunities for Negroes as the general level of employment rose through the Second World War and after; the migration of Negroes from south to north was linked with a reduction in the wage differential between black and white manual workers. Meanwhile the approval of equal absolute rises by the National War Labor Board was an immediate cause of the narrowing of proportional differentials during the Second World War; and after the war the Fair Labor Standards Act with its minimum wage exerted an upward pressure on the lowest rates of pay. But the most pervasive and powerful force was the extension of education. The percentage of boys and girls of high school age who were actually at school was only 7 in 1889–90; by 1952–53 it had reached 77. This numerical expansion went with a shift from academic towards vocational education within the high schools.

That expansion of education has found its counterpart, if not on the same scale, still sufficiently to mark a 'silent social revolution' (Lowndes 1937) in most Western countries. Among manual workers a chief consequence has been the passing of the old dichotomy of craftsman and labourer, and the rise of the semi-skilled. Few workers remain who are unskilled in the old sense of that term. By upbringing and education most manual workers now are capable of learning to perform a variety of operations requiring understanding as well as dexterity, and some of these operations are more complex, and involve no less problem-solving, than the traditional crafts. John Stuart Mill (1848, II. xiv. 2) remarked on the beginnings of this change from stratification to gradation in the England of his own day:

So complete, indeed, has hitherto been the separation, so strongly marked the line of demarcation, between the different grades of labourers, as to be almost equivalent to an hereditary distinction of caste. . . . The changes, however, now so rapidly taking place in usages and ideas, are undermining all these distinctions; the habits or disabilities which chained people to their hereditary condition are fast wearing away, and every class is exposed to increased and increasing competition from at least the class immediately below it. The general relaxation of barriers, and the increased facilities of education which already are, and will be in much greater degree, brought within the reach of all, tend to produce, among many excellent effects, one which is the reverse; they tend to bring down the wages of skilled labour.

This last sentence gives us pause. Why did the tendency that Mill thought he saw so clearly in 1848 take so little effect down to 1914, despite the great extension of education meanwhile? Two answers may be put forward. The first would accept that the pressure from the side of supply was indeed building up as Mill supposed, but its expected effect on relative wages was obstructed by the power of the craft unions and by sheer custom, until the great shake up of these things in the First World War. The second answer, which does not exclude the first, points out that there will have been shifts in demand as well as supply, and suggests that the increased supply of those capable of more skilled manual work was at least balanced by the extension of demand for them. Economists have differed in their assessment of the effects of technical change on the differential for manual skill. Some have seen such change as tending to reduce the differential. 'There are indications that many skilled occupations are becoming less skilled, arduous, and responsible with the improvement of mechanical equipment and working conditions. . . . At the other end of the ladder there are fewer and fewer jobs which are entirely unskilled. Labourers now work with an increasing amount of mechanical equipment, which both lends some element of skill to their work and raises their productivity' (Reynolds & Taft 1956, p. 357). Without calling those observations in question we can also accept Perlman's observations cited above concerning the switch of demand from old forms of skill to new. We have no measure of changes on the side of demand as we have in part at least of those on the side of supply; but the hypothesis of switches within the demand for skill, and of a sufficient extension of it in the aggregate to balance the extensions of the potential supply, does provide an answer to the main question posed by the actual course of events, namely why differentials among manual workers have not contracted more generally and unmistakably than they have done.

Among the factors mentioned as having brought about the contraction in the margin for manual skill in the U.S.A. during and after the Second World War was the enactment, in the Fair Labor Standards Act, of a minimum wage of wide coverage. We also noted the powerful effect ascribed to minimum wage legislation in Brazil. A number of other countries, developing or developed, have been enforcing a national minimum, or have taken statutory action to raise wages of particular groups of the low-paid. Have these measures tended to raise the pay of the unskilled generally relatively to that of the skilled? The British National Board for Prices and Incomes (1971, para. 124(2) and Appx. G), on a survey of the experience of other countries, found that they had not. 'No false hopes', it reported, 'should be attached to a national minimum wage. It does not offer an easy and direct way to effect a permanent improvement in the relative position of the low-paid; experience suggests that it does this only temporarily. . . . Because of the tendency of differentials to reassert themselves, the raising of national minimum wage levels in the wrong circumstances could be a dangerous source of cost inflation.' The finding that differentials tend to reassert themselves rests on U.S. experience. In a study of the effects of the raising of the U.S. minimum rate, Douty (1960) found that in Southern saw-milling the differentials of two skilled occupations over the unskilled rate declined in 1950, following the introduction of the $0·75 minimum in January of that year, but were restored partially by 1953 and completely by 1955. They fell again in 1956 when the minimum rate was raised to $1.00, but the next year, the last for which data were available at the time of report, they had recovered somewhat. It appears that minimum wage regulation is effective in raising the relative pay of isolated persons or groups, or of categories of labour like women or juveniles whose pay is hardly part of a common scale for different grades of labour, but that it is not effective save temporarily in raising the relative pay of the lowest grades within such a scale.

3.2 Changes in the relations between the pay for white-collar and for manual occupations

The term 'white collar' is a convenient label for all the administrative, technical, and clerical occupations that are collectively distinguished from the manual in that they do not transform, handle, or transport materials, but use processes of thought and communication for which a fairly high level of literacy and often also of numeracy are prerequisite. Needless to say, the distinction is not sharp-cut, and there are many borderline or ambiguous cases in the service occupations. But most of the white-collar occupations are distinguished from the manual by the level of education required by entrants, and the graduations of their pay are fairly closely associated with gradations of that level. With the great extension of education in Western countries over the last hundred years, should we not then expect the relative pay of the white-collar occupations to have fallen?

That of some high administrative posts certainly has done. In France the Directeur générale des Finances was paid more than 13 times as much as a

Table 3.3

The Pay Structure of the British Civil Service, 1876–1950

U.K. Civil Service and Post Office: relative pay of ten grades in 1876–79 and 1950, and changes in pay of each grade through four intervening periods.

Grade	1876–79 Av. salary p.a. as % of postman's	1913 / 1876–79	1924 / 1913	1938 / 1924	1950 / 1938	1950 Av. salary p.a. as % of postman's
Treasury classes						
Permanent heads	3,200	102	160	100	148	1,597
Administrative class	883	103	134	94	128	302
Executive class	307	106	197	100	132	174
Clerical officers,						
old 2nd Division	307		145	89	154	} 132
old Asst. Clerks[1]	130	149	243			
Women clerks	132	140	203	92	143	102
Post Office						
Manipulative A[2]	140	123	175	98	151	116
,, B[3]	100	138	186	97	194	100
,, W[4]	85	151	221	89	184	96
Engineering A[5]	440	178	200	101	140	454
,, B[6]	127	126	226	91	207	134
General wage rates		119	196	104	197	

[1] Subsequently Copyists or Abstractors.
[2] Male telegraphists, telephonists, and postal and telegraph officers.
[3] Postmen and sorters.
[4] Women telegraphists, postal and telegraph officers, and telephonists.
[5] Inspectors and above.
[6] Below inspectors.

Source: Routh (1954).

doorkeeper in 1834, more than 14 times as much in 1875, but only about 5 times as much in 1955 (Scitovsky 1966, Table 1). A no less drastic contraction has been found by Routh (1954) in the relative pay of the permanent heads of British civil service departments over the same span between the 1870s and 1950: Table 3.3 shows that from being 32 times that of the postman their pay came down to 16 times.

It might be held that the salaries of these posts in France and the United Kingdom in the earlier years were an inheritance of courtly privilege rather than an indication of the generally prevailing rate in comparable employments. But Table 3.3 shows a fall in the ratio of the pay of all the white-collar grades relatively to the manual: by 1950 the ratio had been reduced to little more than a third for the Administrative class, and little more than a half for the Executive, of what it had been in the 1870s. Between 1913 and the 1950s, the pay of women clerks rose relatively to that of male clerks generally (Routh 1965, Table 37), but in both the Civil Service and the Post Office it still fell relatively to that of male manual workers.

These changes came about mainly in three stages: the pay of the manual workers in the Post Office rose when that of the three Treasury classes hardly changed, in the years before 1914; and through the two World Wars the pay of all grades and occupations rose, but that of the manual workers rose rather more than that of wage-earners generally; in the interwar years it was reduced a little while the general level rose a little from end to end; but through both World Wars the two changed very closely in the same proportion. The extent of agreement here gives us ground to believe that the figures drawn from government service are representative of wider tendencies.

We find similar tendencies in the postal service of Geneva (Girod 1958). In 1860 the superintendents were paid more than three times as much as the postman, and the clerks nearly half as much again; in 1957 the superintendents' ratio was well below two to one, and the clerks' below 1·3.

The estimates of Scitovsky (1966), already drawn upon in Sec. 2.3, show that the reduction in the relative salaries of the higher civil servants was pronounced in a number of countries, and indicate that this was part of a marked general tendency of the higher earned incomes to come down relatively to average incomes. The earnings, it will be remembered, are expressed throughout as multiples of the average income per head of the occupied population of the country at the time concerned. Over the four professions of physician, dentist, lawyer, and university professor, and the eight countries, the median multiple in the 1930s lay between 4·2 and 4·1; in the 1950s it was 2·6. For the higher civil servants, the average multiple was 8·5 in the 1930s, 4·3 in the 1950s. Table 3.4 sets out particulars of the movement of the multiple in those cases in which Scitovsky's first estimate goes back to 1915 or earlier. In these instances the median multiple at the first date, before or early in the First World War, was 7·3, in the 1930s it was about 5·0, in the 1950s it was about 3·0.

Keat (1960) has shown that the halving of the multiple for professors in the U.S.A. extended over high school principals and teachers, though for elementary school teachers the fall was only by a quarter. But the U.S.A. provides a notable exception to the general tendency of the multiple to fall, in an actual rise through the Second World War of the ratios for dentists and physicians. Of the series for physicians, which begins only in 1929, Scitovsky remarks (p. 41):

How this series would look if it could be carried back to 1913 I do not know; but it is worth noting that the number of physicians per population in the United States had been declining at least since 1900, while in all the other countries it has been rising. . . . In general . . . the downward trend of professional incomes is the least pronounced and least well established in the medical profession. Perhaps the great advance in medicine and the resulting greatly increased demand for physicians' services account for this; an important additional factor in the United States is the restriction of entry to the profession.

Table 3.4
Relative Earnings of Professions in
the Twentieth Century

Instances from 8 countries,[*] 5 highly paid occupations, at dates 1915 or earlier, in the 1930s, and in the 1950s: earnings or salary as a multiple of income per head of the occupied population.

Physicians						
U.K.	1911	5·4	1936–38	5·2	1956	4·3
Denmark	1915	4·8	1930	4·9	1954	3·0
Sweden	1913	7·2	1930	4·2		
Dentists						
Sweden	1914	5·9	1930	3·7	1954	2·2
Lawyers						
U.K.	1911	7·3	1936–38	7·5	1956	3·2
Denmark	1915	5·8	1930	4·6	1954	2·6
University professors						
U.S.A.	1904	3·8	1930	3·7	1956	1·9
France	1914	8·5	1930	8·9	1956	2·9
Germany	1897	7·3	1938	5·3	1956	4·1
Denmark	1915	8·5	1935	4·6	1950	2·3
Norway	1910	4·7	1930	3·7	1957	2·1
Higher Civil Servants						
U.S.A.	1900	7·8	1930	6·1	1958	4·1
U.K.	1911	17·8	1936–38	15·2	1956	8·9
France	1914	10·3	1930	11·1	1956	3·7
Germany	1913	14·8	1935	10·6	1956	6·7
Norway	1910	5·3	1930	3·9	1957	2·1

Source: Scitovsky (1966), Tables 5–9.

Friedman and Kuznets (1954, pp. 136–7), finding an anomalously high rate of return on investment for training in medicine in the U.S.A., suggested that the number of practitioners may have been kept down, and their earnings kept up, by 'a scarcity of training facilities' and/or 'a deliberate policy of limiting the total number of physicians to prevent so-called 'overcrowding' of the profession'.

If we accept, [they said] our highly tentative figure of 17 per cent as an upper limit of the excess of mean income in medicine over dentistry consistent with completely free and moderately rational choice of profession, then about half of the observed difference between the mean incomes of physicians and dentists is attributable to the greater difficulty of entry into medicine.

But more recently Psacharopoulos (1975, c. 5), on comparing the rate of return on investment in training for medicine with that offered by other professions, has found that when allowance is made for the longer hours generally worked by doctors, the rate of return they realize does not appear to be higher than the rates in other professions, nor does it seem to have been rising. This leaves open the possibility that there are restrictions on entry throughout all the professions, but to establish this it would be necessary to identify the particular forms that the restrictions took. Since the costs of training are higher for medicine than for most other professions, the further possibility suggests itself that the present training is unnecessarily extensive. This is not an issue on which the economist as such can form' a judgement; were the possibility established, it would show that physicians' earnings were in one sense higher than they need be, but not that there was any monopoly element in the rate of return on their investment in their present training.

When we come to broader groupings the tendency of white-collar earnings to fall relatively to manual is seen to be far from general. The data for the U.S.A. and the U.K. summarized in Tables 3.5 and 3.6 show an actual rise in the ratio of salaries to wages in the United States between 1890 and 1915. Burns (1954), to whom the data of Table 3.5 are due, held that this must be ascribed to a relative extension of the demand for the services of the white-collared, for he notes that the number of clerks increased fourfold between 1890 and 1915 while that of manual workers only doubled. (The inference is the stronger, because any occupation whose relative numbers are growing will generally be drawing in a larger proportion of young people, and this of itself will tend to lower average earnings in the occupation.) After 1915, the ratio of salaries to wages fell on his reckoning through both World Wars. Some of the apparent fall will be due to his salaried employees including both sexes, when the proportion of women was rising. The data for Great Britain in Table 3.6 distinguish men and women, and what stands out here is the absence of any fall through the First

Table 3.5
Salaries Relative to Wages in the U.S.A., 1890–1952

1890–1928:   *Salaried*, weighted average of salaried employees, including managers, in manufacturing; railway clerks; Post Office employees; Federal Government employees.
         Wage earners in manufacturing, steam and street railroads, coal-mining.

1929–2l: *Salaried* in seven sectors.
         Wage earners in nine industries.

	Salary as % of wage		*Salary as % of wage*
1890	188	1929	128
1915	204	1933	158
1920	148	1937	129
1922	169	1939	130
1928	175	1944	97
		1946	107
		1949	102
		1952	96

Source: Burns (1954).

World War in the earnings of professional and clerical men relatively to those of manual workers, and an actual rise meanwhile in the relative earnings of professional and clerical women. For the men the Second World War brought a reduction that was bigger the higher the salary was to start with, and for the higher professionals it was drastic; the relative salaries of the teachers and nurses who made up the lower professional women were also greatly reduced, but those of women clerks appear as a little higher in 1960 than they were before the war.

That the relative pay of clerks has held up as much as it has is remarkable, when already John Stuart Mill (1848, II. xiv. 2) had seen it as dependent on an exclusiveness of education that was fast breaking down in his own day.

Until lately, [he wrote,] all employments which required even the humble education of reading and writing, could be recruited only from a select class, the majority having had no opportunity of acquiring those attainments. All such improvements, accordingly, were immensely overpaid, as measured by the ordinary remuneration of labour. Since reading and writing have been brought within the reach of a multitude, the monopoly price of the lower grade of educated employments has greatly fallen, the competition for them having increased in an almost incredible degree.

The reason we have already noted for the fall not having gone farther and faster is that the extension of supply of educated workers was largely matched by an extension of demand. Everyday knowledge suggests that this has been so. Social and political developments have called for a great expansion of public administration: more and more people have become occupied in the offices of central and local government. At the same time the development of technology and

Table 3.6
Salaries Relative to Wages in Great Britain, 1913–60

Great Britain, at dates from 1913–14 through 1960: average earnings in certain classes of white-collar occupations as relatives to the average earnings of manual workers.

	1913–14	1922–24	1935–37	1955–56	1960
1. Higher professional, men[1]	373	357	409	256	250
2. Lower professional, men[2]	176	197	179	109	121
3. Lower professional, women[3]	101	131	123	79	86
4. Clerical, men[4]	113	112	112	94	97
5. Clerical, women[5]	51	65	58	57	61

[1] Barristers, solicitors, dentists, general practitioners, clergy, army officers, engineers, chemists.
[2] Qualified teachers, draughtsmen, veterinary inspectors, laboratory assistants.
[3] Qualified teachers, nurses.
[4] Civil service clerical officers, railway clerks, clerks in business, bank clerks.
[5] Civil service clerical officers, clerical assistants, shorthand typists, typists; clerks in business and banks.

Source: Routh (1965), Tables 1, 30, 33, 37, 38, 40, 44. Weighted average of manual workers' earnings in 1906 raised to 1913 level by applying the wages index in Table I of Bowley (1937).

of the methods of management, together with great increases in the size of the firm, have expanded the activities of designing, organizing, communicating, and controlling, and progressively raised the number of white-collar workers employed by industry for each hundred manual workers. This has gone much too far for us to ascribe it to the response of an unchanged demand to what fall there has been in the relative price of administrative, technical, and clerical services; and in part, as we have seen, there has been no such fall. There must have been an extension of demand.

But this may not have been the only factor holding up the relative price. The possibility remains that the extension of potential supply, over against the actual extension of demand, would have brought the price down farther, had that not been resisted by some other factor. John Stuart Mill (1848, loc cit.) found this in custom and status. What seemed an anomalously high relative pay for routine clerical work he ascribed partly to the still restricted access to education, but partly also 'to the remaining influence of an ancient custom, which requires that clerks should maintain the dress and appearance of a more highly paid class'. Highly skilled manual workers would be employed in far greater number if their wages were lower, and 'similar considerations apply in a still greater decree to employments which it is attempted to confine to persons of a certain social rank, such as what are called the liberal professions; into which a person of what is considered too low a class of society is not easily admitted, and if admitted, does not easily succeed.'

The influence of custom and status may also be seen in the conditions of work of the white-collar employee having remained superior to those of the manual worker even where his relative pay has been brought down. In the U.K., for instance, it is still often the case that he does not have to clock on and off as the manual worker must; he is more likely to have the benefit of an occupational pension scheme; he has a shorter working week than the manual worker, and longer holidays; his earnings are regular, not fluctuating; he can take a certain amount of time off without loss of pay, as the manual worker cannot, in family crises, or for minor illness, or to go to the dentist, or he will receive sick pay over and above his national insurance benefit. These differences, not in the U.K. alone, are increasingly recognized as anomalous, and they are being reduced, usually on the initiative of government or the employers. That more has not been done in this way before may be explained by the manual workers not having pressed for parity of conditions. This may have been because they preferred to put all the improvement they could obtain in any negotiation into the wage packet, but it may also have owed something to taking customary distinctions of status for granted.

The belief that the attainments of the white-collar worker inherently assigned him a certain status, and this entitled him to commensurate relative pay, may be seen in our own day in the sense of outrage to their personal dignity that drives many white-collar employees such as civil servants and schoolteachers to demand a restoration of their former margin over the manual worker. Similar feelings have been invoked to explain what for the economist is the perverse behaviour of the clerk's differential in many of the less developed countries, where 'the differential for the simpler non-manual skills—for clerks and typists—often remains substantially greater than that for skilled manual or supervisory work despite significant "intellectual" unemployment *and* a shortage of competent craftsmen and chargehands. For Africa South of the Sahara, indeed, such general evidence as can be collected suggests that in recent years the average skilled manual differential has been narrowing while the clerical differential has been widening' (Turner 1962, pp. 12–13). Palekar (1962, pp. 207–16), on setting out the pay structure in Bombay City, noted that the factory worker earned no more than the much less strenuously occupied office peon, and the master turner or fitter no more than the bank clerk. He remarked:

These disparities reflect partly the interplay of market forces but more so a pattern of income distribution based on an age-old and obsolete social structure. It is the man who is paid, not the job. A man sitting behind a desk is paid more than a man working behind a machine, not because the latter's contribution to national output is less than that of the former nor because the desk workers in India are in short supply, none of which is true, but mainly because the man doing the paper work belongs to a social group which has traditionally enjoyed a higher standard of life than the group to which the manual worker belongs. Few Brahmins are to be found today among factory workers in India. The pattern of relative incomes seems to be only some kind of a homage that society pays to this occupational stratification which has behind it the sanction of both religion and time.

The last words suggest a distinct factor that may well have been operative, alike in John Stuart Mill's England and in the less developed countries of recent years. That there is an elbow-joint or ratchet effect in wage movements has long been recognized: even unorganized workers can combine effectively to resist a cut. One feature apparent in Fig. 3.1. is the extraordinary absence of reductions in the course of seven centuries of the pay of building craftsmen; though the way in which the data were collected will have elided ups and downs from year to year, there can be no doubt about the absence of sustained reductions or downward trends. Now it may well be that most of us as employees are not much less sensitive to reductions in our relative pay than in our absolute pay—at least to certain relativities. The pay of clerks may thus be kept near the relative level that prevailed when clerical abilities were scarcer than they are now, partly at least because the clerks already employed act in spontaneous concert to resist reductions in the relative pay to which they are accustomed. Such resistance is easier when pay is rising generally, and the maintenance of relativities is an argument to decide the size of a rise which in some amount or other is recognized as bound to come.

In surveying the changes in differentials over time we have been looking hitherto only at the differentials between broad grades—between the skilled and the other manual occupations, and between white-collar occupations and manual occupations as a whole. But the position of a particular occupation can change independently of the broad grade to which it belongs. A moment's reflection suggests a number of ways in which this may come about. There may be changes in the work performed, and correspondingly in the job requirements—technical advances sometimes simplify and lighten jobs, sometimes call for greater knowledge and impose heavier responsibility. When the requirements of an occupation are unchanged, the supply of labour to it may be varied by shifts in the outlook and preferences of potential entrants: a wider choice of jobs, and greater ability to avoid those with deterrent aspects such as 'unsocial hours', will be conferred by improvements in local transport, including especially the employee's possession of his own car, and by a high level of employment. The supply of labour, notably to some occupations largely filled by women, has been reduced by the lowering of barriers that impeded the entry of women to other occupations, the supply of labour to which has thereby been extended. In Sec. 5.4 we shall consider the effectiveness of minimum wage regulation designed to raise the relative pay of low-paid occupations, and in discussing discrimination in Sec. 5.2 we shall touch on the enforcement of 'equal pay for equal work'.

In these various ways the force of the market or of government may impinge on the relative pay of particular occupations, but the effects can hardly be lifted out of the flux of events for separate record. There are two other sources of change, however, sufficiently general to allow of separate examination. In so far as an occupation is linked with a particular industry, its relative pay may vary with the fortunes of that industry; and unionization, and the ongoing pressures exerted by trade unions and professional associations, have impinged differentially on the pay structure. Let us survey these influences in turn.

3.3. Changes in the relative pay of occupations linked with particular industries

We have noticed the very different position that the pay of a particular occupation can occupy in the structures of different economies, and have associated this with differences in the position in the market, or in planners' priorities, of the industries in which the occupations are mainly engaged. The pay of coal-miners was very much a case in point. Similarly for changes over time within any one economy: the rise or fall of the prosperity of an industry can carry the relative pay of a particular occupation up or down with it.

We may expect this movement to be resisted or reversed by two reactions on the side of supply. One is the endeavour of labour of a given grade to move away from the industries in which it is now paid relatively less towards those in which it is paid more. Whether there will be an actual shift in relative numbers depends on a number of factors; but even if there is no such shift, the greater ease of recruitment in the higher-paid employments, with its converse in the others, will bear on standards of recruitment, and on the relative size of the pay rises obtained by the two sorts of employment at a time when rises are general. The second reaction to be expected on the side of supply is conventional—it springs from the judgements employees form about what relativities or parities are just and reasonable, and their ability to make those judgements good in individual or collective bargaining. If, for instance, they firmly believe that two oc-

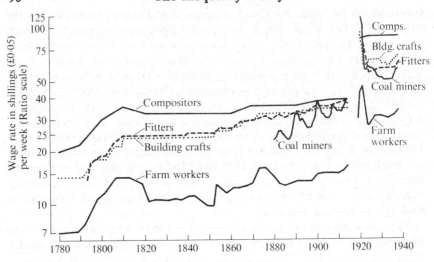

Fig. 3.4. Great Britain, 1780–1938, wages of certain occupations linked with particular industries. *Sources*: as for Table 3.7.

Table 3.7

Relative Levels of Wages in some British Industries
Since 1780

Great Britain, at dates within 1780–1970: relative wages in five occupations each of which is closely associated with a particular industry.

Relatives to average of wages of building craftsmen and fitters = 100

	Weekly wage rate					Median earnings in week of April 1970
	1793	1830	1880	1914	1930	
Compositor	206	138	116	105	145	114 Compositor; typesetter
Building crafts	101	100	104	96	105	90 Bricklayer; carpenter and joiner
Fitters in ship-building and engineering	99	100	96	104	95	110 Fitters—maintenance; production; toolroom
Coal-miner			75	100	86	95 Coal-miner
Agricultural labourer	53	44	47	45	52	65 Stockman; agric. machinery driver/ operator; general farm worker

cupations call for 'equal work' and therefore should receive equal pay, but the pay of one of them is pulled up by a surge of activity in the industry with which it is linked, the pay of the other occupation may be raised in sympathy, without there having been any corresponding extension of demand there; though the relation is not symmetrical—if the initial change is the holding back or forcing down of the pay of one occupation, the other is unlikely to follow.

With these possibilities in mind let us look at the relative movement of wages in five manual occupations, each mainly followed in a particular industry, over a run of years in Great Britain. From the eighteenth century until 1939 we can follow the commonly observed or negotiated wage-rates, and these are displayed in Fig. 3.4. After 1945 the effective pay diverged increasingly from those rates, and the relativities of 1970 which are shown in Table 3.7 together with those of some earlier years are based on actual earnings, including overtime and bonuses.

The remarkably close agreement between the fitters and the building crafts throughout more than a hundred years from the end of the eighteenth century

---

Sources:
B.L.S.: Dept. of Employment and Productivity, *British Labour Statistics: Historical Abstract 1886–1968* (H.M.S.O., London, 1971).
A.B.H.S.: B. R. Mitchell & P. Deane, *Abstract of British Historical Statistics* (Cambridge U.P., 1962).

1780–1938
Compositor: B.L.S., Table 4, London.
Building crafts: Phelps Brown & Hopkins (1955), Table I, wage rate of building craftsmen in southern England in pence per day through 1846, thereafter pence per hour. Weekly rates were obtained by multiplying daily rates by 6, and hourly rates by the hours per week obtained by consideration of Bienefeld (1972), Tables 2, 4, 5, 9, and Fig. 21b, and B.L.S., Table 2, as follows:

1847–63	58·5	1872–1910	54
1864–65	falling to 56	1911–14	falling to 50
1866–71	56	1920–28	44

Fitters: Through 1905, index in *A.B.H.S.,* c.XII, Table 3, converted into money by taking index 107 = 36*s.*, this being the wage of fitters and turners in Birmingham (*B.L.S.,* Table I), in 1905–10 when the index lay around 107.

1906–14, index provided by Guy Routh from A. L. Bowley and G. H. Wood, 'The statistics of Wages in the U.K. during the 19th Century, Part XIV, Engineering and Shipbuilding', *Journal of the Royal Statistical Society,* 69, Mar. 1906, 148–92, and from *18th Abstract of Labour Statistics of the U.K.* (Cmd. 2740, H.M.S.O., London, 1926), this index being spliced with the preceding series at 1905. *1920–38,* index at *A.B.H.S.,* c.XII, Table 3, converted into money by taking index 100 = 56*s.,* this being the wage of fitters and turners in Birmingham (*B.L.S.,* Table I) in 1924 when index was 100.
Coal-miner: 1880–1914, Bowley (1937), Table II, the index being converted into money by taking index 136 = 31·5*s.,* this being the average earnings in full week of males in coal-mining at the Wage Census of 1906 (Bowley, op. cit., p. 50), when the index was 136. *1920–38, A.B.H.S.,* c.XII, Table 38, index converted into money by taking 100 (index at 1924) as = 60·4*s.* which is the wage of 37·1*s.* in 1914 raised by 63 per cent (*A.B.H.S.,* p. 351).
Agricultural Labourer: Through 1914, A.B.H.S., c.XII, Table 3, England and Wales, the index being converted into money by taking 110 at which the index stood in 1905–10 as equal to the approx. 15*s.* given by *B.L.S.,* Table 7, as the average cash wage of ordinary labourers in agriculture in 1905–09. *1920–38, B.L.S.,* Table 8, average minimum wage per week for basic hours, adult male workers.

1970
Department of Employment, *New Earnings Survey 1970* (H.M.S.O., London, 1971), Table 30, median earnings in a week of April 1970 of full-time men aged 21 and over. For all except compositors, the earnings shown are the weighted average of the earnings of the occupations listed on the right-hand side of the present Table, the weights being the numbers in sample given in Table 150 of the same work.

down to 1914 is too sustained to be fortuitous, or to be the outcome of reactions on the side of supply, which must take time to work themselves out and so allow of substantial divergences remaining meanwhile: they seem most likely to be the result of a general judgement that these craftsman's rates should be about the same. But in the interwar years the fitters in engineering were in the exposed sector of the economy, the building crafts in the sheltered, and the fitters' rate ruled lower accordingly. By 1970 the order had been reversed: it is not immediately apparent why this should have been so, after a quarter of a century in which both industries were expansive and craftsmen were in short supply in both.

Between the Napoleonic and the Second World Wars the farm workers' rate kept a fairly steady ratio to the craftsman's, and this may mark the steadiness of the relations between the farm wroker's rate and that of the labourer in engineering and building, and again between the latter and the craftsman's rate. The rise in the farm worker's relative earnings after 1945 may be attributed to the pressure of population in the villages having been reduced while farming became more profitable than before, and technical progress raised productivity in agriculture greatly.

What is quantitatively the most striking feature, the fall in the relative pay of the compositors, is probably to be attributed to the social change observed by J. S. Mill, and not to the factors with which we are concerned at present. The printing industry was not depressed, the numbers engaged in it (together with paper and stationery) expanded in greater proportion between 1841 and 1911 than those in building or in engineering. Its craftsmen were strongly unionized. If their relative pay fell, must it not have been because the prerequisite literacy was rare in the eighteenth century and increasingly plentiful in the nineteenth?

But in the varied fortunes of the coal-miners—the rising trend of their relative pay in the expansive years of their industry down to 1914; the sharp fall in the interwar years; the recovery after 1945—we have a strong case of that dependence of an occupation on the prosperity of a particular industry, which has also been displayed by the fitters and the farm workers.

The extent to which the relative earning of workers of the same grade but in different industries can vary is further illustrated by the data from the Netherlands in Fig. 3.5, and here the variations appear within short spans of years. But, of course, these were unusual years: the first span, 1939–58, included the Second World War and the years that followed it, of centralized control of wage movements; in the later span, 1959–72, wage earnings rose threefold. This Dutch experience, therefore, also throws light on the power of institutional regulation and market forces to shape the occupational pay structure, in so far as occupations are largely identified with particular industries, and wages are adjusted industry by industry. The remarkable reduction of differentials that had come about by 1958, in comparison with 1939, was the outcome of the policy adopted in the time of great hardship at the end of the war: differentials had to be reduced, because when the lower-paid were assured of a social minimum, there was little left over at first to provide more for others.

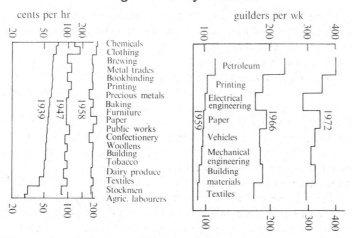

Fig. 3.5. Changes in Dutch inter-industrial wage structure.

Netherlands: average earnings of adult male skilled production workers, in 17 branches of industry and 2 of agriculture, 1939, 1947, 1958; and in 8 branches of industry, 1959, 1966, 1972. *Sources*: Witteveen (1960); Netherlands Central Bureau of Statistics, communicated by P. de Wolff.

Central control of wage movements by the national organizations of employers and trade unions maintained the uniformity that had been established in hard times through years of recovery and rising prosperity. But in 1959 wage policy was changed, and all the forms it subsequently took allowed some divergence. How far this went is shown by the right half of Fig. 3.5.

Two opposed inferences might be drawn from this experience. On the one hand the truly remarkable uniformity brought about in the first period may be seen as a demonstration of the arbitrariness of the differentials that come about in the absence of central regulation, and of the consequent practicability of such regulation. On the other hand the departures from central control in 1959, and the divergences that followed, may be seen as evidence for the strength of market forces and of the bargaining power of employees, as these bear on pay and prices in different industries. From our knowledge of the way in which the successive phases of Dutch wage policy came about, it is the second interpretation that seems more likely. Uniformity was accepted only in the aftermath of war; as those hard years receded, the will to maintain central control weakened relatively to the pressures for freedom of manoeuvre.

What form the ensuing diversity took will have depended on many factors, such as the market for the product, technical change in the industry, its rate of growth or contraction, the supply of labour, the strength and policy of the trade unions, the method of wage payment, and government intervention. We do not know if the differentials opened up by 1972 represented a recovery of relations that would prove more durable than those of 1959, or whether fresh divergences would emerge so long as the inflation went on in which those of 1972 had come about. Earlier in the present section we noticed two ways in which differences between the earnings of a given grade of labour in different industries may be reduced, and one of these was the insistence by the lower-paid on parity with the higher. This in turn is part of the mechanism of cost inflation. The inter-industrial differentials of 1972 are likely to prove less stable than those of 1939, for the same reason as the general level of wages was less stable in 1972.

3.4. The influence of trade unions on occupational differentials

Has unionism any systematic tendency to change the differences in pay between occupations, and, if so, in what ways? Judgements based on general considerations or particular experiences have differed widely. Economists looking to market forces have asked what occupations are confronted with a demand sufficiently inelastic for the loss of employment consequent on the forcing up of pay to be so small as to have little deterrent effect. Believing that skilled workers are generally more strongly placed in this respect than other workers, they have concluded that unionism was likely to widen the differential for skill. This would come about in two ways: the skilled workers would be able to exert greater pressure, and their employers' capacity to pay their less skilled workers would be diminished. Those observers on the other hand who give less weight to the elasticity of the long-run demand curve than to the immediate bargaining power of the parties in confrontation have seen the unskilled worker as weaker than the skilled when standing alone, and as having correspondingly more to gain from combination. What has actually happened?

The question is hard to answer, because to isolate the effect of unionism we need to be able to compare the pay of unionized workers with that of others who are like them in all respects except that they are not unionized. The nearest approach to those circumstances has been found in the very partially unionized economy of the United States, though allowance has still to be made for other sources of differences in pay, such as the unionized workers being located in different regions, or in cities of different size, from the non-unionized. Surveying a considerable number of these American comparisons, H. Gregg Lewis (1963) found that in 1957–58 unionized workers' pay generally stood from 10 to 15 per cent above that of their non-unionized counterparts.

But this was on a comparison of the average earnings of the whole manual labour force in different sectors of a given industry, and not of different occupations. Two later studies, however, have used information concerning individual employees: the 1/1,000 sample of the Census of Population in 1960, and the Michigan Survey of Consumer Finances, provide particulars such as the age, education, and race of particular persons, as well as their occupation and earnings, and whether or not they are union members. This information has made it possible to take account of another factor that may intrude upon the comparison between the pay of members and non-members—a prevailing difference of personal quality between them. The information also makes it possible to estimate the differential effect of unionism within a given occupational grade; if this effect is different for different grades, unionism will be

Table 3.8
The Raising of Wages by Trade Unionism in the U.S.A.

U.S.A. 1960 and 1966: percentage by which the earnings of unionized workers in certain grades of occupation exceeded those of comparable non-unionized workers.

	(1) *1,111 heads of families* *in the Michigan Survey* *of Consumer Finances 1966*	*(2)* *1/1000 sample, Census of Population 1960* *Workers in regulated and unregulated industries*	
		Industries with low *degree of concentration*	*Industries with high* *degree of concentration*
Craftsmen	24	14	9
Operatives	26	10	14
Laborers	52	13	15
Clerical and sales	18	clerical, female −8	+6

Sources: (1) Stafford (1968); (2) Weiss (1966 & 1968).

seen to have altered the differentials between grades. The findings of Weiss (1966 and 1968) and Stafford (1968) are shown in Table 3.8. Weiss assigns to each person the degree of unionization of the industry in which he works, whereas Stafford takes each person's own membership or non-membership. We might then expect a lower effect for unionism on Stafford's reckoning, because the pay of a union member in an industry in which unionization is low may well be raised less than that of a non-member in a highly unionized industry; but on Stafford's reckoning the effect is actually much higher. However this may be, when we take his findings and Weiss's together we can reach a conclusion: there is no ground for holding that unionism has raised the pay of the skilled and semi-skilled in different degree, and some ground for holding that it has raised the pay of the unskilled more than that of the other two grades. Rosen (1970), using aggregative data for U.S. manufacturing industries about 1960, agrees with Weiss's finding that 'unionism has probably increased wage rates of unskilled labourers by at least as much [as] and possibly more than that of skilled craftsmen' (p. 269), but differs in finding that the effect on the semi-skilled has been small.

Both studies drawn on in Table 3.8 show a smaller effect of unionism for clerical than for manual workers. Two other American studies agree with this. Hammermesh (1971), examining the pay of clerical and manual occupations in 70 metropolitan areas, found that unionism raised clerical pay by 5 per cent, against 20 per cent for manual. Johnson and Youmans (1971), also using the wage surveys of those areas, found that 'unions benefit less educated workers to a greater extent than more educated workers'.

We may conclude that, in the U.S.A., unionism has taken more effect on the pay of manual workers than of clerical workers, and that among the manual workers it has raised the relative pay of the unskilled.

It is a further question, how far unions have made the maintenance or change of occupational differentials an object of policy. Observers in the early 1950s were impressed by the narrowing of the differential for manual skill that had come about during and since the Second World War, and though it was clearly attributable to several causes other than union policy, the unions had at least not opposed it, while some had found it convenient (Douty 1953). If there had been no general upward movement of wages and the cost of living, the unions might not have made any egalitarian move on their own; but, argued Turner (1952, p. 279), 'granted that prices *have* increased, the mechanics of unionism has ensured that relative wage-differentials be narrowed'. By the mechanics of unionism he had mainly in mind the numerical preponderance of the less skilled workers within the recently expanded unions, the wish of unions to expand farther by recruiting more such workers, and the virtue of one and the same rise in money for all grades within the union as a means of avoiding dissension between them, and concentrating on the negotiation with the employers. That the form of this common rise should have been an absolute amount and not a proportion implies that the more skilled were either voted down by the less skilled, or regarded their differential as being preserved if it was constant in pence. but we have seen that differentials did not go on narrowing. It seems likely that as continually rising prices began to dissipate the money illusion, the skilled workers came to see their differential as essentially a proportion. Unions, moreover, which had a numerical preponderance of the less skilled might still in practice be run by craftsmen; or their executives might be well aware that they could not depress the relative position of their skilled men far without goading them to break away.

It thus appears that trade unions, though they accepted the narrowing of differentials that came about in the upheavals of the two World Wars, have generally tended to conserve existing differentials. Indeed it may be argued that they are inherently disposed to do this, in so far as they are directed by the immediate interests of their members. These members will generally be concerned that the pay of their own occupation or grade should not fall relatively to that of other groups within their orbit of comparison, and these groups will be equally watchful towards them. It is then much harder to obtain an explicit agreement on a change in relativities, than to maintain a tacit agreement to keep the present ones. One factor in the recent unionization of some white-collar employees in the United Kingdom has been the wish to restore and uphold relativities.

It could be otherwise in a congress or confederation of unions whose legislature, so to speak, adopted an egalitarian policy. The first question is the extent of central control. We have seen how the egalitarian policy of the Histadrut failed for lack of this; but the national organization of the manual workers' trade unions in Sweden, the L.O., has brought the claims of its member unions within 'central framework agreements' negotiated with the national organization of employers, in which the rises to be received by different groups of workers have been fairly closely and effectively apportioned.

Rudolf Meidner, in a study significantly entitled 'Co-ordination and Solidarity' (1974), has shown how these central agreements have been the vehicle of an effective thrust to raise the relative pay of the low-paid. The principle of solidarity that was expounded in a report to the Congress of the L.O. in 1951 meant 'equal pay for work of equal value': relative pay should be fixed by job evaluation, and if that were done, it could be said that all wage differentials had been abolished, even though the absolute pay for jobs of different requirements still differed. The L.O. has in fact never attempted this job evaluation, but the feeling that at least the low-paid received too little in relation to the requirements of their jobs was strong among the activists of the unions, and during the 1960s it took effect through the central agreements. The L.O. did not enter into these agreements of set purposes: it was drawn into them rather by the need of the Social Democratic government, with which it was closely identified, to check inflation, and at some junctures also by the insistence of the employers. But the negotiations once being joined, and the total admissible rise in wages being limited, the question of priorities became inescapable; and when member unions were consulted, it was priority for the lower-paid, as between industries and within particular industries, that they asked for. Women's wages were a matter of special concern, and in 1960 it was agreed that all separate rates for women should be eliminated in the course of the next five years. The effect of the central agreements was thus to reduce the inequality of earnings, both as between the average earnings of different industries, and as between the higher- and lower-paid within any one industry. One measure of the inter-industrial effect is provided by Meidner when he groups industries according as their average earnings were above or below the average of all, and forms a weighted average of the relative earnings in each group, using as weights the number of man-hours worked in each industry. In 1959 the above-average industries came out as 17 per cent above the average of all, and the below-average as 13 per cent below, a spread of 30 per cent; by 1972, through a fairly symmetrical convergence, the spread had become only 15 per cent. For the reduction of inequality within industries, Meidner gives figures only for engineering, from 1961 to 1972. Here, though the earnings of the higher-paid declined only a little relatively to those of the median worker, the earnings of the lowest-paid 30 per cent of the workers moved up markedly towards the median—at the lowest decile earnings were less than 76 per cent of median earnings in 1961, but nearly 84 per cent in 1972.

How far does this experience go towards establishing the malleability of the pay structure? That the difference was really made by the agreements and not by market forces operating in the same direction appears from the observation, stressed by Meidner, that the convergence occurred only in the years on which agreements impinged, and was checked by wage drift in the years between. But one reason for this checking seems to have been the resistance of the higher-paid to the narrowing of their differentials over the less skilled workers in the same firm or industry. The employers certainly feared that an initial relative rise in the lower rates would set up a demand for an equal proportionate rise in the others. 'The method one uses to pay any low wage supplement', said the head of the employers' national association in 1971, 'must agree with the interpretation at the place of work of what are appropriate wage differentials' (Meidner 1974, n. 44). Reviewing 'the attempts to promote equality, which were expressed in increasingly resolute low wage drives', the L.O. Congresses of 1961 and 1966 found that these attempts had not 'achieved the desired results, primarily because of the pull in the opposite direction of "market forces"—a ragbag term for differences in the profitability of branches and firms, increasingly rapid structural change, wider regional disparities and, not least, conflicts between the job evaluation of the market and the wage differentials created by the policy of equalisation' (Meidner 1974, p. 26). The last factor calls attention to a basic obstacle. The zeal for equality which undoubtedly animates many of the activists of the Swedish trade union movement has not carried all their constituents with it so far as to make them accept a standstill of their own real wages in order that more should be available to the lower-paid. The wave of unofficial strikes that began with the highly paid miners of Kiruna in December 1969 showed that many of those whom the policy of solidarity was holding back were chafing under its restraints, and ready to repudiate the central authority by which it had been adopted and applied (Tersmeden 1972).

It therefore remains to be seen how far the compression of the wage structure that had undoubtedly been brought about in the Sweden of the 1960s will persist. The pressures acting on differentials outside the central negotiations will not all have been tending to conserve them: against the narrowing of the spread of earnings in Swedish engineering in the 1960s may be set the similar narrowing that we noted in Coventry engineering in the same decade, and this may be more than a coincidence. Perhaps the imposition of regulation takes its most enduring effect when by breaking down custom it releases pent up forces that work in the same direction as itself.

3.5. Review and discussion

(a) The changes observed in differentials in the course of time can be accounted for by changes in the demand for and supply of labour more readily than by changes in social valuation and esteem. The rise in the differential for skill in the British industrial revolution and its subsequent contraction was mirrored in Russian economic development from the First Five Year Plan to 1956. Similarly, that the differentials for skill are generally wide in the less developed economies, and become narrower as development proceeds, may be ascribed to the initial extension of demand for skills previously little used in the economy, and the subsequent increase in the number acquiring those skills. We have noted the effect of the extended supply of literate workers, and that this may account for the greater contraction since the eighteenth century in the relative pay of compositors. That the relative earnings of physicians in the U.S.A. have risen while those of other learned professions have declined may be attributed to the number of physicians, unlike those of the other professions, having decreased relatively to the population. In all, we have noticed few differentials that have widened in the course of time, and many that have contracted. The contemporary changes that would account for this include the extension of education and the rise in the standard of living, reducing the differences of mental and physical capability between one person and another; the increased quantity and ingenuity of equipment, reducing dependence on the skill of the worker and increasing the productivity of the less skilled; but also the increased unionization of the less skilled; and the policy of governments, and in some times and places of trade unionism, seeking to raise the lowest-paid or maintain a social minimum.

(b) But in so far as we can ascribe observed changes to the operation of supply and demand in the first place, we have also to note that this operation is not symmetrical. The supply price of labour with particular qualification forms a threshold but not a ceiling: if the actual rate of pay falls below it, a fall in the number of persons available for employment will pull it up again, but it can stand above the threshold without the excess of potential workers over the number of jobs pulling it down. An extension of the demand for a particular type of labour will generally pull its pay up, but a contraction of demand will not necessarily or generally pull it down. The factors operative here are the unwillingness of workers to offer themselves for employment at less than the going rate, the power of combinations to resist cuts for those in employment, and the force of custom.

(c) The power of custom to perpetuate differentials, however these may have been established originally, was instanced by the persistence for 500 years of one and the same differential between building craftsman and labourer in southern England; by the upholding of the clerk's differential in the presence of a great extension of the supply of clerical capability; and by the maintenance of the structure of rates for the crafts in British engineering through years in which their work was much diversified. That big changes, not subsequently reversed, came about during the two World Wars, is less likely to have been due to wartime effects being perpetuated by custom, than to the wars having broken up the resistance that custom had been maintaining to the pressure of market forces.

(d) The relative pay of different occupations has been deliberately changed in certain times and places by the policy of government or of trade unionism. We saw an example of the former in the Netherlands, of the latter in Sweden. But both these examples showed that the attempt to change differentials systematically encounters resistance from those, whether employers or employed, who dislike central control, and from the pressure exerted by market forces at particular points.

(e) There is much evidence for the effect of trade unions on differentials. The impact of unionization, though marked, may be transitory, but sustained unionism has been associated with a raising of manual relatively to white-collar pay, and among the manual with a relative raising of the unskilled.

(*f*) The discussion of this and the preceding chapter has left us with a view of differences of pay as determined in the main by market forces, though this determination has limits of tolerance within which other forces take their effect. Certain of these other forces, again, may be the immediate causes of changes that are compatible with underlying shifts of supply and demand. The other forces are national culture and tradition; custom; trade unions; and the policy of governments or pay-negotiating bodies.

But we know that some observers view the pay structure very differently: they see the rank order and stratification of occupations by pay as being determined basically by social forces, while the market forces only impinge here and there to make some displacement, or heighten and counteract tendencies of other origin. These observers may well maintain that if it is the market forces that seem to predominate in the survey we have just made, that is only because we have quite left out of account so far one of the most salient observations open to any such survey, namely the widely prevailing agreement of the ranking orders by pay and by social status. It is to examine the facts and significance of this agreement that we now proceed.

4

Pay Structure and Status

4.1. The ordering of occupations by average earnings

We can arrange occupations in a rank order according to the average earnings in each, and the *New Earnings Survey* in Great Britain enables us to do this for some 166 occupations. Figure 4.1 shows the outcome for a week in April 1970. The occupations have been grouped in intervals of £5, and the length of the horizontal line in each interval is proportional to the number of persons employed in occupations, the *average* earnings in which fell within the interval—though some of those persons' individual earnings will have been above or below it.

What strikes the eye here at once is the peg-top outline—the long spindle, and the bulb below, widening rapidly at first, then narrowing as we go down. The spindle shows the upper half of the scale of earnings as containing relatively few employees: only 1,214 out of every 10,000 were in occupations whose average weekly earnings were £33 and over. The widening below marks the presence of nearly 7 out of every 10 employees in occupations whose average earnings were from £18 up to £33, with the mode in the interval '£23 and less than £28'. Below that again, the narrowing betokens the relatively small numbers—some 1,823 out of every 10,000—in occupations whose average earnings were less than £18, that is, less than about three-quarters of the modal £25.

But which were the particular occupations in each class? When we come to specify them, we notice at once a conflict with our usual way of grouping and ordering occupations. It is true that the occupations in the spindle—small numbers, high pay—are almost all managerial and professional; but not quite all—in '£33 and less than £38', besides the planning engineers, the systems analysts, and the senior foremen, we find the dockers, the steel erectors, and the production electricians. In the interval below, '£27 and less than £33', we find another mixture, in which administrative, clerical, and technical workers are mingled with many skilled manual and some semi-skilled manual workers; and so on.

That we see this as a mixture of different sorts, and an incongruous one at that, implies that we have in mind a way of grouping occupations according to some form of likeness other than in their average earnings. One basis for such grouping is the nature of the work. This gives us a familiar division of occupations into the managerial and professional; the 'white collar', or administrative, clerical, and technical; and the manual, these last being in turn subdivided into skilled, semi-skilled, and unskilled.

In Fig. 4.2. we see the effect of segregating the occupations of Fig. 4.1 into

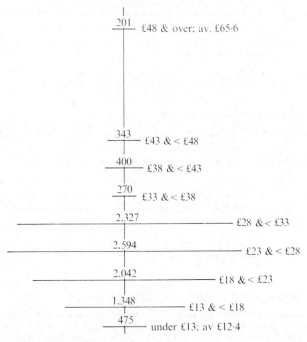

Fig. 4.1. Weekly earnings in Great Britain, 1970.

Great Britain, sample of 116,000 employees in a week of April 1970: average gross weekly earnings in each of 166 occupations, grouped by level of earnings, the number in each group being shown as per 10,000 employees. *Source*: Dept. of Employment, *New Earnings Survey 1970* (H.M.S.O. London, 1971).

those five groups. We have the same class-intervals of weekly earnings as before, and the lengths of the horizontal bars in each group are again proportional to the numbers in the given interval and group, out of 10,000 employees in all. We see now how the managerial and professional occupations stand by themselves, except for the overlap already noticed in the lowest interval in which they appear. But throughout the remaining occupations overlap is general. The administrative, technical, and clerical (ATC) occupations have two modes, the upper one in the same interval as the mode of the skilled manual workers, but the lower one below the mode even of the unskilled manuals. This lower mode of the ATC contains many occupations largely filled by women, such as clerk, routine; secretary, shorthand; office machine operator; and copy/audio typist. The modes of the three levels of skill among manual workers behave systematically, with the semi-skilled mode in the earnings interval next below the skilled, and the unskilled mode in that next below again; but there is overlap throughout between the skilled and the semi-skilled, and not a few of the unskilled earn more than some even of the skilled.

The same divergence between the traditional grouping and ordering of occupations and their ranking by relative pay—in particular, the overlap between

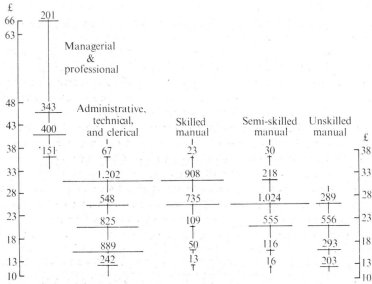

Fig. 4.2. British weekly earnings in occupational groups.

Great Britain, sample of 116,000 employees in 166 occupations, in a week of April 1970: average gross weekly earnings in occupations within each of 5 categories of occupation, grouped by level of earnings, the number in each group being shown as per 10,000 employees in all. *Source*: Dept. of Employment, *New Earnings Survey* 1970 (H.M.S.O. London, 1971).

NOTE ON THE STATISTICS OF FIGS. 4.1 and 4.2 The Dept. of Employment's *New Earnings Survey 1970* (H.M.S.O., London, 1971) gives the gross weekly earnings by occupation of a random sample of some 170,000 employees, or 1 in 130 of all employees in employment in Great Britain, in a week of April 1970. Some 116,000 of these, whose earnings for a full week are reported by occupation, provide the data for the present two Figs. the source arranges them in 16 groups. They are men aged 21+ and women aged 18+. Table 28 of the source gives the numbers in sample in each of the 166 occupations comprised here. Table 34 gives the average gross weekly earnings (excluding those whose pay was affected by absence) in all the groups and in most but by no means all of the occupations. The missing averages for particular occupations have been estimated from the median earnings of the occupations concerned, given with the median earnings of the groups in Table 30, on the assumption that the average earnings bore the same ratio to the median in a given occupation as they did in the aggregate of the group containing that occupation. The intervals in the scale of earnings in the Figs. were chosen so that concentrations of earnings fell as nearly as possible in the middle of intervals—there were minor modes at £12, £15, £20, £24–£26, and £30–£31.

white-collar and manual occupations—appears in the Russian structure reproduced from Shkaratan (1973b) in Table 4.1. Here we see what he regards as 'the principal social groups in the working class' with the average earnings of their members in certain industrial enterprises. At the lower end the distinction between manual and non-manual occupations finds no corresponding differentiation by earnings; skilled manual work earns more in Leningrad, though not in the Tatar Republic, than skilled mental work; only the highly skilled scientists and technologists, and the higher managers, are raised far above the rest by their earnings.

Table 4.1
'Social Groups' and Earnings in Russian Industry

Average earnings of personnel in 'the principal social groups in the working class' in 7 engineering enterprises in Leningrad 1965–66, and as found in surveys of 3 industrial cities of the Tatar Republic, 1967–68 (median of the averages for the three cities).

	Leningrad	Tatar Republic
	(roubles per month)	
Executives of labour collectives, public and state organizations	173	164
Highly skilled scientific and technical personnel	127	157
Personnel in skilled mental work	110	111
Personnel in highly skilled work combining mental and manual functions	129	116
Skilled, primarily manual hand labour	120	96
Skilled, primarily manual labour, employed on machines and mechanisms	108	99
Skilled non-manual labour without special education	84	76
Unskilled manual labour and low-skilled non-manual labour without special training	98	63

Source: Shkaratan (1973b), Table 3.

4.2. The ordering of occupations by status

Many people will feel that there is something anomalous about some of the relations we have just examined—such as that many white-collar workers earn less than many unskilled manual workers. This is felt to be an inversion of the natural order of things, because the nature of each occupation is seen as conferring a certain social status upon it, and an occupation whose status is higher than another's is felt to be inherently entitled to higher pay.

It has in fact been found in a number of countries that if a sample of people drawn from the general population is asked to rank a number of well-known occupations by status or social standing, the terms of the request are broadly intelligible to them. In a British inquiry (Goldthorpe & Hope 1974, Appx. D), the interviewers were told to ask respondents 'to arrange the occupations according to what you think is their *social standing*'. 'If the informant asks what is meant by "social standing" tell him that he should just think of what this means to him and grade the occupations accordingly. If the informant seems in any doubt at all, make clear that what you are interested in is what *he* thinks the social standing of an occupation is—not what the thinks *others* think it is, or what he thinks it *ought* to be.' An American inquiry told the respondents 'Please pick out the statement that best gives your own *personal opinion* of the *general standing* that such a job has', the statements providing a choice of five grades—excellent, good, and average standing; somewhat below average; poor standing. The instruction in a Japanese inquiry—in contrast with the

British—was, 'Think of the general reputation they [the listed occupations] have with people', and sort them into five groups, 'from those people think highly of to those which are not thought so well of' (Inkeles & Rossi 1956). The criterion for ranking has also been given as the extent to which each occupation is 'looked up to' (Canada), as its 'honour or importance' (Turkey), and, in many countries, its 'prestige' or 'social prestige' (Hodge, Treiman, & Rossi 1967). We can infer that the notion of the status, social standing, or prestige of oc- cupations is held in people's minds very widely, and that people feel they can tell from their everyday knowledge of occupations where these stand relatively to one another in the hierarchy of status.

The kind of ranking order that results is illustrated from Poland and from England and Wales, in Table 4.2. The comparison cannot be close, because of uncertainty about the connotation of the Polish occupational titles, but certain points of similarity and contrast are unmistakable. The outstanding similarity is that the respondents in both countries put the professions at the top and the unskilled manual workers at the bottom. For the most part, also, the rankings agree throughout in depending on the extent of education and training that oc- cupations require. But a major exception to this is that the Poles put the skilled and semi-skilled manual workers—the steel workers and the machinists—much higher than did the English and Welsh respondents, and they put white-collar workers correspondingly lower. We remember that this agrees with the relative pay of these two kinds of workers in the Soviet-type economies generally, but it marks a great change from the Poland of 1939 (Sarapata & Wesolowski 1961). Even so, it is a change within the rank order, not an egalitarian revulsion against the very idea of ranking. The sociologist in charge of an inquiry into the ranking of occupations by people in Czechoslovakia in 1967 has reported that 'the inquiry has not confirmed the hypothesis that prestige in socialist societies is formed according to other criteria than in non-socialist societies' (Strmiska & Vavakova 1972, p. 253).

Outside the Soviet-type economies, moreover, what is most striking is the extent of agreement in ranking order between respondents in countries at different levels of economic development and of different culture and political form. Hodge, Treiman, and Rossi (1967) have compared the ranking orders ob- tained in 23 countries—we omit one relating to the U.S.S.R. as having been obtained only from exiles. When the rank order of each of the other countries was correlated with that of the United States, the coefficients of determination (R^2) averaged 0·83; the lowest, for Poland, was 0·62, and the highest, for New Zealand, 0·95. When the correlations were calculated separately for white- collar and manual occupations, rather less agreement was found among the rankings of the manual. But when the countries were divided into the Western and non-western (the latter including the Belgian Congo, Ghana, India, and In- donesia), the non-Western proved to be in as close agreement with the United States as were the Western. This is the more remarkable in that, among the Western Countries, the lower their Gross National Product per head, the less their agreement with the United States, and if we carry this relation down to

Table 4.2
Ranking of Occupations by Status in Warsaw and in England and Wales

The rank order by status of 23 occupations among those ranked by persons in Warsaw in the 1950s, compared with the rank order of the approximately corresponding occupations in a scale covering all occupations and constructed from the responses of a random sample of 620 persons throughout England and Wales in 1972.

Warsaw Occupation	Rank order	Rank order	England and Wales Occupation
University professor	1	1	⎰ Barrister, solicitor
Doctor	2		⎱ doctor
Teacher	3	3	Minister, government
Mechanical engineer	4	4	Pilot, aircraft
Pilot, airline	5	5	Professor, university
Lawyer, attorney	6	6	Engineer, mechanical professional
Minister of the National Government	7	7	Policeman, police force
Journalist	8	8	Clergyman, priest
Skilled steel worker	9	9	Teacher, primary and secondary schools
Priest	10	10	Journalist
Machinist	11	11	Office supervisor
Factory foreman	12	12	Shopkeeper (self-employed, less than 25 employees)
Small farmer	13	13	⎰ Locksmith ⎰ self-employed,
Shopkeeper	14		⎱ Tailor ⎱ less than 25 employees
Tailor with own workshop	15	15	Foreman, engineering
Locksmith with own workshop	16	16	Clerk
Office supervisor	17	17	Rolling, tube mill operators, metal drawers, skilled manual
Railway guard	18	18	Farmer, self-employed, no employees
Policeman	19	19	Machinist, engineer's; machine tool operator
Office clerk	20	20	Shop assistant
Shop assistant	21	21	Labourer, agricultural
Building labourer	22	22	Labourer, bricklayer's
Unskilled farm worker on a state farm	23	23	Railway guard

Sources: Warsaw: Sarapata & Wesolowski (1961). *England and Wales:* Goldthorpe & Hope (1974); Offices of Population Censuses & Surveys (1970).

the low GNPs of the non-Western countries, we should expect a much lower agreement there than we actually find. The authors conjecture that this is because Western evaluations of occupations have penetrated those countries, especially through Western-type education, ahead of the economic development that has been associated with these evaluations in the West.

It is true that any such comparison as this brings out the limitations of the original inquiries between which it is made. The occupations listed for evaluation are not a stratified sample of all occupations, but tend to be weighted towards the extremes, agreement in the ranking of which is not offset by disagreement in the ranking of intermediate, less contrasted occupations. The respondents, again, are not usually a random or stratified sample of the population at large—though in some countries at least it has been found that groups of different types of respondent arrive at much the same rankings (Reiss 1961, pp. 187–90; Svalastoga 1959, p. 107–8; Tiryakian 1962, p. 396). But though the findings of international comparisons must be qualified by these limitations, they are too uniform and pronounced to be disregarded.

That rankings should be similar in countries at different stages of development suggests that they may be similar at different times within any one country. A comparison of findings in the United States between 1925 and 1963 does not conflict with this expectation. It is true that the position of particular occupations changed variously from time to time—in particular, the manual occupations rose relatively to the managerial and clerical between 1947 and 1963; but the movements were all small, and the correlations between the rankings at different dates were all so high that the authors of the study concluded 'that there have been no substantial changes in occupational prestige in the United States since 1925' (Hodge, Siegel, & Rossi 1964).

4.3. Pay differentials and the scale of status

Everyday knowledge indicates that the occupations which hold a high place in a ranking order such as that of Table 4.2 are generally also relatively highly paid, and conversely: but how far does this relation hold in detail? Figure 4.3 enables us to examine it for some 107 occupations. The earnings in these are recorded in the British *New Earnings Survey 1973* (Dept. of Employment 1974). Their status or social standing is found in the scale covering all occupations, constructed by Goldthorpe and Hope (1974) from the rankings made by a random sample of 620 persons interviewed throughout England and Wales in 1972. The scale was constructed so that its values run from 5 to 95 points. Figure 4.3 shows the earnings recorded for groups of occupations having the same or very similar scale values. The earnings are on a logarithmic scale. The vertical lines show the range from the lowest to the highest median earnings by occupation within the group of occupations at the given level in the scale of status, and the spots mark the unweighted means of the median earnings of all occupations in the group.

The first feature to strike the eye is that the spots—the group averages—lie quite closely about a straight line, save for the group whose scale value is between 31 and 32, and whose earnings at only £26 lie far below the line. The line has been fitted to all the spots except the last-mentioned one. The slope of the line implies that throughout all occupations, from sweeper to doctor, a rise of 1 unit in the scale of status is associated with an increase of 1·031 per cent in earnings. The Goldthorpe–Hope (GH) scale is based simply on ranking. In the inquiry by which it was generated, each of the 620 respondents was given a set of cards each bearing the title of an occupation, and was asked to arrange these

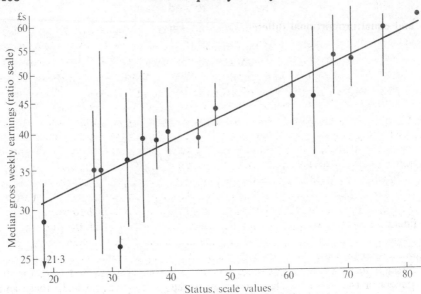

Fig. 4.3. The relation between status and relative pay.

England and Wales, 1972, 1973: Groups of occupations having the same or closely similar status (social standing) in the Goldthorpe–Hope scale, with the range of median earnings by occupation in each group (vertical lines) and unweighted average of the median earnings of the occupations within the group (spots). *Sources*: Goldthorpe & Hope (1974); Dept. of Employment (1974); Office of Population Censuses and Surveys (1970).

cards in order of the social standing of the occupations, either one below the other, or two or more alongside each other if they were assigned the same standing. The ranks were then numbered 1, 2, 3 . . . , and it was ultimately out of these numbers that the values of the single comprehensive scale were built up. So far it appears that the scale values serve only to mark 'higher' and 'lower', and that no significance attaches to the size of the differences between them. But perhaps we might think that when the respondents pondered whether to put a card below or alongside another, they had in mind a unit of difference, a *minimum sensibile*, just sufficient to show that the two occupations concerned must go into distinct though adjacent grades. A counterpart would appear if we provided a respondent with a large number of stones, and asked him to rank them in order of weight by holding them in his hand. On this view we could regard some absolute difference in the GH scale values as marking a unit distinction of grade, that in some sense was the same throughout the scale. Suppose also, as there seems some reason to believe, that a unit distinction of grade is generally associated with a pay differential of 10 or 15 per cent: then Fig. 4.3 suggests that the difference in GH scale values marking the perception of a unit distinction of grade would be from 9 to 13 points, and the whole range of 90 points in the scale would contain from 7 to 10 grades.

This possible relation between what we may regard as unit intervals of grade and equal proportional differences in pay agrees with experience reported by consultants who have worked with the staff of firms to construct a salary structure on consensus. They have found that when the many elements of job requirement have been surveyed in the course of job evaluation, and the outcome in the aggregate is weighed up for two jobs, the notion of 'a difference in job requirements just sufficient to constitute a difference of grade' can in practice be applied as a unit of evaluation at all levels. They have further found agreement that the appropriate difference of pay between two adjacent grades was a constant proportion—between 10 and 15 per cent of the pay of the lower scale—again at all levels.

This in turn puts us in mind of a relation found in experimental psychology. If someone is asked to tell which of two objects is the heavier by lifting them, we can record the actual difference in weight that enables him to say with confidence that one or other is the heavier, and this is called the *jnd* or 'just noticeable difference'. The same process of relating differences in sensation or evaluation to measurable differences in the stimulus or object can be carried through for many qualities—not weight only, but warmth and cold, for instance, or the intensity of light, sound, smell, or electric shock. In these and other instances, we can take the *jnd* as a unit with which to build up a numerical scale of sensation or evaluation. The question then is, what relation do we find between the scale of sensation and that of the stimulus? According to the 'Weber–Fechner law' this relation is generally of such a form that unit differences in the scale of the sensation correspond to equal proportionate differences in the amount of the stimulus: if, for example, the *jnd* between the weights of stones proves to be 1 ounce when stones of about 10 ounces weight are to be compared, it will be found to be 5 ounces around the 50-ounce level, 10 ounces at the 100-ounce level, and so on. Later studies have found that though a relation of this kind obtains very generally for vision and hearing, it does not hold for the higher and lower levels of other forms of sensation, and another formula has been proposed of wider application.[1] Within the middle ranges, however, 'the working area of the senses', the Weber–Fechner relation remains a fair approximation, and the difference between it and the alternative formula is not very great (Woodworth & Schlosberg 1954, pp. 223–4; Stevens 1961; Engen 1971).

---

[1] The Weber–Fechner relation may be written

$$R = K \log S \tag{1}$$

where R is sensation, S is the stimulus, and K is a constant. The formula proposed by Stevens (1961) is

$$\log R = n \log (S - S_0.) \tag{2}$$

where S_0 is the threshold value of the stimulus below which it is not sensed, and n (if the variables are expressed in standard deviation units) is an exponent, a value of which characterizes the sensing of each particular quality or modality. According to (1) the change in sensation per unit change in stimulus is inversely proportional to the stimulus; according to (2) it is likewise inversely proportional to the stimulus but at the same time also directly proportional to the level of sensation. Within a central range of the level of sensation the effective difference between the two formulas will therefore not be great.

If we note the correspondence between the *jnd* and what is felt to be a difference of a grade in job evaluation, we are tempted to see the equal proportional differences in what is felt to be the appropriate pay as the counterpart of the Weber-Fechner equal proportionate differences in the stimulus. This would be intelligible if it were felt that to make the same difference throughout to the benefit of pay to the recipient we should have to raise pay at all levels by the same percentage, not the same absolute amount. Equal proportional differences in the stimulus, pay, would then go with equal absolute differences in benefit or real reward, to match equal absolute differences in job requirements.

So far we have been considering the relation between the status of a grade and some average of the earnings obtained in it: Fig. 4.3 shows that the relation between the status and the earnings of particular occupations is far less regular. We have noted already the low earnings of the occupations whose scale value is between 31 and 32: these are the general farm workers, stockmen, and driver/operators of agricultural machinery. Some part of the displacement may be due to the earnings of farm workers in one week of April, the period of the *New Earnings Survey*, being less than a proportionate part of their annual earnings; and to money earnings being generally more supplemented in kind in agriculture than in other industries. But the group with the lowest status also has lower pay than would be expected from the general relation shown by the line of regression: this group is made up of the unskilled labourers—kitchen porters, road sweepers, railway porters, roadmen, dustmen, and general labourers. It appears that the general relation between intervals on the scale of status and differences of pay does not hold for those traditionally classified as labourers.

But the looseness of the relation between the status of a particular occupation and its relative pay is shown most clearly in Fig. 4.3 by the vertical lines that mark the range of pay received by occupations with the same or closely similar status. Here, for example, are the 13 occupations all with a scale value of 32·61, arranged in order of median weekly earnings:

	£s
Butchers, meat cutters	28·1
Bakers, confectioners	32·5
Tailors, cutters, dressmakers, etc.	32·7
Bleachers, dyers, finishers	34·3
Footwear workers	34·9
Weavers	35·7
Woodworking machinists and sawyers	36·6
Forklift etc. drivers/operators	37·3
Cutting and slitting machine operators (paper etc.)	38·3
Smiths, forgemen	38·5
Paper and board makers	38·7
Moulders, coremakers, diecasters	40·3
Furnacemen	41·8

Evidently occupations the nature and requirements of whose work lead to similar perceptions of status can be very differently paid according as they are carried on in different industries.

These and other causes of the divergences between status and pay have their significance for the interpretation of the prevailing association between the two. The strength of this association remains the outstanding feature of Fig. 4.3. How can we account for it? Let us take this question up by considering the nature of status.

4.4. The nature of status

Status as Max Weber saw it is many-sided. A *status situation*, he wrote (1968, p. 932), is constituted by 'every typical component of the life of man that is determined by a specific, positive or negative, social estimation of *honour*. . . . In content, status honour is normally expressed by the fact that above all else a specific *style of life* is expected from all those who wish to belong to the circle.' Hence, more formally (pp. 305–6), "status" (ständische Lage) shall mean an effective claim to social esteem in terms of positive or negative privileges; it is typically founded on:

(*a*) style of life, hence
(*b*) formal education, which may be
    α) empirical training or
    β) rational instruction, and the corresponding forms of behaviour,
(*c*) hereditary or occupational prestige.'

Thus Weber sees the prestige or esteem attaching to occupations as only one source of status among others: status groups may come into being, he says (ibid.), not only as occupational groups with 'their own style of life'—though this he puts first—but also 'through hereditary charisma, by virtue of successful claims to higher-ranking descent,' and also 'through monopolistic appropriation of political or hierocratic powers'.

There are two strands of thought here. First, persons of the same status are seen as forming a social stratum, in the sense that they are treated and treat themselves as standing in relations of inferiority and superiority to groups of different status. In this respect status as Weber sees it merges with one aspect of class. Our present concern is only with the relation between the status of occupations and their pay; but we shall see that judgements about what pay is 'right and proper' are sometimes based on the 'station in life' that is deemed necessary for those who are to follow the occupation in question, or is customarily associated with it, and this 'station in life' is tantamount to status as a social stratum.

The second strand of thought concerns the characteristics that Weber sees as determining the attribution of status. 'Occupational prestige' is only one of them. But the other two, 'style of life, and 'formal education', are also closely connected with occupation—'style of life', because it depends in great part on the income that an occupation affords, and 'formal education', because occupations have their educational thresholds.

From Weber's account of the varied ways in which *persons* attain status we can therefore derive an account of the basis on which status is attributed to those who follow particular *occupations*. Each occupation, we may take him to say, is associated with a certain life-style, by reason of the income and education of those who follow it, and perhaps by certain traditions of activities and interests that those persons enter into by joining the occupation. This life-style may be seen as associated in turn with a station in life, that is, a certain level within a stratification of society by income, manners, and mutual regard. But the attribution of status is also founded on 'occupational prestige', by which we may understand the admiration generally felt for the degree of skill an occupation requires, and the extent to which the exercise of that skill is conspicuous.

The identification with occupation is the basis of the Russian sociologists' account of status under socialism (Shkaratan 1973a). As they see it, the abolition of private ownership of the means of production has done away with class antagonism, but though all workers share in the utilization of social property, some utilize it more fully than others: their labour is more complex, and the 'most appropriate' method of social evaluation 'is based on the degree of complexity of labour (its degree of skill in the broad sense of the word)' (p. 13). Occupations thus divide workers into groups differentiated by their earnings and 'their social status, the nature of their interpersonal contacts, the structure of their leisure, their social and political functions, their informal production and managerial functions—in short, everything that transforms a category of individuals into a social group with its own specific characteristics' (p. 14). Though there are thus many aspects of differentiation by status, all 'are subordinate to the skill-occupational structure' (p. 21). In sum, 'when socialism liquidates private property, it eliminates the consequences of private property—antagonistic classes—but it does not eliminate the original cause of social inequality: the division of labour into socially heterogeneous types' (p. 11).

Another account of the basis on which status is attributed begins by asking why, when occupations are ranked by status, the resultant order should be largely the same in countries that differ widely in culture and economic development. Hodge, Treiman, and Rossi (1967) find the answer in the division of labour and the provision for the functions of social administration that come about in all organized communities. They say (1967, p. 310),

Specialized institutions to carry out political, religious, and economic functions, and to provide for the health, education and welfare of the population exist in one form or another in all national societies. Considering the importance of these functions to the maintenance of complex social systems, it is not surprising that occupations at the top of these institutional structures should be highly regarded. Moreover, these are the very occupations which require the greatest training and skill to which the greatest material rewards accrue.

Considering later the smaller degree of similarity between the rankings of manual than of white-collar occupations, they add (p. 318),

Major institutional complexes serving central societal needs which exist in all societies, and the common bureaucratic hierarchy imposed by the nation state, act to ensure (despite vast differences in level of economic development) similarity between nations in the white-collar prestige hierarchy of doctors, scientists, teachers, public officials, and clerks, but these factors cannot be expected to induce a corresponding degree of prestige similarity at the blue-collar level.

The argument is not just that the same occupations exist in different societies—the comparisons of rankings in any case require a common list of occupations—but that given occupations have the same evident importance everywhere in maintaining the social system, the same usefulness in meeting social needs; and that their ranking by status follows their place in the bureaucratic hierarchy that is common to the nation states. But when in one of their inquiries Goldthorpe and Hope (1974, Table A4) asked respondents to grade occupations separately by value to society, as well as by standard of living, power and influence over other people, and level of qualifications, it was the gradings by value to society that showed the lowest correlation with the mean grading overall. It also seems doubtful whether people generally see occupations outside public administration as having the function of maintaining the social system: everyday knowledge suggests that they look more directly at the work that those who follow the occupation perform, and the qualities they must have if they are to be able to perform it.

What in particular it is that they look at is indicated, for one group of respondents at least, in Table 4.3. This gives the list of occupational attributes that the respondents to a well-known American inquiry (N.O.R.C. 1947) were

Table 4.3
Job Attributes that Indicate Status

Percentage of respondents to inquiry into standing of jobs (National Opinion Research Centre 1947) giving each of the listed attributes as their main ground for attributing 'excellent standing' to a job.

	%
The job pays so well	18
It serves humanity: it is an essential job	16
Preparation requires much education hard work and money	14
The job carries social prestige	14
It requires high moral standards, honesty, responsibility	9
It requires intelligence and ability	9
It provides security, steady work	5
The job has a good future; the field is not overcrowded	3
The job is pleasant, safe and easy	2
It affords maximum chance for initiative and freedom	less than 0·5
Don't know, no answer	10
	100

Source: N.O.R.C. (1947).

asked to choose from in order to answer the question, 'When you say that certain jobs have "excellent standing", what do you think is the one main thing about such jobs that gives this standing?' Against each attribute appears the percentage of respondents who selected it as their 'one main thing'. It will be seen that the usefulness to society on which Hodge, Treiman, and Rossi laid their stress appears in the second place. But Duncan (1961) found that he needed to take into account only the first and third considerations, namely pay and education, in order to predict the N.O.R.C. rankings with great accuracy for the most part, even though in a few occupations there were divergences—the predicted standing being, for example, lower than that ascribed by the N.O.R.C. respondents for clergymen and building contractors, and higher for newspaper reporters, insurance agents, and shop assistants.

Considering such evidence as that of Table 4.3 has led some sociologists to sceptical conclusions about what it is that is really being assessed in the name of status or social standing. Thus Goldthorpe and Hope (1972, 1974) maintain that status in the strict and proper sense is not at issue in these assessments, but only some notion of the 'general desirability' of occupations. When people are asked to grade occupations by prestige, 'this does *not*, in the majority of cases, lead them to adopt a distinctively "prestige" frame of reference: that is, a frame of mind in which they respond primarily in terms of symbolic indications of social superiority or inferiority'. In that frame of mind, the people in a given occupation are seen as having attitudes of deference, acceptance, and derogation towards those in occupations respectively of higher, equal, and lower prestige. 'Rather,' the authors continue, 'most respondents assess the occupations presented to them on the basis of what they know, or think they know, about a *variety* of more "objective" occupational attributes—most often, perhaps, job rewards or requirements—which they see as relevant to the ordering of occupations *simply in terms of some rather unspecific "better-worse" dimension*' (1974, p. 11). It is as if they had been asked to arrange a number of houses, with all their various amenities and drawbacks, in order of general desirability.

The same concept appears in an inquiry into the rating of occupations by graduates in 1965 from Leningrad secondary schools (Vodzinskaia 1973). The respondents rated the occupations separately by the possibilities they offered for creativity; by the possibilities again for personal development—that is, for 'raising skills in the broadest sense of the word'; by pay; and by 'social prestige—the authority of an occupation in public opinion'. But these were seen only as the 'basic components of the concept "attractiveness of an occupation" ', which the respondents also rated. The ratings under the four component heads were in fact highly correlated by the rating of general attractiveness, those under creativity most highly of all. But there were enough divergences between the rankings by general attractiveness and by social prestige to show that, at least in the eyes of these Leningrad school-leavers, prestige was distinct. Thus prestige was markedly greater than attractiveness for secondary and primary school-teachers, and for shop assistants—perhaps because prestige attached to the nature of the work or the clean working conditions, but attractiveness was reduced by low pay. The high prestige of the steel founder will mark the importance of the skilled manual worker in general, and the steel industry in particular, in the Five-year Plans; but that the occupation was ranked much lower by attractiveness may show the effect of arduous working conditions, despite high pay. On the other hand there were occupations whose ranking by attractiveness was markedly higher than their ranking by prestige—radio technician, mechanical engineer, driver, toolmaker or maintenance fitter, chemical worker, railway worker, and cook, waiter. Here it may have been the pay that boosted the attractiveness.

Besides discussion of what it is that gets assessed under the name of status, there have been doubts about the possibility of arranging the variety of occupations in any one ordinal scale. Hatt (1950) remarked that one cannot attach much meaning to the finding, in one well-known inquiry, that 'airline pilot', 'artist who paints pictures', 'owner of a factory employing about 100 people', and 'sociologist' had the same 'general social standing'. Two opposite conclusions have been drawn about the possibility of assigning each occupation to some level in a single stratification by status. One is that such assignment is possible as between broad groups of occupations, but not within them. 'There probably is an ordinal scale of occupational "prestige" for major occupational groups . . .' but occupations within these groups 'do not form ordinal scales, nor do [they] always scale with those from other major occupational groups' (Reiss 1961, p. 105). But as against this it has been pointed out that, even as between the major groups, it is hard to say which of the lower white-collar and higher manual groups has the higher status. It is also observed that the reported rankings of the whole list of occupations are the averages of individual rankings that differ widely: the correlation between the rank orders of individual respondents is generally found to be not more than 0.6. If then we regard the order established by respondents as significant only where they are in substantial agreement, we cannot go beyond smaller groups of cognate occupations, clustered here and there in the occupational field (Hatt 1950). The conclusion must be that comparisons of status are possible within groups but not between them.

The complexities that this discussion reveals may be reduced if we distinguish at least provisionally between two settings each containing its own sort of status. The first setting is that of the group made up of people with a common interest or activity: here status is tantamount to prestige, and it is conferred by performance. The second setting is that of a whole society: here status is tantamount to social standing, and it is conferred by life-style. Let us consider these in turn.

There are many kinds of group with their own internal rankings by status. They range from the local darts club to the international golf circuit, and from horticultural associations to learned societies; they include all the professions and indeed all skilled occupations, or at least all those groups of their members within which one member's performance is known to the others. These groups may have their own forms of government, with officers of various degree, but it is not that form of ranking which concerns us here. The rank order that does concern us is that based on the skill shown in the activity, a common interest in which constitutes the group. Status, that is to say, is founded on performance, and is conferred by the admiration that high performance calls forth. Since performance generally improves, up to a point, with experience, and in those activities that do not depend too much on bodily agility experience continues through the middle years of life, status rises with age. This has been well put by Lloyd Warner and Low (1947, pp. 87–8) in their account of the shoe-making craftsman in the days before much of his work was taken over by machine:

The hierarchy of crafts which once organized the relations of the workers and provided a way of life for the shoe workers was really an age-grade system. Youngsters served their hard apprenticeship, and as neophytes, learned their task; even more importantly they were taught to respect the skills they had learned and those they looked forward to learning. Above all, they acquired respect and admiration for the older men above them who had acquired the skills and who occupied the proud positions of journeymen and master craftsmen.... In learning to respect the skill of the master craftsman, the apprentice learned to respect himself.... He spent his life acquiring virtue, prestige and respect, learning as he aged and climbed upward, and at the same time teaching those who were younger than he and who aspired to be like him.

These observations remind us that the admiration accorded to skill in such a setting is not merely such as is aroused by some work of craftsmanship that has come down to us from the past: it is a relation between people. Warner and Low speak of respect, and respect is admiration tinged with deference. Yet when we speak of one footballer, one mathematician, or one advocate as being better than another, or even as being superior to him, we mean 'more skilful', and not 'socially superior'.

It is only in the second sort of setting that the category of social superiority and inferiority appears. Just as the groups we have been considering are constituted by a common interest or activity, so the wider and comprehensive group we call a society is a unity because certain values and attitudes are held in common by its member. One of these values is that set upon life-style, and the associated attitude is that of deference. We have seen what are the characteristics that make up life-style, and how predominant occupation is among these, for more than one reason. There can be no question of arranging all the myriad different occupations of a contemporary society in a single rank order; we have seen reason to doubt the significance of the detailed ordering even of a comparatively short list of distinctive occupations. But it is found that most occupations can be readily assigned to one of a small number of groups, and these groups are of distinct social standing. Frequent use has been made in American studies of the 'Edwards occupational index' set out in the report of the 1940 Census (Edwards 1938; U.S. Govt. 1943):

1. Professional persons
2. Proprietors, managers & officials

    (*a*) Farmers (owners and tenants)
    (*b*) Wholesale and retail dealers
    (*c*) Other proprietors, managers, & officials
3. Clerks and other kindred workers
4. Skilled workers and foremen
5. Semi-skilled workers
6. Unskilled workers
    (*a*) Farm labourers
    (*b*) Labourers, except farm
    (*c*) Servant classes.

Each of these groups, Edwards observed (p. 170), has 'a somewhat distinct standard of life, economically, and, to a considerable extent, intellectually and socially. In some measure, also, each group has characteristic interests and convictions as to numerous public questions—social, economic, and political. Each of them is thus a really distinct and highly significant social-economic group.'

As status within the special interest group is conferred by admiration, within the wider society it is manifest by deference. In deference there may well be an element of admiration, but the essence of it is a perception not of the performance of those to whom one defers but of their dignity, of the claim that they can make on others: not of their contribution but of their inherent entitlement. The nature of this perception is made clearer by its opposite, in which we look down on those whose life-style is humble or whose occupation is degrading. Some occupations, irrespective of the skill they call for, are seen as inherently noble, and others are inherently demeaning. 'I shall never believe', Tolstoy wrote to Romain Rolland, 'the sincerity of the Christian, philosophical or humanitarian pretensions of a person who sends a servant to empty his chamberpot' (Troyat 1970, p. 653). This sense that some occupations dignify and others shame those engaged in them is seen at its strongest in the Indian caste system. Generally, 'dirty work'—as the metaphoric use of the term implies—is seen as being of lower status than clean. And as the nature of the work done may confer social standing, so the members of an organization may seek to differentiate their standing, or have it customarily differentiated for them, by signal differences in the conditions in which the work is done, and in the manners and dress of those who do it, which are not essential to the performance of the task. This appears clearly in the segregation of staff and manual workers in a Western factory—the separate entrances, lavatories, canteens; the differences of dress signalized by the very term 'white collar'; and, within the staff itself, the 'status symbols'—of office furniture, for instance—associated with gradations of rank.

This discussion of the nature of status has thus brought us back to Weber's view of it that we noted at the outset. We have come to see the essence of status as the stratification of society by honour, by deference, by a relation of superior to inferior that is a subjective relation between persons and not merely an objective relation between qualifications or attainments. To condense this description of status, we can indicate it by 'station in life', stations being distinguished by their 'life-style'.

Weber saw various ways in which persons might attain to or be assigned to a station in life, and one of these was by following a certain occupation. It is this link between occupation and station in life that concerns us here. A given occupation connotes a certain station in life for its members. It also commands a relative pay, which places it in a certain level of the pay structure. We have seen how closely these two stratifications, by status and by pay, generally agree, so that occupations can be assorted in 'socio-economic groups' that are ordered in the same way in both those dimensions. Our basic problem is, why this agreement? Does it come about because status determines pay? or because pay determines status? or because both are determined by some other element? In the next three sections we shall examine the case for the first of these possibilities.

4.5. Station in life as a basis of assigned income

In the notion that each occupation assigns to those who follow it *a station in life*, and that their pay should be such as to enable them to maintain that station, there are several strands.

One was given by Adam Smith (1776, Bk. I, c. X, Pt. I) when he cited 'the small or great trust which must be reposed in the workman' as a cause of inequalities of pay. 'The wages of goldsmiths and jewellers', he wrote, 'are everywhere superior to those of many other workmen, not only of equal, but of much superior ingenuity, on account of the precious materials with which they are necessarily entrusted.' Similarly it has been held that civil servants and judges should be assured of an income that will enable them to deal impartially with issues involving large sums of money, and help to set their integrity above all suspicion of venality.

Adam Smith went on to a second consideration. 'We trust our health to the physician,' he wrote; 'our fortune and sometimes our life and reputation to the lawyer and attorney. Such confidence could not safely be reposed in people of a very low or mean condition. Their reward must be such, therefore, as may give them that rank in society which so important a trust requires.' The argument is that we cannot believe in the professional skill of those who evidently are earning little by it: so we must assure consultants of a high income if they are to be able to do their work. There is a circularity here that we have met before: the status determines the pay because the pay determines the status. But this is still how many people think—the capability that cônfers high status also commonly, as a fact of the market, commands high pay, and the association is taken to mark a causal relation, so that we cannot believe in the high capability of anyone whose high status is not shown by a prosperous appearance. We therefore have to pay consultants highly in order to be assured that we are getting value for our money.

This way of envisaging the association between high levels of capability, pay, and status shades into another that applies to all levels. In the third and longest strand of thought about stations in life, each occupation is seen as set in a stratum of society defined by income and way of life; and so set not merely as a fact, but rightfully, so that the pay for each occupation ought to be that which would enable those who follow it to live in the station of life appropriate to the occupation. The justice here is not Marx's 'bourgeois equity' according to which each man should be paid what he produces, but resides in compliance with the ordering of man's estate, which is seen as part of the natural order which it would be disastrous to subvert. But even where the philosophical foundations are never thought of, there has been a widespread feeling that it is what is needed to enable the worker to maintain his station in life, be that high or low, that should determine his pay.

That this is the essential interpretation of the appeal to station in life is brought out by Haber's account (1974) of the professions in the U.K. and the American colonies in the eighteenth century. The three learned professions—law, medicine, and the church—were an estate of the realm. Those who followed them were gentlemen who had received a liberal education: thus the barrister was marked off as such from the solicitor, and the physician who did not work with his hands from the surgeon who did so work and who had learned his trade by apprenticeship. Gentlemen received honoraria rather than charge fees; barristers would not sue clients who failed to pay. Of Smith's argument—the second strand above—that we can place great trust only in those who hold a sufficient rank in society, Haber remarks that 'somehow locksmiths, shipwrights, coachmen, mushroom gatherers and jewellers were relied on in matters gravely affecting many lives and fortunes without being granted the kind of trust Smith intended or the high standing in society that he thought it required. This trust implied not simply reliability, but a relationship of authority and dependence. And that relationship owed more to the rank of the men who customarily did the work than the nature of the work itself.'

On this view, the rank was given independently of and prior to the pay, by such criteria as birth and the attainment of a liberal education: it was then only right and fitting that the pay should be commensurate with the rank. This held for all ranks. The British Corn Production Act of 1917 provided that the Board it set up to fix wages in agriculture should 'as far as practicable, secure for able-bodied men wages which, in the opinion of the Board, are adequate to promote efficiency and to enable a man in an ordinary case to maintain himself and his family in accordance with such standard of comfort as may be reasonable in relation to the nature of his occupation'. This directive was repeated in the Agricultural Wages Act passed under a Labour governemnt in 1924. As late as 1946, a committee set up to advise on the appropriate pay for dentists in the British National Health Service was instructed to pay due regard 'to the desirability of maintaining in the future the proper social and economic status of general dental practice and its power to attract a suitable type of recruit to the profession' (B.P.P. 1948)—the wording seeming to imply that adequate recruitment depended on the maintenance of the proper status.

Closely linked with the notion of the pay appropriate to a station in life is that of the social minimum—the pay appropriate to those of the lowliest station. Reder (1955) has suggested that before ever a minimum wage was enacted federally this notion took effect in the U.S.A. to fix effectively, not a minimum to which society should make up family income in one way or another, but 'the minimum (straight time) hourly wage rate at which a business firm or government—as distinguished from a household or family farm—can hire an hour of labour'. The First World War, he considers, lifted the actual wage rate of the unskilled well above the social minimum; but 'the ideology of "welfare capitalism" and the general social climate of the 1920's so raised (that minimum) that, by 1929, it had more or less caught up with the prevailing wage rates for unskilled labour'.

The blending of the status accorded to an occupation with the station in life of those who follow it, and the belief that the occupation tends to get the level of pay that fits the station, are illustrated in a letter from a British train driver to *The Times* (29 Nov. 1972). 'Train drivers', wrote Mr. J. R. Clack, 'have long been regarded by the public as cloth-capped uneducated peasants content to rub along on a pint and a fag: well, I've news for all we are the fastest land bound travellers in the country and are soon to be expected to career about the countryside at speeds in excess of 100 m.p.h. ... We have progressed from clanking steam engines and grime-laden workmen to highly skilled technicians.'

The Webbs saw the principle of payment according to status as one widely accepted by wage-earners, and applied by them even when that meant foregoing a possible rise. To trade unionists it seems obvious, they wrote (1926, p. 332), 'that the actual earnings of any class of workers are largely determined by its Standard of Comfort, that is to say, the kind and amount of food, clothing, and other commodities to which the class has become firmly accustomed. It would not be easy to persuade an English engineer to work at this trade for thirteen shillings a week, however excessive might be the supply of engineers. Rather than do such violence to his own self-respect, he would work as a labourer, or even sweep a crossing.' When the Webbs first wrote, thirteen shillings was the wage of the Dorsetshire labourer, of whom they went on to say that 'however much in request [he] might find himself it would not enter his head to ask two pounds a week for his work'. Hence, in effect, a tacit agreement to maintain the rate of pay of each occupation at or about a certain level; or a tacit combination among workers to uphold a minimum for it. 'There is, in fact ... in each occupation a customary standard of livelihood, which is, within a specific range of variation, tacitly recognised by both employers and employed.' Again (op. cit., pp 696–7), 'to the modern observer it is obvious that the existence, among all the workmen of a particular grade, of an identical notion as to what amount and kind of weekly expenditure constitutes subsistence, is in itself equivalent to a tacit combination. It is, in fact, however it may have come about, an incipient Common Rule, supported by a universal and prolonged refusal to work, which is none the less a strike in that it is unconcerted and undeliberate.'

It remains for us to consider what seems at first the clearest expression of the conviction that each man's pay should be set to enable him to maintain the station in life to which he is assigned by his occupation—namely the scholastic doctrine of the Just Wage. In his account of that doctrine, Fogarty (1961, pp. 257–83) has a section headed 'To each according to his status'. The tradition is clear, he says, 'especially in the Middle Ages and in the last seventy or eighty years, that a Just Wage is one which allows an employee of normal earning capacity ... to earn enough to keep himself and his wife and children at the standard customary in his social class.' A wage is 'an expression of employees' status in the social order as a whole'. Nor does this mean only that the lower-paid should be assured of a decent minimum: those of higher status should be paid highly enough to enable them to maintain the appropriate way of life.

But the doctrine was at once more sophisticated and more practical than this. Since the Schoolmen also held that the wage should vary with the valuation set by the market on the work done, a problem arose when this valuation differed from the pay that was commensurate with status. The way in which this problem was solved is illuminating. For the doctors and lawyers and others of higher income it was pointed out that 'the status that they have a right to maintain [was] derived from the value of their services', so there was no risk of status and income diverging in the long run. And similarly for the low-paid labourer: the customary standard to which he has a right depends on the average value in the long run of his kind of services. So the case for the Just Wage runs, in effect, as follows: the pay of workers in a given occupation, averaged over a number of workers and years, provides a standard of living that confers on the occupation a certain status; in enjoining each employer, in whatever particular circumstances, to pay the wage commensurate with that status, the principle of the Just Wage takes the status as an index of the normal wage, in order to protect the worker from exploitation by particular employers and from buffeting by fluctuations of the market. But this is very different from holding that the wage must be set to match a status that is established quite independently of the market, and will be the same whether the qualities that confer the status are scarce or plentiful relatively to the demand for them.

The principle of the Just Wage was thus based on a relation between income and station in life that was regarded as normal because it had long obtained, and there was no apparent reason why it should not continue to obtain. But this very stability precluded inferences about causality—it would have been otherwise if both income and station had varied from time to time, and varied together. The stability would have come about in an economy that was not changing greatly and in which accordingly the market forces determined relative incomes that also did not change greatly, while life-styles and stations in life followed from the relative incomes. In all instances of a perceived link between pay and station, the link may really be of this kind: however durable it may seem, economic changes may break it. The station in life assigned to farm labourers did not keep their wages above the starvation level when the numbers seeking work in the English villages increased rapidly at the end of the eighteenth century; nor has it kept their wages down when evident market forces have been pulling them up in the last thirty years. In all employments, these years of a general rise in real incomes together with shifts in the demand for particular kinds of labour have made the attribution of differences in pay to differences of station increasingly implausible.

The breaking-up of the once settled notions of the station in life of those who followed this or that occupation has not disrupted the corresponding notions of status. Though in this discussion, following some of our sources, we have sometimes used 'station in life' and 'status' interchangeably, a distinction between them appears when we follow Haber (1974), in his study already cited, in tracing the breaking up in the U.S.A. of the old gentlemanly conception of the learned callings and the struggle of those who followed them to attain and defend what we now call professional status. There came in the 1830s a period of liberalization, and attack on privilege in the name of both equality and liberty: entry to occupations must be open to all—let any man practise who can induce others to pay him for his services. But there followed a period in which the impulses that had formed the guilds of old led to the formation of professional associations, whose animating principles were 'a dislike of competition, an affirmation of occupational autonomy and esprit de corps, and an assertion that a special authority and benevolence towards the client was intrinsic to the occupation' (p. 267). The acceptance of these claims by legislatures and the public owed much to the growth of professional training—as witness the rise of the professional engineer—and in medicine to the great advances in knowledge that gave the trained physician and surgeon a vastly greater power to heal. Thus after station in life was broken up by a turbulent individualism, status was accorded to manifest skill acquired by long study and experience.

4.6. Is status prior to pay?

An affirmative answer is suggested by the observation that stratification by status has existed and exists today in societies that in other respects differ very widely. An American anthropologist, Lloyd Fallers, whose own fieldwork was in East Africa and Turkey, has traced this to one of the categories of human perception, the propensity of mankind everywhere to form moral judgements. 'The heart of stratification', he wrote (1964, p. 113), 'what makes it universal in human societies—is man's tendency to evaluate his fellows, and himself, as "better" or "worse" in terms of some cultural notion of "the good". To be sure, the content of such notions varies over a wide spectrum, but the universality of moral ideas forms one of the common roots of stratification.' These moral ideas, we may add, include the propriety of deference to those of higher status. An English exponent of linguistic philosophy (Frayn, 1974, 5.9) has observed, 'Our reading of the world and our mastery of notations are intimately linked. We read the world in the way that we read a notation—we make sense of it, we place constructions upon it. . . . Our ability to read the phenomena around us depends upon our ability to differentiate them. So, obsessively, we classify and order. And we judge, and rank by merit. We find everything better or worse, more beautiful or less beautiful, socially superior or inferior, approvable or disapprovable.' Talcott Parsons, again, in his 'analytical approach to the theory of social stratification' (1954), has argued that inherent in the very possibility of rational action is the evaluation of ends and means: 'but given the process of evaluation, the probability is that it will serve to differentiate entities in a rank order of some kind' (p. 93).

The view that ranking by status is a propensity inherent in human nature—more exactly, a genetically programmed propensity—is linked with the observation that it serves to promote the order and cohesion that are indispensable for the very existence of any society. In his study of the Indian caste system, significantly entitled *Homo Hierarchicus*, Dumont (1970, p. 252) contends that it is the essential function of stratification (or, as he says, of hierarchy) in any complex society to express 'the unity of such a society whilst connecting it to what appears to it to be universal, namely a conception of the cosmic order, whether or not it includes a God, or a King as mediator. If one likes, hierarchy integrates the society by reference to its values.' This is only to repeat what Shakespeare put into the mouth of Ulysses:

> The heavens themselves, the planets and this centre
> Observe degree, priority and place,
> Insisture, course, proportion, season, form,
> Office, and custom, in all line of order . . .
>
> . . . .
>
> Oh! when degree is shak'd,
> Which is the ladder to all high designs,
> The enterprise is sick. How could communities,
> Degrees in schools, and brotherhoods in cities,
> Peaceful commerce from dividable shores,
> The primogenitive and due of birth,
> Prerogative of age, crowns, sceptres, laurels,
> But by degree, stand in authentic place?
> Take but degree away, untune that string,
> And, hark! what discord follows . . .
>
> . . . .
>
> Then everything includes itself in power,
> Power into will, will into appetite;
> And appetite, a universal wolf,
> So doubly seconded with will and power
> Must make perforce a universal prey,
> And last eat up himself . . .

(Troilus and Cressida, Act I, scene 3.)

Now if the observance of degree has this function of preserving society, we might suppose that the requirements of survival will have selected our forebears towards an innate propensity to such observance, during the millenniums in which, as we might also suppose, their hunting-gathering bands needed cohesion for protection against predators, and sometimes also for the pursuit of their own prey and defence against other bands. We do well to remind ourselves of how large a part of human existence has been passed in the conditions of hunters and gatherers. 'Cultural man has been on earth for some 2,000,000 years; for over 99 per cent of this period he has lived as a hunter-gatherer .... Of the estimated 80,000,000,000 men who have ever lived out a life span on earth, over 90 per cent have lived as hunters and gatherers; about 6 per cent have lived by agriculture and the remaining few per cent have lived in industrial societies' (Lee & Devore 1968, p. 3). It is therefore natural to conjecture that we who are descended from so long a line of survivors in such conditions should be genetically programmed to behave in ways that promoted survival in just those conditions. Did these ways include 'the observance of degree'?

We have no direct knowledge of how our hunter-gatherer forebears behaved, but we do know a good deal about the behaviour of hunter-gatherers today. True, these may not be typical of our forebears, by the very fact of their not having experienced the neolithic revolution that our forebears proved capable of initiating or adopting; yet if they were indeed found to be stratified by status, the case for regarding status as prior to pay in developed societies would be strengthened. The fact, moreover, that though found in different continents and very diverse settings—tundra, tropical forest, desert—they are strikingly similar in social structure (Bicchieri 1972) makes it more likely that this structure was associated with the hunting and gathering of our forebears. But this structure, and the norms of behaviour that go with it, are very different from those associated with stratification by status. The common characteristics of these present-day societies of hunters and gatherers are fluidity, the absence of structured authority or personal dominance, and egalitarianism.

The fluidity is possible because these people move in bands whose size is variable within limits, and which are not closely circumscribed spatially. Groups may come together at one season of the year and separate at another. Disputes within a group can be dealt with by the dissidents going off to join another group or form the nucleus of a new group: of the G/Wi bushmen of the Kalahari we are told that 'compatibility of personality is the expressed motive for migration to a band and is the qualification for acceptance of a recruit' (Silberbauer 1972, p. 308). What the same author tells us of these bushmen's society applies to the hunter-gatherers very widely. It is 'loosely structured', he says (p. 304), '... the social system is flexible and versatile ... It is a high-valency society, permitting fusion and fission at many points.' The forms of association within this fluidity are varied (Steward 1968, p. 322). There may be sodalities, totemic clans, moieties, task groups, dyadic relations; but the one universal and dominant tie is kinship. What we do not find is the relation of superior and inferior status.

This is so, even though there are recognized leaders, for the leader owes his position to his personal qualities in a particular capacity, and he exercises no general or constituted authority. Among the Dogrib of the Canadian North-West Territories the term K'awo means 'the temporary travelling or hunting "boss" selected by group consensus' or 'an executive officer, either temporary or "permanent", appointed by chief or headman to organize and direct group events'. There are seven councillors under a chief, but their authority 'rests solely in the respect and deference granted by their followers. A councillor can be thrown out upon the consensual decision of his people' (Helm 1972, p. 77). Among the Copper Eskimos, 'persistent questioning of older informants failed to reveal any structurally defined institution of leadership. All informants stressed egalitarianism. But there was a term for "the organizer of a hunt" ' (Damas 1972, p. 32).

That egalitarianism is the third salient characteristic of these peoples It expresses itself positively in co-operativeness Of some Australian Aborigines we are told that 'the horde or band is not just a group made up of nucleated family units ... It is a cooperative unit, with each member caught up in an intimate network of responsibilities and obligations, depending on others as others depend on him' (Berndt 1972, pp. 198–9). It is because co-operation means dependence that the Paliyans of South India form an exception in their avoidance of it; but this springs from their wish to combine equality with autonomy, not from any lack of concern for equality, still less from any bent towards competitive individualism (Gardner 1972, pp. 424–5). It is common for food to be shared, not merely with dependants, but between hunter and hunter. The Guayaki of Paraguay even have a taboo against the hunter eating any part of his own catch: he must live on what other hunters give him (Clastres 1972, pp. 168–70). Egalitarianism is also expressed positively by the requirement of consensus. The Dogribs hold that 'because all men are equal, they should equally agree. Dogribs should "listen to one another". Thereby is achieved the ideal of consensus in group affairs. To ignore the interests and opinions of members of the group or pit one's will against them is antipathetic to Dogrib ethos. So also is ego aggrandizement at the expense of others (as in Latin *machismo*)' (Helm 1972, p. 80). This introduces the negative expression of egalitarianism: resentment of and opposition to anything that tends to make anyone superior to or better off or more powerful than others. Of the Ik and Mbuti in Africa we are told that 'there is a strong hostility felt towards any individual who aspires to a position of authority or leadership. Hostility is even shown towards those who, without any such aspirations, are plainly better fitted to lead than others by virtue of sheer ability' (Turnbull 1968, p. 136).

To these considerations we may add that conflict, whether within or between the hunter-gatherer bands, does not call for discipline and subordination. We have seen how conflict within the band can be dealt with by fission. Conflict between bands is generally avoided: there are no fixed boundaries to defend, and no overspill of population to set up a struggle for scarce resources. Each tribe of the Guayaki 'considers the others as dangerous cannibals, and if two strange bands meet by chance in the forest, they either try to massacre each other or flee in opposite directions'; but such encounters are rare, for 'the moment a travelling group discovers the tracks of a foreign band, it goes back the way it came' (Clastres 1972, p. 163). When fighting does occur it does not take the form of battles between disciplined forces.

The evidence is thus powerful, that contemporary societies of hunter-gatherers are in no wise stratified by status. One basic consideration makes it likely that this also held of our forebears' societies: all hunter-gatherers, because they have to move around, are inherently prevented from accumulating much in the way of personal possessions, and so from becoming differentiated one from another in respect of wealth. This appears by force of an exception; in one instance we do find stratification among hunter-gatherers, and this is where the food supply is big enough for people without agriculture or herds to establish permanent settlements and accumulate property. Of the Indians of the north-west coast of America, Suttles (1968, pp. 56–68) observes, 'Here were people with permanent houses in villages of more than a thousand; social stratification, including a hereditary caste of slaves and ranked nobility; specialization in several kinds of hunting and fishing, crafts and curing; social units larger than villages; elaborate ceremonies; and one of the world's great art styles.' Property (in some sense) in the means of production, together with specialization among adult males, created the role of leader or manager: on the central coast (p. 65), though social organization was loose and 'in general the household was autonomous', 'task groups were directed by the "owners" of resources such as fishing sites and clam beds; by owners of special gear, as the net for a deer drive; or simply by skilled specialists in the activity'. Occasional surpluses in the food supply made it possible to acquire prestige by wealth: (p. 60) among the Tolowa '. . . storing food to sell to others was recognized as an important method of acquiring wealth. . . . Wealth is converted into prestige by its use in ceremonial displays and in payment of bride price, which establishes the social status of children to the marriage'. It is significant that three things appear together here—differences in property, the division of labour among adult males, and social stratification.

Contemporary groups of non-human primates are even farther away from our own forebears than contemporary human hunter-gatherers, yet if we found that where these groups of primates needed to co-operate in order to get food or to defend themselves against predators or other groups they adopted an ordering by rank, it would seem more likely that our own forebears had adopted ranking under similar pressures. But what we know of primate groups is far from bearing this out. Like those of the hunter-gatherers, these groups are marked by great diversity and flexibility, with only kinship as a basic and general tie. It is true that relations of dominance—popularly instanced by the 'pecking order' among hens in captivity—are often found in the primate groups, and that they do serve the purpose there of avoiding the strife through which they are sometimes arrived at. The form they take, moreover—the inferior 'keeps his distance', or approaches the dominant animal with gestures of humility—is very like the bearing expected of human inferiors towards their social superiors. Yet Hinde, in his work on 'The Biological Bases of Human Social Behaviour' (1974), remarks (p. 347),

While the establishment of dominance relations accepted by the individuals concerned is accompanied by a reduction in intra-group strife and tension, a dominance order cannot in itself be responsible for group cohesiveness. Hierarchical structuring is to be regarded rather as the consequence of the responses of individuals to potentially agonistic situations when withdrawal is rendered impossible either by physical barriers or by other facets of their own behaviour. Agonistic interactions form only one aspect of the inter-relationships between individuals, and a dominance hierarchy is only one aspect of the total pattern of relationships.

Where there is leadership, moreover, such as in the guidance of the group towards scarce or scattered supplies of food or water, or away from danger, the leader may be an old hand, who is respected for his wisdom, and is not the dominant member of the group. Thus it is not by dominance and deference that the group meets the needs of survival that we began by supposing might be at the origin of ranking order.

In sum, what we know of contemporary hunter-gatherers and non-human primates is very far from encouraging us to believe that our forebears were selected for a genetic propensity to stratify by status. On the contrary, if there is a propensity of social behaviour that was selected for in them and programmed genetically in us their descendants, it is a propensity to prefer associating in small groups, and working co-operatively and taking decisions by consensus, without imposed or constituted authority, and without stratification—on the contrary, setting a conscious value upon equality. We might even conjecture that the social tensions of our own day might be ascribed to the conflict between this inherent propensity towards co-operative and egalitarian association, and the inequality and subordination inherent in the methods of production that have been developed from the neolithic revolution onwards.

The neolithic revolution opened very widely the possibility of economic differentiation that had been exceptional before. In the societies that had undergone this revolution, we find the stratification that is so conspicuous by its absence in the hunter-gatherer societies known to us. Burt (1959, p. 23 n.1) has suggested that the neolithic revolution brought differentiation by skill. He saw this in terms of class, but his suggestion applies equally to status:

The most primitive communities of which we have knowledge—the so-called 'foodgatherers'—had no class-system' A class-system only appears among the so-called 'food-producers', and seems to have arisen out of the need for a controlled organization of labour as a prerequisite to the successful development of a large agricultural community. In Sumer, Egypt, India, Mexico, and Peru the emergence of a ruling group is associated with the emergence of a routine and a ceremonial governing the provision of an adequate food supply, and particularly with the invention of an efficient calendar, which in the words of an eminent anthropologist must have been 'one of the greatest intellectual feats ever accomplished'. Thus the ruling group at the outset was a highly intelligent group.

We have seen (Sec. 2.6) that in the Kibbutzim in which tasks have become technically differentiated, some of the younger members at least have felt that differentiation by skill ought to be accompanied by differentiation of income.

We may conclude that, instead of status being prior to pay, it is much more likely that economic differentiation came first, and that higher status then came to be attributed to greater wealth or income or proficiency. But we have still to examine the grounds for believing that, however we settle the question of origins, in modern societies a status that is determined independently of pay often provides the basis for fixing pay.

4.7. Evidence for status moulding pay in modern societies

We have seen already (pp. 87–88) how Mill in the England of the 1840s and Palekar in the India of the 1950s saw the pay of clerks as being held up much above the level at which it would have settled under the play of supply and demand, by the continuing attribution of high status to literacy. Such determination of pay by status has been held to operate extensively. A British economist, for instance, with a wide experience of pay fixing in both the private and public sectors, has written that '... what is anomalous to the economist may make perfectly good sense to the sociologist. In a hierarchical society such as ours, large issues of social status are involved in wage and salary scales. Pay and prestige are closely linked; and (in spite of some exceptions) it is the rule that the high prestige person should be also the highly-paid person; and vice versa' (Wootton 1955, p. 68). Certainly it is not hard to find instances of status acting as an independent factor in pay fixing or of its being expected to do so.

At a time when the pay of doctors in the British National Health Service was in dispute, a leader of the medical profession, Lord Segal (1965), maintained that 'the real crisis in general practice today is primarily one of status, rather than pay. By insisting upon the pecuniary aspect of the doctor's case, medical leadership has allowed the true claims of the general practitioner to go largely by default. Had emphasis throughout been laid upon raising the status of general practitioners, they would long ago have been able to command a salary commensurate with their enhanced status.' The crisis of status Lord Segal regarded as arising from the capitation list, on the length of which the doctor's income depends, and its vitiating effect on the relation between doctor and patient—in particular, its requiring the doctor to submit himself to the patient's demands, under pain, if he will not, of the patient's transferring himself to the list of another doctor who will. The argument was, in our terms, that instead of the patient deferring to the doctor, the doctor had to defer to the patient; and that only when the old relation was restored would the community see it as fit and proper to provide doctors with 'a salary commensurate with their enhanced status'.

Two instances may be cited in which status has been held to be an actual determinant of pay. Sadler (1970) has described how compositors have retained their top status, and pay, in printing, despite the Linotype and Monotype, and the fact that 'it would take longer today to re-train a compositor to be a machine minder than *vice versa*'. For two English bakeries the remarkable finding is reported (Lerner, Cable, & Gupta 1969, p. 225) that workers whose relative pay lay below their status themselves chose to work more overtime in order to bring their earnings up to the commensurate level. 'In general the status hierarchy coincided with the national job-rate structure; but where the methods and the organization of work conferred upon different groups of workers rewards which were not regarded as commensurate with the status of the job performed, there was adjustment of earnings to fulfil expectations. The most important, but not the only means by which customary earnings differentials were adjusted was by working more overtime.' Where 'jobs were of equal status, but the organization of production conferred on one group of workers greater opportunity for shiftwork, the other tended to work more overtime and thus keep its earnings in line'.

Here the reference group by which the fairness of pay was judged consisted in jobs of equal status. A remarkable study of British airline pilots by Blain (1972) shows us how status matters greatly or little according as the comparison of status is made with the members of a reference group or of society at large. When Blain asked the British pilots whether they 'felt that their social status was relevant in salary determination', only 47 per cent considered that it was, and 42 per cent thought it irrelevant—many of these very much so, for 'as many as 12 per cent of pilots in all airlines, and 32 per cent in B.O.A.C. felt that their status in the community was the single most irrelevant factor in the list of sixteen items' submitted to them (p. 235). 'The main explanation of this result', Blain suggests, 'is that pilots, generally speaking, receive higher salaries than other professionals'; but we may also surmise that the nature of their own work is so different from that of other professionals, or of the neighbours in their places of residence, that they do not regard these as constituting a reference group. In the relations with two other groups, however, they were acutely conscious of status. One of these consisted of the managers of the airlines. The pilot's claim to full professional status had brought them into conflict with a management that was disposed, as they saw it, to treat them as 'drivers airframe'. Their sense that technical and administrative changes had lowered their status within the organization heightened their militancy. Their other reference group consisted of the pilots of European (but not the American) airlines, and here again they smarted under a loss of status, in this case through a fall in their relative pay: this was the main instigation of their pay claim.

Whereas Lord Segal's advice to the doctors was, 'Restore your status and you will raise your pay', the pilots' claim was 'Raise our pay in order to restore our status'. In part, at least, they seem to have attached importance to status for its own sake, and sought higher pay because they saw it as an affimation and public recognition of status. This attitude may well be common. In particular, an employee in the higher ranks may regard his own relative pay as his 'score', with which he is credited; a group of employees may regard the relative pay of their occupation as the measure of the value that society sets upon their qualifications. This belief that status is conferred or at least has to be upheld by relative pay appears in a view attributed to the chairman of an organization of British professional engineers; he was adamant, it was said, 'about the need for something to be done about salaries as one leg of a campaign to upgrade engineering and its public image generally' (Harris 1975).

The two-way connection between status and pay is found especially in what is called 'the internal labour market' (Doeringer & Piore 1971). To call this any kind of market is perhaps inappropriate, for it consists of those employments within any firm or organization that are largely insulated from market forces. The insulation is most apparent where the skill the employee has acquired within the firm is specific to that firm's processes and of no use to other firms. Two consequences follow—the trained worker is unlikely to leave unless his present earnings fall below what he could earn elsewhere as a beginner; but he does not have to compete with outsiders for higher-grade posts that become vacant within the firm, for most of these can only be filled by promotion from within, and this provides the captive worker with the prospect of a career of advancement within the firm. There is also insulation when skills are not specific but an employee's capability is vouched for by no diploma, and is known with certainty only to the firm in which he has developed it: he will find it hard to better himself by moving, at least in the short run. In these circumstances the pay can be fixed job by job without close regard to what must be paid to attract and retain the worker, or to the immediate value to the firm of the work done at that point. There are certain 'ports of entry', through which the firm recruits outsiders, and what it pays here will depend on the state of the external market; but in other parts of its job structure it can vary pay within wide limits at its discretion, or by agreement with the employees concerned. Evidently the scope for discretion at any point will be wider, the more closely the employees concerned are attached to the firm, and the more they themselves are concerned with their long-run prospects rather than their pay there and then. In industry, these conditions are seen at their fullest in Japan. The outstanding comparison of two Japanese firms with their English counterparts in electrical engineering by Dore (1973, c. 3) has shown how the difference between the ways of fixing differentials for skill in the two settings sprang from the very different degrees of attachment of employees to the firm. In the English firms both management and employees saw the rate of pay appropriate to each grade of skill as a market price, dependent on supply and demand: they believed 'that the market does more or less determine a going price for a particular skill, and that employers ought to pay that price, not merely because it is "just" but for the self-interested reason that workers will drift away elsewhere if they do not'. But the Japanese firms generally had to take account of the market only when engaging new entrants: once a man was hired, the total pay due for the whole working life of a man of his quality could be allocated to the successive stages of his career without much need to have regard to what was being paid for his kind of work in other firms, or to the match between what he was getting and the value of his work to the firm at any one time. In fact each man's basic wage or salary rose annually, while from time to time, according to his merit but without regard to the work he was doing or post he held, he was advanced to a higher grade. There were recognized maximum ages by which the worker was assured of reaching a certain grade. In both ways pay was thus made to rise with age, which together with merit was seen as conferring status.

The connection between relative pay, place in an organization, and self-respect appears at its clearest wherever there is a chain of command, in management, the armed forces, and administration generally. For most people it is as incontestable that someone who has authority over others must in the nature of things be paid more than they, as that any two sides of a triangle are together greater than the third. At first this seems a strong case of status determining pay. But the principle that higher authority must have higher pay is not given categorically; it rests rather on the premisses, first, that this authority can be exercised efficiently, and can command the respect of subordinates, only if those in whom it is vested are of greater capability; and, second, that greater capability should and generally does receive higher pay. If relative pay, in other words, is justified only by relative capability, and is generally taken to be an index of it, then the effective authority of a superior over his subordinates, and their ability to accept his orders without loss of their own self-respect, would both be vitiated if he were not seen to be 'worth more than they'. On this view, it is not his status that confers his pay: status and pay alike are conferred by the capability he must have to do his job.

But this argument concerns only the rank order, and not the size of the differentials between the ranks. It may be contended that these are set as status symbols. Certainly they appear to be conventional, when we read of the officers of American corporations that 'generally speaking, a president will receive in salary about a third more than his No. 2 man, about twice what his No 3 man gets, and some three times the salaries paid to those on the fourth rung of management' (The editor of *Fortune, The Executive Life* (New York, 1956), p. 100, quoted here from Hall 1969, p. 154).

Marris (1964, pp. 89–99) has developed a theory of managers' salaries, according to which they are economically indeterminate. The theory is based on the bureaucratic element in management, with a hierarchy of posts relating superiors to subordinates, and the impossibility, for a variety of reasons, of not paying the superior more than the subordinate. The question then is, how much more? Within each organization, Marris suggests, a convention is established about the rate at which pay shall rise per unit increase in responsibility, as that is measured by the number of people at the bottom level who report to a manager directly or through intermediate management. This convention is 'sociologically determined', Marris does not say just how; but he does say (p. 97) that

the system as such merely lays down a set of relativities, and there is no indication that the absolute income of a person of given ability must take on any particular value. Consequently, the general level of corporate salaries, like that of most other incomes, is left indeterminate. If all executive salaries were halved tomorrow, although some effects might be felt at the lowest levels, neither in the short nor the long run would any effects be felt at the top, i.e. if the average corporate officer in the U.S. were brought down to a gross compensation of $30,000 per annum, he would continue to function efficiently and no special difficulty would be experienced in finding his successors.

Yet, once established, the sociological convention takes on an economic function: 'within organisations of similar types both seniors and subordinates will come to expect and accept a conventional rate of gradation; if this is not obeyed, authority may break down. Thus observance becomes a functional necessity' (p. 93).

But an alternative account of executive salaries suggests a less arbitrary origin. It ascribes the relative sizes of these salaries to what has been called the 'scale of operations' effect (Tuck 1954; Mayer 1960; Reder 1968, pp. 589–95; Reder 1969, pp. 219–21). The initial presumption here is that the amount a job is worth depends on the difference the holder of it can make to the product by doing it ably or not so ably. In Mayer's words, 'If, because of differences in ability, one man completes 90 per cent of his tasks successfully and another completes only 80 per cent and the total potential value of their output is $10, the difference in ability will lead to a $1 difference in earnings. But if the total potential value of their output is $1,000, then the difference in ability is worth $100.' A study of sales, profits, and executive incomes in 45 of the largest 100 U.S. corporations in 1953–9 found evidence for 'the likelihood that there is a valid relationship between sales and executive incomes ... but not between profits and executive incomes, although, because of the statistical problems involved, the tests employed do not completely rule out the possibility of a valid relationship between profits and executive incomes too' (McGuire, Chiu, & Elbing 1962). As Reder has argued cogently (1968, p. 590),

If we suppose that executive skill and capital are co-operant factors in producing profits (i.e. a given degree of skill can generate more profit the greater the value of the resources over which it is exercised), it follows that the marginal product of an executive would have a strong positive association with the value of the resources under his control; i.e. with his 'scale of operations'. The current profits of the firm need not, in the first approximation have anything to do with his compensation; a good executive is worth as much to a company in holding its losses to $10 million when, with ordinary management they might have been $15 million, as in augmenting its profits by $5 million.

Lydall (1968, p. 132) cites surveys of chief executives' salaries in France, Germany, Great Britain, and the United States which find a general tendency of these salaries to vary with the sales of the firm: as between one firm and another, the proportionate difference between the salaries of the chief executives was from a quarter to a third of the proportionate difference between the firms' sales.

The factor here called the 'scale of operations' is much the same as that called 'responsibility' in job evaluation. Under the application of job evaluation in the American steel industry it was found that though automation reduced the skill requirements of some jobs, at the same time it increased the responsibility they imposed (Stieber 1959). If we consider the increase in throughput and in the amount of capital used, this is readily understood as a 'scale of operations' effect.

The possibility that it is on the evaluation of responsibility that differences between the pay of managers at different levels are based, has been developed by Simon (1957) and Lydall (1959; 1968, pp. 127–33). Lydall makes two assumptions. First there is what appears to be the simplifying and heuristic assumption that 'each supervisor controls—on the average—a fixed number of persons in the next lower grade'. Second, the pay of each supervisor is proportional to the aggregate pay of those he supervises. This is plausible, because 'the income paid to a manager depends on the extent of his responsibility; and this can resonably be measured by the aggregate income of the people whom he directly controls. If either their number or their average income goes up, it would be only natural for the manager to expect an increase in his salary' (1959, pp. 111–12). On these assumptions Lydall shows that we should expect a distribution of the higher earned incomes of the Pareto form, in which when we plot the logarithm of the number of incomes about a certain level against the logarithm of that level we find a straight line. But this is the form we actually find in the higher earned incomes of Western countries, though not in the Soviet-type economies where, Lydall says, 'it has been the official policy . . . to pay salaries according to "ability" rather than respnsibility' (1968, p. 130).

Consideration of the pay of top executives brings out one function of pay, the possibility of which we have already raised in the case of the airline pilots—namely, pay as a form of recognition. For this purpose it is irrelevant that pay takes the form of purchasing power, and equally that most of the amount by which the top salaries rise out of the ruck is lopped off by tax. What matters is that the high salary distinguishes the recipient as bearing no less high responsibility. It is an announcement to the world of the exacting requirements of his office, and an assurance to him that his energy and ability in meeting those requirements are recognized. In this it is like badges of rank in the armed forces, and the familiar 'status symbols', such as office furniture or access to particular dining-rooms, by which grades are distinguished in civilian organizations. A man might rise to the challenge of an exacting job, and be willing to do it, so far as his 'compensation' went, for no more than was being paid for an easier job: but then the world would not know how exacting his job was. He would not want to be hitting the runs without the score going up on the board.

This perception of relative pay as a public evaluation or recognition of capability and performance can uphold differentials in any part of the pay structure. The familiar objection of the skilled manual worker to a rise in the pay of the unskilled that he does not share cannot arise from any reduction in his purchasing power, but does express resentment of a reduction in the recognition accorded to his skill. In this way, relative pay neither confers status nor is conferred by it, but is an announcement and confirmation of status.

We have now examined the three grounds that have been cited for believing that status determines pay. At a number of points this examination has raised the possibility that status appears as a determinant of pay because, whatever the origin of the link between the two, it has been evident so long as to become regarded as part of the natural order, which if ever disturbed must be restored. We go on, therefore, to ask how far the influence of status is explicable as that of custom.

4.8. The influence of custom

We have already seen (Sec. 3.1) how the differential between craftsman and labourer in building in Southern England remained at or close to the same round figure for five centuries. Whether custom stabilized the differential indirectly, by way of stabilizing status, or simply inhibited change in both differential and status, the possibility is apparent of an association between status and relative pay being maintained by custom in defiance of the shifting play of market forces. We have also drawn in Sec. 3.1 on Rowe's discussion of the stability of differentials in British engineering workers in the thirty years down to 1914. In the passage already quoted (1928, p. 111) he remarks, 'A cursory examination of the problem of wage differentials in other industries strongly emphasizes the far-reaching effects of sheer custom, and its domination over men's minds. The fact that all the so-called skilled grades in an industry'—that is, we may interject, those who customarily are accorded the same status—'usually get approximately the same wage rates, is at least prima facie evidence of a certain artificial element in the wage structure. It is extremely unlikely that the economic factors of supply and demand would automatically produce this exact similarity of wage rates.' 'We do not realise', Rowe remarks in conclusion, 'the little changes in everyday life which sap the logical foundations of our ideas, and custom has time to consolidate the structure before those foundations have completely crumbled. And so the structure remains resting on the surface of the ground, to outward appearance as solid as ever, until there comes a hurricane.'

An American economist, Piore, who has made a special study of the wage structure internal to the firm, has suggested that this structure is largely determined by custom, which the entrant is taught during his training on the job to accept as morally binding, and which he consequently feels entitled to defend ruthlessly against attempts to change it. Piore has written (1972, p. 289):

The environment in which on the job training can successfully occur is one in which a customary law tends to develop and prevail. Among the tenets of the law are a series of relationships among the wages of the members of the group and between the group members and other workers. These relationships generally establish a fixed structure of relative wages ... The structure is imposed upon individual management by the moral commitment of the work group to it and their willingness to undertake actions in its support which would otherwise be deterred by law and by a commitment to a higher morality and code of behaviour. But the structure achieves its larger moral significance from the fact that the commitment to it is intrinsic in the process through which the supply of labour is generated and, hence, it is difficult to generate a set of competitive pressures which will undermine it.

(See also Doeringer & Piore 1971, pp. 39–40, 85–9.)

There is reason also to believe that customary notions of status, with the unquestioning sense of something being very wrong when status and pay do not agree, have survived until recently in one at least of the Soviet-type economies. Reflecting on the complaints about excessive wage equalization that met her on a visit to Czechoslovakia in 1965, McAuley (1966) wondered whether the real ground of complaint was not that the pay of administrative and professional workers did not conform with traditional notions of status.

> Doctors, we were repeatedly told, earn far too little—the salaries are indeed low ...—but there is no shortage of people wishing to enter the medical profession. ... Do the low salaries for teachers damp down demand for university education? ... Somehow one got tired of being told that a skilled worker could earn more than a university graduate, a bus driver more than a primary school teacher ... and a coal cutter more than an engineer, as though *a priori* this was a bad policy, a ridiculous policy. Would the engineer willingly change places with the coal cutter, or the primary school teacher with the bus driver? ... Is it really economic reasons that have prompted the incessant preoccupation with wage equalization (and if so are these convincing) or is it the result of social attitudes to job status and the kind of salary that 'ought' to go with it? (pp. 182–3.)

The hurricane that upset the British differentials which Rowe had surveyed was the inflation of the First World War: when this had ended the reign of custom, other forces could impinge. We have seen how they took effect to reduce substantially the differentials between skilled and unskilled manual rates, and between clerical and manual rates generally. So long as custom rules, and holds pay and status together, we cannot infer causality. When custom breaks up, and relative pay changes, we can look to see what forces cause the change. In the present case, these forces evidently included public policy, trade unionism, and shifts in the supply of and demand for particular qualifications: it is not at all clear that they included any prior changes in status.

Our examination of the apparently causal link between status and pay has thus brought us to conclusions that are largely negative. Given that, for whatever reason, the rank orders of status and pay are once brought into conformity with one another, anyone wishing to raise his pay can make out a good case for it if he can show that it is less than commensurate with his status. A customary association becomes accepted as inherently right and proper. It is seen as part of the natural order of things that those who follow certain occupations should hold a certain station in life, that is, are entitled to a certain relative income. Here again, where the notional station in life and the actual income have long been adjusted to one another, those who can show that their incomes are less than commensurate with their station have a strong case at the bar of public opinion, and are likely to be able to bring their incomes up. But all this throws no light on the nature of the general link between status and pay. It is not more compatible with status determining pay than with pay determining status, or with each having some influence on the other within a system of forces in which other factors operate on both. In periods when the hold of custom is loosened, and in parts of 'the labour market' where the conditions that constitute a market do in some measure obtain, we see what some of those factors are.

These negative conclusions are reinforced by the instances we go on to cite of divergence between the two rank orders.

4.9. Divergences between the rank orders of status and pay

4.9.1. *Instances of status and pay offsetting one another.*

'Honour', said Adam Smith (1776, Bk. I, c. I, Pt. I), 'makes a great part of the reward of all honourable professions. In point of pecuniary gain, all things considered, they are generally under-recompensed. ...' 'The office of judge', he remarks later in the same work (Bk. V, c. I, Pt. II), 'is in itself so very honourable that men are willing to accept of it, though accompanied with very small emoluments.'

But if high status makes lower pay possible, low status raises pay. 'Disgrace', he continues in the passage first cited, 'has the contrary effect. The trade of a butcher is a brutal and an odious business; but it is in most places more profitable than the greater part of common trades. The most detestable of all employments, that of public executioner, is, in the proportion to the quantity of work done, better paid than any common trade whatever.'

Adam Smith made it clear how he saw the adjustment of pay as being brought about. The mechanism was not that people generally held that low status, for instance, deserved compensation, and set pay higher by common accord. What he saw happening was rather that the low status of an occupation kept down the supply of entrants to it, and thus raised the rate of pay that those who did enter could command; and conversely where high status attracted numerous entrants. He observed (Bk. I, c. I, Pt. I):

There are some very agreeable and beautiful talents, of which the possession commands a certain sort of admiration; but of which the exercise for the sake of gain is considered, whether from reason or prejudice, as a sort of public prostitution. The pecuniary recompense, therefore, of those who exercise them in this manner, must be sufficient, not only to pay for the time, labour, and expense of acquiring the talents, but for the discredit which attends the employment of them as the means of subsistence. The exorbitant rewards of players, opera singers, opera-dancers, etc. are founded upon those two principles; the rarity and beauty of the talents, and the discredit of employing them in this manner. It seems absurd at first sight that we should despise their persons, and yet reward their talents with the most profuse liberality. While we do the one, however, we must of necessity do the other. Should the public opinion or prejudice ever alter with regard to such occupations, their pecuniary recompense would quickly diminish. More people would apply to them, and the competition would quickly reduce the price of their labour.

On this view, the status of at least some occupations depends on the nature of the work done and the qualities required of those who do it, while the pay depends on the balance of supply and demand. Status affects pay only indirectly, through its effect on supply. Pay has no effect on status. Status and pay together make up the net advantage which must cover the supply price of labour to an occupation.

This view is borne out by the experience of the Kibbutzim in filling their posts of responsibility (Tannenbaum *et al.* 1974, p. 121). In great part, status is its own reward. Those who take their turn as managers feel themselves recompensed by the prestige and approval they enjoy among their fellow members if they do their work well. They derive satisfaction also from their ability to contribute notably to the common purpose, and from the variety of their work and the independence in which they can go about it. Yet, though the members of the Kibbutz are dedicated to its ideals or they would hardly remain in it, many of them are still reluctant to undertake the cares of office, with its burden of responsibility, and the fret of dealing with difficult members, and exposure to criticism; at least it has been found that members generally are not so anxious to rise to 'higher' posts as are workers in plants in other countries where those posts carry higher pay. This is evidence for the reality both of the non-pecuniary rewards linked with status, and of deterrents that are also linked with it and that may need to be offset by pay if a sufficient supply of able entrants is to be maintained.

Indeed, it is the experience of the Soviet-type economies that some differentiation by pay, albeit not altogether on the same pattern or on the same scale as in the West, is essential as an incentive; the rewards of status, and the consciousness of social usefulness, are not enough. We are going on to consider a study of the social structure of Czechoslovakia. Commenting on this, and on the attitude towards differentials of the sociologists of the Soviet-type economies generally, two Czech sociologists working in France have written (Strmiska & Vavakova 1972, pp. 246, 247):

Inadequate pay differentials within and between occupations bring a lowering of interest and a disturbance of morale in work, a general fall in performance, a lack of interest in occupational careers and in attaining higher qualifications. ... It is generally recognised that the ideological motivations to work become more effective if they are combined with the influence of a material interest; in themselves, and apart from other influences, they can determine the behaviour of ideological elites, but they are not wholly sufficient for the bulk of society.

4.9.2. *Stratification by status differing from ranking by pay*

Discussions of status usually notice the exceptional cases of disparities between status and income—the 'gentlewoman in reduced circumstances', or the *nouveau riche*; but these are to be regarded as instances of a person's income diverging from the level at which that person's life-style and so status were originally fashioned. There are such cases also as the poor scholar, or the priest whose life of service is led upon a pittance; but of these cases too it can be said that they are striking precisely because they are unusual—what these folk are doing is intelligible, in that they are choosing to give up income in order to devote their powers to what they value more, but not many people so choose. Yet though these cases are exceptional, and perfectly consistent with status and income being closely linked for most people, the fact that they do occur, however rarely, shows that status and income can be separated.

This separation has been shown to extend quite widely in one Soviet-type economy. The Czech sociologist Machonin (1970) made a study of the life-style of a large sample of his fellow countrymen in 1967, by placing each respondent in one of six grades under each of the headings:

    I. Complexity of work
   II. Cultural level of leisure: activities and consumption (life-style)
  III. Participation in management: position within the management of the work organization, level of elected bodies in which the respondent develops voluntary political activities
  IV. Accomplished education—higher, secondary, lower vocational, elementary, etc.
   V. Income.

Thus under the first heading, Complexity of Work, the six grades are examplified by:

    1. Physician-Specialist, director of an industrial enterprise
    2. Engineer, secondary school teacher
    3. Foreman, maintenance fitter
    4. Skilled factory worker
    5. Semi-skilled factory worker
    6. Unskilled worker.

And under II, Cultural Level of Leisure, the grades range from
    1. Owners of cars, people spending their leave abroad
to 5. Owners of TV sets, living in an apartment with basic equipment
and 6. People without 'positive' characteristics.

These particulars having been gathered, the next step was to see how far respondents in effect grouped themselves by the similarity of their ratings—were there many, for instance, who were in the first or second grade under all five headings? In fact there were; and at one level or another, a majority of the respondents showed much the same rating throughout. It will be seen that the question of stratification was not prejudged—the respondents were not assigned to strata on the basis, say, of occupation and income, but were grouped only in so far as they resembled each other closely in five respects. But four such groups were in fact found, with median grades 1·6, 2·8, 4·2, and 5·3. These contained nearly 70 per cent of the population. The grade under Participation in Management was often lower than the grades of the same respondent under other headings, and the income of persons in the third stratum was 'a little higher than corresponds to their average complexity of work, and education'. But these things apart, Machonin concludes, 'it is possible to refer to Czechoslovak society in 1967 as a stratified society, that is, one possessing a certain amount of consistency of social status for the overwhelming majority of population studied' (p. 735).

The average earnings of the four strata were themselves arrayed in the same order: to that extent there was no divergence between pay and status. But this was a society in which a reduction in the inequality of incomes had been a main object and conspicuous achievement of public policy. The range of average income from the highest to the lowest of the four strata was only about 2 to 1. That this narrowing of the range of income had not been accompanied by a greater equalization in other characteristics evidently surprised the investigators. 'Income equalization', Machonin concluded, '. . . was far from leading to corresponding standardization of consumption or of cultural activities during leisure. In brief, the egalitarian arrangement was not such a significant aspect of the social structure of Czechoslovakia as we had assumed initially: and this was perhaps one of the most interesting findings of our study' (pp. 739–40).

There were significant divergences between status and income, moreover, at particular points. Within each stratum individual income varied relatively to the grading under other heads. Besides the four strata there were three groups, well-defined by the consistency of their characteristics other than income, where incomes were inconsistent:

I. Semi-skilled or sometimes skilled industrial workers, mostly in small towns; their earnings were high for their qualifications, and they did not use them for the life-style that usually goes with them.

II. Typically clerks in big cities; their earnings were low for their qualifications, but did not bring their life-style down.

III. Skilled or semi-skilled workers in big cities; their earnings were high for their qualifications, and so was their life-style.

The first of the three inconsistent groups reminds us of the affluent semi-skilled English factory workers studied by Goldthorpe et al. (1969): these too had earnings that were high for their level of training, but had not changed their life-style to that commonly associated with such earnings. Of their affluence it might be remarked that they had not experienced if for very long, and perhaps would adapt their life-style to it in time. Similarly we might comment on Machonin's findings, that the compression of income differentials was still only twenty years old in 1967. People aged over 40 had reached adult stature under the old regime, and may well have maintained the life-styles and distinctions of status that had been linked with the greater differentiation of income then. As the proportion of the population who had grown up under 'equalization' rose year by year, perhaps here too there would be an adjustment of life-style to income.

On the other hand, the divergence between grouping by earnings and by other criteria of affinity may mark not a lag of adjustment of the other criteria to earnings, but an inherent tendency of developing societies. This is the interpretation offered by Gordon and Klopov (1973) of their observations, very similar to Machonin's (1970) in Czechoslovakia, about 'the social structure of the Soviet working class'. In 'the early stages of socialism, the boundaries of the socio-occupational grid have a distinct culture-forming character, and therefore divisions on the other levels coincide with these first ones . . . a social group distinguished by a particular position in the sphere of production generally has a more or less identical level of culture, lives in comparatively similar cultural and daily life conditions, and is distinguished by approximately the same tenor of family life.' But now this was changing: 'the structure of the Soviet working class is ceasing primarily to be production-based, socio-occupational in nature. It presents itself today in the form of a complicated interweaving of socio-occupational layers with socio-cultural, socio-daily life, socio-demographic strata ...'

Whether the divergence marks a lag in adjustment or a persistent development, clearly it is possible, and possible for a good many years. We must infer that there are factors besides income on which status depends, and that they are independent of income even if generally correlated with it.

We also learn how status becomes differentiated even in a society of egalitarian ideals. Two major sources and axes of vertical social distancing have been observed in Czechoslovakia (Strmiska & Varakova 1972, p. 224). One is differentiation by fine gradations according to education, qualifications, and leisure interests. Here, as we have seen, there is no settled relation with the pay structure: at least in such a transitional society as this, life-style has considerable independence of income. The second form of vertical distancing is the hierarchy of more sharp-cut differences that is formed by the bureaucratic structure of public administration and industrial management. Though the levels of this structure are matched by levels of pay, the status and the pay are the joint products of the function of the officeholder, and neither is prior to or a determinant of the other.

That status is in this way a direct outcome of organization, quite apart from inequalities of income, also appears from the need felt by Chairman Mao to close the social distance between the élite and the masses by a direct attack on the separation of technical and administrative functions—for example, by ordaining that political zeal and purity be regarded as qualifications for appointments no less than functional proficiency; and by requiring technologists and managers to bring manual workers into their problem-solving, and themselves from time to time to put in a spell at the manual worker's job (Whyte 1973). Mao probably observed in China what has been observed in Czechoslovakia, a development of 'the technocratic ("culturocratic") type of stratification and management. The "culturocratic" tendencies increase the rationality and efficiency of management, as likewise the qualification and specialization of the managers' (Strmiska & Vavakova 1972, p. 226). The consequent differentiation of managers by status was one target of Mao's Cultural Revolution of 1966. Its significance in our present context lies in its implication that differences of status are largely independent of differences of pay.

A British instance suggests the independence of status as a motivation to the worker. The technical director of a British engineering firm, considering what he saw as 'a slow but resolute drift of talent away from industry (and farm work) and into the more glamorous and traditionally respected vocations', suggested that 'the reason is not so much the poor financial rewards of British industry, but rather that people are motivated more by esteem than by money. Of seven graduates of the Cambridge Faculty of Engineering who were my colleagues in 1957, all have eschewed and taken leave of British industry. I cannot censure them: our society did that to them years ago.' (Rilett 1975.)

4.10. Review and discussion

(a) The problem of this chapter was set by the observation that the grouping of occupations by their average earnings formed much the same structure as the grading of occupations by status. This grading seemed to be a basic human propensity, because people in different times and places respond readily to the invitation to rank occupations by status or social standing, and the outcome is broadly similar even as between very different societies. This raised the question of the nature of the link between pay and status.

(b) Light could be thrown on this question by ascertaining what it is that those who rank by status have in view. They have been held to assess only the general desirability of jobs in this and that occupation, but they seem to be concerned also with the life-style of the job holders, and life-style is seen in its setting of social stratification and the personal relation of superior and inferior in esteem. Our task therefore has been to examine the agreement between ranking by pay and an ordering by status that is not a rank order merely but a hierarchy.

(c) We examined this agreement to see whether it arose and persisted because the relative pay prevailing in each occupation was adjusted to that occupation's status. That this is so has been held on several grounds. One is that each occupation is seen as belonging to a certain station in life, and the pay appropriate to it is that which will suffice to maintain the life-style of the station. On a second ground, man as *homo hierarchicus* is seen as inherently disposed to rank and order his fellows so that social stratification is anterior to economic relations, which will have adapted themselves to stratification. A third ground cites numerous modern instances of status evidently influencing claims and decisions about pay. But we found no reason to conclude that the association betwen pay and status was maintained because the pay was adjusted to the status: apparent instances of this being done might only show a customary association being accepted as normative. The association, moreover, has not been invariable: we noticed cases of pay and status being related inversely, and of ranking by pay differing from stratification by status. Nor did what we know of the societies of hunters and gatherers today suggest that such societies had been hierarchical in the past: it seemed probable that differentiation by status followed rather than preceded the economic differentiation first made possible by the neolithic revolution.

(d) So far the evidence has led to negative conclusions, but a positive statement that is not in conflict with it is as follows.

Where there is an effective market for labour, in that the workers concerned have effective access to alternative employers or customers, who for their part can bid up the pay of workers in short supply, the relative pay of occupations varies with (among other factors) the natural ability, the education and training, and the experience they call for, and the responsibility they impose.

But it is upon these factors that the status attributed to an occupation mainly depends. Generally, then, the rank order of occupations by status will be much the same as that by pay. The similarity in this respect of societies that differ widely in respect of culture and of political and economic organization indicates a general agreement about which qualities are worth paying more for and which attract the attribution of higher status.

This *de facto* association being formed over a sufficient number of occupations comes to be seen as a causal connection: the pay is regarded as the natural complement to or outcome of the status. This is supported by a feedback: the members of an occupation that attains relatively high pay by the working of the market will be enabled by that pay to maintain the kind of lifestyle to which high status is attributed. The association also tends to maintain itself as it becomes hallowed by custom. Those whose relative pay has fallen are able to appeal to the status customarily attributed to their occupation, as a ground for raising their pay; or they may denounce the present rate as unfair, because it denotes a loss of status. Some occupations endeavour to raise their status in the expectation that higher pay will follow. To the extent that these endeavours succeed, status appears as the effective basis of pay, as indeed it is, in the sense that the widespread acceptance of the principle that pay ought to be commensurate with status has been a necessary condition of the rise.

The same customary association finds even readier application to those occupations or employments whose pay, within limits, is insulated from the forces of the market, and is little influenced by changes in the availability of or demand for the labour concerned. Such rates of pay are fixed by custom, administrative decision, or negotiation. In all these processes the principle that gradations of status must be marked by differentials of pay provides a guide to actual rates and a basis of agreement. Here, though always within the limits set by the potential breaking-in of market forces, status is indeed the basis of relative pay.

The present statement of the parts played by status and market forces in shaping occupational differences of pay is borne out by our study of differentials in Secs. 3.1 and 3.2. We saw there that the customary attribution of status was a conservative force, whereas the forces making for change came from supply and demand, and especially from supply.

(*e*) The question that gives practical interest to this discussion is whether the relative pay of occupations could be changed, and in particular be made more equal, if there were a change in the attitudes and evaluations by which status is attributed. The answer depends on the relative extent of the sectors of employment subject to and insulated from market forces, and the width of the limits within which the insulation is effective. A fall in the status of an occupation would not allow its relative pay to be lowered if the demand for its work continued to keep it fully employed at the existing rate. A general agreement that one occupation was deserving of no less honour than another, when the former required little ability or training and the latter required much of both, could hardly maintain the pay of the two in equality in any society that allowed its members to choose and change their jobs. At any one time there is always likely to be room for changes in differentials, because attributions of status, it may be, as well as market forces have shifted while customary differentials have persisted, and because the limits within which market forces fix differentials are in any case often wide. But no society could fix differentials simply according to its ideas of status, if the valuation these ideas set upon the personal qualities required by different occupations diverged widely from the willingness of employers and consumers to pay for those qualities, unless (as in the Kibbutzim) the society ceased to relate income to employment altogether, and made alternative arrangements for allocating persons to particular employments.

(f) The above argument has rested throughout on a distinction between assessing the qualities an occupation requires, in order to decide its status, and evaluating the productivity of those qualities, in order to decide how much it is worth paying for them. We may call these the social and the economic judgements. Holding them apart as we have done here can be impugned on two grounds—that the social depends on the economic judgement, and that the economic is in practice interfused with the social. The first of these is of philosophic interest, but the second is pertinent to pay determination in practice.

That the social judgement depends on the economic, or has an economic component, might be maintained on the ground that our admiration for the qualities that attract high status really depends no less than our willingness to pay for them on their being scarce. If in the course of social development the rare qualities of skill, expert knowledge, and creativity become less scarce, the relative pay they command will fall: will their desirability in the general view show itself then as truly intrinsic, and remain unchanged, or will plentifulness bring commonness in both senses of that term? This raises the whole question of the basis of our admiring judgements. If artistic ability came to be widely diffused, and there was a Michelangelo, a Vermeer, or a Renoir in every street, would 'great art' still be 'great'? This issue carried here to an extreme has already been raised in a milder form by the extension of secondary and tertiary education. Time will show whether certain qualities will always be seen as admirable in themselves, however common they may be, so that as more people come to possess them the status they attract will persist although the pay they command falls: or whether to excel is essentially to be exceptional, and rarity is an essential condition of high status.

That the economic judgement is in practice interfused with the social can be maintained as a matter of everyday knowledge. There is one passage in which Adam Smith (1776, Bk. I, c. VI) virtually maintains that it is esteem for the workman that sets the price on his product. If one kind of labour, he says, 'requires an uncommon degree of dexterity and ingenuity, the esteem which men have for such talents, will naturally give a value to their produce, superior to what would be due to the time employed about it'. We can easily point out that however uncommon, for instance, the degree of dexterity and ingenuity required to compose elegant Latin hexameters, they will not sell for a high price today: it must be that the employer's valuation of the workman proceeds from the consumer's valuation of the product, and not the other way about. Yet how much the work of a particular occupation is worth, when it is only one of many contributions to the making of the product, is bound to depend in practice on an estimate into which subjective elements of appraisal may enter. An employer's estimate may well be influenced by the view he shares with all around him of the status of the worker. In particular, he may well undervalue the work of persons—notably women and racial minorities—to whom low status has been ascribed on grounds other than their occupational capability. Such undervaluation is one form of discrimination.

Discrimination is many-sided, and it has to do with differences of class as well as of status. We shall therefore treat it separately in the following chapter, which links the present discussion with that of Class in Chapter 6.

(g) The inquiry of this chapter has led us to the conclusion that though the monetary valuation set upon work usually agrees with the status accorded to the worker, that valuation is not derived from the status, but is formed independently, according ultimately to the willingness of the public to pay for the services or product of the worker. We can then take it that what will be paid for a unit of a given kind of work will tend, in a given state of demand, to vary inversely with the amount of that work supplied. Prompt adjustments of this kind are rare in the labour market, and there are strong resistances to any cuts even in the long run; but where the supply of a given kind of work extends without a corresponding extension of demand we shall expect the pay in question to rise less than other pay in the course of time, and where the supply is contracted relatively to the demand we can readily envisage the bidding-up of pay by the competition of employers. In our further inquiry we shall therefore be begging no question if we assume that whatever reduces the supply of labour to a given occupation relatively to the supplies to other occupations tends to raise its relative pay, and whatever extends that supply tends to reduce it; though the tendency may take effect only if and when other changes occur that break up the rule of custom.

5

Discrimination

5.1. Forms of discrimination

Discrimination has been stigmatized as an outstanding source of unfairness in contemporary societies. In various ways, people to whom those societies accord an inferior status are seen to be denied an equal opportunity to develop their potential capability and to use what capability they have in advantageous employment; and, in any given employment to which they are admitted, they are seen to be paid less than others who are of no greater capability but of higher status. The lack of equal opportunity for development concerns especially the minorities marked off by colour, national origin, speech, or religion, but the perpetuation in contemporary society of the traditional division of labour between men and women in the homestead has come under increasing attack as a denial to daughters of life-chances that are open to sons. Minorities and women alike are observed to receive lower pay in many instances than members of the majority, or men, receive for the same work. The ending of these various forms of discrimination has become a major issue of public policy in societies many of whose members have come to see it as incompatible alike with democratic citizenship and common humanity.

It interests us on that account, but also because, if it can be established in these outstanding cases, its significance extends much more widely: for if it is effective as between, say, a white majority, and a black minority, it may also operate as between occupations of different status within that majority, or indeed as between any persons of different status in any part of society. The difference in the pay of occupations of different status may be largely due to the value the market sets on the work done, without regard to who does it; but can we be sure that it is so due in its entirety?—may it not have been widened by the ability to discriminate against the occupation of lower status?

Implicit in this initial account of discrimination is a distinction between 'discrimination *before* the market' and 'discrimination *within* the market'. Discrimination *before* the market denies those who are discriminated against the same opportunities as others have to develop their capability, and to use so much capability as they do develop in the most advantageous employments for which it qualifies them. By discrimination *within* the market, workers who are distinguished by some characteristic that does not directly affect their present capability are treated less favourably in a given employment than others who are of no greater capability but are not marked off by that characteristic. In each of these two fields discrimination may take two forms, so that there are four forms in all.

(*a*) *Discrimination in upbringing*. The differential provision of social services, especially education, and the segregation of residence, prevent the children of a group from developing their potential capability. They are at a further disadvantage through their parents having been similarly situated, and so having a limited ability to develop and motivate them; this kind of discrimination, once imposed, is thus in a measure self-perpetuating. Though it affects the development of the capability of those who suffer it, it does not in itself cause whatever capability is developed under it to command lower pay than the same level of capability in an unaffected person would command.

(b) *Discrimination in opportunity.* The entry of persons having some characteristic into a given occupation is hampered or prevented, when there is no such hindrance to the entry of persons of no greater capability but without that characteristic. Those excluded increase the number of entrants into those occupations that they can enter freely, and the rate of pay in these is consequently lower.

These first two forms of discrimination lower the relative pay of those discriminated against, the first by restricting the development of their capability, the second by affecting their allocation between different occupations; but neither implies that when with given capabilities they are taken into employment in given occupations they will be paid less than other persons would be in the like case. The possibility of just this happening, however, is raised by two other forms of discrimination.

(c) *Monopsonistic discrimination.* When a buyer of labour, as of any material product, is able to deal separately with each of a number of suppliers, he will minimize the cost of a given total supply if he buys from each supplier at that supplier's minimum supply price. Generally it is expected that people of minority groups, and more generally people of lower status, will be 'weak sellers' of their labour, unable to hold out for the same pay as the employer must give others for labour that is no better than theirs. The employer is able to discriminate in this way because the 'weak sellers' are unlikely or unable to demand equal pay with those of higher status, even though the difference of status does not actually affect the capability of doing the work. But the employer must also be secure from the interloping of other buyers, who would compete with him for the workers whose labour is cheap, and bid up the pay for it.

He will be secure from competition in this way if he is a monopsonist in the strict sense of the term, the sole buyer of labour to whom a given group of workers have access. But competition will be equally well excluded for the present purpose in the more likely case of there being a number of potential employers of the same persons, but these employers agreeing overtly or tacitly not to bid up the prevailing rates of pay in order to attract to their employment more of the labour that it is profitable to employ. The collectivity of employers then becomes a kind of monopsonist. To refrain in this way from 'spoiling the market' is only the counterpart of a tacit agreement to refrain from cutting the price of a product that in other respects is sold competitively.

The possibility of such local combinations of employers was illustrated by Marshall (1892, VI. xiii. 4) from his own observation in the English countryside of his time. A farmer might calculate, he said, that it would be worth his while, other things being equal, to pay 14s. a week to secure an additional labourer.

But other things are very likely not to be equal. If the current rate in the parish is 12s. a week he could not bid 14s. without incurring odium among his brother farmers, and perhaps tempting the labourers already in his employ to demand 14s. So he will probably offer only 12s. and complain of the scarcity of labour. The price of 12s. will be maintained because competition is not perfectly free; because the labourers have not much choice as to the market in which they sell their labour; and because they cannot hold back their labour at a reserve price equal to the highest wage which the employer can afford to pay.

By a tacit agreement of this kind, employers could keep down the pay of any kind of labour, of high status just as well as of low, provided always it was in inelastic supply. But they are much more likely to follow the same course without overt combination if the labour is of low status and they spontaneously concur in believing that, in the natural order of things, low status is appropriately recompensed by low pay. It is also much more likely to be persons of low status who give the discriminating employer his opportunity, by having a lower reserve supply price for their labour. The present form of discrimination thus merges with the fourth form.

(*d*) *Discrimination by status.* Though merged with monopsonistic discrimination in practice, it is distinct in principle, in that it can occur where employers are effectively competing with one another, and their competition ensures that each pays for the services of any worker the full amount that he reckons those services are worth to him. In such a case the employer will pay a worker of the disfavoured type less than he would pay others for doing the same work only if he reckons the services of that type worth less to him. There are three ways in which he may come to such a reckoning.

The first is a matter of taste. He himself may have some aversion to working with persons of the disfavoured type; or his other employees may have such an aversion, and so work less well, or have to be paid more, if they are to work with those persons; or his customers may be less willing to buy the products of those persons or have dealings with them. The employer will then set off these psychic and/or monetary costs of employing the disfavoured persons against their value productivity, and be willing to employ them only at a lower rate of pay than he reckons others worth who do the same work no better but who do not set up these costs (Becker 1971; Arrow 1972).

Secondly, the employer will be led to discount the value of the services of disfavoured persons if his assessment of that value is not firmly based on the actual results of their work, but is guided and biased by their status. He may simply see it as in the nature of things that lower status should be matched by lower pay, or he may assume that the lower pay that already prevails is the reliable outcome of general experience of what the work is worth.

Thirdly, knowing it as a fact that a number of persons of the disfavoured type have some disabilities as employees, and being unable to distinguish among applicants between those who will and those who will not prove to have these disabilities, he will be willing to pay no more to those who prove not to have them than to those who do. Thus if he knows that a number of the young women he engages will leave on marriage just when the experience they have gained is making them really useful, he may pay those who in fact stay on at rates justified for the early leavers.

With these forms of discrimination in mind, let us go on to consider two leading cases—discrimination against women, and against minorities.

5.2. Discrimination against women

5.2.1. *Discrimination against women before the market.* Daughters are distributed over households of different socio-economic levels in the same way as sons, but in the aggregate they are less well prepared for paid employment: not so many of them as of the sons are maintained through high school and college, or receive vocational training of a professional kind. Perhaps the main reason for this is the persistence of the traditional conception of the division of labour between men and women, which puts women's work in the home. The expectation that a daughter will marry, and if she does not withdraw from paid · employment altogether at least cease to depend on it for her main livelihood, gives the parents a reasonable ground for devoting a smaller part of scarce resources to her preparation than to that of a son, who is likely to be the breadwinner of a family. The same consideration gives girls less incentive than boys have to enter and persist in exacting courses of preparation. There is also a feedback from the restricted employment of the preceding generation of women: because few women of that generation qualified for certain occupations, there seems little opening for women in them, and the succeeding generation sees no purpose in qualifying. Not long since, moreover, in most Western countries there were many colleges and professional schools to which women were simply not admitted; and though many of those outright barriers to entry have gone down now, the admission of women may still be subject to a quota.

So though half the intelligence of every country is in women's heads—in I.Q. tests the average scores of girls and boys are the same—that half does not develop the same qualification for paid employment as the men's half. This is partly reasonable, because most women will spend fewer years in employment outside the home than men do, and many will choose to treat such employment as subsidiary to their concern for their family. But the lesser preparation of girls is also due in part to discrimination, in the family and in education and training, by which girls are denied as much preparation as boys get.

But this difference in preparation is far from accounting for the whole difference in pay between women and men. Figure 5.1 shows, for a sample of British employed and self-employed persons in 1966–67, how far and con-

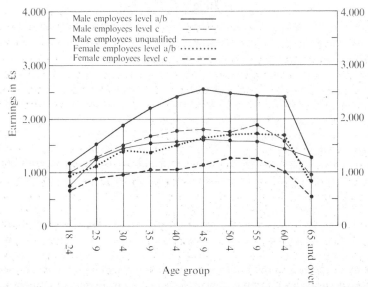

Fig. 5.1. Median earnings by level of qualification and sex in England and Wales, 1966–67.

Levels of qualification
a Higher university degrees, and Membership of College of Technologists.
b First degrees and all other qualifications of that standard.
a/b = a + b.
c Below first degree level: including Higher National Diploma, Higher National Certificate, Teaching Certificates, Nursing Awards, City & Guilds Higher Grade Technicians Certificates, and memberships of some professional institutions.
Source: Survey of Earnings of Qualified Manpower in England and Wales 1966–67 (Dept. of Education and Science, Statistics of Education, Special Series No. 3, H.M.S.O., London, 1971). In a follow-up of the 1966 10 per cent sample census of population, questionnaires concerning pay in money and kind, and income from self-employment, were sent to 15,000 qualified and 5,000 unqualified persons in occupations that contained appreciable numbers of both sorts. The response rate was 66 per cent for men and 60 per cent for women.

sistently the women's earnings lay below those of men at the same level of qualification. If, for instance, we take those with a first degree or higher qualification, the median earnings of the women lay 25 per cent below those of the men in the age group 30–4 years, 38 per cent in the age group 40–4 years, and 31 per cent in the age group 50–4 years. Up to age 45, moreover, the gap widens with age—the women's 'age-earnings profiles' rise less steeply in the earlier years; they are flatter than the men's. These observations suggest two kinds of discrimination in opportunity.

The first would account for the comparative flatness of the women's age-earnings profiles. Part of this will be due to the interruption of women's employment during the years of family formation, so that on the average a woman of a given age has fewer years of work experience than a man of the same age. Where promotion depends on work-experience employers are likely to treat young women as having less potential for advancement than young men of no greater ability, and will therefore be less willing to place them on the lower rungs of ladders of advancement, or to invest in their training on the job. Such unwillingness has a rational base; but discrimination against women in opportunity for advancement may also be due to a prejudice on the part of the employers, or of their work-people—not excluding the women among them—against women as supervisors. In an econometric analysis of the background, qualifications, and earnings of heads of households in a sample drawn from the data bank of the Michigan Survey Research Center, Blinder (1973) found that almost two-thirds of the shortfall of women's earnings below men's was due to the flatness of the women's age-earnings profile: 'the failure of women *in the same education-occupation category* [as men] to rise [as much as the men] on the economic ladder over their working lives is seen to be the single largest cause of the male-female differential among whites' (p. 448). One factor here is that the employments accessible to married women are limited spatially, because where they live is generally determined by their husband's job, and they are not able to take opportunities for promotion that would involve a change of place. This is thought to be a reason why the percentage of married women teachers who become heads of British primary and secondary schools has been much lower than that of single women who do so (Turnbull & Williams 1974).

The second kind of discrimination in opportunity prevents women from starting level with men in the first place, by denying them equal freedom in the choice of occupation. There is much evidence for the obstacles and inhibitions that obstruct the entry of women into employments they are well capable of following. Particularly among manual workers, women are debarred from work which they could do perfectly well by the deliberate opposition of the men, often with the agreement of employers, or by the tacit acceptance of customary lines of demarcation between what is and what is not 'women's work'. Much evidence of this was given to the inquiries set up in the United Kingdom towards the end of each of the two World Wars, the Atkin Committee on Women in Industry (War Cabinet 1919) and the Asquith Commission on Equal Pay (Royal Commission 1946). The Atkin Committee cited a written agreement in the boot and shoe trade for the 'gradual cessation of the employment of female amongst male operatives in the clicking, press lasting and finishing departments'. The Trades Union Congress in its evidence to the Asquith Commission reported an agreement between the packing case makers and two trade unions, by which an arbitrary line was drawn to prevent the extension of women's work where they were already working alongside men—'no female shall be allowed to use nails longer than $1\frac{3}{4}$ inches'; and similarly an agreement in 1939 in the clothing trade specified trimming and fitting-up 'as jobs on which women were and would continue to be employed', but 'expressly provided that neither would men so employed be replaced by women nor would the employment of women on these operations be extended on any scale'. Giving evidence before the Asquith Commission, a spokesman of the Engineering Employers said,

I can assure you that it would be very easy for you to take the pre-war years when we had recognized women's jobs and recognized men's jobs, and for you to confirm that such men's and women's jobs were regarded as such on the factory floor itself by the people who were actually involved. The people on the factory floor assess these things in their own way, and any effort that might have been made to dispose of a man and put a woman on his job in order to save money . . . would be instantly taken up by the workpeople themselves through their trade unions. It was just not possible for such a thing to happen, and it did not happen. (Minutes of Evidence, 12, Q.2860.)

In printing, the Atkin Committee reported (para. 36) that 'exclusion [of women] from the trade was ensured by the London Society of Compositors by allowing their admission upon the same conditions as journeymen to be paid strictly the same rate'. A later official study of women in industry (Ministry of Labour 1930, p. 26) stated, 'It is estimated that in 1910 there were about 1,100 women compositors in Edinburgh alone, but now as a result of the Unions' opposition there are said to be only about 200 in the whole of Scotland.' Of compositors' work two economists have written more recently (Polanyi & Wood 1974, p. 74), 'By 1974 some London daily newspapers were having to pay £8,000–£9,000 a year to their compositors . . . The job is one which can be learned with a far shorter period of training than imposed by the union in Britain and could, in practice, be done by a competent shorthand typist or any other keyboard operator. In Russia, for instance, the composing rooms at *Pravda* and *Izvestia* are largely staffed by women who undertake six months' training.'

The evidence of the Trades Union Congress to the Asquith Commission accepted the reality of the demarcation of 'women's work', and its consequences for women's wages:

The trade unions have been compelled not only to uphold, but to promote, a clear demarcation between men's and women's work—where such demarcation was possible—in order to protect the men's and thus indirectly the women's rates of pay. Admittedly there is something like a vicious circle involved in this situation, since the limited opportunities for industrial employment that were available to women have tended to crowd them into certain occupations and to keep down the rates of wages paid in those occupations. (Appx. VIII to Minutes of Evidence, para. 17.)

The same crowding was observed by John Stuart Mill a hundred years before (1848, II. xiv. 5). Asking why pay in the 'peculiar employments of women' was always 'greatly below that of employments of equal skill and equal disagreeableness, carried on by men', he answered:

In the occupations in which employers take full advantage of competition, the low wages of women as compared with the ordinary earnings of men are a proof that the employments are overstocked: that although so much smaller a number of women, than of men, support themselves by wages, the occupations which law and usage make accessible to them are comparatively so few, that the field of their employment is still more overcrowded.

Mill went on to observe that because few women had a family to support, the

reserve price to which competition beat their wage down was much lower than
that of the men.

So women have been segregated in employment. In the United States, for instance, women made up 38 per cent of the whole labour force in 1970, as
against only 18 per cent in 1900; but

well over half of all working women in both 1900 and 1960 were employed in jobs in
which 70 per cent or more of the workers were female . . . The increasing numbers of
women have been absorbed into the labour force not through an across-the-board
expansion of employment opportunities, but rather through a growth in traditionally
female jobs, particularly in the clerical and service category, through the emergence of
new occupations that rapidly became female, and, in some cases, through a shift in the
sexual composition of an occupation from male to female. (Weisskoff 1972, p. 163.)

This last-mentioned shift has been compared with the rapid change from white
to black that follows an initial penetration by blacks into a housing area.

Is this segregation by occupation sufficient to account for differences such as
Fig. 5.1 illustrated between the earnings of women and men with similar
educational qualifications? Sawhill (1973) surveys six American estimates of
the size of the differential against women's pay that remains after allowance
has been made for such factors as occupation, hours worked, age, education,
colour, size of city, region, and migrancy. Five of these studies arrived at a
residual differential of between 29 and 37 per cent of the comparable men's pay.
An essential element here is the allowance for occupation, that is, for the
segregation of women in certain generally low-paid occupations. If this
allowance is all it should be, then—having regard also to the other factors
whose influence has been allowed for—the residual differential can be ascribed
only to discrimination within the market, by which work of given value is paid
less for when a women performs it than when a man does. But the sixth estimate (Sanborn 1964) brought the residual differential down to only 12 per
cent by basing the allowance for occupation on a *detailed* classification of occupations. This raises a crucial and embarrassing question. Sawhill herself,
having found a residual differential of 44 per cent after allowance for race,
region, age, education, weeks worked per year, and hours worked per week, but
not for occupation, remarked that 'it would, of course, be quite easy to substantially reduce the remaining differential by resorting to an occupational adjustment, and the finer the occupational classification used, the smaller the differential would be' (p. 391). If the classification is coarse, we shall find women being
paid less than men for 'the same work' when the actual work done by the
women is distinctly different, and would command less pay if it were done by
men. If the classification is fine enough, there will be no 'same work' left, and
the whole differential will be due to the allocation of women to jobs that are
different from the men's, and lower paid. But part of the differential surely
arises otherwise than from allocation. If we cannot tell how big that part is, we
have reason to believe that it exists—that the relative pay of women is
depressed in some measure by discrimination within the market, that is, by
monopsonistic discrimination and discrimination by status.

5.2.2. *Discrimination against women within the market*. A number of observations suggest that, in some times and places at least, the employer has paid
women not according to what is required to attract and retain them in his
employ, and what he reckons their work is worth to him, but according to a
conventional valuation of women's labour at large. The Atkin Committee (War
Cabinet 1919), surveying the wages recorded in the Wage Census of 1906,
remarked on 'the comparatively small range of average wages for women and
the persistence in this connection of a figure in the neighbourhood of 12s. in the
most widely different trades and industries . . . . A similar level of wages
prevailed in the years immediately preceding the war [i.e. before 1914] all over
Western Europe'. This is the level for women's unskilled manual work; but
when we consider semi-skilled and skilled manual work, and rise through the
clerical, administrative, and professional occupations, we have to account for
women being paid less than men even in the 'overlap areas' where they are
working alongside men and doing work that is indistinguishable from the men's
hour by hour. The findings in this respect of the Asquith Commission (Royal
Commission 1946) have been summarized as follows (Phelps Brown 1949, pp.
391–2). In clothing and engineering, piece-rates were set in accordance with
unequal time-rates.

Here the understanding is that a piece-rate shall be set to as in practice to yield the
representative worker not less than an agreed rate of earning per hour. That hourly rate
is lower for women: if their rate of output were lower in the same proportion, then the
same piece-rate as the men's would give them no more than their hourly rate; but, in
fact, their rate of output often runs higher than this, and their piece-rates are correspondingly lower. But most often 'unequal pay' in the overlap areas comes through
unequal time-rates. In manual work it is so in french polishing and (partially) in wool-
combing and clothing. In clerical and administrative work and in retailing it holds
almost universally.

One explanation that has been offered for those observations is that the
women's labour was available at a lower supply price. This brings us back to
status. We have seen how status merges into station in life, and this in turn implies a standard of living which is regarded as a minimum which carries with it
an entitlement to be paid at least enough to cover that minimum. Sir David
Ross, reflecting on his experience as Chairman of the Trade Boards whose
function was to fix minimum wages for lower-paid workers, many of them
women, found in this principle of the supply price of labour based on station in
life an explanation not of women's wages alone but of the whole wage structure. 'I doubt', he wrote (Royal Commission 1946, IX, 10, para. 12),

whether employers in general are able to estimate with accuracy the value to them of
the work of particular workers. This is particularly so with regard to the completely unskilled workers . . . For [these] are for the most part engaged in doing odd jobs in and
about the works, whose commercial value to the employer is obviously very difficult to
estimate. I suspect that the wage paid to the unskilled workers is not fixed by any
attempt to estimate at all exactly the value of their work, but rather by the rate at
which they are willing to offer their services, and that this in turn is determined largely
by their unwillingness to work for a wage insufficient to support an average family . . .

So long as his total wages bill allows him to make a profit, the employer probably does not ask himself very closely whether each of his employees is worth to him the wages he is receiving. I suspect that the wages given to different classes of labour are determined at least as much by the rates at which the different classes are willing to offer their services, as by any attempt to estimate accurately the comparative value of those services to the employer. If this be so, the fact that women earn lower wages than men because, not having families to support, they are willing to work for lower wages, will not be an isolated feature of the wage structure but will fall in line with a more widespread feature of it.

An alternative explanation was put forward by another member of the Trade Boards—that the employer does form an estimate of the value of the women's work, but he bases this estimate on the pay: so the low pay of women is justified by the low value of the work, which itself is inferred from the low pay—a circularity that perpetuates the existing state of affairs. 'I think', wrote D. H. Macgregor (Royal Commission 1946, IX, 9, para. 6),

that there still remain conventional attitudes towards rates of pay which are women's rates; and that they derive from social attitudes . . . My reflection on the matter is, that the conventions lead to the restrictions [on the jobs open to women] and so verify themselves. If women's rates are assumed lower than men's, by a significant margin, the women are put on the processes which are low-paid as a market fact, and are employed there as far as they are worth the rate. Some degree of 'crowding' exists, which keeps the rate down. Since, with this restriction, they are getting what they are worth, it is taken to verify what women's work is worth. I am not able to say that this is due to a man's point of view about women's work; there are women on all Trade Boards, but I cannot recall any argument for equal pay. If it is a man's attitude, it is not so consciously, but rather traditionally.

If the employers are not concerned or able to compare the pay of particular workers with an independent assessment of the value of their work, that would explain why they do not compete for low-paid labour and so bid its price up, for they cannot tell whether it is cheap at its present price or not. We may add that even when they do have reason to believe that it is cheap, they may have no reason in the way their production is organized to employ more women relatively to men, or they may know that any attempted extension of jobs for women at the expense of men's would be blocked by the men. But the same assumption about the employers' behaviour would allow women to be paid more, within a limit set only by the profitability of the business overall, without loss of jobs, and we have to explain why the women have not pressed for more. The reasons have been found in their lack of organization, which in turn has been attributed to their comparative lack of concern with the terms of an employment which they do not expect to last long, or which they look to only for a supplement to an already assured household income. The women authors of a study of wage drift, noting that there had been little drift of women's wages even though a higher proportion of women than of men were working on piece-rates which lend themselves especially to drift, found the explanation in the shop stewards' 'attitude that women do not really need to earn as much as men', and to the women being less aggressive than men in pressing their claims themselves (Lerner & Marquand 1962, pp. 37–8). We might add that any claim that was put forward would be likely to be resisted by the employer in the knowledge that if he did accede to it he would at once be confronted by a claim from his men for the restoration of their customary differential.

The explanation of women's lower pay developed in this way thus rests on the assumption that employers are unable to estimate the value of women's work, so that they do not bid against one another for it until they have raised the wage to as much as the work is worth; while the women themselves do not push, singly or in combination, to raise it. Employers then apply a conventional valuation of women's work, that is based on the three-sided notion of status, station in life, and the minimal expenditure required to maintain that station. Alternatively, whether or not employers are able to estimate the value of women's work, they are held to agree spontaneously in applying the conventional valuation, so that they enter tacitly into monopsonistic discrimination against women. An employer who did judge that women's work was 'cheap at the price' would still be restrained from bidding in more women, by the resistance of the men.

If the view that employers simply follow a conventional valuation of women's work were called in question because they evidently are willing to pay more for some kinds of women's work than others, the answer might be that the conventional valuation is based on status: the status accorded to the ability to do more skilled work being higher, correspondingly higher must be the station in life of the skilled woman, and what she needs to earn to be able to maintain that station. For all grades of labour above the unskilled, the conventional valuation based on the lower status of women would thus be applied in practice as a discount on what is paid to men doing similar work.

But when the explanation is set out in this way, much that seemed illuminating at particular points fails to carry conviction as a general theory, for there is much other evidence in conflict with it. This evidence shows that there are objective reasons for the value of women's work in certain jobs being less than that of men's; that employers are in fact able to estimate that value; and that some measure of 'unequal pay' is therefore economically appropriate, as being 'equal pay for work of equal value'; though it does not show that the actual extent of inequality does not exceed that.

In some manual work, to begin with, women are handicapped by lack of physical strength. An inquiry into British farmers' estimates of women's work outputs as a percentage of men's in 49 tasks on the farm (Smith 1943) found that though in one or two tasks, such as attending poultry and picking fruit, women's output was higher than men's, in the others it was lower. At the lowest, in heavy tasks, it was less than half; in the middle third of the tasks the percentage lay between 70 and 90; the median percentage was 79. The average minimum hourly rate for women in British agriculture was 72 per cent of the men's in 1938, rising to 82 per cent in 1941. The source already cited for wages in Mao's China quotes a scale that gave women in agriculture seven-tenths of the man's day rate, this being justified on the ground that women's output was lower in the same proportion (Mehnert 1972, pp. 52–3).

There is evidence also concerning manual work in industry. Among the cottom beamers, twisters and drawers in, it was reported to the Atkin Committee of 1919 (Minority Report, p. 280), 'men and women are paid the same rate, but the women pay the men a certain sum each week in order to lift for them'. The same Committee recorded (p. 185) that

a woman working at the draw-bench of a cold solid-drawn tube works . . . would be paid the same piece-rates as the men, and might handle as much total weight of light tubes per day as the latter, and so receive the same daily earnings; but she would not be able to draw the heavier class of tube; and this lack of adaptability would make her less valuable, under competitive conditions, than a man who could, though he rarely did, spend short periods at the heavy tube benches.

The effect of this handicap is measured by the extent to which women's earnings fell short of the men's when both were working at the same piece-rates. The Asquith Commission found this shortfall to be from 16 to 35 per cent of the men's earnings in the weaving of woollens, and 28 per cent in making raincoats; but the most extensive evidence, from cotton weaving, shows the shortfall there as only 12 per cent (Gray 1937). The handicap can often be overcome by providing more equipment: reporting on British experience during the Second World War, the Minister of Labour said, 'We thought it would need three women for the output of two men, but, by the help of our production engineers, new devices and labour aids in one way and another, I am glad to say that the output is almost equal one for one' (Royal Commission 1946, Appx. VII, para. 22). But the cost of these adjuncts reduces the net value of the women's work.

There is evidence that employers have in fact been able to estimate this net value. The Atkin Committee (para, 116) reported that

according to employers' statements, at the present time there is, if anything, an advantage of employing women rather than men in cotton-weaving when they get the same piece-rates; in the rather heavier woollen weaving, where their piece-rates are 10 per cent less than the men's, it is a matter of indifference to the employers whether men or women are at the looms; while in engineering, they say that payment to the women of more than two-thirds of the men's wages would lead them at once to prefer boys or men.

In the U.S.A. Sanborn (1964) used an inquiry by the Bureau of Labor Statistics into earnings in two industries, to infer the relative outputs of men and women employed on the same tasks at the same piece-rates. In furniture, the women's outputs were about 13 per cent below the men's—the same differential as for earnings in the industry as a whole. In the shoe industry the shortfall of women's outputs was about 10 per cent, which compared with a 12–13 per cent differential in earnings in the Great Lakes and Midwest regions of the industry.

It is significant that the differential between the pay of men and women for similar work has not been the same at all levels of qualification and earnings, but has varied inversely with that level. In the United Kingdom, down to the end of the Second World War, 'the spread of the differential [was] from some 50 per cent of the men's rate in the lower ranks of industry to 10 per cent or nothing at all in the higher ranks of some of the professions' (Royal Commission 1946, para. 337). If the differential depended throughout simply on status, this would be hard to account for, but it is intelligible if we suppose that the differential was based on differences in the value of men and women as employees. For if we consider the relative importance of two factors on which that value depends, physical strength and intelligence, we see that physical strength, in which women are generally inferior to men, becomes of less importance as we rise in the scale of qualifications and earnings, while intelligence, in which women are equal to men, becomes of progressively greater importance. So far as the capability of the worker depends on these two factors, therefore, the difference between the capabilities of women and men, and their values in similar employment, will be less, the higher the qualifications that the employment requires.

To the differences in the value of work that make themselves felt at any one time must be added one, already touched on, that in the past at least has appeared in the value of employees reckoned over their whole period of service. It has arisen especially in the white-collar occupations in which physical strength is not required, but the usefulness of the employee does depend very much on his training and experience on the job. In such employments the value of a type of labour depends on the length of service to be expected from it; or, inversely, on its rate of turnover. Most women get married, and most of these again leave paid employment at least for a time in order to raise a family. Employers given a choice between engaging men and women for a given type of work must expect that on the average they will receive a smaller return on investment in the training of women than of men, and that fewer of the women will be available for advancement on the basis of the experience they have gained with the firm. The effect has been to make employers prefer men to women as entrants where the rate of pay is the same for both, or to regard a lower rate for the women as a necessary offset to the lower value of their work as reckoned over their expected period of service; in particular, it has made them reluctant to admit women on equal pay with men, or admit them at all, to jobs requiring any considerable period of on-the-job training. The women who will in fact give long service suffer because they cannot be distinguished initially from the others (Phelps 1972). True, in the United States at least, 'the differences in worklife expectancy between men and women have narrowed quite dramatically in the postwar period': it has been estimated, on the basis of 1966 mortality and labour force participation rates, that at 25 years of age the expected working life of a woman who marries is about 30 years, that of a man about 38 years (Sawhill 1973, pp. 394, 388). But any one employer has still to reckon with more discontinuities and interruptions of the services of women than of men in his employ. In 1968, in American manufacturing industries, the median number of years during which employees had been in their current job was 4·8 for men but only 2·4 for women (O'Boyle 1969).

That in these ways the net value of women's work may be reduced is borne out, for some employments in which men and women work together, by the belief of those concerned that to require equal pay for the women would be to exclude them from employment. We have already seen how the London Society of Compositors secured the exclusion of women by so requiring. The great advocate of Family Allowances in the United Kingdom, Eleanor Rathbone, writing from a close acquaintance with the labour market in Liverpool, held that unless the drawbacks of women's work were allowed for, 'equal pay' 'will prove in practice the equivalent of total exclusion': she therefore formulated the aim as 'equal wages to workers of equal value' (1917, pp. 59–60).

The policy of male trade unionists towards women's wages reveals the interplay of social and market forces. On the one hand the men have felt that the maintenance of their own status required them to uphold their customary differentials over women's rates, so that employers have had reason to expect that to raise the women's rates alone would prompt a demand from the men for equal proportional rises. The men have also felt it unfair that they as the main breadwinners and support of their households should have to make do with less in order to give more to women, most of whom are working only for supplementary income—'pin money', it is sometimes said. But the men have also recognized that low rates for women's work could threaten the security of men's jobs, by offering the employer an inducement to substitute women for men. The conflict has been resolved by resort to the second form of discrimination, discrimination in opportunity: a line is drawn between the jobs recognized as men's work and those allowed to women, and the men will stop women being moved across that line.

From this discussion we can draw two conclusions. First, in more than one way judgements of status have made people regard it as only right and proper that women should be paid less than men in similar employment. But, second, in many employments there are objective reasons for the work of women being of lower net value than that of men; and employers do estimate such net value and take it into account. If then (a) competition between employers for labour, and (b) the pressure of labour itself for higher pay, were effective in keeping women's rates up to the limit set by the net value of women's work; and if (c) the employers' estimate of that limit were unbiased by masculine prejudice: then there would be no discrimination against women. But we do not know how far any of these three conditions is satisfied. We have reason to think that none of them is satisfied fully in all cases, but the outcome will differ in different places, employments, and periods. In particular, it seems probable that the upheavals of the two World Wars, both of which in the United Kingdom brought a rise in the general level of women's rates relatively to men's, will have given market forces freer play as against the conventional. We remain uncertain how far, if at all, existing differentials exceed differences in net value. But it seems highly probable that the disabilities of women workers spring far more from our first two forms of discrimination, in upbringing and in opportunity, rather than in the two with which we have dealt here, discrimination by monopsony and according to status.

It might be thought that a test of whether women's pay is depressed more than can generally be accounted for by the lower value of their work, would be provided by the equalization of women's rates, or the elimination of all separate rates for women by title, that has been ordained in a number of Western countries in recent years. If the raising of women's relative rates were not followed by any reduction in the number of women employed, we might infer that the old rates had been below the value of the work. But to be sure of that we shall have to wait until it is clear that the cost of the hour of women's labour to the employer has been raised permanently relatively to that of the men's and that, whatever has happened to rates, the men (and their employers) have not found ways of restoring the old differential in earnings. By that time, however, other developments will have affected the demand for women's labour. Investigation of all the circumstances of particular cases would be needed to form even a judgement of probability about the effects attributable specifically to the change in relative pay.

One such case—the application of 'equal pay' in the British state-maintained schools from 1961 onwards—has revealed one way in which married women continue to be disadvantaged. The age-earnings profiles of teachers, calculated as at 1970, showed that men were systematically earning more than women of the same age. But as we have seen, Turnbull and Williams (1974) found that whereas most if not all of the differences between men and single women could be accounted for by differences in qualifications and length of service, the further shortfall of married below single women could be accounted for only by a difference of career prospects—taking primary and secondary schools together, more than 15 per cent of the single women were deputy heads or heads, but less than 10 per cent of the married women. This may be attributed in part to the married women being able to seek promotion only in openings within the areas to which they were confined by residence with their husbands: this is a factor on the supply side, implying no discrimination on the side of demand. It is also possible that married women were regarded as less eligible for promotion because their family responsibilities were liable to interfere with their work for the school. This, whether right or wrong, is a judgement of objective capability. But—we may add—discrimination based on social values would also enter if the scale was turned against married women applicants by the consideration, in the minds of the appointing bodies, that 'they did not need the money so much'.

The present discussion throws some light on the possiblity already noticed, that the bearing of women's status on their pay is only one instance of a possible relation between status and pay throughout society. If women's pay is depressed relatively to men's because of the lower status of women, may not the pay of the labourer equally be depressed relatively to that of the skilled manual worker, or the pay of manual workers as a whole be depressed relatively to that of the white-collared? But we have seen that in many instances there are objective differences in the value of work to account for women's labour being at some discount against men's. Though we do not know that this discount is as big as the difference in pay, there is at least no encouragement here to believe that differentials throughout the pay structure are imposed wholly or even mainly by differences of status.

5.3. Discrimination against minorities

We are to consider the pay of minorities marked off by race, religion, regional origin or language, in so far as their social status is inferior. Not all minorities are in that position: there are some that hold political power over the majority, and others that are socially integrated with it. Whatever their social and political position, moreover, some minorities—like the Chinese in South-East Asia—enjoy higher incomes than the majority. To be in a minority is therefore not a source of weakness in itself. But some minorities have characteristics that the majority regard as inferior—their members are poorly educated, and taken to be of inferior intelligence; their appearance, their speech, their ways of life are unaccustomed and in many situations unacceptable; they do not apply themselves to work in the way the majority expects. In so far as these characteristics put the minority at a disadvantage in the labour market, they also appear in some members of the majority; but in the minority they are associated with the distinguishing features, in themselves of no effect on economic performance, by which the minority is marked off. In that way a *type* is created—in the minds of the majority the colour of skin, for instance, becomes linked with an expectation of poor economic performance, and the evaluation of actual performance becomes biased by distaste for the colour of skin. All members of the minority are then likely to be treated by the majority according to its perception of the type. It is in this way that the minority, as we are concerned with it here, differs from the statistical class of 'workers with a given grade, or given distribution of grades, of capability': the latter have no feature in common, such as colour of skin, by which they are marked off, and which has its own effect on the assessment others make of their suitability as workers. Members of the majority are therefore likely to agree spontaneously in treating any member of the minority as a worker on terms less favourable than those they would accord to a person of equal capability but without the stigmata of the minority.

These possiblities of discrimination will be examined with reference to the blacks in the U.S.A.

5.3.1. *Discrimination against blacks before the market.* There is social discrimination against the members of a group when they receive a less than proportionate share of the public provision for welfare. The pay they will be able to earn depends especially upon the part of such provision that is devoted to education.

In the past, the resources allocated to education were smaller per black child in the U.S.A. than per white child, and some differences persist, but they are decreasing. It is still the case that black children on the average attend schools that receive less financial support than those attended by whites, but that is mainly because a higher proportion of black children than of white live in the South, where there is less financial support for schools for black and white alike. Within any one district, though districts vary, the differences between the schools mainly attended by blacks and whites are generally small, except in the South, and there they are declining as desegregation proceeds. Taking the distributions between North and South and within particular districts together, Jencks (1972, p. 28) concludes, 'Our best guess is that America spends about 15–20 per cent more per year on the average white child than on the average black school child.' But the level of education of the black workers of today depends on the provision made for the education of black children in the past, and this was much smaller than for the white. Taking account of this together with the greater number of years that white children spent in school, Jencks (loc. cit.) estimates that whereas 'blacks now in school will probably have three-quarters to four-fifths as much spent on them as whites do', the proportion for children born during the Second World War was two-thirds, and for those born around 1900 it was probably less than half.

It has been held that the schooling of the black child has been inferior not only in quantity but in quality, but the smallness of the increases in the achievement test scores of black children after desegregation suggests that the difference of quality has not been great in recent years. The evidence generally cited for it was that black children scored lower in achievement tests than white children with the same number of years of schooling. But a major influence on these scores for black and white alike seems to be the socio-economic level of the child's home: if that level were no higher for the average white child than for the average black, the white children's test score might be no higher too. The homes of the black children were in fact at a lower socio-economic level in great part because the parents were less educated and earned less. In so far as this was due to discrimination against the parents in the past, their children's inability to make as good use of their schooling as white children did is an effect of discrimination; in this way discrimination once set up is self-perpetuating. This is so likewise if part of the inability lies in the black child's lack of incentive to apply himself at school, through his awareness that, if he does achieve a high level of education, it will profit him less than it would a white, because he has less expectation of advancing himself by his exertions. The Coleman report (1966) on an inquiry into the educational opportunities of minority groups in the U.S.A. found that when socio-economic background was held constant, 'differences between schools account for only a small fraction of differences in pupil achievement'; and 'a pupil attitude factor, which appears to have a stronger relationship to achievement than do all the "school" factors together, is the extent to which an individual feels that he has some control over his own destiny . . . The responses of pupils to questions in the survey show that minority pupils, except for Orientals, have far less conviction than whites that they can affect their own environments and futures. When they do, however, their achievement is higher than that of whites who lack that conviction' (pp. 21–3).

We have touched here on an issue that extends beyond discrimination against minorities into differences of class. A minority that suffers social discrimination, and a lower class in a racially homogeneous society, resemble each other in one important way: the children born into them get a worse start in life than children of equal genetic endowment born into other sectors of the society, and this is a factor making for the perpetuation of a disadvantaged group. A major factor in this worse start, moreover, as we shall see in Sec. 7.3, is the culture of the home and the tradition of child upbringing. In this respect the disabilities of the black child, in respect particularly of ability to profit by schooling, are of the same kind as those that 'working-class children' have been liable to suffer, in comparison with 'middle-class children', in white societies.

What has been said so far about the quality of black schooling has implicitly concerned only the primary and secondary school. That until recently Negroes have been at a considerable disadvantage in college education is clear in that they found it difficult to gain admission to white colleges, while the black colleges prepared their students for 'teaching and preaching' rather than for business and the professions. That a number of studies have found the increment of earnings associated with further education for blacks rising after the first degree has been attributed to the black's postgraduate studies having been mostly carried out in white colleges whose curricula lead into a wider range of employment (Wohlstetter & Coleman 1972).

So far we have seen how social discrimination has reduced the capability that a black child would develop by the time of entry to the labour market, in comparison with that developed by the white child of no greater potential. That, at least, is how it has acted in the past; in recent years the changes have been great. We have now to add the discrimination in opportunity for employment, by which the range of jobs open to the black entrant who has attained a given capability is more restricted than that open to the white entrant whose capability is not superior.

The extent and incidence of such discrimination are indicated in a study by Bergmann (1971). She took 29 occupations in which the majority of workers in 1960 were not high school graduates, and compared the actual number of non-whites in each occupation with the number who would be found in it if the proportion of non-whites in it were equal to that among all persons in the U.S.A. having the 'educational achievement' prevailing in it. In 18 of the occupations the actual number of non-whites fell short of the number calculated on that assumption of 'proportional representation'. These were mainly the crafts in engineering and printing, and some but not all of the building crafts; together with machinists, locomotive engineers, miners, and farmers. In four occupations the difference between the actual and hypothetical numbers of non-whites was insignificant. Eight occupations had significant surpluses of non-whites, and more than four-fifths of the aggregate surplus was found in only two of them—service workers, and non-farm labourers. Two others of these occupations were farm labourers, and truck and tractor drivers. But the eight also included, albeit with only small surpluses, masons, cement and concrete finishers and plasterers. It is interesting that these building crafts contained more than the hypothetical proportion, whereas the carpenters, electricians, and painters contained much less: was it for historical reasons, or because the three occupations with surpluses are all heavy work?

This kind of discrimination takes much of its effect on the pay of blacks by denying them entry into lines of advancement in which substantial on-the-job training in the earlier years of employment leads to a progressive rise, at least up to the employee's mid-40s, in his grade and pay. Just as the age-earnings profiles of women are flat compared with those of men, so those of blacks are flat compared with those of whites. Mincer (1962, pp. 568–9) made estimates of the amounts invested in the schooling and the on-the-job training of non-whites

Table 5.1

Cost of Schooling and Training for Non-White and for All Males in U.S.A.

U.S.A. 1949: estimated total cost per non-white male and for all males of schooling and on-the-job training, by educational level

Educational level	Total costs of schooling per		Total costs of on-the-job training per	
	non-white male	all males	non-white males	all males
		$'000s		
College	13·20	15·9	7·87	24·3
High School	5·15	5·7	3·89	8·6
Elementary School	1·23	1·6	3·43	3·9

Source: Mincer (1962), Table 6.

that are reproduced here in Table 5.1, together with the corresponding estimates for all males in the U.S.A. The on-the-job training of the non-whites is much smaller than that of all males, and the disparity is much greater here than in education. This finding for the non-whites, Mincer says, is the implication of 'the relative flatness of their age-income profiles and the smaller differentials in earnings by education . . .' That non-whites get less on-the-job training for a given level of education 'creates an even lower skill concentration in the occupational distribution than would be predicted by the educational distribution . . . this results in a statistical finding that the ratio of non-white to white incomes declines with increasing level of formal education.'

Using mainly the data for 1966–8 in some 50,000 households sampled by the Current Population Survey in the United States, Wohlstetter and Coleman (1972) estimated the extent to which occupational segregation reduced the earnings of blacks. They examined the distributions of earnings that are formed by setting against each level of earnings the percentage of persons with incomes above that level. The earnings level exceeded by the top 1 per cent of the persons in the sample was found to be lower for blacks than for whites; similarly for the top 2 per cent, the top 3 per cent, and so on throughout the sample. This gap between the two distributions was reduced considerably by adjustment for the proportions in which blacks and whites were spread over higher- and lower-paid occupations. For men, the adjustment removed 'about a third of the disparity on the average throughout the distribution and almost half the disparity in the lowest fifth'. The smaller initial disparity for women was 'erased altogether in the lower half of the distribution', and in the upper half it was much reduced, except in the top decile.

Evidently there was segregation *within* occupations as well as between them. Table 5.2, drawn from Wohlstetter and Coleman, shows that very generally the

Table 5.2

Earnings and Representation of Non-whites in Various Groups of Occupations in U.S.A.

U.S.A. 1967: earnings and representation of non-whites relatively to those of whites, by non-farm occupational group.

Occupational group	Median white earnings	Ratio of non-white to white earnings	Relative representation of non-whites[1]
	$		
Managers, officials and proprietors	8,897	0·655	0·27
Professional, technical and kindred	9,090	0·657	0·54
Craftsmen, foremen and kindred	7,089	0·708	0·61
Sales workers	6,103	0·764	0·30
Operatives and kindred	5,677	0·779	1·26
Service workers, except private household	3,886	0·810	2·27
Clerical and kindred	6,088	0·838	0·96
Labourers, except farm and mine	2,472	1·179	2·76

[1] (Proportion of all non-whites in given group) divided by (Proportion of all whites in given group).

Source: Wohlstetter and Coleman (1972), Table 1–1. Lexington Books, D. C. Heath and Company. Copyright by the RAND Corporation, 1972.

higher the level of white earnings in an occupational group, the lower both the relative representation of non-whites and the ratio of non-white to white earnings. The exceptions are the sales workers and the clerks. Generally, such blacks as did enter the higher-paid occupations must have been concentrated in the lower-paid posts within them.

Further estimates of the effect of discrimination in opportunity are provided in the studies by Duncan, Featherman, and Duncan (1948), Duncan (1968), and Blinder (1973) that we cite later, in Table 5.3. In Blinder's study the effect of discrimination is analysed in so far as it affects not only 'attainment of occupational status' but also educational attainment, vocational training, trade union membership, and tenure on present job. The total effect through these factors comes out at about 30 per cent of the initial differential between the wage rates of blacks and whites. Blinder points out (p. 447) that this estimate is also close to that of Duncan, who, 'using a somewhat different specification and different statistical methods, but a decomposition technique which is almost the same as mine', attributed some 35 per cent of the initial differential between black and white incomes to 'divergent attainments of education and occupational status which could not be predicted by family background'.

What are the causes of this discrimination in opportunity, that is, of segregation? The most evident is custom. Just as it is often taken for granted that there is 'men's work' and 'women's work', so in the past at least it has been seen as in the nature of things that some kinds of work should be done by blacks and others by whites. 'In the South', a Southern economist wrote (Dewey 1952, p. 280), '. . . a rigid division of labour is a striking feature of the everyday business life in almost every town from Maryland to Western Texas. I believe it no exaggeration to say that most Southerners view their economy as divided into "white" and "Negro jobs'." As with women again, blacks have had to crowd into the limited number of occupations that were open to them, so that the pay they could command in them had to be low even if they received the full value of their work. The origins of this segregation might be found in the spontaneously concerted action of the whites, when blacks first entered the market for free labour, to prevent blacks taking their jobs, and to keep high status jobs untarnished by black participation. Marshall in his survey of the economics of racial discrimination (1974, p. 860) has maintained that 'whites clearly have been more motivated to bar blacks from such status jobs as mechanical craft workers in the construction industry, railroad conductors and engineers, and managers and supervisors of integrated work forces than they have from such jobs as hod carriers (not a low-wage job), foundry work (also not low-wage), cement masons, service workers, and labourers, all of which are considered to have lower status.'

The lines of demarcation so established could be maintained in more recent years, despite the rapid extension of industrial employment in the South, because of the big inflow of white labour from the countryside to the towns there.

Yet if we accept this account of the origins and persistence of segregation we have still to explain why there were not some employers at least who took advantage of the cheapness of black labour; and if only a few did so at first, would not their competition force others to follow? Dewey (1952, n. 14) thought that 'cases where employers deliberately sacrifice profits in order to indulge an animosity towards Negroes are extremely rare', and that the community would disapprove of employers moving blacks across demarcation lines only when the condition of the market was such that the employer would have no incentive to move them in any case. The effective restraint on employers he believed to be their ignorance of the capability of blacks.

But he recorded the dissenting opinion of a colleague, who held that in a small Southern town employers would feel an obligation to maintain lines of demarcation. That the sentiment of the community does take effect in this way is suggested by the finding in a more recent study by Bergmann and Lyle (1971, p. 433) that 'variables bearing on the quantity and quality of education do not help in predicting Negro occupational standing by area', whereas the size of the vote for Governor Wallace in the Presidential election of 1968 'explains a major portion of the variance among area scores'. But this 'explanation' is a matter of correlation, and Flanagan (1973, p. 463) finds that the Wallace vote is so highly negatively correlated with the median income for a family of four, that the two are 'virtually interchangeable' as independent variables in regressions designed to account for the relative demand for black labour.

That lines of demarcation can be maintained by a tacit agreement among employers who are highly competitive in other respects, and who do not discriminate in pay, is indicated by a study of organized baseball by Pascal and Rapping (1972). They found that the proportion of black players in the major leagues was higher than in the working population as a whole, and that as players tended to be paid in accordance with their performance no matter whether they were black or white, and the black performed better than the white, the average salaries of the blacks were the higher. None the less there was evidence of discrimination. The facts just cited imply that only those blacks are engaged 'who are demonstrably superior to their white counterparts' (p. 149). The proportion of black players was much the same in all teams within each of the two leagues, but significantly different as between the leagues. Blacks were 'under represented as outfielders and first basemen' (ibid.); and very few were managers, coaches, or umpires. Pascal and Rapping suggest that their findings for baseball apply to other fields of employment. 'If racism is as subtly pervasive as it appears to be on the diamond, it is likely to be exceedingly powerful in the plants, offices, and stores where discriminatory treatment can still be masked by complaints about the absence of qualified applicants' (p. 150).

Whatever the origins of segregation, once set up it tends to reinforce itself, because young blacks will have little inducement to prepare themselves for occupations in which there are few jobs for blacks, and which hardly enter their field of view as they grow up. Fein (1967) has pointed out the effect on their aspirations. 'In 1960', he has written (p. 117), 'when 10 per cent of the male experienced labour force was non-white, only 3·5 per cent of male professionals, technical and kindred workers were non-white (and perhaps a quarter of these were not Negro) . . . When a non-white child met an employed non-white, the chances that he was meeting a janitor were six times as great and the chances that he was meeting an engineer were only one-sixth as great as when a white child met a white employee.'

5.3.2. *Discrimination against blacks within the market.* We have been studying discrimination in so far as it bears on the capability acquired by the black up to his entering the labour market, and the range of occupations accessible to him there. This is discrimination *before* the market. There follows the possibility of discrimination *within* the market, by monopsony or according to status: this is often referred to as 'outright discrimination' or 'pay discrimination'. The question is whether the black worker will be paid the full market value of his capability in the job he takes, or whether pay discrimination results in his being paid less than a white worker of the same capability would get for doing the same job.

The studies by Duncan and Blinder cited in Table 5.3 provide one answer to this question. The principle on which they proceed can be illustrated if we suppose that the worker's level of capability is sufficiently indicated simply by his years of schooling. Let the average years of schooling be 11 for the white workers and 8 for the black, and the average earnings be $7,000 and $4,000. We find for the white workers alone the functional relation between years of schooling and earnings; in this function the average 11 years of schooling are associated with the average earnings of $7,000. If instead of these 11 years we put in the blacks' 8 years, the same function might give, say, earnings of $6,000: the difference of $1,000, or one-third of the whole shortfall of black average earnings below white, can thus be attributed to the blacks being persons who have had fewer years of schooling, and would therefore have earned that much less even if they had been white. The remaining $2,000 of the shortfall must be attributed to a given level of capability commanding lower earnings for a black than for a white.

In the usual case, in which capability is indicated by a number of factors such as the socio-economic level of the worker's parents and the occupation he attains to as well as his years of schooling, the black average values for these factors can be inserted in the now more comprehensive white function one at a time, successively. After inserting years of schooling as above, for instance, we might insert an index of the average black parents' socio-economic level: if the earnings were thereby brought down from the $6,000 they stood at when only the years of schooling had been inserted to say $5,500, we could infer that another $500 of the whole shortfall of the blacks' average earnings was due to their average parental socio-economic status being lower and carrying lower earnings just as it would for white workers. And so on.

We have seen already that Duncan and Blinder agree in attributing about a third of the shortfall of black average earnings below white to the blacks having attained lower levels of education and being concentrated in the lower paying occupations. We can now ask how these studies account for the remainder of the shortfall: in particular, do they attribute any part of it to discrimination within the market, that is, to blacks being paid less than whites of no greater capability in the same occupation?

The findings of Duncan and Blinder are summarized in Table 5.3. They agree in attributing about 40 per cent of the gross differential to discrimination within the market. In Blinder's sample the average gross differential was about 49 per cent of white earnings, so it appears that the average black worker was paid about 20 per cent less than a white worker of equal capability in the same occupation.

Wohlstetter and Coleman, however, give reasons for regarding these analyses

Table 5.3
Analysis of Difference in Pay Between Black and White Workers in U.S.A.

U.S.A. 1960s: attribution of the gross pay differential between black and white workers to three groups of factors, by O. D. Duncan and A. S. Blinder.

Duncan	%	%	Blinder
Family background	27	30	Family background, age, health, residence, local labour market conditions
Extent of attainment of occupational and educational status, from given family background	35	30	Extent of attainment in occupation, education, vocational training, trade union membership, war veteran status, and tenure on present job
Outright discrimination in rates of pay	38	40	Outright discrimination in rates of pay
	100	100	

Sources: Duncan, Featherman and Duncan (1968); Duncan (1968); Blinder (1973).

as unreliable. For one thing, as we have seen already, how much effect is ascribed to occupational segregation depends on the fineness of the classification of occupations. We have seen evidence in Table 5.2 for the blacks in a given occupational group being concentrated on the lower-paid posts within it; and the coarser the classification, the less of this effect will be brought to light, and the more of the gross differential will be left to be attributed to factors other than segregation. It is thus difficult to separate 'pay discrimination' from discrimination in opportunity. But it is also difficult to separate it from the effects of family background. Wohlstetter and Coleman point out that the statistical procedure used for this separation is formally the same as that used to separate hereditarily transmitted differences in ability from the effects of environmental factors. The pay, or the performance in I.Q. tests, associated with given levels of such factors as the income of the parents and the number of years of schooling completed by the child, is compared for blacks and whites. If the pay of the blacks is lower, that is a measure of 'outright discrimination'; similarly, if the I.Q.s associated with given levels of environmental factors are different for blacks and whites, that is taken to be a measure of the difference in genetic endowment. 'Colour prejudice', Wohlstetter and Coleman observe, '. . . has much the same effect on the earnings of non-whites as would a difference in ability', and we cannot tell if an observed difference in earnings is due to one or the other, or to both: 'the forces that affect learning and the ability to earn money in the market place are highly confounded' (1972 p. 45).

This brings up the possibility that the parts of the differential attributed to social discrimination in schooling, and to 'outright discrimination' by status, may in fact be due to black parents transmitting to their children a potential different from that transmitted by white parents. Any group that is largely endogamous is likely to have a gene pool that is differentiated in ways that endow the children with a potential for the development of capability that differs from the potential of the surrounding population. The genetic endowment is hard to separate from the effects of the family environment in the early years of the child's life: the differentiation of potential in the gene pool is liable to be increased or offset by ways in which the culture of the group is distinguished—especially by the prevailing structure of the family, and the pattern of child upbringing. The resultant differentiation may well be qualitative, so that the numerical results of the same tests of ability and aptitude applied to people of the two cultures cannot place them one above the other on a common scale. But since these tests are found to be predictive, in the aggregate, of the kind of performance on which pay depends in the economy containing the group, lower scores in the tests do show that members of the group are at a disadvantage in respect of characteristics transmitted to them genetically and through upbringing. It is therefore significant for our present purpose that the average scores of blacks in these tests have been found to be lower than those of whites at the same levels of family income and with the same number of years of schooling (Jensen 1969). This difference, like those between the average scores of other ethnic groups, is small in comparison with the range of individual scores within any one group. Nevertheless we have to allow that some part—we cannot say how great a part, or how little—of the pay differential between black and white that the statistical analyses cannot account for as a result of the factors they list may be due to the potential transmitted from parent to child, of which there is no indicator among the listed factors.

The upshot is that it is hard to separate the effects of discrimination *before* the market from those of discrimination *within* the market—that is, to form an independent estimate of the value of blacks' work after the first sort of discrimination has taken its effect, in order to see how far if at all the actual pay falls short of that value. How much the black worker has suffered from outright discrimination in pay, indeed whether he has suffered from it at all, we cannot be sure.

That he has so suffered, however, has been very widely believed, has indeed been regarded as self-evident. The black minority has been seen to be exploited by the white majority. The two communities can be regarded as two economies that trade with one another, and in the theory of international trade it has been shown that in certain circumstances one economy can gain at the expense of the other by changing the terms of trade between them, as it might do by imposing a general tariff on imports from the other country. The counterpart in the exchanges between the black and white communities would be a general agreement on the part of the whites to keep down the price at which they will buy black labour relatively to that at which they sell their own services, including the provision of capital, to the blacks (Krueger 1963). But what evidence is there of any such general agreement with intent to exploit? As Arrow has pointed out (1972, p. 99), it could hardly hold against the evident self-interest of particular employers in departing from it and hiring more of the cheap type of labour. A majority could always adopt a deliberate policy in order to exploit a minority of any kind, in whatever way it was distinguished, but we do not find that happening. If then we do find the white community following a policy that is exploitative of the black, we cannot think they follow it of set intent. It arises rather from history, from traditional attitudes and the emotive aspects of race. If it results in the whites gaining at the expense of the blacks, the outcome is unforeseen. The behaviour that yields the gain would be the same did the whites lose by it.

It may be asked, however, if there has not been intent to gain at the black workers' expense in the policy of trade unions towards them. In respect of admission to the union, that policy has depended on whether the unions were of the craft type that defends its members' pay by restricting entry to the job, or the 'industrial' type that defends it by ensuring that all entrants are paid not less than the union rate. Ashenfelter (1972) found that among the crafts the proportion of black workers in union membership was about half that of the whites, whereas in the sector of industrial unionism the two proportions were the same. He also found that the ratio of black to white wages in labour markets organized by craft unions consistently differed little from that in unorganized markets of the kind, but in the labour markets organized by industrial unions the ratio was consistently higher than in the unorganized. 'Under certain simplifying assumptions,' he concluded (p. 463), 'these results taken together imply that in 1967 the ratio of black to white male wages might have been 4 per cent higher in the industrial union sector and 5 per cent lower in the craft union sector than they would have been in the absence of all unionism.' But the possibility remains of discrimination between black and white members of a union in its local administration, as for instance in the priorities observed for overtime and lay offs; when agreements are negotiated for the reckoning and application of seniority within the shop as distinct from the whole plant, the shops may be defined so as to segregate blacks (Dewey 1952). In these ways unions may discriminate in earnings even where there is no difference in rates.

But if there is thus on the whole little evidence for deliberate exploitation, everyday knowledge has given reason to believe that a general tendency to discriminate has in fact sprung from widely held prejudice. We have already noticed the possible workings of prejudice, of distaste for association with blacks on the part of white employers, their employees, or their customers. A theory has been developed, notably by Becker (1971), in which the consequences are worked out on the neoclassical assumption of behaviour that—granted the distaste—is rational and maximizing. An employer who has a distaste for association with blacks, as compared with whites, will employ a black, instead of a white of equal capability, only if the black is available at lower pay. The difference of the pay in money is not a source of benefit to the employer, but is needed to offset the disutility to him of association with the black worker. He is thus in equilibrium, although he is paying the black worker less than the monetary value of his work, that is, less than his marginal value product. If white employees have a distaste for association with black, the introduction of a black employee will require the employer to pay his white employees more to compensate them for their distaste, if they are not to move to firms in which only whites are employed; or, it may be, he does not pay them more, and they do stay with him, but his costs are raised by friction over working arrangements and a fall in morale. Again, therefore, he will not be willing to engage the black worker, unless the extra costs his entry will set up are offset by his accepting a wage lower than his marginal value product. If again it is the customer who has some distaste for the products of black workers, or for contact with blacks when they make their purchases, the employer of blacks can sell in competition with all-white enterprises only if his products are lower priced; and he must make good this discount by paying less than their marginal value products to the black workers whose presence makes the discount necessary.

This theory rests on an account of the origins of discrimination in the tastes or prejudices of whites; and by incorporating these tastes in the calculus of the benefit that people seek to maximize as employers, employees, or consumers, it shows how the discrimination by which some workers are paid less than their marginal value products can persist in competitive equilibrium.

It is an inference from this theory that legislation requiring 'equal pay' for blacks and whites, or enforcing a minimum wage for both sorts of worker, will increase segregation. If the extra costs, psychic or monetary, that are set up by the introduction of black workers can no longer be offset by their being paid less, they will not be engaged except in conditions of scarcity, when no whites are available, and higher product prices can be obtained to cover the higher costs of a mixed labour force. What has actually happened under fair employment laws appears consistent with this expectation. Landes (1968) noted that 29 states had enacted laws 'prohibiting discrimination in employment on the grounds of race, creed, colour or national origin'. The gross differential between non-white and white wages was from 11 to 15 per cent smaller in the states that had such fair employment laws in 1959 than in those without them then; but from 1939 to 1959 the excess of the non-white over the white unemployment rate was growing in the fair employment states relatively to the others, and this divergence was particularly marked in the states which adopted laws between 1949 and 1959.

None the less, the distaste theory of discrimination can be criticized on the grounds of inconsistency between the workings of competition that it embodies and the likely distribution of distaste in the community. Arrow (1972) has pointed out that any employers who lack this distaste, or have less of it, will be able to undersell the others. 'In the long run, the less discriminatory will either drive the more discriminatory out of business or, if not, will cause the wage differential to fall. If we suppose that there are some actual or potential

employers who do not discriminate at all, then the wage differential should, in
the long run, fall to zero. The discriminating employers will possibly continue
to operate, but they will employ only white labour' (p. 90).

Flanagan (1973) assesses the theory based on distaste—the utility theory of
discrimination, as he calls it—by testing its implication that 'if the dispersion
of employer tastes is similar in major labour markets, the racial income ratio
should vary inversely with the proportion of blacks in the market, since blacks
will be forced to seek employment in firms which have relatively large tastes for
discrimination in markets where they comprise a relatively large share of the
labour force' (p. 465). This implies a negatively sloped demand curve, where
the price is the ratio of blacks' pay to whites', and the quantity is the proportion of blacks in the labour force. Flanagan looks for this relation first in a
cross-section analysis of the labour market state by state, using data from the
1960 Census. He takes the black/white wage ratio in each of a number of
groups of occupations, and after allowance for the influence of some other factors on it looks to the way in which it varies with the proportion of blacks in
the occupational group and state. He finds that, for males at least, the two do
not vary together at all but seem to be independent of one another, except
among the salesmen and craftsmen, and here the bigger the proportion of
blacks, the higher, not the lower, the blacks' relative wage.

If then we leave employers' distaste aside, and rest the theory on the distaste
of employees, we encounter another difficulty, for it appears that the operations
of this factor would lead to complete segregation, some firms or departments
being all-white and some all-black, and blacks being paid the same as whites for
work of equal value. This has been put by Arrow in the paper just cited, in
which it will be remembered he assumes that the capabilities of black and white
workers are the same at each level of skill. He has argued:

At a general equilibrium with full employment of both types of labour . . . it would
never pay a firm to have a mixed labour force, since they would have to raise the wages
of their white workers above the level for the all-white option. The firms would also
have to find the two types of segregation equally profitable; otherwise, they would all
switch to one or the other. This requires that wages paid to whites in the all-white
firms equal that paid to blacks in the all-black firms (p. 92).

The expected effect of complete segregation is not so far from the facts, if our
units of employment include the department, shop, or process as well as the
whole firm; but the expected absence of pay discrimination means the disappearance of what the theory sets out to account for.

To explain the persistence of this discrimination, without firms all trying to
go over to the cheaper type of labour, Arrow has invoked the 'personal investment' involved in the engagement, settling in, and training of a new employee:
any substitution of one worker for another imposes a cost in this way, which
must be more than offset by the cheapness of the newcomer's labour if the substitution is to be profitable. A differential not big enough to do this can then
persist. Arrow has also suggested that differentials can persist if employers

generally believe that the pay of black labour is no more than it is worth—simply because of prejudice; or because they have reason to believe that some blacks are not worth more, and regard any black applicant as liable to be like that; or need to rationalize their prejudice—'precisely the fact that discriminatory behaviour is in conflict with an important segment of our ethical beliefs will . . . intensify the willingness to entertain cognitive beliefs that will supply a socially acceptable justification for this conduct' (p. 97).

The appeal here is, in effect, to the existence of demarcation lines and employers' acceptance of conventional valuations. But these constitute a sufficient explanation of discrimination in themselves, and we can dispense with the theory that they have been brought in to prop up. When one considers the willingness of whites to employ black domestic servants, prevalence of distaste for association does not seem more acceptable as an assumption of fact than a general attribution of lower value to the work of persons of lower status. We have one significant study, moreover, that indicates the persistence of discrimination in a sector where distaste seems unlikely to take effect. Taylor (1968) studied two unskilled male occupations—the materials handlers and the janitors—in 80 firms in Chicago. In these occupations, he pointed out, the black is not handicapped by his prevailing lack of education and training on the job, for among the whites they attract only the unskilled. They are occupations, too, in which there is little opportunity for friction between white and black: the employer is remote, and the white employee would see no threat in the employment of blacks in jobs that are traditionally theirs. Yet after allowance for a number of personal characteristics such as age, education, and seniority that affect individual pay, and for a number of characteristics of the establishment in which each man worked, such as also account for pay differences, Taylor found differentials against the blacks of some 5 per cent of the mean hourly rate among the materials handlers, and 3·3 percent among the janitors. Such differentials, found consistently in a field of employment in which the black is at little or no disadvantage by reason of the whites' perception of his characteristics and does not impinge on white susceptibilities, indicate the possibility of pay discrimination rooted not in distaste for associaton with the black but in the black's status.

We may conclude that discrimination against blacks within the market is best accounted for by the prevalence of a traditional ascription of lower value to the work of persons of lower status—an ascription in which our earlier discussion suggests there are mingled a sense that lower pay is proper for those whose station in life is lower, the assumption that what costs less is worth less, and the apprehension that any black applicant for employment may prove to have shortcomings that are perceived as the objective characteristics of certain blacks. The measurement of the resultant outright discrimination is difficult, because it requires us first to separate out those parts of the gross differential between black and white pay that are due to any objective disabilities of the blacks, and to their being segregated into the jobs within any one occupation that are less well paid and offer less prospect of advancement. The effects of these factors are likely to vary from one employment to another, and are hazardous to estimate everywhere. The studies we have noted, of various coverage and method, have found the part left for outright discrimination to be as much as 30 per cent of the white pay in one case, and in another as little as 3·3 per cent of the average pay of whites and blacks together.

5.4. The effects of raising minimum wages, as a test for the presence of discrimination

Minimum wages have been enforced in many countries, by statute or decree of wide application, or by the decisions of boards having jurisdiction over particular groups of workers. The raising of these minima has generally brought about an immediate rise in the wages of some low-paid workers. These workers have commonly included a high proportion of women, juveniles, and, in the U.S.A., of non-whites. If the raising of these workers' wages was closely followed by a reduction in the number employed, we might infer that the workers were previously being paid as much as they were worth to the employer, and their pay was not low by reason of discrimination against them within the market: unless indeed the employers were all undervaluing their work by reason of a prejudice whose hold on their judgement was not loosened by the shock of the raising of the wage. If, on the other hand, the raising of the wage was not associated with any reduction of employment, it would seem probable that the workers concerned were previously being paid less than the employer was prepared to pay them, and one reason for this would be that they were being discriminated against. But it is not the only possible reason. In his study of 'economic adjustments to changes in wage differentials', Lester (1957) has given a detailed account of the various ways in which employers can absorb or pass on a rise of limited amount in the pay of one group of workers, so as not to have to dismiss any of them. These possibilities place the going rate of pay for any one group of workers in a zone of indeterminacy, rather than at a single point of equilibrium. The finding that the wages of some low-paid workers had been pushed up without any of them losing their jobs would therefore not necessarily show that their rate of pay had previously stood lower, relatively to the employer's judgement of what their work was worth, than did that of other workers.

None the less we are bound to want to know what changes in employment have been associated with the raising of minimum wages. An abrupt and externally imposed change of this kind, even though far from being imposed under experimental conditions, should provide opportunity for insight into the forces bearing on wages and employment.

Yet the many studies of the needed kind that have been made suffer from the limitations common to all attempts to trace cause and effect in the flux of economic affairs. If the effects on employment are looked for in the one or two months immediately following a rise in the minimum, there may not have been time for the employer's reactions to it to be worked out and put into effect; if the effects are looked for over a longer run, much else may have been happening to affect employment meanwhile. A rapid drop in 1920–1 in the employment of workers for whom minimum wages were prescribed—many of them for the first time quite recently—by the British Trade Boards led to the setting up of a committee of inquiry (Ministry of Labour 1922); but this drop came at a time of mounting unemployment generally, and in a period too when factories capable of mass production were in any case taking output away from the little local workshops in which many of the workers concerned were employed. Similarly to the perplexity of the inquirer, though with the opposite effect on employment, the rises in the minimum under the U.S. Fair Labor Standards Act mostly came into effect at times of rising general activity. The problems of sequence in time can be avoided by cross-section studies—by comparing the changes in employments affected by a rise in the minimum with those occurring at the same time in other employments not so affected. But here again there is the problem of 'other things not being equal'; the two sorts of employment may be subject to different extraneous influences, even when they are in the same locality, or in establishments of different size but in the same industry. The difficulty of controlling for other influences arises even more severely if comparison is made between regions—such as states in the U.S.A.—some of which have their own minimum wage laws and others not. The comparison, again, of the unemployment rates of adults and juveniles in the U.S.A. suggests that the higher rates of juveniles owes something to the higher impact on juvenile than on adult wages of the federal minimum; and so it may, but we have also to remember that between 1958 and 1968 the number of teenagers in the U.S.A. rose by nearly a half, that of adults by less than a seventh (Kosters & Welch 1972, p. 328 n. 11).

Tracing the effects of rises in the minimum wage is also made more difficult by the generally small impact of those rises. Of the impact of the federal minimum in the U.S.A., O'Herlihy has observed (1969, p. 4) that 'at no time have more than 10 per cent of employees covered by the Act been directly affected by a change in the minimum wage in the sense that their wages had to be increased to comply with the law; indeed at no time has a change in the minimum wage directly caused an increase of over 1 per cent in the total wage bill of the covered industries'. 'In even the most affected low wage industries', Peterson (1957, p. 414) reports of the rises of 1938–50, 'to have raised all workers to the minimum would have required only a 5–15 per cent increase in pay-rolls and a 1–3 per cent increase in total cost.'

These considerations go some way to explain why Secretaries of Labor in the U.S.A. have been able to report very differently on the effects of the minimum wage on employment. In transmitting his annual report in January 1959 on the application of the Fair Labor Standards Act, the then Secretary observed of the rise in the minimum from 75 cents to $1·00 in 1956 that 'the surveys present evidence of disemployment apparently related to the increase in the $1·00 minimum, despite the fact that the economy was rising at the time and there were increases in the general level of prices which facilitated adjustment to the $1·00 minimum. Employment tended to decline in the low-wage industries, and in most cases markedly in those segments of the low-wage industries where wage-rates had been increased most' (U.S. Dept. of Labor 1959). But a later Secretary observed, in transmitting his report in January 1966, that 'there is clearly no evidence in the 28 years of experience of unemployment resulting from statutory minimum wage rate increases. The strong—and only—indication from the record is that reasonable increases in the minimum rate have no retarding effect on an expanding economy and do not result in larger unemployment than there would have been in the absence of such increases' (U.S. Dept of Labor 1966, p. 6).

None the less there are two types of study of the effects of minimum wages in the U.S.A. that escape in some measure the inherent difficulties of observation. Certain macro-economic studies have endeavoured to separate the effects of general and persistent factors affecting employment from those attributable to the incidence of particular rises in the minimum wage. Studies in the field have provided detailed information about factors affecting employment in particular firms, and recorded employers' statements about their reactions.

In one macro-economic study, Moore (1971) controlled for the general level of unemployment, and looked for the net effect of the federal minimum wage, as its ratio to the general level of wages varied month by month through 1954–68, on the unemployment rates of various types of employee aged 16–19; the effect was looked for according to a 'distributed lag'. He found that the ratio was positively associated with the unemployment rates of the teenagers of all types, though not with the rate for males aged 20–24; it was associated more closely for non-whites than for whites, and for females than for males. Kosters and Welch (1972) took account of the long-term trends and cyclical movements of the numbers employed from among various demographic groups in U.S. civilian employment 1954–68. 'In this framework', they say (p. 324), 'we estimate the effects of minimum wage legislation on the distribution of employment and on the distribution of changes in employment between whites and non-whites, between males and females, and between teenages and adults.' They find (p. 330) that 'minimum wage legislation has had the effect of decreasing the share of normal employment and increasing vulnerability to cyclical changes in employment for the group most "marginal" to the work force—teenagers. Thus, as a result of increased minimum wages, teenagers are able to obtain fewer jobs during periods of normal employment growth and their jobs are less secure in the face of short-term employment changes.'

The local detail of employment changes has been inquired into mostly by the Department of Labor. The earlier inquiries have been surveyed by Blum (1947), and those concerning the impact of the $1·00 minimum in 1956 have been reported by Samuels (1957) and Badenhoop (1958). These surveys agree in finding that reactions to rises in the minimum rate varied from one employer to another even in the same industry and locality. Among seven low-wage industries the proportion of the employers interviewed who said they had discharged workers because of the rise to $1·00 was nil in footwear and about two-fifths in seamless hosiery; in the others it ranged from 6 to 25 per cent (Samuels, p. 328). Some of those who said they had discharged workers replaced them presumably with more efficient workers. Other ways reported of raising efficiency so as to offset the higher wage rate included 'closer control of overtime work, higher production standards, more rigid hiring and lay-off practices, reorganization of plant layout . . . redesign of product, installation of labour-saving machinery'. But 'employers frequently indicated that some of the changes being made were part of a long-range program' and not necessarily due to the rise in the minimum wage (Badenhoop, p. 743).

From the macro and micro studies we can draw two conclusions. One is that the application of the minimum wage to teenagers has reduced the number of jobs available to them. The other concerns the reactions of the employers of workers whose wages are required to be raised: they react variously, and many of them have ways of absorbing the not very great rise in the pay roll generally called for, but a substantial number also find it necessary and possible to raise the productivity of the workers concerned, and in a limited number of cases workers have been discharged.

From these conclusions in turn we can draw an inference concerning discrimination within the market. If we found that when the minimum was raised an employer simply paid the higher rate without much other reaction of any kind, we could infer that previously he had been paying the workers concerned less than he judged them to be worth, or that the higher rate had shocked him into revising his judgement. But what we do find is a variety of reactions whose common property is that they are calculated to maintain or restore an existing equation between the worker's wage and his productivity: thus jobs are not extended to teenagers as they otherwise might be, and some low-paid workers are discharged; or steps are taken to raise the productivity of the worker. The existence of that equation is inconsistent with the prevalence of any substantial discrimination within the market against the workers concerned.

5.5. Review and discussion

(a) Our initial problem was whether persons regarded as of lower status were paid less for doing given work than would have been paid for the same work if it were done by persons of higher status. If that were so, it would be an instance of relative pay being not so much determined by market forces, as set to match the hierarchy of status. We shall have demonstrated that status determines relative pay by way of discrimination, if we have both established the fact of discrimination, and shown reason to believe this discrimination is due to the inferior status of those discriminated against, and not to some other factor.

(b) We have found abundant evidence for the existence of discrimination *before* the market, and this as a cause of lower pay for both women and blacks. Both types suffer from inferior education, training, and instilled motivation in their preparation for employment; both are largely segregated and indeed crowded into certain employments; both tend to be denied entry into those

avenues that provide considerable training on the job with prospect of subsequent progressive advancement. Many of the reasons for these things are
different in the two instances: in particular it is to be noted that the reluctance
to provide on the job training for women springs from the fact, specific to
women, that most of them withdraw from paid employment, be it only for a
limited number of years, in order to raise a family. No doubt too the sense in
which the status of women has been inferior to that of men is different from
that in which the status of blacks has been inferior to that of whites. But much
of the discrimination before the market against women and blacks alike is most
readily understood as the natural counterpart of the belief that in one way or
another their status is inferior. This is especially clear in the segregation of
'men's work' and 'women's work', and of 'white jobs' and 'Negro jobs', which
is probably the major cause of the lower average earnings of women and
blacks.

(c) The evidence concerning discrimination *within* the market cannot in the
nature of things be so clear. Discrimination before the market can be established by pointing to evident differences in education and training and job
opportunities; but to establish the existence of discrimination within the
market we have to show first that some persons who are differentiated by
stigmata that do not affect their capability are being paid less than others in the
same occupation who are of no greater capability but who do not bear those
stigmata. But any actual differential between men and women, or whites and
blacks, is likely to be made up at least in part of systematic differences in
capability that affect the value of their work. These in turn may be due to discrimination before the market, but we have to separate their effects out before
we can arrive at discrimination within the market, or outright discrimination,
the giving of different pay for products of equal value. How hard it is to effect
this separation we have seen. The evidence concerning women does not allow
us to conclude that there is any outright discrimination: even where men and
women were performing the same work with equal efficiency hour by hour, and
the women were paid less, it was still possible that their work was worth less to
the employer over a longer span of time, because they were more liable to leave
when their experience was making them increasingly useful. The statistical
analysis of the evidence concerning blacks, however, does yield estimates of a
sometimes wide margin of outright discrimination, though we do not know
how far this margin would be reduced if more of the factors affecting the value
of the work—for example, the intelligence of the worker, his motivation, and
his steadiness of application—could be entered in the regressions. The effects
of rises in minimum wages on employment are hard to analyse in the nature of
things, and employers' reactions vary widely, but there are more grounds to infer that employers aim at maintaining an equality between the productivity of
the low-paid worker and his wage, than that they discriminate against him by
paying him less than they judge him to be worth. We have seen that this last
possibility depends either on employers everywhere maintaining a common and
in effect monopsonistic policy in their hiring of the labour concerned, or on

their all, though acting independently, being in fact alike in undervaluing that labour, and in not being spurred to revalue it by the rise in the minimum.

(*d*) That prejudices held in common do lead in that way to unconcerted but parallel behaviour does seem to be indicated by what we know of prevailing attitudes. We have seen (p. 173) how blacks may be paid less for work of equal value for three reasons—because of 'a sense that lower pay is proper for those whose station in life is lower, the assumption that what costs less is worth less, and the apprehension that any black applicant for employment may prove to have shortcomings that are perceived as the objective characteristics of certain blacks'. But the last two reasons do not lead to discrimination proper, though they do lead to certain blacks being paid less than they are or could be made capable of producing. The assumption 'that what costs less is worth less' may apply to labour of any kind; it will lead to the work being so slackly organized that the worker's product is no more than enough to cover his wage, and this may be less than the worker is capable of producing under other arrangements, but he is not being paid less than the employer judges him to be worth where he is. The use of a characteristic such as skin colour as a means of estimating an applicant's potential is a negative form of 'credentialism', and need not have anything to do with the status of those concerned (Reder 1969, pp. 240–2). The estimate will do less than justice to some applicants, but there is no implication that the pay will be below the estimate. In the first reason, however, in the 'sense that lower pay is proper for those whose station in life is lower', we do have a divorce between pay and productivity: workers are to be paid according to their status, and if that is low the wage should be low, irrespective of how productive the worker may be.

(*e*) So far, then, as the evidence goes in the cases of discrimination examined here, status appears to affect relative pay in two ways. The evidence is cogent that lower status keeps down the value of some people's work by limiting their education and training, and their access to jobs. There is no implication so far that status supersedes the market forces of supply and demand, which for all we know may set the same price on the work of persons who have been discriminated against in this way as they set on the same work done by other people. In that case there is equal pay for work of equal value; what discrimination has done is to prevent persons of lower status from doing work of higher value that they could do, given the needed preparation and access to jobs. But there is evidence also, albeit not so unmistakable, that status affects relative pay in a second way, in which market forces are set aside to some extent, and persons of lower status are paid less for their work than is paid for the same work when it is done by others. Here we have unequal pay for work of equal value. The amount of the differential against those of lower status varies inversely with the extent of competition between employers, and their ability to assess the value of work objectively. Even in a competitive labour market, custom and prejudice may set some discount on the value of the work of persons of lower status; but only where employers do not compete for cheap labour, or do not know cheap labour when they see it, will any considerable discount persist.

(f) In sum, we find that status affects relative pay within the zones of indeterminacy that are left by the working of market forces, and can affect it to the extent that any such zone is broad or narrow. But there is no indication here that the main lines of the pay structure are fixed to match the hierarchy of status.

In the course of the preceding study of black workers, we saw how some of their disabilities arose from the poorer start in life generally given to the children born into black homes, through inferior access to education, weaker motivation, and upbringing in a culture that might not be well adapted to work in industry. We also touched on the possibility of differences between largely endogamous groups in the qualities transmitted by parents to their children, genetically and by early upbringing. These issues raised peripherally by the discussion of status enter basically into that of class. We go on now to examine the effect of class on the pay structure through its influence on the supply of labour to different occupations.

6

Social Class and
Intergenerational Mobility

6.1. The assignment of occupations to social classes

The notion of social class is as many-sided as that of social status (Dahrendorf 1959, pp. 74–6), but there is one aspect that concerns us here above all—the extent to which the kind of occupation into which young persons find their way is linked with their parents' class. If that extent is considerable, and we shall see that it is so, then the class structure is evidently an important influence on the relative supplies of labour to different occupations. This means in turn that it may prove to be an important influence on relative pay. We must ask, for instance, whether it keeps the supply of labour to some occupations below the number of those capable of learning to perform the work, and so keeps up the relative pay there; and to what extent young people are in practice confined to the same kind of occupation as their parents', so that—as has been held—the different classes form 'non-competing groups', each with its own insulated level of pay.

Our initial link between occupation and class might be expressed by saying that the life-chances of young persons depend in no small measure on the socio-economic class of their homes. One way of finding the class to which a given home belongs is to ask what occupations its children are most likely to enter. For we find that occupations group themselves, in that the children of parents following any of the occupations in the group are more likely themselves to enter one of the occupations in the group than any outside it. This form of grouping constitutes the aspect of the social class that we need to explore for the purposes of our present inquiry. It is closely connected with social mobility and the supply of labour to different occupations, and hence—at least in so far as we find that supply and demand take effect here—with the relative pay in those occupations. It calls for a full examination accordingly.

We begin with the possibility of forming an index of the likelihood that the son of a father at a certain occupational level will himself enter a given occupation—an index, that is to say, of the affinity between the father's occupation and the son's.

Let us take an economy in which there are only eight occupations, A, B, C ... H. A labour force of 1,000 men is divided among them, 80 in occupation A, 200 in B, 120 in C, and so on. Each man has one son, and the sons find their way into the eight occupations, some following their fathers, but most entering one of the other occupations. There is no change in the occupational structure between generations—the 80 fathers in occupation A, for instance, will be

Table 6.1

Index of Affinity—Numerical Example
of Intergenerational Mobility

Example of allocation of the labour force between 8 occupations in 2 generations.

No. of sons having fathers in given occupation		No. of sons entering given occupation							
		A	B	C	D	E	F	G	H
A	80	10	12	12	3	15	6	4	18
B	200	12	34	20	10	72	30	7	15
C	120	20	18	10	3	20	9	4	36
D	60	2	9	5	3	14	6	15	6
E	240	12	64	24	12	44	43	11	30
F	100	4	40	8	4	40	4	—	—
G	50	2	3	5	18	8	—	8	6
H	150	18	20	36	7	27	2	1	39
	1,000	80	200	120	60	240	100	50	150

succeeded in that occupation by 80 sons, though most of these sons will have had fathers in other occupations. What happens may be as in Table 6.1. Here, looking along the rows, we see, for instance, that of the 80 sons of fathers in occupation A, 10 followed their fathers in that occupation, 12 went into B, 12 into C, 3 into D, and so on. Looking down the columns, we see that of the 240 sons who entered occupation E, 15 had fathers in A, 72 had fathers in B, and so on. Thus the entry 30 in column F, row B, means that of the sons of fathers in occupation B, 30 entered F.

How much affinity is apparent within this mobility? Whether the entry of 30 we have just noticed marks any affinity between occupations B and F depends on how many sons of fathers in B we should expect to enter F if they were no more and no less likely to enter F than any other occupation. Of the 1,000 jobs, 100 or 10 per cent are in F, so on the condition just stated we should expect 10 per cent of the 200 sons of fathers in B, i.e. 20, to go into F. In fact we find that 30 did so go. The ratio of 30 to 20, or 1·5, we take as the index of affinity between occupations B and F. Calculating the corresponding indexes for all the other cells, we get the figures of Table 6.2.

If the number following the path from their father's occupation to their own is no more than we should expect if there was no attraction or repulsion between the two occupations, the index is 1·0; a positive affinity is marked by an index greater than 1·0, and if the index is less than 1·0 then there is some resistance to movement along that path. But this holds strictly only in such a case as the present example, which has been simplified by two unrealistic assumptions—that each father has one son, or, more generally, that the propor-

Table 6.2
Index of Affinity—Calculation of Indexes
from Numerical Example

Indexes of affinity between occupations, calculated as the ratio of the actual number, as shown in Table 6.1, of sons of fathers in occupation X who themselves entered occupation Y, to the number of those sons who would have entered Y if they had been equally likely to enter any occupation.

		Occupations entered by sons							
		A	B	C	D	E	F	G	H
	A	1·56	0·75	1·25	0·63	0·78	0·75	1·00	1·50
	B	0·75	0·85	0·83	0·83	1·50	1·50	0·70	0·50
	C	2·08	0·75	0·69	0·42	0·70	0·75	0·67	2·00
Fathers'	D	0·42	0·75	0·69	0·83	0·97	1·00	5·00	0·67
occupations	E	0·63	1·33	0·83	0·83	0·77	1·79	0·92	0·83
	F	0·50	2·00	0·67	0·67	1·67	0·40	—	—
	G	0·50	0·30	0·83	6·00	0·67	—	3·20	0·80
	H	1·50	0·67	2·00	0·78	0·75	0·13	0·13	1·73

tion of sons to fathers is the same in all the fathers' occupations; and secondly, that the proportionate distribution of sons between occupations is the same as that of the fathers. When we remove these assumptions, the significance of any given numerical value of the index changes, and 'neutrality' is no longer necessarily represented by 1·0. The formula for the index, in terms of the instance just calculated, is

$$\frac{\text{sons of B fathers entering F (30)}}{\text{all sons of B fathers (200)}} \div \frac{\text{all sons entering F (100)}}{\text{all sons (1,000)}}.$$

Suppose now that by reason of differential fertility the number of sons of B fathers rose above 200: the number of such sons entering F might rise in consequence above the present 30, but not necessarily in the same proportion. Suppose again that by reason of differential mortality among those already working in F, or a change in demand on the part of employers or consumers, the number of vacancies in F increased, so that the number of all sons entering F rose above the present 100: this might be associated with some rise above 30 in the number of sons of B fathers entering F, but again we have no reason to expect any rise to be in the same proportion. In these two ways the value of the index might change although there was no change in the underlying affinity, that is, in the extent to which upbringing as the sons of a B father and the requirements of occupation F made it easy or difficult for such sons to move into F. We must bear this in mind as we go on to apply the concept of affinity to statistics of social mobility.

But for the purpose of our present inquiry into the principle of the grouping of occupations to form classes, we can return to our example, in which we can take it that an index of 1·0 between two occupations marks 'neutrality'. Between each two occupations there are two paths along which the index can be calculated. Thus we have seen that the index for the sons of B fathers entering F is 1·50, and in Table 6.2 we also see that the index for the sons of F fathers entering B is 2·00. The sum, 3·50, we can regard as an index of the cohesion between B and F, that is, of the extent to which persons following occupations B and F belong to the same class. We can also adopt the convention that a sum of 2·0 or less marks the absence of cohesion. We then calculate all the two-way sums—they are set out in Table 6.3—and look for those that are greater than 2·0. By this test we find affinity between:

(1) A and C;   A and H;   C and H
(2) B and E;   B and F;   E and F
(3) D and G

All the other indexes are less than 2·0: that is, there is no cohesion between the above three groups, which thus stand apart from one another. But they do not form 'non-competing groups' in the full sense of that term, for there is some movement along all but three of the paths between the father's occupation and the son's. Here, then, we may say, are three classes, defined by the proclivity of the children of fathers following any occupation within the class to enter the occupations within it rather than those outside it.

But there is nothing here to show us how these three classes will be ranked. Ranking will be provided only if we can add the finding that the occupations placed in a given class by this test of cohesion generally require an extent of education and training, and command a level of pay, in which they resemble one another, and differ from the occupations in the other classes. In this way

Table 6.3

Indexes of Cohesion Formed from Numerical Example

Indexes of cohesion formed by adding the two indexes of affinity for each pair of occupations in Table 6.2.

Pair of occupations	Index	Pair of occupations	Index	Pair of occupations	Index	Pair of occupations	Index
A, B	1·50	B, C	1·58	C, E	1·53	D, H	1·45
A, C	3·33	B, D	1·58	C, F	1·42	E, F	3·46
A, D	1·05	B, E	2·85	C, G	1·50	E, G	1·59
A, E	1·41	B, F	2·50	C, H	4·00	E, H	1·58
A, F	1·25	B, G	1·00	D, E	1·80	F, G	—
A, G	1·50	B, H	1·17	D, F	1·67	F, H	0·13
A, H	3·00	C, D	1·11	D, G	11·00	G, H	0·93

we should arrive at Weber's definition of social class. 'A "social class" ', he says (1968, p. 302), 'makes up the totality of those class situations within which individual and generational mobility is easy and typical.' This is our notion of affinity; but Weber's definition of 'class situation' adds the characteristics by which classes are ranked—' "Class situation" means the typical probability of

1. procuring goods
2. gaining a position in life and
3. finding inner satisfactions,

a probability which derives from the relative control over goods and skills and from their income-producing uses within a given economic order.'

In the history of statistical practice, however, assigning by such characteristics as these has come first, and what we have called cohesion—except in so far as it is a matter of common knowledge—has been revealed only by the subsequent study of mobility between classes so defined. The reports of the British census of population assign occupations to *five social classes* (General Register Office 1966):

   I. Professional etc., wholly non-manual
  II. Intermediate ⎫
 III. Skilled   ⎬ each divided into manual, non-manual, agricultural
  IV. Partly skilled ⎭
   V. Unskilled, wholly manual

Occupations are assigned to these classes 'so as to ensure that, so far as is possible, each category is homogeneous in relation to the basic criterion of the general standing within the community of the occupations concerned. This criterion is naturally correlated with, and the application of the criterion conditioned by, other factors such as education and economic environment, but it has no direct relationship to the average level of remuneration of particular occupations' (pp. x–xi). In addition, the British census distinguishes 16 *socio-economic groups*, each of which 'should contain people whose social, cultural and recreational standards and behaviour are similar'. The assignment of occupied persons 'is determined by considering their employment status and occupation' (p. xi).

Let us see what is known about intergenerational mobility between classes or groups so defined.

6.2. Intergenerational mobility between occupations

A number of inquiries enable us to compare the occupations of the respondents with those of their fathers. Most of these inquiries depend for the father's occupation on the son's recollection, and this may be faulty, or biased; and even where the father's occupation is taken from the son's birth certificate, it may not be the most representative of the occupations he followed at different times of life. But inquiries made in different countries and different generations show results so strikingly similar that we cannot call their main findings in question.

We can illustrate them from a British and an American inquiry.

Glass and Hall (1953) studied a sample of 3,700 males in England and Wales in 1949. They used a grouping of occupations into 7 'status categories' worked out by Hall and Caradog Jones (1950) as agreeing with what seemed to be a consensus about the social standing of some leading occupations, and the grounds on which that standing appeared to be attributed, namely length of education and training required, and administrative responsibility and authority. Their Category 1 'includes all occupations calling for highly specialized experience and frequently . . . a long period of education or training'. The distinction between their Categories 2 and 3 is that Category 2 'includes persons responsible for initiating and/or implementing policy . . . while those in Category 3 have no such responsibility but they may have some degree of authority over others'. The skilled manual work of Category 5 is distinguished from the semi-skilled of Category 6 by its requiring 'special training, adaptability and responsibility for the process and material'. From the findings of Glass and Hall, indexes of affinity between these classes have been calculated in the same way as for Table 6.2, but here, in Fig. 6.1, they are displayed graphically.

Our first interest is in the diagonal of cells, Category 1 sons of Category 1 fathers and so on, which shows the extent to which the entrants to a given stratum of occupations came from the sons of fathers in that stratum—the extent to which those sons could be seen as advantaged by access to their fathers' level of occupation if this was a high one, or restricted to it if it was low. A first glance at the Figure shows that it is in these cells that the index is at its highest, save only that the sons of fathers in Category 3—'inspectional, supervisory and other non-manual, higher grade'—showed slightly more proclivity to enter the occupations of Category 2—'managerial and executive'—than those of their fathers' category. The tendency to self-recruitment, that is, for the categories to form 'non-competing groups', is at its strongest in the two top categories—in Category 1, indeed, the index is much too high to be contained within the Figure as drawn. The tendency is also marked in the two lowest categories; but the sons of fathers in the intermediate categories—generally the administrative, technical, and clerical, with the skilled manual—were spread more widely over other destinations. If we illustrate these tendencies by figures, we must remember that a given amount of mobility will appear as a higher or lower figure according as our categories are narrow or broad, the likelihood of any move being recorded as a change of category being greater or less accordingly. But if we bear in mind that the present figures relate to a 7-category framework, we can use them for internal comparisons. Table 6.4 shows that the actual proportion of sons in occupations of the same category as their fathers' ranged from less than 19 per cent where the fathers were in Category 3 to over 47 per cent where the fathers were in Category 5. In the whole sample, 35 per cent were in the same category as their fathers.

This means that 65 per cent had moved upwards or downwards; in fact, about 30 per cent moved upwards, and 35 per cent downwards. Figure 6.1,

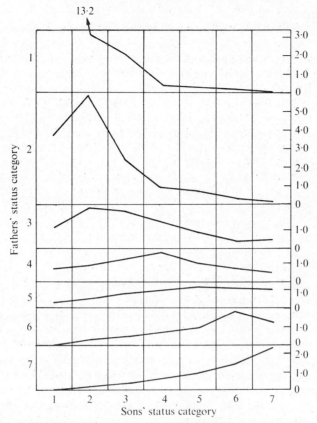

Fig. 6.1. Indexes of affinity in England and Wales, 1949.

England and Wales, 1949: Indexes of affinity between 'status categories' of fathers and of sons, in sample of 3,700 sons. *Source*: calculated from Glass & Hall (1953), Table 2.

Status categories: 1. Professional and high admin; 2. Managerial and executive; 3. Inspectional, supervisory and other non-manual, higher grade; 4. Inspectional, supervisory and other non-manual, lower grade; 5. Skilled manual and routine non-manual; 6. Semi-skilled manual; 7. Unskilled manual.

with the curves falling away on either side of the peak, shows that most of the movement was short-distance, and that generally the greater the distance, the less was the proclivity to move either up or down. Of all those who moved, more than half went only into the category immediately above or below their fathers'. No son of any father in Categories 6 and 7 rose to Category 1, though a few of the sons of fathers in that category did come down to 6 and 7. That we can speak of distance as we have done here, and that the proclivity to move was generally lower the greater the distance to be traversed, validates the initial stratification.

An ingenious way of assessing the extent of the mobility found in this sample, by comparison with what we should have found if the father's status

Table 6.4

Indexes of Affinity in England and Wales 1949

England and Wales, 1949: proportions of sons in sample who entered same category of occupations as their fathers, with implied indexes of affinity in these cases between father's occupation and son's.

	Category of occupations						
	1	*2*	*3*	*4*	*5*	*6*	*7*
1. Proportion of sons with fathers in given category who entered the same category as their fathers	0·388	0·267	0·188	0·212	0·473	0·312	0·274
2. Proportion of all sons who entered given category	0·029	0·045	0·094	0·131	0·409	0·170	0·121
3. Index of affinity, (1) ÷ (2)	13·17	5·87	1·99	1·62	1·16	1·84	2·26

Source: Calculated from Glass and Hall (1953), Table 2.

category had no influence on his son's, was developed by Prais (1955). He began by asking what would happen to a family line—father, son, grandson, and so on—if the proportion of sons becoming occupied in their father's category remained the same in each succeeding generation. In Table 6.4, for instance, we see that the proportion of sons with fathers in Category 1 who themselves became occupied in that category was 0·388, which we may round to 0·4. If we begin with 100 men in that category, and suppose the proportion 0·4 to hold throughout, the numbers of lineal descendants in Category 1 in successive generations will be

     100   40   16   6·4 . . . . .

—a geometric progression that sums to 167. This is the total number of men belonging to 100 family lines who will be in Category 1: so the average family will spend less than two generations—1·67 on the present assumption—in Category 1. Column (1) of Table 6.5 shows the average length of stay within a given category, calculated in this way, for each of Glass and Hall's seven categories.

These figures can be compared with those we should obtain, by the same method, if we supposed that every son, no matter what his father's category might be, had an equal chance of entering any category. On this supposition the chance of any son entering his father's category would be the proportion of men in that category in the sons' generation. Hence col. (2) of Table 6.5. Column (3) compares the average lengths of stay found from the actual sample with those obtained on the assumption that there is no intergenerational link. The strength of the link is outstanding in the top two categories, and marked in the bottom two.

Table 6.5
Length of Stay of a Family Line in a Status Category

England and Wales, 1949: average number of generations in which any one family line will be found in the same status category, on the assumptions (col. (1)) that the proportions of sons entering their father's category are those of row 1 of Table 6.4, and (col. (2)) that the numbers of sons in different categories are the same as for Table 6.4, but the father's category has no influence on his son's.

Status category	Average no. of generations. Intergenerational link as in actual sample (1)	supposed nil (2)	(1) ÷ (2) (3)
1. Professional and high administrative	1·63	1·02	1·60
2. Managerial and executive	1·36	1·04	1·31
3. Inspectional, supervisory and other non-manual, higher grade	1·23	1·10	1·12
4. Ditto, lower grade	1·27	1·15	1·10
5. Skilled manual and routine non-manual	1·90	1·69	1·12
6. Semi-skilled manual	1·45	1·22	1·19
7. Unskilled manual	1·38	1·15	1·20

Source: Prais (1955), Table 3.

Our American illustration of findings on intergenerational mobility comes from a study by Blau and Duncan (1967). The U.S. Bureau of the Census conducts a monthly Current Population Survey (C.P.S.), which in March 1962 was used to obtain particulars of the occupation as well as of a number of other characteristics, including income and years of schooling, of persons in the households drawn in the sample. Among these some 20,700 men aged 20–64 provided further particulars, including father's occupation. The sample figures were then weighted by the relevant proportions, by age and colour, in the U.S. adult male population. The respondents and their fathers were then allocated among the 17 occupational categories, ranked according to median income and median years of schooling as in Table 6.6. From the resultant matrix Blau and Duncan calculated what we have called indexes of affinity, and they call 'ratios of observed frequencies to frequencies expected on the assumption of independence', or 'mobility ratios'. Some of these are displayed in Fig. 6.2.

The main features of the movement between generations so revealed are the same as those found in the British sample—the son being most drawn towards his father's occupation, and after that towards the occupations on either side of his father's in the rank order, with the affinity between father's occupation and son's decreasing with the distance between the two in that order. Again, as in the British sample, this peaking of the index of affinity—as it appears in the Figures—is more marked for the occupational categories at the top and bottom

Table 6.6

Occupations in U.S. Study of Intergenerational Mobility

U.S.A. 1962: 17 occupational categories, ranked according to median income and median years
of schooling, used by Blau and Duncan for classification of particulars of respondent's occupation
and father's occupation obtained by Current Population Survey.

Occupational category	Median income	Median years of schooling
	$ p.a.	
1. Professionals, self-employed	12,048 ⎫	16·4
2. Professionals, salaried	6,842 ⎭	
3. Managers	7,238	12·8
4. Salesmen, other than retail	6,008	13·0
5. Proprietors	5,548	12·1
6. Clerical	5,173	12·5
7. Salesmen, retail	3,044	12·3
8. Craftsmen, manufacturing ⎫	5,482	11·2
9. Craftsmen, other ⎭		
10. Craftsmen, construction	5,265	10·2
11. Operatives, manufacturing	4,636	10·0
12. Operatives, other	4,206	10·4
13. Service	3,233	10·3
14. Labourers, manufacturing ⎫	2,189	8·9
15. Labourers, other ⎭		
16. Farmers	1,992	8·8
17. Farm labourers	488	8·3

Source: Blau and Duncan (1967), Table 2.1.

of the rank order than for those in between. But because we have 17 categories
for these materials, instead of 7 for the British, we shall not be surprised to find
more exceptions here. In four categories the peak is not in the diagonal, that is,
the occupation towards which the son is most drawn is not his father's: the
clericals' sons, for instance, tend most strongly to become managers, and the
manufacturing operatives' sons to enter an occupation actually lower in the
rank order than their fathers', and become labourers in manufacturing. But in
contrast with the British sample, it is movement upward that predominates
here. One particular manifestation of this predominance is seen in the effect of
the boundary between white-collar and blue-collar which lies between
categories 7 and 8, and that between blue-collar and farm which lies between
categories 15 and 16: both these boundaries are found to impede downward
mobility, but not upwards.

A French inquiry of 1964 (Praderie & Passagez 1966; Praderie, Salais, &
Passagez 1967) into the father's occupation and the current occupation of a
large sample of men and women shows just the same pattern of intergenerational mobility for men as Figs. 6.1 and 6.2 have illustrated for
England and Wales and for the U.S.A. But the inquiry is specially valuable as a

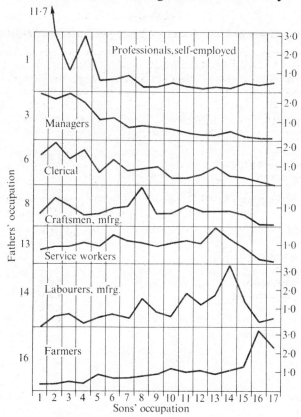

Fig. 6.2. Indexes of affinity in U.S.A., 1962.

U.S.A. 1962: indexes of affinity between occupations of fathers and of sons, in a weighted sample of 20,700 sons. *Source*: Blau & Duncan (1967), Table 2.5.

Occupations:
1. Professionals, self-employed
2. Professionals, salaried
3. Managers
4. Salesmen, other
5. Proprietors
6. Clerical
7. Salesmen, retail

8. Craftsmen, manufacturing
9. Craftsmen, other
10. Craftsmen, construction
11. Operatives, manufacturing
12. Operatives, other
13. Service workers
14. Labourers, manufacturing

15. Labourers, other
16. Farmers
17. Farm labourers

source, rare if not unique, for the intergenerational mobility of women. Some of the findings are illustrated in Fig. 6.3. In calculating these indexes, we have compared the proportion of a given group of women entering a certain occupation with the proportion of all women, not of all persons, in that occupation: so the entry of women to an occupation might be restricted, and indeed restricted arbitrarily, without the restriction appearing in the index of affinity. But with that proviso, what is remarkable is how closely the pattern of the women's indexes resembles that of the men's. The women, for instance, are most drawn

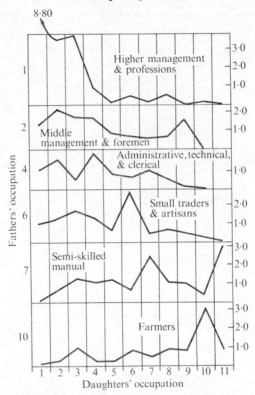

Fig. 6.3. Indexes of affinity for daughters in France, 1964.

France, 1964: indexes of affinity between occupations of fathers and of daughters, in a weighted sample of women aged 15–65 in 1963. *Source*: Praderie, Salais & Passagez (1967), Annexes 2A, 2B.

Occupations:
1. Higher management and professions
2. Middle management and foremen
3. Proprietors of industrial and large wholesale and retail establishments
4. Administrative, technical and clerical
5. Skilled manual

6. Small traders and artisans
7. Semi-skilled manual
8. Others gainfully occupied
9. Labourers
10. Farmers
11. Agricultural labourers

towards their fathers' occupations, and after that to the occupations next above and below their fathers' in the conventional ranking order by extent of education and training and level of earnings. The daughters of fathers in higher management and the professions are more drawn than the sons towards middle management and the category of industrial and commercial proprietors. The daughters of fathers in middle management have less tendency than the sons to move upwards into higher management and the professions. There are other divergences at particular points. But no systematic difference appears.

After reviewing the qualitative evidence for intergenerational mobility in the U.S.S.R., Inkeles (1950) concluded that it was unlikely to be less, and might

Table 6.7

Indexes of Affinity in U.S.S.R.

Kazan, U.S.S.R. 1967: indexes of affinity between five occupational grades, from the occupations of 3,642 children and the heads of their families of origin.

Index of affinity between Grades A and B given by (per cent of children of family heads in grade A themselves occupied in grade B) ÷ (per cent of all children occupied in grade B).

	Occupation of head of family				
Occupation of child	Agricultural and unskilled	Skilled manual	Skilled non-manual	Technicians	Administrative, technological, and professional
Unskilled manual and low-skilled non-manual	1·30	0·91	0·37	0·51	0·17
Skilled manual	1·13	1·11	0·75	0·58	0·40
Skilled non-manual	0·91	1·29	1·10	1·05	0·38
Technicians	1·00	1·00	0·57	1·29	2·14
Administrative, techno-logical, and professional	0·50	0·61	2·07	2·40	3·49

Source: Shkaratan (1973c), Table 4.

well be greater, than in the U.S.A. The numerical data provided by Shkaratan (1973c) from a more recent study of occupied persons in Kazan do not conflict with that conclusion. In Table 6.7 the more numerous grades that Shkaratan details, in somewhat different form for the children and their parents, have been condensed into five; the procedure is rough and in part conjectural, but should serve to present the main features in a form comparable with the findings for other countries. A marked similarity with these appears in the concentration of high values on or near the NW.–SE. diagonal: we notice especially the high proportion in which the workers in the highest grade are recruited from the children of parents in that grade. But we also see to what an extent the entrants with an agricultural background were being brought on into all the skilled occupations except the highest grade; how the children of skilled manual parents were entering skilled non-manual occupations; and how the children of skilled non-manuals and technicians were entering the highest grade. These are all marks of high intergenerational mobility. They can be seen as not specific to a Soviet-type economy, but as what we expect to find in any economy that is drawing on great reserves of rural labour for the expansion of industry, and in the development of industry itself is increasing the relative numbers of technicians and professionals generally.

That the similarities we have found so far extend to other countries is indicated by the work of Miller (1960) in collating inquiries of various forms, and drawing from them common measures of the movement upwards and downwards across the line between manual and non-manual occupations.

Table 6.8
International Comparison of Intergenerational Mobility

Inquiries in 13 countries, relating to dates within 1946–57: intergenerational mobility between manual and non-manual occupations.

Inquiry	Date to which inquiry relates	Proportion of sons of manual fathers themselves in non-manual occupations	Proportion of sons of non-manual fathers themselves in manual occupations
		%	%
France I	1948	30·1	20·5
France II	1953	29·6	26·9
U.S.A. I	1946	28·8	19·7
U.S.A. II	1956	28·7	22·6
Sweden		25·5	27·7
England and Wales	1949	24·8	42·1
Denmark	1954–55	24·1	36·8
Japan	1955	23·7	29·7
Norway	1954	23·2	28·6
West Germany	1955	20·0	29·0
Netherlands	1954	19·6	43·2
Hungary	1949	14·5	27·5
Puerto Rico		14·3	42·7
Finland	1951?	11	24
Italy		8·5	34·4

Source: Miller (1960), Tables I and II and Statistical Appendix.

These are shown in Table 6.8. The terms 'upwards' and 'downwards' can be used here only in a conventional sense, for not a few manual occupations overlap the non-manual in point of pay, and it is between the skilled manual and the lower white-collared occupations that most of the movement across the line occurs. Differences of classification in this region may account for some of the apparent differences in mobility. What is striking for the most part, however, is the extent of similarity: in nine of the countries the percentage representing upward mobility lies in the approximate range 20–30 per cent, and that representing downward mobility lies in the same range in seven of these countries and in two others. But no systematic relation appears between the extent of the two sorts of movement country by country, and downward movements of over 40 per cent stand out in England and Wales, the Netherlands, and Puerto Rico, with Denmark not far below. Much here is unexplained; but the findings have made a marked impression by their showing for the most part far less difference between countries than had been expected from the apparent diversity of their societies. In particular, the U.S.A. does not stand out as 'the land of opportunity' in contrast with European countries.

We can see in general terms that the movements we have been looking at here are the outcome of three forces. First, there are *shifts in demand* for the work of different occupations, shifts whose impact tends to increase the number of jobs in some occupations and decrease it in others. Second, *differential fertility and mortality* as between occupations bring it about that, supposing every child to follow an occupation in the same grade as his parents', the relative numbers in different grades would change, and if they are not to change in that way, there will have to be some movement of children into grades other than their parents'. A third factor consists in the tendency of persons 'to find their own level', through the ability of some to make their way into occupations higher in the scale than their parents', and the inability of others to get or keep jobs at their parents' occupational level: this we may call the *sorting* factor.

It is hard, if not impossible, to divide a given flow into components corresponding with these three forces. Supposing the data were available from which we could calculate the effects year by year of differential fertility and mortality: we should then know how many persons a given occupation must receive from other occupations or send out to them if it was to keep its own relative numbers unchanged, but we could not infer that a corresponding part of the actual flows, no more and no less, arose from this sort of attraction or impulsion. Those who are counted as having entered to make good a gap in the numbers in an occupation might have arrived there by reason of their personal capability, gap or no gap. Though an excess of children over deaths and retirements, for example, does exert a pressure towards outward movement, there is no presumption that this pressure will effect the movement of precisely the calculated excess: how many move and to what destination depends also on the capabilities of the children and on the state of demand elsewhere—that is, on the third and first of the factors mentioned above. Nor can we separate the workings of these two factors. How many persons a given extension of demand for an occupation draws into it will depend on whether competition for applicants raises the relative pay much or little, which in turn will depend on the supply, in the short and the longer run, of persons with the needed capability—that is, on the sorting factor. An extension of demand for a low-paid occupation will hardly, by the mere creation of vacancies, draw in more of the children of fathers in higher-paid occupations than would enter it otherwise: a more likely effect is a raising of the relative pay of the occupation as a whole. We cannot take the change in the relative numbers in an occupation as a measure of the shift in demand for it.

Nevertheless there is one way in which we can make a rough estimate of the contribution of the sorting factor, relatively to the joint contribution of shifts in demand and differential fertility and mortality. This estimate depends on the assumption that the sorting factor makes equally for movement in both directions. Over the population as a whole, that is to say, upward moves by children whose capabilities fit them for levels above their parents' will just offset the downward moves by those whose capabilities fall short of the requirements of their parents' level. This is what would come about if the distribution of capabilities among the children at each level were normal, with those who were to various extents above the average balancing those who were to corresponding extents below it. On this assumption, then, we can say that it is in the nature of the sorting factor to make no change in the relative numbers at different levels. But the opposite is true of shifts in demand, which tend to change the relative number of jobs at different levels; and of differential fertility and mortality, which tend to push persons out from or draw them into a given level without any offsetting flow in the opposite direction. It is thus in the nature of these two factors to set up one-way movements that change the relative numbers at different levels. (Cases are conceivable in which the movements they set up in this way offset one another, leaving the relative numbers unchanged. The most likely is a shortfall of children at one level being made good by the 'immigration' of an equal surplus of children occurring at other levels. But this apart, cases of these factors operating without any change coming about in relative numbers are unlikely.) If, then, we found in a particular instance that the relative numbers at different levels were the same in the children's generation as in their parents', we could infer with a fair degree of probability that there had been no shifts in demand or differences of fertility and mortality, and we could ascribe the whole of the observed mobility to the sorting factor.

But usually the relative numbers change considerably between generations, and how in that case can we separate the effects of the sorting factor? It has been suggested that we can still do this, if we adjust the figures hypothetically, making the smallest changes in their internal proportions that will yield unchanged relative numbers. Suppose, for example, that in a society with only two levels, X and Y, the fathers' occupational distribution and the sons' were as in Table A. 30 of the fathers, but only 20 of the sons, were occupied at the X level; 40 of the fathers, but 50 of the sons, were occupied at the Y level. The intergenerational mobility is made up of the movement of 20 sons of X fathers to the Y level, and 10 sons of Y fathers to the X level. Suppose now that while keeping unchanged the proportions of the sons occupied at the X level who had X fathers and Y fathers, we raised the total number of such sons by a half, from 20 to 30, to equalize it with the number of fathers at the X level; and suppose we scaled down the number of sons at the Y level from 50 to 40, on the same principle. The result would be as in Table B. Here the distribution of the sons is in the required proportions, but in making it so we have upset the original distribution of the fathers. So the next step will be to multiply the X row through by 30/31, and the Y row by 40/39; and so on, until the remaining discrepancies are negligible. If we were prepared to accept those of Table B as already negligible, we could see that Table as recording intergenerational mobility made up of the movement of 16 sons of X fathers to the Y level, and 15 sons of Y fathers to the X level. This we should ascribe to the sorting factor. The difference between this and the greater mobility recorded in Table A we should ascribe in unknown proportions to the other two factors, shifts in demand and differential fertility and mortality.

Table A

		Sons		
		X	Y	Σ
Fathers	X	10	20	30
	Y	10	30	40
	Σ	20	50	70

Table B

		Sons		
		X	Y	Σ
Fathers	X	15	16	31
	Y	15	24	39
	Σ	30	40	70

Hazelrigg (1974) has applied this form of analysis to Miller's survey data for eight countries, together with more recent surveys for another four—Australia, France, Italy, and U.S.A. In each country he has taken the intergenerational movements between only three levels of occupation. Table 6.9 shows the proportions of the sons of fathers at each level who themselves became occupied at a different level, together with the proportions who are estimated to have so moved after elimination of the movements hypothetically attributed to the intergenerational change in the relative numbers in occupations, brought about by shifts in demand and differential fertility and mortality.

The effects of that elimination are seen to be that in all the countries except Israel the downward movement is increased, while to a much greater extent the upward movement is decreased.

The movement with which we are left is that attributable to the sorting factor. We see that it is generally large, in comparison with the movement attributable to the other factors. Is it large in comparison with our expectations? We find an outward movement, taking upward and downward together, and excluding Hungary, of from 28 to 30 per cent of sons of fathers at a given level, on the average of the three levels. This movement we take to arise from the matching of capability and temperament with job requirements. That so much movement of this kind occurs makes it clear that these societies are far from being divided into castes; but some observers may point to the other side of the medal—that from 61 to 72 per cent of the sons remain at their fathers' level—and see in this, even when the groups are as wide as they are here, an indication that some who have the ability to rise are denied the opportunity of doing so, and some are kept up who ought to go down. There can be a similar difference of views as to whether the fact of eleven countries, in some ways so

The Inequality of Pay

Table 6.9

International Comparison of Adjusted Intergenerational Mobility

Twelve countries, sample surveys at dates within 1949–64: intergenerational mobility between three groups of occupations—non-manual, manual, and farm, (a) as found in a sample survey, (b) after adjustment of (a) by Hazelrigg's method, to remove that part of (a) which is deemed to be linked with intergenerational changes in the relative numbers in the occupational groups.

| | | Percentage of sons moving out of their father's group of occupations | | | |
| | | (a) as found in sample survey | | (b) after adjustment of (a) to remove part linked with change in relative numbers | |
Country	Date of survey	Upwards	Downwards	Upwards	Downwards
Sweden	1950	38	9	20	19
Australia	1965	29	13	20	19
U.S.A.	1962	33	11	19	18
Norway	1957	33	11	19	19
W. Germany	1955	27	12	17	18
Puerto Rico	1954	41	10	17	17
Japan	1955	29	11	16	17
France	1964	28	12	16	15
Yugoslavia	1962	38	7	15	14
Italy	1963–64	29	8	14	14
Israel	1962	8	30	14	14
Hungary	1949	24	5	11	11

Source: adapted from Hazlerigg (1974), Table 2.5.

different, all lying within the range of 28 to 39 per cent is more remarkable than their being spread over a range of that extent.

The second effect, the reduction of the upward movement and increase of the downward, shows how much of the movements found in the survey depended upon the expansion of the non-manual group and the contraction of the farm group. Israel is an exception, because here many immigrant sons of non-farm fathers went into farming. Since the samples being all of father-and-son allow of no intergenerational change in total numbers, the numbers entering and leaving each group, in the adjusted systems, must exactly offset each other. If the adjusted rates of upward and downward movement in Table 6.9 are not always equal, that is because some movements are across one boundary only and others across two boundaries.

6.3. Changes in intergenerational mobility over time

What evidence we have for the course of mobility over time does not, at least so far as it extends, bear out the expectation that intergenerational mobility will have increased with the widening of the labour market and the extension of education. No inquiry has found evidence of any significant change in the extent and pattern of mobility. Glass and Hall (1955) examined the experience of successive cohorts of sons in England and Wales, and found no course of change between those born before 1890 and in the 1920s. An inquiry by Ginsberg (1929) covering the parents and grand-parents of persons occupied in 1927–28, mainly in England, found some indication of an increase in upward mobility, but none of any change in downward. Blau and Duncan (1967), on a review of recent retrospective studies in the U.S.A. and the division of their own respondents into four cohorts, the earliest those born in 1897–1906, found no indication, at least on the face of the evidence, of changing mobility: 'What is most striking in a regression framework', they say (p. 113), 'is the essential invariance of the father–son correlation over a period of nearly 40 years.'

A comparison of the mobility shown by the occupations of father and son recorded on marriage licence applications in Indianapolis in 1905–12 and 1938–41 (Rogoff 1953) found that though there were changes in the mobility rates attaching to particular categories of father's occupation, the variance of those rates was similar in the two periods, and the over-all mobility rates were the same—in both, 'about 70 per cent of the men were in occupations different from those of their fathers' (p. 107). The longest retrospect is for Copenhagen, where Rishøj (1971) used the military enrolment lists to obtain particulars of the occupations of the fathers of males born in 1838–42, whom he followed up to find their own occupations at ages 22–26. The intergenerational mobility revealed here he compared with that shown by particulars recorded in marriage licences in 1901, and again with that found for young men in the national sample studied by Svalastoga (1959). Over his span of a hundred years Rishøj found that 'there has been no increase in the social mobility, and that in a preindustrial or early industrial community of Copenhagen we find the same rate of mobility as in the modern industrial Copenhagen' (p. 139).

In all, we find a remarkable degree of similarity between a number of countries in recent years in the extents to which sons enter the same category of occupations as their father's, or move into categories adjacent or more distant in rank order, whether above their fathers' category or below it. Such evidence as we have for this sort of mobility in earlier years has revealed no course of change. We seem to be in the presence of a social process of much generality and persistence in the Western economies. But the broad lines of our comparisons may conceal differences which though relatively small quantitatively are of considerable significance in their effect on the perceived openness of the societies concerned. The chances of long-distance movement, particularly from 'humble origins' into the highest category or 'élite', deserve separate notice as being possibly of that kind.

6.4. The extent of intergenerational movement into and out of the top grade

One common feature noticed above was that self-recruitment—the entrants to a grade being found from the children of parents in that grade—was high for the top grade, indeed often very much higher than for any other grade. The extent to which the grade of highest pay and status is in practice accessible from below has great social significance: there might be a great deal of intergenerational movement between manual and clerical occupations and middle management, but the society might still figure in many people's minds as one of entrenched privilege if few people whose parents were not in the top grade themselves achieved entry to it, while those who were in that grade could rely on most of their children succeeding them in it. Let us look into the evidence more closely at this point.

It would be well if we could begin by comparing the extent to which the top grade was recruited from lower grades in different countries. But the difficulty is that the bounds of the top grade, or 'élite', have been drawn very differently in different studies. In those assembled by Miller (1960), for example, the élite made up 13·8 per cent of all occupied males in Puerto Rico but only 2·8 per cent in Italy; and it seems very likely that the greater part of such differences as these arises from a difference in definition rather than in the actual structure. The broader the definition of the élite, the greater the possibility of moving up

Table 6.10

International Comparison of Intergenerational Mobility into the Élite

Two groups of countries, in which the definition of 'the élite' includes similar proportions of all occupied males, at dates between 1945 and 1960: facility of movement into élite occupations by the sons of fathers in manual and middle-class occupations.

	Per cent of all men in élite	*Index of affinity for sons of* manual fathers	*middle-class fathers*
Group I			
U.S.A.	11·60	0·85	1·80
Netherlands	11·08	0·60	1·04
Japan	11·74	0·59	1·29
Group II			
Sweden	6·66	0·53	2·72
France I (Bresard)	8·53	0·41	1·46
Great Britain	7·49	0·30	1·15
France II (Desabie)	6·12	0·25	1·71

Source: Blau and Duncan (1967), Table 12.1, p. 434.

The *élite* were described in the original studies as 'professional, technical and kindred' for the U.S.A.; for the other countries they are made up of 'the occupational grouping with the highest standing'—containing, for example, professional and high administrative employments, manufacturers and independent professionals—and 'the grouping with somewhat less standing but of distinctly higher standing than other occupational groupings'—containing, for example, managerial and executive occupations, and medium grade technicians (Miller 1960).

Manual: 'blue-collar and farm labourers'.

Middle class: 'white-collar excluding the élite'.

into it will seem to be, partly because the wider the terrain the more places there are to fill, partly because the part of the terrain brought in when the definition is broadened is in any case easier of access. The first of these factors is cancelled out when we calculate an index of affinity; but not the second.

It happens, however, that the proportion of all males in the élite was much the same—between 11 and 12 per cent—in studies of the U.S.A. the Netherlands, and Japan; and also much the same through smaller—between 6 and $8\frac{1}{2}$ per cent—in studies of France, Sweden, and Great Britain. Table 6.10 enables comparisons to be made within each of these groups. Comparisons between them would not be significant, unless allowance were made for the difference between them in the proportionate size of the élite; when this is done, most though not all of the apparent greater mobility of the first group disappears. The index of affinity of 0·60 for the sons of manual fathers in the Netherlands means, it will be remembered, that the proportion of such sons making their way into the élite, as here defined, was 0·60 of what it would have been if such sons had been as likely to enter the élite as any other grade. It is no surprise that the index is much higher throughout for the sons of middle class than for those of manual fathers. By the test of both indexes, the élite was most accessible in the U.S.A. among the first three countries, and in Sweden in the other group. But the figures for the U.S.A. are subject to this qualification, that they come from a span in which access to the élite was being facilitated by its doubling in size, as a proportion of the whole occupied population, within one generation. When this happens there can be a high rate of upward mobility into the élite at the same time as a high level of self-recruitment, and so it was in the U.S.A. (Fox & Miller 1966).

We see that in none of these countries was the top grade an enclave, but again we find that those who made their way into it were proportionately fewer, the lower their parents' grade. This is brought out by Table 6.11, which

Table 6.11

Comparative Mobility into Élite, by Father's Grade

Japan (1955), Netherlands (1965), U.S.A. (1956): proportion of sons of fathers in given occupational grade, themselves entering élite occupations, as relative to proportion of sons of élite fathers, themselves entering élite occupations.

Occupational grade of father	Japan	Netherlands	U.S.A.
Élite	100	100	100
Middle class	39	22	37
Manual			
skilled	21	20	22
semi-skilled	17	6	6
unskilled	18	5	9

Source: Fox and Miller (1966), Table 7.

for each of the countries in our first group compares the proportions of the sons
of middle class and of skilled, semi-skilled, and unskilled manual workers who
themselves enter the top grade, with the proportion of sons of fathers in that
grade who themselves become occupied in it. The comparative facility of movement into the top grade is generally lower, the lower the father's grade, but it is
noticeable how little difference appears between the sons of the three grades of
manual worker in Japan, and between the sons of skilled manual workers and
the middle class in the Netherlands.

There is some long-range downward movement from the top grades as well
as long-range upward movement into it. The studies already cited have found
that the proportion of the sons of fathers in élite occupations who themselves
entered manual occupations was 15 per cent in the U.S.A., 18 per cent in Great
Britain, 24 per cent in the Netherlands, and 27 per cent in Japan (Fox & Miller
1966, Table 5). In France, however, though half of all the sons born between
the First and Second World Wars to fathers in the élite (the 'classe dirigeante')
themselves entered occupations of lower grade, they mostly worked in middle
management and white-collar jobs; hardly any became manual workers (Bertaux 1970). A dam across downward movement appears here that has been
observed as lying along the boundary between white-collar and blue-collar occupations in the U.S.A. This boundary and that between blue-collar and farm occupations 'restrict downward mobility between virtually any two categories below
the level expected on the assumption of indepence [that is, the assumption that
movement into all categories is equally likely] although they permit upward
mobility in excess of this level' (Blau & Duncan 1967, p. 420).

Table 6.12
Comparative Intergenerational Mobility into
Upper Non-manual Occupations

Eight countries, sample surveys at dates between 1950 and 1965: proportions of sons of fathers
in given groups of occupations, themselves occupied in the upper non-manual group.

| Country | Date of survey | Per cent of sons of fathers in given group of occupations, themselves occupied in upper non-manual group | | | |
		Upper non-manual	Lower non-manual	Manual	Farm
Puerto Rico	1954	35	24	11	10
Australia	1965	43	32	17	12
W. Germany	1955	54	9	2	2
Sweden	1950	55	18	5	2
France	1964	57	41	19	11
U.S.A.	1962	59	44	22	11
Israel	1962	63	24	10	15
Italy	1963–64	70	24	12	5

Source: Hazelrigg (1974), Table 6.

For eight of the twelve countries in his study already referred to, Hazlerigg (1974) has separated the upper non-manual from the lower non-manual group of occupations, and taking these together with the manual and the farm groups has calculated the proportions of the sons of fathers in each group who themselves entered upper non-manual occupations. Table 6.12 presents some of his findings. We have seen that the extent of movement into the top group depends in part on its relative size, which may be a matter of definition that varies from one survey to another. With any definition the chances of movement vary with the expansion of the relative numbers of the upper group so defined. A third factor is the extent of assortment, of how far the sons of fathers in the top group, themselves lacking the required capability, have to move down, leaving places to be filled by those who have that capability and are the sons of fathers in other groups. In making comparison between countries in the extent of upward movement shown in Table 6.11 we must bear these considerations in mind: the first of them, for instance, may account for the outstanding figure for Puerto Rico. Of the rest, Australia shows the greatest movement into the top group, with 57 per cent of those occupied in it being the sons of fathers in lower groups. The corresponding percentages for the remaining countries lie between 30 (in Italy) and 46 (in West Germany). In all countries except Australia the proportion of the sons of lower non-manual fathers who themselves entered upper non-manual occupations was at least twice as great as the corresponding proportion for the sons of manual fathers; and this last proportion was bigger than that for the sons of farming fathers, except in Israel and West Germany.

For more detailed accounts of movement into the top grade we turn to particular studies in France and Great Britain.

Table 6.13 gives particulars of the socio-economic origins of those among a sample of 27,000 French men and women who were occupied in higher management and the liberal professions in both of the years 1959 and 1964. It is perplexing that such high proportions of these persons' fathers were classified as 'not gainfully occupied'. If we exclude the sons and daughters of these 'inactifs', and consider only the remainder, we find that about 26 per cent of the men's fathers, and 37 per cent of the women's, were themselves in higher management or the liberal professions. Such, then, was the extent of self-recruitment, of which the obverse is, that nearly three-quarters of the men in that top grade in 1959, 1964 (within our restricted sample), and more than 60 per cent of the women, had come from homes where the father was in a lower grade. The chief contributory grades were the small-scale traders and artisans, middle management and foremen, and the white-collar employees. Manual workers made up 9·5 per cent of the fathers of the men, and 6·2 per cent of those of the women. In all, the impression is one of considerable upward mobility, but from the lower middle class rather than from the manuals. No doubt this was helped by an expansion of the relative number of top-grade posts after 1945.

Another view of the extent of long-range mobility in France is afforded by

Table 6.13
Socio-economic Origins of French Men and Women in High-grade Occupations

France: occupations of fathers of sample of men and women who in both 1959 and 1964 were occupied in higher management and the liberal professions.

	Men	Women
Higher management and the liberal professions as per cent of all occupied	5·7	2·0

	Fathers of	
	Men	Women
	%	%
Of the fathers of the men and women occupied in higher management and the liberal professions, the percentages classified as 'inactifs' were	17·8	26·4
Of the remaining fathers, the percentages in given occupations were:		
Higher management and the liberal professions	25·9	36·7
Middle management and foremen	16·8	12·1
White collar	9·4	12·9
Skilled manual workers	6·3	4·2
Semi-skilled manual workers, miners, fishermen	1·8	1·2
Unskilled manual workers	0·7	0·8
Agricultural wage-earners	0·7	—
Industrials and large-scale traders	8·3	9·3
Small traders and artisans	17·6	14·1
Farmers	7·8	5·8
Other occupations	4·6	2·9
	100·0	100·0

Source: Praderie, Salais, and Passagez (1967).

starting at the other end. Of nearly 2 million sons born to manual workers between the First and Second World Wars, about 70 per cent became manual workers themselves, and 23 per cent became technicians or entered white-collar occupations or lower management; 5 per cent reached higher management (Bertaux 1970). The 70 per cent compares with an estimate of 75 per cent for Great Britain (Stacey 1968).

A number of studies of the social origins of British managers since 1950 show a different extent of mobility according as they consider top management or other grades of management, and big firms or other sizes of firm. A study covering 27 big manufacturing companies, each with more than 10,000 employees, but confined to grades of management above foreman but below the board, found that by the test of education more than half came from manual or lower-middle-class homes—20 per cent had attended only elementary schools, and a further 33 per cent had not gone beyond an ordinary secondary school—not a grammar school (Acton Society Trust 1956). The finding was very different in an inquiry confined to the directors of large companies: of the minority who responded, nearly two-thirds were the sons of businessmen, and only 8 per cent came from manual or lower-middle-class homes (Copeman 1955).

The difference between the top and other grades of management is brought out by the two studies from which Table 6.14 is drawn. In both the proportion of top managers whose homes were in the highest of the Registrar-General's five socio-economic classes was half as great again as that of all managers, and the proportion of directors was nearly treble in one sample, double in the other.

Table 6.14
Socio-economic Origins of British Managers

Great Britain, sample of 646 managers and directors in 28 firms, mostly in textiles and engineering in the vicinity of Manchester, 1958; and sample of 804 managers and directors in private and nationalized industries, 1966: distribution by class of father.

Father's class, by Registrar-General's classification	1958			1966		
	Managers			Managers		
	All	Top	Directors	All	Top	Directors
	%	%	%	%	%	%
I. Professional etc.	20	34	57	8	12	17
II. Intermediate	28	38	30	35	33	44
III. Skilled manual	44	25	13	44	41	25
IV. Semi-skilled manual	6	2	—	11	12	12
V. Unskilled manual	2	1	—	2	2	2
	100	100	100	100	100	100

Source: Stacey (1968), after Clements (1958) and Clark (1966).

The size of firm and the mass of capital required account for the difference found by Erickson (1959) between the steel and hosiery industries. In 1865–1925 nine-tenths of the leaders in steel came from business, land-owning, or professional families, though by 1953 the proportion had fallen to near six-tenths, as more came up from the homes of clerks, traders, and skilled manual workers. In hosiery, the leaders were drawn much more throughout from families already in the industry and from the homes at the lower socio-economic levels.

That of the two samples in Table 6.14 Clark's shows much more upward mobility has been attributed to his sample containing more firms which of their nature used more scientists and technologists (Stacey 1968). As industry generally comes to use more specialists who must have had advanced education and training, the upward mobility of those who mount the educational ladder is increased, but those who do not mount it have less chance of rising. Stacey cites the experience of a steel firm, reported by Scott et al. (1956): in the early

1950s more than a third of its top managers came from manual homes, but technical development had doubled the proportion of professionally qualified managers between 1935 and 1954, and it was becoming more difficult to rise from the shop floor.

Where high educational attainment is a prerequisite for entry to a profession, long-range occupational mobility depends upon the proportion of children in manual homes who have the ability and motivation to attain university honours, and an effective opportunity to follow courses leading to them. Kelsall (1955) found that of entrants by open competition to the administrative class of the British Civil Service, 7 per cent came from manual homes in 1929, but 27 per cent in 1949–52.

The various studies cited in this and the preceding section do not enable us to answer the question whether occupational mobility in Western societies is big or small. That question implies a standard of size, perhaps 'perfect mobility' as a limiting case. We might think of this as attained in a society in which every person was able to reach the 'highest' occupation that he or she was capable of following; but we do not know how much intergenerational mobility that would call for, in successive generations, or how far mobility in existing societies falls short of it. That it does fall some way short we can be sure. The evidence we have surveyed shows that the present extent of intergenerational mobility in Western societies makes it a factor of the first importance for the efficient use of labour, and probably also for the acceptability of the structure of society to its members; but the prospects of a child's advancement are still closely linked with its parents' class.

6.5. Review and discussion

(a) We have been concerned with the effect of the class structure upon relative pay in so far as that structure affects the supply of labour to different occupations. Is the pay of those who follow certain occupations high because others who are potentially just as able to follow them are kept out by inability to acquire the needed education, training, and life-style? The aspect of class that has concerned us here is therefore the effect of being born into a family of a given class on the occupation that the child will enter. Accordingly we envisaged classes as groups of occupations such that the children of parents working in any occupation in the group were more likely to enter an occupation in the group than any outside it.

(b) We took it on trust that this cohesion of occupations was associated with certain features of life-style, and it is by these in practice that occupations have been assigned to social classes or socio-economic groups. We could then see whether the pattern of intergenerational mobility between classes of occupations formed in that way was consistent with the concept of class in (a). We found that it was, in the sense that children were more likely to enter an occupation in their father's class than in any other, and also that the farther removed in either direction an occupation was from the father's class in the conventional class structure, the less likely in general the children were to enter it.

(c) The element of self-recruitment, i.e. the proportion of those in a given grade whose fathers were themselves in that grade, is highest in the top classes. But there is still a substantial movement into those classes. This movement is subject to the general rule that the numbers moving vary inversely with the social distance moved, though with the exception that a relatively high proportion of the sons of independent tradesmen and small employers move to the top.

(d) The pattern of intergenerational mobility appears to be much the same in a number of countries, including the U.S.S.R. What evidence there is for past years indicates that at least until a recent date the changes in the pattern have been small. These findings suggest that the pattern depends upon properties of society or human nature that are not greatly affected by differences in educational opportunity, standard of living, social philosophy, or economic organization.

(e) Downward intergenerational mobility is of the same substantial order as upward—indeed it must be so save in so far as the relative numbers in the different classes change between the generations. It also obeys the same rule as upward mobility—the numbers making a given move vary inversely with the social distance moved. We may therefore expand the reference to persistent 'properties of society or human nature' in (d) above by observing that the parents' class delimits the span of social distance that most of their children will move through, but that which children move, in which direction and how far, depends on factors and processes that operate in much the same way in all classes, to differentiate children. In the following chapters we shall explore this combination of delimitation by class with individual differentiation.

7

Social class, mental ability, and education

In the last chapter we have considered social class in so far as it is defined by life-chances: we have brought out the extent to which young persons' chances of attaining a given occupational level are linked with their parents' occupations. We shall now examine the ways in which this link is forged.

7.1. The association between occupation and I.Q.

A number of inquiries in the U.K. and the U.S.A. have found a consistent and positive association between the level of an occupation in the socio-economic structure and the average I.Q. of those who work in it. 'The relationship of measured intelligence to socio-economic level is one of the best documented findings in mental-test history' (Tyler 1965, p. 336). In particular, the results have been recorded of tests of mental ability administered to U.S. servicemen in both World Wars, and to British in the Second; we have data from the Second World War, for instance on the civilian occupations and test scores of more than 18,000 white men enlisted into the U.S. Army Air Force (Harrell & Harrell 1945), nearly 90,000 British naval candidates (Vernon 1947, 1949), amd 10,000 British army recruits (Himmelweit & Whitfield 1944). Table 7.1 shows the scores in two of the 'higher' occupations, recorded only in the U.S. data, and in 16 other occupations for which we also have a score in the British Navy or Army data, or both. The occupations are arranged in descending order of the U.S. scores. The scales of the three tests used are different, and our interest is in the rank order of the scores. There are some differences in this between the British orders and the American—the retail tradesman or shop assistant, the electrician, and the labourer, are differently placed in both the British orders; likewise the lorry driver in the British Army order. But that is all. For the rest, the agreement between the three orders, even where gradations are fine, is outstanding.

The score for each occupation, however, is an average of a wide distribution, so that there is much overlap between occupations. The extent of this is illustrated by Fig. 7.1. Here the upper part shows the range of test scores of eight occupations among those followed by men enlisted in the U.S. Army Air Force. These occupations are stacked in order of the median score, from accountants at the top with 128 to farmers at the bottom with 93. The lower the medians, the wider generally is the range. This comes about through the least score becoming smaller as we descend the stack while the top score falls little: the farmers' lowest score, for example, at 24, is 70 points below the accountants' lowest, but the farmers' top score at 147 is only 10 points below the ac-

Table 7.1

Test Scores of Entrants to U.S. and
U.K. Armed Forces

U.S.A. and U.K. during the Second World War: average scores obtained by men in given civilian occupation, in General Classification Test (U.S. Army Air Force), Progressive Matrices Test (British Navy), and paper and pencil intelligence test (British Army).

| U.S. Army Air Force | | British Navy | British Army | Title of occupation if other than in U.S. | |
| | | | | British Navy | British Army |
Occupation	Score	Score	Score		
Accountant	128·1				
Engineer	126·6				
Teacher	122·8		39·68		
Clerk, general	117·5	42·43	28·93	Clerk	Clerk
Tool maker	112·5		20·48		Fitter
Machinist	110·1		20·33		Wood machinist
Sales clerk	109·2	35·27	22·76	Retail tradesman	Shop assistant
Electrician	109·0	30·20	25·78	Electrical worker	
Sheet metal worker	107·5	36·56			
Mechanic	106·3		19·16		
Machine operator	104·8	35·58			
Butcher	102·9		17·73		
Plumber; carpenter, construction; painter, general (weighted average)	100·5	35·07	17·51	Builder	Carpenter; builder's labourer; painter (weighted average)
Truck driver	96·2	33·63	17·94	Driver	Lorry driver
Labourer	95·8	31·85	13·40		
Farmhand	91·4	32·33		Farm worker	
Miner	90·6		14·90		
Teamster	87·7		12·04		

Sources: U.S.A.A.F., Harrell and Harrell (1945); *British Navy*, Vernon (1947); *British Army*, Himmelweit and Whitfield (1944).

countants'. This is a general feature of these distributions: some persons who score high are to be found in almost all occupations, whereas the low scorers are concentrated in the lower part of the structure. The other part of Fig. 7.1 shows the distribution of test scores made in 1943 by British naval candidates coming from two groups of civilian occupations, clerks and labourers, both sorts being composed of men in their forties. Here again the overlap is conspicuous: the modes of the two distributions are far apart, but more than half the clerks scored no more than some of the labourers.

A more comprehensive view of the overlap between grades whose mean

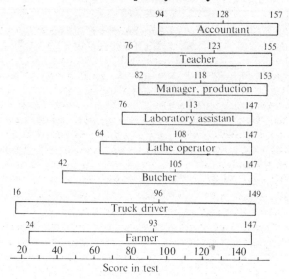

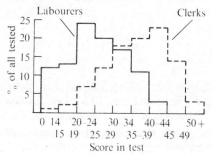

Fig. 7.1. Test scores by occupation.

Fig. 7.1.1. Range and median of scores in General Classification Test of white men from certain civilian occupations enlisted in the U.S. Army Air Force in the Second World War. *Source*: Harrell & Harrell (1945).

Fig. 7.1.2. Distribution of scores in Progressive Matrices Test of British naval candidates aged 40–49 in 1943 and coming from two groups of civilian occupations. *Source*: Vernon (1949), Table II.

scores are systematically arrayed is afforded by Table 7.2, in which we see the distributions of the test scores of men enlisted in the U.S. Army Air Force, in each of six grades of civilian occupation. The extent of the spread within each occupational grade was also brought out by Vernon's finding (1947) that of the variance of the test scores of British naval candidates, nearly 78 per cent was due to individual differences, as against less than 13 per cent to differences of occupation.

Part of the difference in each occupation will be due to differences of age, for scores generally fall with age. Thus among the British naval candidates, those who scored 40 or more made up 77 per cent of the clerks aged 17–19. but only

Table 7.2

Distribution of Mental Ability by Occupation

White men enlisted in U.S. Army Air Force in Second World War: distribution of General Classification Test scores in each of six grades of civilian occupation.

Occupational grade	Mean score	Under 60	60–79	80–99	100–109	110–119	120–139	140+
				per cent of all in grade				
I	122		1	5	10	25	50	9
II	117		1	10	18	25	43	3
III	115		2	12	17	29	36	4
IV	105	1	8	24	24	24	18	1
V	99	3	14	32	21	16	13	1
VI	96	5	17	32	21	15	9	1

Occupational grades according to the Edwards Occupational Status Scale (Edwards 1938):

  I Professional
 II Proprietors, managers and officials
III Clerks and other kindred workers
IV Skilled workers and foremen
 V Semi-skilled workers
VI Unskilled workers

Source: Anderson, Brown and Bowman (1952).

40 per cent of those in their 40s; among the machine operators, they made up 39 per cent of those aged 17–19, but only 10 per cent of those in their 40s (Vernon 1949). This may be attributed to three factors. There is first the general effect of ageing (Birren 1954). We lack evidence for cohorts at adult ages; if we fall back on cross-sections, then we have to allow that the older persons at any one date will have been born and grown up when the general standards of living and of education were lower than those enjoyed by the younger persons studied at that date. But the 7,000 British civil servants studied by Vincent (1952) will all have had an education enabling them to satisfy the same relatively high requirements, and their scores in a verbal intelligence test fall almost linearly with age, from over 75 for those aged 20–24 to less than 60 for those aged 55–59. This is strong evidence, because these civil servants will have had had the higher I.Q.s, and the continued mental exercise, that have been found to be associated with a slow decline with age, or none (Butcher 1968). The second factor has just been mentioned: the young naval candidates were born in the early 1920s, those in their 40s in the early 1900s, and the young ones may have enjoyed somewhat higher standards of living in the home and considerably higher standards of schooling. It is noteworthy that when a version of the test used for men enlisted in the U.S. army in the First World War was given to a representative sample of those enlisted in the Second World War, their median score was at a level higher than the score achieved by 83 per cent

of those tested in the First World War (Tuddenham 1948). Thirdly, Vernon's data show not only a fall in the average score with age, but a change in the shape of the distribution of the scores—in each occupation scores above the mode are sharply reduced, and there is a general rise in the proportion of lower scores. This suggests a twofold process: some of those with higher mental ability leave the occupation; those who remain in it lose some of their facility or nimbleness in performing this sort of test, while not necessarily losing any of their capability in the occupation itself, indeed quite likely increasing it through experience. That a loss of facility arising out of adaptation to the occupation rather than any loss of ability is to be reckoned with, is suggested by the low scores of miners (see Table 7.1) and also of farmers—a standing that everyday knowledge suggests by no means represents their ability. It is noteworthy that differences between occupations are less marked in the scores in non-verbal than in verbal tests (Vernon 1947).

These observations raise, and help to answer, two questions—what is the nature of the mental ability that is associated with occupation? and how does the association come about?

Our ideas about what it is that tests of mental ability indicate have been much influenced since the 1940s by factor analysis (Vernon 1950). If we find a high correlation between the performances of a large number of persons in, for example, arithmetical, verbal, and spatial tests, we look for a common factor; factor analysis, using these correlations, shows us how far performances of a particular kind can be accounted for as the outcome of factors operative also in other kinds of performance, and how far they can only be attributed to a factor specific to the particular kind. Here we have envisaged a mental structure of two levels, one holding factors common to performance in a number of different activities, the other mounted on it and holding factors specific to performance in particular activities. Factor analysis of ability actually suggests three or more levels. Thus we can envisage the broad common factor (usually called 'g') as bearing groups of more specific factors—Vernon suggests two main groups, one verbal-numerical-educational, the other practical-mechanical-spatial-physical; and these groups in turn as bearing or splitting up into factors more specific still. This hierarchical picture, Vernon points out, is over rigid, for how we distinguish between group and specific factors will vary, with a given test, from one population to another, and with a given population from one test to another. But we can infer that the tests with which we are concerned here have it in common to assess the 'g' factor, while they differ in their sensitiveness to this or that group or specific factor in addition. Thus the type of tests used for the Stanford–Binet I.Q. will be more sensitive to the verbal-numerical-educational group, those of the Progressive Matrices type to the practical-mechanical-spatial-physical group. But scores in the two types are highly correlated: in both it is the 'g' factor that predominates.

The ability represented by this 'g' factor is best described as the ability to perceive relations. This means the ability to abstract and to conceptualize, to use abstractions as an instrument of problem-solving, to reason and to envisage in general terms, as distinct from perceiving only particulars, and such of these mainly as are before one's eyes. The ability to compare and generalize and to use concepts is evidently bound up with the ability to communicate and receive information, and relate things seen with things not seen. To apprehend relations and reason with concepts is to form schemata, and Vernon (1960, pp. 35–6) observes that a person's intelligence corresponds with the complexity and flexibility of his schemata.

We come to our second question. If the mental ability indicated by the test scores is of the kind just described, how comes it that the rank order of occupations according to the average scores of those who follow them is closely the same as their rank order by status and earnings? We have seen that the dispersion about the average is always wide, but is generally wider the lower an occupation stands in the scale of status and earnings. We have also seen that there are far fewer low scores in the higher occupations than high scores in the lower ones.

The following hypotheses are consistent with these observations. We note first that an occupational title often covers a variety of jobs, requiring different capabilities; and this in itself will account for some of the spread of the scores in each occupation. Setting that consideration aside, and treating occupations as homogeneous, we may suppose that each has a certain threshold of capability—only those persons who have at least that degree of capability can continue to follow it. But this capability does not consist solely in mental ability: it is a package that also contains characteristics of personality such as energy and reliability. Throughout the middle range of the structure, a plus of these characteristics can effectively offset some shortfall of mental ability. This will account for the extent of overlap between the scores of occupations in that range, and the small differences between their averages. In the higher occupations, however, particularly those entered by examination, there is less scope for compensation of lower mental ability by personality: anyone with an I.Q. below 115 is unlikely to be able to qualify as a doctor, however strong his personality. This will account for the exclusion of the lower scores from these occupations. Though strength of personality will not offset lack of mental ability, weakness of personality does offset high mental ability, so that some persons with high scores but unsuitable traits will be able to find employment only in a 'lower' occupation. This will account, in part at least, for the range of scores widening as we go down the conventional structure, and for the presence of more high scores in the 'lower' occupations than low scores in the 'higher'.

These considerations make it surprising that the rank order of the average scores in occupations should prove to be as systematically related as they are with the rank order by status and pay. That this should be so is made more intelligible when we catch glimpses of the sorting-out process, in which those whose capabilities lie outside the band suited to an occupation move out of it. A study of students in a British training school for mental nurses, for example, found that a high score was associated with voluntary withdrawal from the course, a low score with being asked to leave (Crookes & French 1961). Those selecting boys as apprentices in a British electrical engineering firm are reported to have soon discovered that boys with scores above the level suited to the occupation either must be promoted, or else their performance would fall off through boredom (Montgomery 1962). A study of typists reports that

the few typists with a mental ratio [I.Q. score] below 105 failed to give satisfaction even in the mechanical work of copying; clerks with a mental ratio above this level but below 120 could do routine typing satisfactorily, but failed in the speed and accuracy of their shorthand and in spelling and display; clerks with a mental ratio of between 120 and 135 made excellent shorthand typists, and the brighter could compose business letters on their own initiative. Clerks with a mental ratio above 135 were generally promoted almost at once to more responsible work, or else became discontented. (Burt, Spielman, & Gaw 1926.)

This process of assortment can hardly ever be complete. Later in this chapter we shall show how access to occupations depends not only on the capability of the entrant but on the household from which he or she sets out. Some people manage to stay in occupations to which they have had access but for which they are not capable enough. Others—probably a good many more—not having had access to an occupation whose requirements are equal to their capability, do not rise out of the lower occupation they have entered. Here is another cause of the dispersion of the scores found in each occupation; for how much of that dispersion it is responsible we do not know.

But the process of assortment is still effective in bringing about the systematic gradation of average score by occupation found in comprehensive data for the U.K. and the U.S.A. This finding provides the first step in our present argument: on the average, the mental ability of the persons in an occupation varies positively with the level of that occupation in the conventional structure.

Nothing in this argument so far shows us how those persons come by their mental abilities. We go on to cite evidence to show that a substantial part of mental ability is formed by a potential with which each person is genetically endowed, while the extent to which that potential is developed depends on early upbringing and on education; and we shall see that both endowment and development are differentiated by class.

7.2. Evidence for the genetic determination of I.Q. potential

Because consistent indications of I.Q. cannot be obtained before the age of 5, and most tests are taken by those who have been at school at least for some years, we cannot observe directly the I.Q. potential with which a child is born, before environment has taken effect. We should, however, be able to learn something from the comparative method, by observing the variance of the I.Q.s either of children who are of different parentage but brought up in the same environment, or of children with the same genetic formation or genotype who are brought up in different environments. The first of these methods is hardly practicable, because of the difficulty of finding 'the same environment'. Within any one family different children may be treated differently by their parents, and may find themselves in different family circumstances at a given age; generally it proves an advantage for educational achievement to be the eldest or the youngest. Institutions such as orphanages provide the same environment in a material sense, but here again different children may be differently handled, by different members of the staff, and they may have had different experiences before entering. The second method, however, has been found practicable. Identical twins have identical genotypes—they are called monozygotic (MZ) because they are formed by the splitting of one ovum after fertilization, as distinct from the dizygotic (DZ) or fraternal twins that are formed by the separate fertilization of two ova. A number of cases have been found and studied, moreover, of identical twins being separated at birth or soon after, and brought up in different families. When later their I.Q.s are tested, how like or unlike are their scores, and how do they compare with those of other pairs—dizygotic twins, it may be, or simply siblings—who are brought up together?

Table 7.3
Correlation Between Characteristics of Twins

U.S.A. (reported 1937): correlations between physical measurements and scores in tests of I.Q. and achievement of pairs of identical twins (monozygotic, MZ) brought up together and apart, and of fraternal twins (dizygotic, DZ) brought up together.

U.S.A.	Monozyotic brought up together	apart	Dizygotic brought up together
Number of pairs	50	19	51
Height	0·932	0·969	0·645
Weight	0·917	0·886	0·631
Head length	0·910	0·917	0·691
Binet mental age	0·922	0·637	0·831
Binet I.Q.	0·910	0·670	0·640
Otis I.Q.	0·922	0·727	0·621
Stanford achievement	0·955	0·507	0·883

Source: Newman, Freeman & Holzinger (1937).

Table 7.3 provides the answers found in studies carried out in the U.S.A. If we take first the I.Q. scores, we see that the correlation between the MZ twins brought up together was the highest; next (though not for Binet mental age) came the correlation between the MZ twins brought up apart; lower than this again was the correlation between the DZ twins, even though they had been brought up together. The outstanding finding is that being brought up apart made so little difference to the I.Q. scores of the MZ twins. The homes they went to were sometimes very dissimilar, and even when they were at the same socio-economic level they must have provided more difference of environment than will generally have been experienced by children brought up in the same home: yet their I.Q. scores (the Binet mental age always excepted) were much more alike than those of children of different genotype brought up in the same home. We are bound to infer that the genotype plays a significant part in the determination of I.Q. as tested.

With achievement it is otherwise. Being brought up apart pulls the achievement scores of the pairs of MZ twins well away from one another, and they resemble one another a good deal less than do those of children of different genotype brought up in the same home. We learn, not surprisingly, that upbringing and schooling take a substantial effect on the acquisition of what is taught in school. We are also encouraged to believe that the I.Q. tests do get through to an underlying mental ability that is what it is in substantial though not complete independence of the particular applications in which it has been exercised.

The data in Table 7.3 include some physical measurements, and we see how what has been said about I.Q. applies to height and head length—here the genotype is preponderant—but not so much so to weight—here other factors take more effect. Evidence such as this has led geneticists to suppose that I.Q. is inherited in the same way as height. It appears, that is, to depend upon the conjunction of a number of genes, and the pairs of allelomorphic genes contain neither a dominant nor a recessive, but may be said to be additive. If men whose height is above or below the men's average in a certain proportion marry women whose own height differs from the women's average in the same proportion—that is, if mating is assortative—then the average height of the sons or daughters will be the same as that of the father or mother; and similarly for potential I.Q. Now given the formation of a characteristic by polygenes, and absence or limited extent of dominance and assortative mating, the geneticist can work out the correlations that he expects to find on the average between the size of the characteristic in a person and not only his parent but also his grandparent, his uncle or aunt, or his cousin, When these expected correlations are set against those actually found for I.Q.s the two prove to be close together throughout. This is impressive evidence, arising as it does from a strong test of the hypothesis that I.Q. as tested is in substantial part genetically determined in the same way as a physical characteristic like height. Evidence from U.S. sources is set out in Table 7.4. Baker (1974, p. 461) finds that the evidence

suggests that cognitive ability, in so far as it is inherited, resembles most measurable physical characters of man in that it is controlled by the cumulative action of a considerable number of genes, each having such small effect that its passage from generation to generation cannot be traced separately. It is agreed by those who have studied the subject that the genetic control of such characters as, for instance, structure (body height), span (greatest distance between middle finger-tips when the arms are held horizontally), and length of forearm (middle finger-tip to bent elbow) is of this nature.

But the same materials also reinforce the inference from materials already cited, that I.Q. as measured also depends on environment. In each comparison of pairs reared together and reared apart, whether unrelated children, siblings, or twins, it

Table 7.4
Correlations Between the Test Scores of
Unrelated and Related Persons

Correlations between scores of pairs of persons in tests of mental ability, as expected on the assumption of polygenic formation, partial or no dominance, and assortative or random mating, and as found in 52 studies covering more than 30,000 pairs, in 8 countries.

| | | | Correlation | |
| | No. of | Median | Expected | |
Pairs	studies	observed	Assumptions 1	Assumptions 2
Unrelated persons				
Children reared apart	4	−0·01	0·00	0·00
Foster-parent and child	3	0·20	0·00	0·00
Children reared together	5	0·24	0·00	0·00
Collaterals				
Second cousins	1	0·16	0·14	0·063
First cousins	3	0·26	0·18	0·125
Uncle/aunt and nephew/niece	1	0·34	0·31	0·25
Siblings, reared apart	3	0·47	0·52	0·50
Siblings, reared together	36	0·55	0·52	0·50
Twins				
Dizygotic, different sex	9	0·49	0·50	0·50
Dizygotic, same sex	11	0·56	0·54	0·50
Monozygotic, reared apart	4	0·75	1·00	1·00
Monozygotic, reared together	14	0·87	1·00	1·00
Direct line				
Grandparent and grandchild	3	0·27	0·31	0·25
Parent (as adult) and child	13	0·50	0·49	0·50
Parent (as child) and child	1	0·56	0·49	0·50

Assumptions 1: assortative mating and partial dominance.
Assumptions 2: random mating and additive genes.

Source: Jensen (1969), Table 2. Copyright © 1969, by the President and Fellows of Harvard College.

is the pairs reared together whose scores show the higher correlation. Specially noteworthy is the correlation of 0·20 between the scores of the unrelated foster-parent and child; it is much lower than the correlation of 0·50 very widely found between the I.Q.s of natural parent and child, but it is far from negligible. Might we not suppose, then, that the prevailing differences between the average I.Q.s of those following occupations at different socio-economic levels are wholly due to the differences in the upbringing and education linked with those levels? and that the average and the distribution of the properly genetic potential is much the same at all levels? This possibility was urged by Halsey (1959).

The issue is one of great social significance. For some observers it has been the clear implication of the evidence for the genetic component in I.Q. and the assortment of I.Q. by socio-economic level, that however much the health and education of the 'lower classes' were improved, their average I.Q. could not be raised by more than a few points. Halsey, however, in effect raised the possibility that if a batch of manual workers' babies were exchanged at birth with a batch of professional workers', those who grew up in the manual workers' homes would not score more in I.Q. tests, and those who grew up in the professionals' homes would not score less, than did the natural children of their adoptive parents. The economist will observe that if such a possibility really obtained, the supply of persons capable of following the 'higher' occupations could be greatly increased by improving the upbringing and education of the children of those who follow 'lower' occupations; and the 'higher' occupations would no longer be able to command the high pay they receive by virtue of the limited supply of labour to them.

How then, can we assess the possibility that the average potential I.Q. of the children born at all socio-economic levels is the same, and the differences in the I.Q. scores they subsequently attain is due wholly to upbringing and education? If this really were so, the average adopted child would have inherited the same I.Q. potential whatever the social class of his parents, and would develop the I.Q. prevailing in the class of his adoptive parents; and presumably the longer he lived with them the stronger this effect would be. But Butcher (1968, p. 170) cites a study by Lawrence (1931) of children who had never lived with their natural father at all, which found a correlation between the child's I.Q. and the natural father's social class; and a study by Skodak and Skeels (1949) of children placed within a few months of birth with foster-parents generally of different social class, which found that the correlation between their I.Q.s and those of their natural parents increased as they grew older. Further, the observed assortment of I.Q. by socio-economic level could be due entirely to environment and owe nothing to differences of genotype, only if the effects of environment were found to be big enough to cover such observed differences as those of 26 points between the average scores of grades I and VI in the U.S. Army Air Force (Table 7.2).

How can we estimate the possible magnitude of the effects of environment? The most direct way is to compare persons with the same genotype who have grown up in different environments. The evidence of Table 7.5 comes from the U.S.A., and most of it was gathered in the first half of the present century: it shows us the effect of the same genetic potential, that of identical twins, being exposed to different environments in the society. For each pair we have an assessment of the extent of difference between the educational and social advantages afforded to its two members by their separate homes, and the difference in their years of schooling is recorded. The question for us is, how far these differences are representative of those between socio-economic levels. The two cases at the top, with differences of 14 and 15 in years of schooling, are clearly exceptional. In all but one of the last 17 cases the differences in years of schooling are small, but those in social advantages are still often substantial. Perhaps on this evidence we might put the greatest difference likely to have been made by environment, in the span between the averages of the highest and lowest socio-economic levels of U.S. society at the time, at about 17 points.

There is no question here of partitioning an actual score between the contributions of genotype and environment, for these contributions are not simply additive: the form of their combination may well be complicated, and include an important joint term, according to which part of the effect taken by either factor depends on the associated value of the other. But the difference between the extent of variation found when the genotype is held constant, and the range of ± 30 points

Table 7.5
Environment and I.Q. of Identical Twins

U.S.A., within 1900–40: differences in environment and I.Q. scores of 22 pairs of identical (MZ) twins brought up apart.

The indexes of differences in educational and social advantages were obtained by summing the ratings given on a 10-point scale by five judges who studied the case material; the maximum is therefore 50.

The I.Q. difference is negative where the twin adjudged to have had the greater educational advantages made the lower I.Q. score.

			Environmental Differences			
Sex	Age at separation	Age at testing	1. in years of schooling	2. in estimated educational advantages	3. in estimated social advantages	I.Q. difference
f	18 mo.	35	14	37	25	24
f	18 mo.	27	15	32	14	12
m	1 yr.	27	4	28	31	19
f	5 mo.	29	4	22	15	17
f	18 mo.	29	5	19	13	7
f	18 mo.	19	1	15	27	12
m	2 yr.	14	0	15	15	10
f	3 mo.	15	1	14	32	15
m	2 mo.	23	1	12	15	−2
f	6 mo.	39	0	12	15	−1
f	14 mo.	38	1	11	26	4
m	1 mo.	19	0	11	13	1
f	1 yr.	12	1	10	15	5
m	1 yr.	26	2	9	7	1
m	1 mo.	13	0	9	27	−1
f	6 yr.	41	0	9	14	−9
f	2 yr.	11	0	8	12	2
f	3 yr.	59	0	7	10	8
m	1 mo.	19	0	7	14	6
f	1 mo.	30	9	?	?	−1
f	1 mo.	19	0	2	?	−3
m	1 mo.	20	0	?	?	−4

Source: Woodworth (1941, p. 23); taken here from Tyler (1965, Table 49).

that may be found in the same scale when genotype as well as environment can vary, indicates the significance of differences in genotype.

We go on to study upbringing and the transmission of genotype in so far as they are differentiated by class.

7.3. The effect of differences between classes in the upbringing of children on the development of I.Q.

The profound importance of home influences in the first five years of life has been emphasized by Bloom in his study of 'Stability and Change in Human Characteristics' (1964). 'The prolongation of the period of dependency for youth in the Western cultures', he says (p. 214) 'has undoubtedly been a factor in desensitizing parents, school workers, and behavioural scientists to the full importance of the very early environmental and experiential influences.' Also we have only 'limited evidence on the effects of the early environment', and such as it is it has been taken to show that early measures of intelligence and personality have little predictive power. Hence 'an implicit assumption running through the culture that . . . the developments at one age or stage are no more significant than those that take place at another.' But Bloom's study of the course of development of five characteristics—height, general intelligence, aggressiveness in males, dependence in females, intellectuality in males and females, general school achievement—led him to conclude that for these characteristics 'there is a negatively accelerated curve of development which reaches its midpoint before age 5. We have reasoned that the environment would have its greatest effect on a characteristic during the period of its most rapid development.'

Observers in the U.K. and the U.S.A. are agreed in finding systematic differences between classes in the ways in which children are treated by their parents (Bronfenbrenner 1958; J. and E. Newson 1963). In their study of the English city of Nottingham, the Newsons found three styles of upbringing. 'The most obvious distinction', they reported, 'is between middle-class and working-class attitudes: almost every area of behaviour shows a broad gulf between professional-managerial class practices and those of the skilled manual group'. White-collar workers generally followed the same practices as the former class, except that in some respects the shop and office workers resembled the manuals. 'The other main rift, between unskilled workers and the rest, can sometimes be linked with lower material or educational standards . . . but this does not always apply; and it is tempting to suppose some basic difference, in personality or in occupational ethos or in both' as the source of the rift (pp. 214, 316).

There are several ways in which differences in the style of upbringing have been found to affect the development of the child's I.Q. Much in this development has been seen to depend on the stimulus that the parents impart by the interest they show in the child's awareness, play, and learning. Generally, the middle-class mother in the U.K. and the U.S.A. interacts more with her child than does the working-class mother. She does more to encourage her children to explore and to engage in new activities. In eliciting responses from them and in responding to their overtures, she helps them to perceive meanings and convey them; they are led to use thinking as a means of envisaging what lies beyond their immediate senses. There are two ways in which they are more prompted than is the working-class child to see relations between objects and to generalize. One lies in their being given reasons—explanations of how things work, rather than instructions for carrying out a particular task; rules of conduct, rather than 'Stop that', 'Do this'. The other way is the use of language. Middle-class mothers talk more with their children, partly because only by using language can they give reasons; and the language they use contains more abstract and general terms, and is more structured. Here again awareness of relations is fostered. Middle-class children are equipped with a better instrument of problem-solving; they can refine their perceptions of the world about them and of themselves because they can conceptualize, and discriminate among a variety of concepts; the range of their interests is widened, as they move from the immediate to the remote in time and space (Bernstein 1961; Bernstein & Henderson 1969; Bruner 1970; Robinson & Rackstraw 1967).

The effect of parental interest on the development of I.Q. during the school years was observed by Douglas (1964) in his cohort. 'Children, when their parents take an interest in their work and encourage them, improve their scores in tests of school performance and mental ability between the ages of 8 and 11 years . . . When parents take little interest their children lose ground in the tests . . .' (1967 edn., p. 88.)

In a study of 12-year-olds in secondary schools in the Scottish city of Aberdeen, Fraser (1959) calculated the correlations between the child's I.Q. and a number of 'background factors' such as family income, family size, living space, and parents' education: much the highest correlation was with parental encouragement. But only those parents who feel it is within their own power to achieve goals that they set before themselves are likely to set goals before their children that they encourage them to achieve. Parents with low incomes are more likely to feel themselves helpless in the grip of circumstance. Among the evidence for this surveyed by Bruner (1970; p. 156 of reprint 1974) is a study that he reports as finding that 'the more a mother feels externally controlled when her child is four years old, the more likely the child is to have a low I.Q. and a poor academic record at age six or seven'.

The importance of the sheer amount of interaction between parent and child is brought out by the well-established effect of family size on test scores. Nisbet (1961) noted that at least 33 surveys over the preceding 30 years, and especially the Scottish Mental Survey with its 70,000 cases, had found a negative correlation between the size of the family and the intelligence of the children. Douglas found that in all the four classes he distinguished test scores fell with family size. That among the working-class families some of the effect may have been due to insufficiency of house room and even of nourishment is suggested by his finding that in the middle classes, by contrast, 'it is not until families of 4 or more children are reached that there is a substantial fall in score and even beyond this size the fall is gradual up to families of 8 or more' (1967 edn., pp. 124–5). Especially when the children come close together, the mother of a numerous brood is remarkable if she is not overburdened and sometimes overwrought, unable even if she had the time to give her children the emotional support they need. In the homes once amply supplied with servants, the parents of a large family could still not give much attention to any one child, and the relations between the children and nursemaids were insecure. But the major factor, common to large families in all classes, seems likely to have been the reduction in the interest and encouragement that each child can get as the number of children grows. The scores of Army tests of 9,000 young Englishmen and Welshmen who began their National Service in Great Britain between 1956 and 1958 show the same pattern of effects of family size as Douglas noted; the effect of there being four or more children in the family is striking throughout—in the professional class the average score of recruits who were one of six children was about three-quarters that of those who were 'onlies', and among all the others the proportion was two-thirds or less (Ministry of Education 1960, p. 125). Lipset and Bendix (1959, c. IX) after noting a number of other studies that have found large families to be associated with lower test scores, remark also on the findings in these studies that 'the more successful among Methodist ministers, top scientists, and a sample of extremely gifted children in New York, were all more likely to be only children, oldest children, or children with longer than average distance between themselves and the next older child, than could be explained by chance.' The reason may well be that these children enjoyed more interaction with adults. But it must be added that though Blau and Duncan (1967, p. 410), considering subsequent occupational achievement rather than test scores, found the same association between higher performance and small size of family, or being the first born—and they add, the youngest—in the family, they had reason to believe that the connection ran through the amount of education received; when this was held constant, the differences largely disappeared.

A number of studies in the U.K. and the U.S.A. have found that at least during the first half of the present century the average number of children in the family was greater, the lower the socio-economic level. The study cited above of the English and Welsh recruits of 1956–7, for instance, found a systematic relation between the occupational level of the recruit's father and the size of his family—the proportion of families with no more than two children ranged from 62 per cent among the professional and managerial class to 24 per cent among the unskilled manual, and the proportion with six or more children from 4 per cent among the former to 28 per cent among the latter. When a cohort of British children born in one week of 1958 had reached the age of 7, the number of their families with four or more children made up about 20 per cent of all the non-manual families, but over 30 per cent of the skilled manual, 35 per cent of the semi-skilled, and over 50 per cent of the unskilled (Davie, Butler, & Goldstein 1972, p. 31). Here, then, has been an additional cause of lower I.Q.s among the children of semi-skilled and unskilled manual workers. But we know that in England and Wales and in the U.S.A. class differences in size of family have been decreasing since the Second World War, through the more educated parents having larger families again, while family planning extends among the semi-skilled and unskilled. A closely associated factor is the adequacy of housing. In his study of the progress of a cohort of children born in England and Wales in 1946, Douglas (1964) observed that 'when housing conditions are unsatisfactory, children make relatively low scores in the tests. This is so in each social class but whereas the middle-class children, as they get older, reduce this handicap, the manual working-class children from unsatisfactory homes fall even further behind' (1967 edn., p. 67).

7.4. The relation between parents' class and their children's I.Q.

The evidence discussed in the preceding sections leads us to expect a connection between the I.Q. of the child and the parent's class as indicated by occupation, own education, or income. We have seen that the higher the class, the higher is the average I.Q. of its adult members. We have seen that the higher is the I.Q.s of the parents, the higher will be the average I.Q. potential that is transmitted genetically to their children. We have also seen that class differences in the early upbringing of children work in the same way, towards

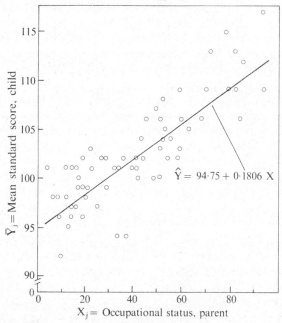

Fig. 7.2. Parent's occupation and child's test score.

Wisconsin, 1929–33: regression on a socio-economic index of parent's occupation of scores in tests of scholastic aptitude of 88, 883 high school seniors, grouped according to their parents' occupations. *Sources:* original data, Byrns & Henmon (1936); socio-economic index, Duncan (1961); calculations and Fig., Duncan, Featherman & Duncan (1968), c.6. 2.

raising the average test scores of the children who grow up in the homes of parents who, always by the criteria of occupation, own education, or income, are assignable to a higher class. Taken together, these observations lead us to expect a systematic relation between the parents' class and the average test scores of the children. A number of studies in the U.K. and the U.S.A. have confirmed this expectation. When the parents are arranged in five or six classes, the differences found in the average test scores of their children are in some instances not very great, but they are remarkably consistent.

A study that related the scores of nearly 90,000 high school seniors in Wisconsin to the occupations of their parents is illustrated in Fig. 7.2. Here the parents have been assorted to sixty-four socio-economic groups, to each of which a value has been assigned in the numerical scale of occupational status constructed by Duncan (1961); this scale is based on the three criteria already mentioned, of occupation, own education, and income. The children being all high school seniors accounts for most of the scores being above the mean, and very few falling below 95. But within that range, though the numerous observations show no little variousness, the pervasive relation indicated by the line of regression is unmistakable.

Table 7.6
Child's I.Q. and Family Income

U.S.A., 1963–65, sample of 7,417 children representative of 24 million children (other than those in institutions) aged 6–11: scores in vocabulary and block design tests, and their combination to form equivalent I.Q. scores, by income of the child's family.

| | Raw Score | | Equivalent |
Annual family income	Vocabulary	Block design	I.Q.*
Less than $3,000	19·9	7·8	89·2
$3,000 and less than $5,000	23·5	10·7	96·1
$5,000 and less than $7,000	25·8	13·5	101·1
$7,000 and less than $10,000	28·3	14·7	104·7
$10,000 and less than $15,000	30·4	16·5	108·4
$15,000 and over	31·8	17·8	111·2

* *Equivalent I.Q.*: the raw scores having been transformed to put the mean of each at 10 and the standard deviation at 3, the scores of each child in the transformed scales were added, and the resultant totals were in turn transformed to put the mean at 100 and standard deviation at 15, as in the Stanford–Binet I.Q. Distribution.

Source: U.S. Dept. of Health, Education and Welfare (1971), Table 25.

Another U.S. study is cited in Table 7.6. Here a random sample has been drawn so as to be representative of American children aged 6–11 as a whole. The children are grouped according to six categories of the income of their families, and the average scores group by group prove to range from 11 points below the mean for the children of the lowest family income, to 11 points above for those of the highest. Here as before it is not surprising that there should be a

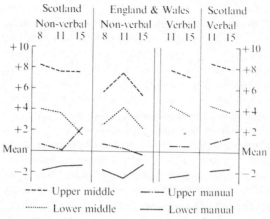

Fig. 7.3. Scores in intelligence tests by children of different social class.

Average scores in T tests of cohort of children born in 1946, in England and Wales, and in Scotland, in each of four social classes, at ages 8, 11, 15 (non-verbal tests) and 11, 15 (verbal tests). I.Q. score = 25 + 1·5 (T score). *Source*: Douglas, Ross & Simpson (1968), Diagrams I, II.

difference of this kind between the extremes; less expected perhaps, and more significant, is the systematic nature of the smaller differences between adjacent groups.

The cohort of children born in Great Britain in a week of 1946 and followed by Douglas (1964, 1968) provides the evidence shown in Fig. 7.3. Here are the average scores of the children from four social classes. The 'middle class' children were those whose fathers were in non-manual occupations. If both parents went to secondary school or 'were brought up in middle class families', the child was assigned to the 'upper middle class'; the remaining children of non-manual fathers were assigned to the 'lower middle class'. The 'upper manual working class' is differentiated from the lower by one or both of the parents having had a secondary education or having been brought up in a middle-class family. The scores are those in T tests, which have a mean of 50 points; a difference of one point corresponds with 1·5 points on the usual I.Q. scale, so that a spread of 10 points, for instance, between the T scores of upper-middle-class and lower-manual children corresponds with one of 15 I.Q. points. It will be seen that in England and Wales the scores of the middle-class children in the non-verbal tests went up between the ages of 8 and 11, whereas those of the manual workers' children went down; while between 11 and 15 the middle-class children fell back, and those of the lower-manual workers' children rose. This was not so in Scotland. Douglas notes that entry into grammar schools came a year later in Scotland, where there were in any case relatively more grammar school places, and this is consistent with the hypothesis that the movements of the middle-class children's scores in England and Wales were due to the greater pressure brought to bear on those children to perform well in the more competitive selection tests they took at the age of 11. This suggests the importance of parental interest as a factor increasing the differences between the test scores of children from homes at different social levels. When Douglas took out the scores of the children of two groups of parents, differentiated regardless of class according as they were or were not ambitious for their children's education, he found the same pattern of divergence between 8 and 11, and convergence afterwards.

The association shown by these and other studies between the test scores of children and their parents' occupational class has been called in question on the ground that the tests are biased towards the culture of the middle class, so that children raised in a working-class culture do not score as highly even though they are of equal or greater ability. There have been endeavours to devise 'culture-free' tests. But the many experiments that have been made with a wide variety of tests have reinforced the view that performance in the usual type of I.Q. test does not depend on familiarity with the materials, on verbal facility, or on styles of communication, but indicates the power to abstract and relate that is common to understanding and problem-solving in every kind of setting. It is true that the extent to which scores are differentiated by social background varies from test to test, but the tests in which no such differentiation appears are few. Some such tests have been devised, but it has been remarked of these that it is not clear what they are tests of: unlike the I.Q. they are not predictive of scholastic achievement. Those tests, on the other hand, in which scores are markedly differentiated by class do not appear on examination to depend on familiarity with words or materials such as is itself differentiated by class (Tyler 1965, pp. 346–8). The evidence does not preclude the possibility that children with the same ability to abstract, notice relations, and solve problems, but raised in different social settings, will perform differently in I.Q. tests, if only because they perceive the taking of tests differently, or are differently motivated to perform; but the observed differences in performance are too large, and too consistent over different communities and tests, for this possibility to account for any great part of them. The suggestion is appealing that high and low scores in an I.Q. test mark, not the possession of more or less of a common property, but a difference in kind that makes the outcome of a common test meaningless. There is humanitarian force in the proposal to devise styles of schooling that will be more helpful to the children whose kind of mind is stigmatized as of 'low I.Q.' than the present ones to which all children are subjected, but which are in fact suited only to the kind that scores 'high I.Q.s'. Such developments may make schooling helpful and encouraging for those to whom too often now it is humiliating. But we do not know whether this will enable these children to develop greater mental ability of the kind that is required to follow particular occupations.

The evidence we have cited so far has concerned only the average scores of groups of children, but now we must take account of the facts that the individual scores of the children of parents in any one class are distributed over a wide range, and that the mean score of the children of a given parent will be nearer than that parent's score to the mean of the whole population. The wide range follows from the polymorphic determination of the genotype I.Q. The 'regression towards the mean' follows on the assumption that mating is not perfectly assortative, that is, persons do not invariably take spouses of the same I.Q. as themselves. On this assumption, the likelihood of a person taking a spouse with, say, a lower I.Q. than his or her own depends to some extent on the proportion, among all persons of the opposite sex, of those having a lower I.Q. If the I.Q. of one person is above the mean of the whole population, more than half the persons of the opposite sex will have a lower I.Q. than that person; and conversely. Subject always, then, to the tendency of like to mate with like, the I.Q. of the person's spouse is more likely than not to be nearer the mean of the whole population than is that person's own I.Q. It follows that the mean of the parents' I.Q.s, the 'midparental I.Q.', will also be nearer the mean of the whole population, though to a lesser extent. Now the mean genotype I.Q. of the children will approximate to the midparental I.Q. Hence the 'regression towards the mean'.

Table 7.7
The Intergenerational Transmission of Genotype I.Q.s

Model of polymorphic transmission of genotype I.Q. from father to son, on certain assumptions concerning the patterns of genes and of mating.

Fathers				Sons					
No.	I.Q.	80	90	100	110	120	Av. I.Q.	No.
16	80	4	8	4			90	16
64	90	8	24	24	8		95	64
96	100	4	24	40	24	4	100	96
64	110		8	24	24	8	105	64
16	120			4	8	4	110	16
256		16	64	96	64	16		256

Source: Carter (1976), pp. 106–08.

Both effects, the range of the distribution of the children's I.Q.s and the regression of their mean I.Q. towards the mean of the whole population, are illustrated by Table 7.7 This 'much oversimplified model' derived from Carter (1976) shows the distribution of the genotype I.Q.s of the sons of fathers at each of five levels of I.Q. It is assumed that genotype I.Q. is determined at only one gene locus. Here there are three alleles, with relative frequencies $\frac{1}{4}, \frac{1}{2}, \frac{1}{4}$, such that the first contributes 60, the second 50, and the third 40 I.Q. points. Their contributions are simply additive. Table 7.7 shows the intergenerational transmission of genotype I.Q. that will come about on the above assumptions together with that of non-assortative, indeed random mating. We see how the sons of fathers at a given I.Q. level will themselves have I.Q.s spread over a number of levels; and how their mean I.Q. is nearer than their fathers' to the mean of the whole population.

Table 7.7 illustrates a further property of the genetic process, that is described more fully in Carter (1970), c. 6. We might expect that the regression towards the mean, repeated in successive generations, would result in an eventual convergence of all members of the population on a single central value. But this is not so at all. The distribution of genotype I.Q.s in the population as a whole, in any generation, depends on the pattern of the relevant alleles in its gene pool, and so long as this pattern remains unchanged it will set the same imprint on the distribution of genotype I.Q.s in each succeeding generation. Any one parent may possess a higher or lower genotype I.Q. than another, but the parents as a whole will transmit I.Q.s to their children in a distribution determined by the relative frequency of the relevant alleles in the population as a whole, together with the extent to which mating is random or assortative. The pattern of alleles may be such, for example, that only a minority of the children of high I.Q. parents are themselves of the same high I.Q., and here we see the regression towards the mean; but the same pattern would bring it about that the parents of moderately high I.Q. would beget a larger absolute number of children of high I.Q. and the parents of average I.Q. a substantial number, and here we see the basic distribution asserting itself. So it is in Table 7.7: of the sons with I.Q. 120 only a quarter are the sons of fathers with that I.Q.; half of them are the sons of fathers with I.Q. 110, and the remaining quarter are the sons of fathers of only average I.Q. So it comes about that despite the regression towards the mean shown by the column giving the average I.Q.s of the sons, the bottom row of the table shows the distribution of the sons' I.Q.s as a whole to be the same as that of the fathers'.

None the less it is true that if all the children of Table 7.7 entered the same classes of occupations as their parents', the kind of intergenerational transmission of I.Q.s that it illustrates would in a few generations remove all differences of I.Q. between the classes—the I.Q.s in each class would become simply a small-scale replica of those of the whole population. Evidently this has not come about. That it has not must be due to one of two reasons. It may be that the stratification of occupations by I.Q. is of recent origin, so that the process of assimilation though currently active has not had time to work itself out; but this seems unlikely. The alternative explanation is that there has been continual mobility by I.Q.: the children whose I.Q.s are higher or lower than those associated with their parents' occupations have been moving upwards or downwards in sufficient number to maintain the stratification of occupations by I.Q. much as it was in their parents' day (Gibson & Young 1968).

At the end of Section 7.1 we noted the remarkable finding that when occupations are stratified by pay and status, the average I.Q.s of those engaged in them are found to be stratified in the same order, despite much overlap between the different levels. Now we have to note that any allocation of I.Q.s of this kind once established between different levels will be continually disturbed by the inter-generational regression and dispersion of I.Q.s, so that to maintain an existing allocation requires some children to enter occupations at higher or lower levels than their parents'. In addition, changes economic and political will generally be varying the relative numbers required at different levels: in recent years they will have increased the relative number of jobs at levels associated with the higher I.Q.s. From U.S. data of the 1940s Anderson, Brown, and Bowman (1952) concluded that some 40 per cent of the actual intergenerational moves between the six levels they considered were required to offset these last two shifts, and maintain the existing extent of match and mismatch between occupational level and I.Q. The remaining 60 per cent of intergenerational moves will have been 'random with respect to intelligence'.

To establish the fact of intergenerational mobility by I.Q. is not to show that disparities of I.Q. exert a sufficient propulsion of themselves. But there is a case for regarding them as making for mobility, whereas other components of heredity and upbringing tend to keep children in the same class of occupations as their parents'. Their analysis of U.S. materials leads Bowles and Nelson (1974) to conclude that in so far as the I.Q.s of children resemble their parents', they play only a small part in 'the intergenerational reproduction of economic inequality', which appears to be 'attributable primarily to the direct impact of socio-economic background and its indirect impact operating via unequal educational attainments'. This leaves it open for disparities between the I.Q. of the child and the I.Q. level of the parents' occupation to be a factor disturbing the correlation between the occupational class of parent and child, and making instead for intergenerational mobility upwards and downwards.

7.5. Class differences in the use made of education

Different styles of upbringing, such as we noticed in Section 7.3, have their effect on the children's will and capacity to learn, and on their adaptability to the requirements of the school.

Middle-class parents have been found to expect more of their children, who internalize those expectations—expecting more of themselves, they care more about achievement at school. In a survey of fifteen U.S. studies, Bronfenbrenner (1958) found that

though more tolerant of expressed impulses and desires, the middle-class parent, throughout the period covered by this survey [mostly down to the Second World War] has higher expectations for the child. The middle-class youngster is expected to learn to take care of himself earlier, to accept more responsibilities about the home, and—above all—to progress further in school. In matters of discipline, working-class parents are consistently more likely to employ physical punishment, while middle-class families rely more on reasoning, isolation, appeals to guilt, and other methods involving the threat of loss of love. At least two independent lines of evidence suggest that the techniques preferred by middle-class parents are more likely to bring about the development of internalized values and controls.

In the middle-class style of upbringing, moreover, the children will generally have been better prepared to make good use of school, because their relations with their parents will have prepared them for relations with their teachers, and the activities their parents encourage will have resembled those of the school. The National Child Development Study, in reporting on the progress of a cohort made up of almost every child born in Great Britain in one week of 1958, noted 'a strong association between social class and reading and arithmetic attainment at seven years of age. The chances of an unskilled manual worker's child . . . being a poor reader are six times greater than those of a professional worker's child.' And such observations the authors of the report would account for as follows:

A home conducive to learning is one where there is a feeling for the spoken and written word as a tool for conveying precise meaning; and where children are stimulated to question the world around them and receive explanations appropriate to their age. There are two senses in which a child from such a home comes to school ready to learn. He is intellectually ready in that his language and concepts are already well structured . . . But he is also psychologically ready to acquire new skills. For example, he has learned that reading provides pleasure and he wants to be a part of the literate community as soon as possible. (Davie, Butler, & Goldstein 1972, pp. 102–3, 100–1.)

The use of language—vocabulary, structure, signals—is of the first importance. Children of manual workers are liable to be disadvantaged because the forms of speech they have learned differ from the teacher's. They may seem unused to speech—they 'may not respond in a normal way to the teacher's requests or be able to offer explanations or to express their needs adequately or even to make appropriate comments on what they see happening in school'. But this does not mean that they are not used to talking and being talked to: it is rather that in their homes 'the attitudes which are expressed through speech, and the attitudes towards language and the purposes for which language is used may be very different from the teacher's own practices' (Tough 1973). The bright child may soon pick up a mode of speech to use with the teacher that is distinct from the one it uses with its parents and with other children. But then it is, so to speak, going to school in a foreign land, and learning is divorced from living.

There are also differences in the code of acceptable and unacceptable behaviour that the child has learned by the age of entry into school. The National Child Development Study found that the proportion of children judged by their teachers to be 'maladjusted' was much lower among those of non-manual than of manual parents, and it was highest among those of the unskilled manual. But this, the authors of the report observe, is maladjustment according to the standards of the school and not necessarily those of the home. In the homes of manual workers, the mother may not be so much concerned about tantrums and fighting. Destruction of others' belongings was found to be five times as frequent among the children of unskilled manual workers as among those of the higher professionals, but 'this may only indicate that this particular behaviour is more accepted at home' (Davie, Butler and Goldstein 1972, pp. 143–5).

To the evidence already cited that children from smaller families make higher test scores, there is evidence to be added that they do better at school. In a sample of grammar school pupils from manual workers' families, Jackson and

Marsden (1962, p. 76) found that these families averaged less than two children, about half the average for manual workers' families as a whole. Analysing extensive U.S. data, B. Duncan (1967) found that large families exerted a consistently depressing effect on educational attainment, relatively to the attainments of children from small families. It is understandable that where there are fewer children in the family, the parents have more resources with which to support the education of each child, and more time in which to attend to the progress of each. But they will not do this simply because their children are few: they must also have the will to do it. Blau and Duncan (1967, p. 413) found that with parents at a given socio-economic level, the boys from small families where the eldest brother did not go beyond elementary school enjoyed no educational advantage over the boys from large families. The inference that these were small families in which the parents were not concerned to advance their children's education is borne out by the further finding that the educational advantage of coming from a small family increased with the level of education of the eldest brother. It seems that the smallness of the family and the scholastic achievement of the children are the joint products of the parents' concern for education.

This concern also takes effect through the choice of school. Douglas (1964, p. 143) noted that British primary schools differed in the extent of the improvement they effected in their pupils' intelligence test scores between the ages of 8 and 11, and in the proportion of their pupils with given test scores who in fact gained grammar school places. 'The primary schools with the best records of grammar school awards attract pupils from the middle-class, and those whose parents are anxious for them to succeed.' Jackson and Marsden (1962) in their study of working-class children in an industrial city of the north of England who completed a grammar school education, found that most of them had attended 5 out of the 29 primary schools in the city: these 5 had a 'large middle-class intake'.

Class differences also appear in the relations between the parents and the school once chosen. Among the parents of the cohort of British children born in 1958, 76 per cent of the upper professionals had visited their children's school but only 43 per cent of the manual workers (Davie, Butler, & Goldstein 1972, p. 39). Middle-class parents are more able to take up their children's problems with their teachers, and bring pressure to bear for changes they want to see for their children's sake.

Class difference in parental concern may well be a cause of differences in the scholastic achievement of children of the same ability. Thus among the cohort of British children born in 1946 who attended secondary modern schools, when the test scores of the pupils and the quality of the school attended were held constant, the middle-class pupils were found to be twice as likely as those of the working-class to obtain an 'O' level certificate by the examination normally taken in the fifth year of secondary education (Douglas, Ross & Simpson 1968, p. 48).

In respect at least of reading, moreover, it appears that differences in achievement depend more on difference between homes than between schools. In a study of reading achievement in eleven developed countries, Thorndike (1973, c. 6 and p. 98) found a fairly consistent association between the individual achievements of children aged 10 and 14 and the socio-economic level of their parents, together with the resources—such as dictionary, books and newspapers—available in their homes: in all these countries it appeared that when account was taken in this way of the home influences on the pupils, the type and quality of the school made little difference to their reading achievement.

7.6. Class differences in extent of education

It is widely observed that the age of leaving school varies with the class of the pupil's family. Thus Douglas found in his British cohort that the proportion who left at the legally minimum age, which at the relevant time was 15, varied from 16 per cent of the upper-middle-class pupils to 77 per cent of the lower-working-class. These differences could not be attributed entirely to the association between class and I.Q., for of the pupils in the top sixth of the I.Q. distribution those who left before or immediately after the fifth year of secondary education made up 10 per cent of the upper-middle-class, 22 per cent of the lower middle, 33 per cent of the upper-working-class, and 50 per cent of the lower-middle-class (Douglas 1964, pp. 157, 24–5). For France the sample of the gainfully occupied population aged 15–65 in 1963 provides the particulars of the ages at which those persons completed their education, subdivided according to twelve occupational classes of their fathers, that are cited in Table 7.8. Of the children in Moscow secondary schools Shkaratan (1973c, p. 302) reports that as one moves up through the school from form to form, 'a considerable number of children whose parents are employed in unskilled and average-paid work drop out, and the percentage of children whose parents are employed in highly skilled work increases sharply'.

These systematic differences may be attributed to three causes.

The first and most evident is that the families with smaller incomes are less able to maintain a child while it continues to study, and stand in greater need of what it can earn forthwith.

Second, the child itself is less likely to want to stay on at school if it is not doing well there, or finding the work interesting; but its experience in these respects will depend in great part on its I.Q., and we have seen the extent to which the I.Q. of the children is correlated with the class of their parents. In post-secondary education, moreover, even those who want to stay on may have to leave if their work does not reach a sufficient standard. In Russia in the 1950s, when the proportion of the children of the intelligentsia in the colleges and technical schools rose sharply, the authorities provided that applicants with not less than two years of experience in paid employment should be admitted even though their performance at the entrance examination was only moderately satisfactory; but too many of the students thus admitted dropped out. 'The result', say Rutkevich and Filippov (1973, p. 256), 'was a sharpening

. . . of a most important contradiction inherent in socialism—that between the full legal equality of citizens and their incomplete actual equality.' They point out that socialist society needs to select for training in its higher schools those who will make the most skilled specialists; but the potential of an applicant depends, among other factors, 'on the material and cultural level of the family in which he was raised . . . Other things being equal, therefore, greater opportunities for admission to higher schools are available to children from more well-to-do families, especially from families in which the parents' educational level is higher . . .'

The third cause of class differences in the extent of education lies in the parents' aspirations for the child, in their and his perception of what careers are open to him. Parents who have the means to support the further education of their children sometimes see no point in it, because the kind of career to which it could lead is not within their field of view, and they simply do not envisage it for their children, or encourage them to look towards it. The importance attached to further education generally varies with the occupational level of the parent. Thus in a U.S. survey of 1947 which put the question 'About how much schooling do you think young men need these days to get along well in the world?' the percentages of the respondents who chose the answer 'Some college training' was 74 among the professionals, 53 among the skilled manuals, and 35 among the non-farm labourers (Hyman 1967). Just the same stratification, with similar percentages, was found by Martin (1953) among parents in a part of Southern England, when they were asked whether they felt strongly about their child going to a grammar school. The inhibiting factor seems to be not lack of interest in getting on, but lack of knowledge of the careers open to ability beyond a certain level: from a number of U.S. studies Havighurst and Rogers (1952) concluded that the youths of high ability who did not go on to college almost all had parents with less than high school education, and that though the parents wanted to see their sons attain high earnings, they did not look beyond high school for them. It also appears that children generally adopt their parents' horizons; there is evidence that the mothers attach more value to education than the fathers, and are the more influential (Hyman 1967; Jackson & Marsden 1962).

In these ways it comes about that the extent of children's education varies with their parents' class. A number of children with the ability to profit by higher education do not proceed to it, but enter manual work. From observation of the cohort of British children born in 1946, Douglas, Ross, and Simpson (1968, p. 100) estimated that among the manual workers of those children's generation 18 per cent would be in the top third of measured ability, and 5 per cent in the top sixth. 'More than half of the boys of high ability from working class homes are unlikely to move out of the social class into which they were born.' The particulars of their own education and their father's occupation obtained from a large sample of French occupied persons in 1964, cited in Table 7.8, show how systematically the extent of education of the children was linked with the father's occupation, and how wide the differences were between the

Table 7.8
Father's Occupation and Extent of Child's Education

France, 1964, sample of occupied persons aged 15–65 at 1 January 1963: proportion having extended their education beyond each of three ages, in each of twelve grades of father's occupation.

	Males			Females		
Age:	15	18	22	15	18	22
	%	%	%	%	%	%
Father's occupation						
1. Liberal professions	88	85	58	90	75	31
2. Higher management	87	79	38	88	77	30
3. Industrials and large-scale traders	77	60	16	75	57	17
4. Middle management	67	50	13	70	47	7
5. Others economically active	53	39	5	56	41	7
6. Administrative, technical, and clerical	53	39	5	63	41	4
7. Small traders and artisans	45	33	5	57	36	3
8. Skilled manual	36	22	2	45	26	2
9. Semi-skilled manual	29	18	1	38	18	2
10. Non-farm labourers	30	18	1	30	13	2
11. Farmers and peasants	17	12	3	22	12	2
12. Agricultural labourers	16	12	3	16	8	1

Source: Praderie, Salais, and Passagez (1967), Figs 5, 6.

higher and the lower grades of occupation. They also show, what may be less expected, that in a population whose years of birth lay within 1897–1947 the education of the women had generally extended as far as that of the men, and sometimes farther; but these were all gainfully occupied women.

In so far as educational courses of different length lead to occupations at different levels, the shorter courses generally completed by the children of parents in the lower occupational grades appear as a mechanism by which inequalities of earnings are transmitted from one generation to the next. The link between the extent of a young person's education and the level of occupation he or she attains is a matter of everyday knowledge. Data collected by the U.S. Bureau of the Census provide the quantitative measure of the link shown in Table 7.9. Here we come upon estimates of lifetime earnings. We lack records of what those now retiring have earned year by year through their working lives, and do not know what those now at work will earn in the future. Instead, in the present study, the earnings reported by persons who had had a given extent of education but were of different ages were treated as showing the flow of earnings year by future year to which a person of that kind at the beginning of his working life today could look forward; each future year's income was then discounted to give a present value, and the sum of the present values provided a single future estimate of lifetime earnings. These calculations reveal a systematic relation between those earnings and extent of education. For those

Table 7.9

Extent of Education and Lifetime Earnings

U.S.A., 1960s, surveyed group of full-time men working full year: average lifetime earnings of men having different extents of education, expressed as relatives to average lifetime earnings of all men in U.S.A.

Extent of education	Relative lifetime earnings
Elementary	
less than 8 years	62
8 years	74
High school	
1–3 years	84
4 years	98
Average of all	100
College	
1–3 years	114
4 years	152
5 years and over	162

Source: U.S. Dept. of Commerce, Bureau of the Census (1970).

who have completed four years of college the prospective lifetime earnings are more than twice as great as for those with no more than an elementary schooling.

From such observed connections as these—the more extensive the education, the higher the subsequent earnings—the inference has been drawn that educating a human being resembles the building of a machine, in that it creates a productive capacity that will yield an output to society and a return to its possessor over its working life. Adam Smith set this out (1776, Bk I, c. X, Pt. I):

When an expensive machine is erected, the extraordinary work to be performed by it before it is worn out, it must be expected, will replace the capital laid out upon it, with at least the ordinary profits. A man educated at the expense of much labour and time to any of these employments which require extraordinary dexterity and skill, may be compared to one of those expensive machines. The work which he learns to perform, it must be expected, over and above the wages of common labour, will replace to him the whole expenses of his education, with at least the ordinary profits of an equally valuable capital. It must do this too in a reasonable time, regard being had to the very uncertain duration of human life, in the same manner as to the more certain duration of the machine. The differences between the wages of skilled labour and those of common labour are founded upon this principle.

There are several thoughts here—that schooling and training implant in the student an earning power that he would not otherwise possess; that their cost should consequently be regarded as an investment, on which the greater earnings subsequently received are the return; that the rate of return on this kind of investment can be calculated for the courses leading to each level or type of occupation; that young people, or their parents, will have regard to these rates of return in their choice of vocation; so that, finally, their avoiding those courses that for the time being offer lower rates of return, and moving into those that offer higher ones, will tend to equalize the rates of return realized in different occupations, and in doing so adjust and determine the relative earnings they afford.

In more recent years economists have given these thoughts both theoretical rigour and statistical application, first and foremost in the U.S.A. (Mincer 1958, 1962, 1970; Becker 1962, 1964; Schultz 1961). We go on to examine the contribution of this development of human capital theory to our understanding of the differences of earnings between occupations.

7.7. Education as investment: human capital theory

A first question to ask about the treatment of education as a form of investment is whether its statistical applications yield intelligible results. These applications consist in tracing the association between the extent of a person's education and the size of his subsequent earnings. But the interpretation of any such association is difficult. In particular, the extent of education completed by any young person is linked with the socio-economic level of his parents and with his own mental ability, personality, and motivation; and any effects these take on his earning power have to be disentangled from the contribution of education. At the outset, however, let us put this difficulty aside, and see only what we find when we ask how far those who have completed more education earn more than others subsequently.

In two respects the findings do support the treatment of education as a form of investment: the rates of return calculated in a number of inquiries have proved to be not unlike one another, and of the same order of magnitude as the rates obtained on other forms of investment; and the returns to successive stages of education generally diminish.

Both these findings are illustrated by Table 7.10. Here one set of rates comes from U.S. data, the other from British. The U.S. rates are 'private' in that they take account of only those costs of education that are borne by the student; these costs include the foregoing of earnings immediately available, as well as actual outlays. The British rates are 'social', in that they include in the costs those that are borne by institutions or the state. To that extent we expect the British rates of return to rule lower than the six comparable rates in the bottom right-hand corner of the U.S. table, and this on the whole they do. In the U.S. estimates we notice the high rate of return afforded by literacy—that is, by carrying an elementary education through to the age of 15. We see also how successive extensions beyond that age generally yield lower returns, with the exception that continuing to 21 offers higher returns than continuing only to 19—presumably because 21 brings a degree, a credential, as the earlier stopping point does not. The diminishing marginal rate of return to the number of

Table 7.10

Private and Social Rates of Return on Extensions of Education

Private rates of return are reckoned on those costs only that are borne by the student and his family. Social rates of return are reckoned on all the costs of the student's education, including those borne by charities and government.

Table 7.10.1

U.S. males, 1949: estimated private rates of return, taking income after tax, on given extensions of education.

	Education extended to age			
Age from which education is extended	15 %	17 %	19 %	21 %
6	27·9	25·2	17·2	17·2
8	33·0	28·2	17·5	17·3
12	24·8	22·2	13·7	14·4
14	12·3	14·5	9·4	11·5
16		17·5	8·5	11·4
18			· 5·1	10·1
20				16·7

Source: Hansen (1963).

Table 7.10.2

G.B. 1966–67: sample of 15,000 persons drawn from the Sample Census of Population: social rates of return from extensions of education beyond age 15.

Extension to	Rate of return
	%
'A level'[1]	7·7
National Certificate[2]—ordinary	7·9
higher	14·4
University	
first degree	10·0
Master's degree	8·6
Doctorate	7·6

[1] Completion of secondary education, with possible qualification for admission to university.
[2] Higher manual skills and technicians.

Source: Morris and Ziderman (1971), Table E.

years of schooling is shown by the fall in the average rate as the span from a given starting-point extends (that is, as we move to the right along the rows, with the exception just noted of the last entries), and by the fall as the starting-point moves towards a given terminal age (that is, as we move down the columns): in each case the movement takes us into spans containing a smaller proportion of the earlier years. The British study was designed to isolate the association between education and earnings, by omitting those persons drawn in the sample who had acquired professional qualifications otherwise than through the educational system; those like members of the armed forces, clergymen, and school teachers whose occupations were seen as differentiated by the extent of their non-pecuniary benefits; and those whose earnings were thought to be much affected by monopoly or monopsony power or administrative rate-fixing. The salient rate of return that this study found for the Higher National Certificate and the first degree suggest, like the return to the continuance of education to age 21 in the U.S. data, the market value of a certificate or credential.

Many other inquiries of this kind were surveyed by Blaug (1972, pp. 224–34). The private rates of return they showed were of the same order as the rates charged on personal loans—a report on consumer credit in the U.S.A. gave the rates charged on such loans as ranging from 12 to 28 per cent (U.S. Federal Reserve System 1957, Vol. I, Pt. 1). The social rates of return, Blaug found, 'are either roughly the same as the yield of alternative public and private investment (as in the U.S.A. and the U.K.), or are sometimes clearly below alternative yields (as in Israel and India)' (1972, p. 231). These are remarkable findings. At first sight it does not seem impossible that the returns on the cost of education and training should be far above those on other forms of investment: most entrants to the labour market might not be able to command resources in sufficient amounts to increase the numbers obtaining further education, and so bring down the earnings that the products of that education could obtain. But equally, since much education in the developed countries is provided at the public expense, or paid for by those who could afford it privately, as a means of widening interests and enriching cultural life—in economic terms, as a consumption good and not as an investment in productive equipment—it seems quite possible that no measurable increase in output is looked for to compensate the outlay on education, any more than that on public libraries and art galleries. But neither of these possibilities is in fact realized. The most natural explanation of the actual state of affairs is that the entrants to employment, or their parents, do weigh the prospective lifetime earnings in different occupations against the cost of the courses of education and training that will give access to them; and that sufficient of them can command the resources needed to meet such cost, to prevent the rate of return on preparation for this or that occupation remaining for long above other rates, or the generally prevailing rate remaining above that obtaining for personal loans.

To this extent the statistical application of human capital theory bears out the assumption on which the theory rests, that the entrant or his or her family is a maximizer, concerned to extend investment in the form of education, as in other forms, up to the point at which the falling marginal return to it comes down to equality with the rising marginal cost of borrowing. But the studies on which this conclusion rests are those of the returns to different extents of education when the earnings of those who have completed each given extent are averaged over all the various occupations they follow. An alternative form of calculation is to take those who are following a given occupation, and relate their earnings to the average costs of the various extents of education they had previously completed.

When we do this, do we find that the returns offered by different occupations to prospective entrants are nearly equal after the different costs of preparation have been taken into account? We might expect this on the ground that if people, at least in the aggregate, adjust their investment in education in the way just noticed, they would also be vigilant enough to notice differences in the returns offered by different courses of education and subsequent occupation, and would move away from the lower returns and towards the higher so as to keep returns to any course from diverging far from the general level. In that case differences between the earnings in different occupations would only be such as were needed to compensate differences in the educational investment they required. We have seen how Adam Smith held that 'the differences between the wages of skilled labour and those of common labour are founded upon' the cost of the training in which the skill was acquired. This principle can be extended to the differences in earnings between all occupations requiring less or more extensive education and training. Do the facts accord with it? Estimates made in Canada and the U.S.A. and drawn on in Table 7.11 agree in their answer. In each case, the prospective lifetime earnings in an occupation were taken from the earnings reported in a recent census by persons in the successive stages of working life. (This use of a simultaneous cross-section to chart the course of a cohort through time neglects any differences there may be other than age between the persons at different stages of working life in the year of the census, but there is no other available basis of estimate.) Certain costs of education and entry into the occupation are treated as negative earnings or a reduction of earnings in the years in which they are incurred. The resultant stream of earnings, negative or small in the earlier years and positive and bigger in the later, is then discounted at a rate of interest deemed appropriate in the context, to arrive at the net capital value of the return offered by the occupation to someone considering preparing for it at age 14. If Adam Smith was right, these capital values should not be very different from one another. Table 7.11 shows that for given occupations they are in fact very different. The higher the earnings in an occupation, the higher was its capital value after offsetting the generally higher cost of education and training for it. The net capital value of the whole lifetime course of preparation and earnings comes out as nearly twice as great for the engineer as for the labourer.

This finding will not surprise us. The supposed process of equalization assumes that higher returns in any occupation will draw in an increased number of entrants, and this extension of the supply of labour will reduce the relative pay that it commands. Everyday experience indicates that this process is operative in some measure, but there are several reasons why it does not go so far as to remove all inequalities. The last section noted the ways in which the class of the parents affected the educational attainment of the child: a chief of these lies in the ability to bear the costs of maintaining the child, and

Table 7.11
Lifetime Earnings Offered by Different Extents of
Education and Different Occupations

U.S.A., males, 1960: prospective lifetime earnings before tax, net of any graduate school costs and costs of entry into occupation, discounted at 5 per cent to age 14.

Canada, males who had attended high school for 4 years, 1961: prospective lifetime earnings, after income tax, adjusted for life expectancy, and net of costs of education and training after age 14, discounted at 8 per cent to age 14.

Capital values in each country expressed as relatives to average capital values in that country of engineers, technicians, draughtsmen, carpenters, and labourers.

U.S.A.			*Canada*
Dentists	146		
Salaried managers and officials in manufacturing	139		
Electrical and mechanical engineers	131	131	Engineers
Physicians and surgeons	127		
Toolmakers, diemakers, and setters	119		
Designers and draughtsmen	110	110	Draughtsmen
Accountants	109		
Technicians, electrical, electronic, engineering, and other	105	113	Technicians
		105	Compositors and typesetters
Plumbers and pipefitters	104		
Machinists and job setters	101		
Masons, tile setters, and stone cutters	95		
Carpenters	85	79	Carpenters
Shipping and receiving clerks	79		
Teachers, elementary school	79		
Labourers, except farm and mine	70	68	Labourers

Sources: U.S.A., Carol and Parry (1968), Table I; *Canada*, Wilkinson (1966), Table 3.

foregoing potential earnings, through the years of further education, but there are other, non-pecuniary links that are hardly less strong. The difficulty of 'finding the money' might be overcome by borrowing, and in the U.S.A it is possible for some young people to finance their education and training by a loan from a local banker; but more generally entrants depend on their families and on grants from the public purse. Even were there no financial limitations, there may still be a limited supply of the personal qualities needed for particular occupations: earnings in those occupations that can be followed only by persons with I.Q.s, say, of 115 and over—one-sixth of the whole population—may contain a 'rent of ability'. The number of entrants may further be limited by lack of knowledge or by spatial immobility. There may also be obstacles to entry erected by those already engaged in an occupation. Even where there is no overt obstacle, if those already engaged in an occupation combine to maintain high rates of pay in it, this will keep the number of jobs available in it down, however many would be willing to work in it at those rates.

So far our discussion of the evidence has shown that the cost of extensions of education can be treated as an investment, in that the returns on it are found to be of the same order as those on other forms of investment; but that the returns offered to those who prepare themselves for different occupations remain very different. Common to the studies from which both these findings are drawn is the assumption that it is the extra education that embodies the extra earning power in the student, but this assumption we must now scrutinize.

At the outset we noted that extent of education is linked with other factors that must also be expected to affect earning power: those who complete longer courses of education generally have higher I.Q.s, come from homes at a higher socio-economic level, and are more highly motivated. Instead, then, of simply recording the association between extent of education and subsequent earnings, we must resort to a more complex analysis, designed to discover how much is contributed to earning power by education when allowance is made for the simultaneous contributions of the associated factors. One way in which this has been attempted has been to take a number of young people whose all-round performance, say, at secondary school indicated similar personal capacity, and then see how far differences in the extent of their further education were associated with differences in subsequent earnings (Wolfe & Smith 1956, cited in Becker 1964, p. 83; Husèn, cited in Blaug 1972, pp. 40–1). These studies have found that extension of education is in fact associated with higher earnings; but possibly the very fact of extension marks a difference of motivation. Alternatively, multiple regressions have been fitted, in which the partial coefficient of the factor education should show by how much a given extension of education will raise subsequent earnings when the other factors affecting earnings are held constant in given amounts. We shall consider these studies more fully when we come in the next chapter to consider variations in individual earnings. Here we can note that all the recorded factors together, education included, have been found to account for not more than half, and sometimes much less than half, of the variance of earnings. (Adams 1958; Morgan & David 1963; Hanoch, cited by Mincer 1970; Taubman & Wales 1973, 1974). Evidently much more enters into the determination of earnings than meets the statistician's eye; amongst the factors he can take account of, education makes a positive contribution, but it is a modest one. From their study of a wide and exceptionally fully recorded sample of U.S. males in the upper half of the I.Q. distribution, Taubman and Wales (1973, pp. 30, 35) concluded that 'it is almost certain that for those who are at least high school graduates, ability is a more important determinant of the range of income distribution than is education'. The efficiency of young executives in a big U.S. firm, as judged by their superiors, was found to be associated with their academic performance (not just the extent of their education), but it was associated no less closely with personal qualities that were correlated with that performance only slightly (Wise 1973). The effect of I.Q., and of the personal qualities that spring from socio-economic background, is also shown by the finding that the standing of the college attended, as distinct from the number of years of attendance, was closely associated with subsequent advancement (Weisbrod & Karpoff 1968; Taubman & Wales 1973; Wise 1973).

There are further grounds for doubting how far any association between extent of education and earnings is due to productive capacity that education builds into the student. It is an implication of the findings of the multiple regressions noted above that one and the same extent of education is associated with a wide range of individual earnings (see also Becker 1964, pp. 104–13). In the U.S.A. in 1969 the median money income of white adult males with college education was some 37 per cent higher than that of those who had not gone beyond high school, but the incomes of about 30 per cent of the college educated were below the high school median, and those of about 26 per cent of the high school educated were above the college median (U.S. Bureau of the Census 1970, p. 124; Thurow & Lucas 1972, p. 18). It has also been found that those now filling a given position adequately have very various educational attainments, many of them a good deal slighter than those stated as prerequisite for the position. Surveying 15 firms in the British electrical engineering industry, Blaug et al. (1967, pp. 49–50) reported that 'over two-thirds of the jobs for which educational requirements were specified are filled by underqualified men, or else by men with the right level of but wrong type of qualification. It is noteworthy that only one-fifth of the occupants of jobs were observed to have the precise qualification corresponding to the job-analysis conception of what was required by the job.' When the survey was extended to cover 68 factories, Layard et al. (1971, c. 9) found no systematic relation between occupation and level of education, or between the subject studied in education and the subject-matter of the present job. This is intelligible if we allow for the extent to which practical experience will provide needed qualifications for those who bring resources of personality to it. Thus Clements (1958, p. 77) remarked of the managers in the region of Manchester who had had no more than an elementary schooling, 'Many find that moral qualities, strength of character, ability to make decisions, hard work and conscientiousness are adequate substitutes for training if allied with experience.'

We may conclude that it is hard to separate the effect of the extent of education from that of personal qualities, both because those qualities that are recorded are associated with extension of education and, even more, because other qualities are not recorded at all. So far as the separation can be made, the influence of extent of education per se appears positive but not outstanding.

Even the undoubted over-all association between educational attainment and level of earnings has been attributed to employers accepting such attainment as evidence of personal qualities that have made the attainment possible and that the course leading up to it has tested but has not necessarily increased (Miller & Reissman 1972; Thurow & Lucas 1972). Degrees and diplomas, that is to say, are accepted as credentials of the qualities that the employer is really looking for, such as motivation and the capacity for persistent application. In effect, he is trusting the schools and colleges to carry out a protracted and thoroughgoing selection procedure for him without charge. The recruit will in any case have to learn the job after he joins the firm, and his academic achievement is evidence of his capacity to learn. So, say Thurow and Lucas (1972, p. 21), 'the labour market is not primarily a market for matching the demands and supplies of different job skills, but a matter for matching trainable individuals with training ladders'. They see jobs as stacked in order of general desirability, and over against this job stack is a queue of applicants with those whom employers judge most trainable at the head.

In judging trainability, the employers are mainly guided by educational attainment, If, then, the applicants come to contain a higher proportion of college graduates, instead of these graduates' competition for the same jobs as before lowering the pay for those jobs, what will actually happen is that some college graduates will now be available for the best jobs formerly held by those who had not gone beyond high school, and will be preferred for these jobs. Similarly, high school graduates will now extend downwards into the best jobs formerly held by those with no more than an elementary education. The average earnings of college graduates and high school graduates will both fall, but those of high school graduates in greater proportion, so that what has been taken as the differential return to further education will actually increase.

During the 1950s and 1960s the proportions of the U.S. white male labour force with high school and college education increased greatly, as note 1 shows in Table 7.12. Drawing on the particulars of their individual education and income which members of that labour force provided in the Censuses of 1950 and 1970, Thurow and Lucas ranked all the jobs held in order of income, and divided them into tenths. The question then is, what proportion of those with each of the three levels of education held jobs in the top tenth, the second tenth, and so on, in 1950, and how had these proportions changed by 1970? Table 7.12 shows how those with college education had become increasingly occupied in the lower income tenths; relatively fewer of those with high school education had been able to find jobs in the top tenths, and there was now much more concentration in the bottom half of the job stack; and for those with elementary education this last shift was marked even more. This accords, say Thurow and Lucas, with the expectations derived from the hypothesis that jobs are allocated by the interaction between the job stack and the educationally ordered queue. They cite particulars of changes in the relative median incomes of those with different education, which also accord with such expectations.

Against the view that the difference made by education is in the initial access to jobs, it has been pointed out that the earnings of the more educated diverge increasingly from other workers' as time goes on (Layard & Psacharopoulos 1974; and see Sec. 8.3 following). If this comes about because further education has built in a greater capability that shows itself by a sustained capacity for relative advancement, it certainly counts against 'credentialism'. But there is the alternative explanation, that the relative rise in earnings in the course of working life is a characteristic of certain 'career paths', up which those who once gain admittance may expect to make their way without exceptional exertions or superior ability, and the function of educational qualifications is to gain admittance in the first place.

Table 7.12
Effect of Greater Education of the Labour Force
on Jobs Obtained

U.S.A., 1950 and 1970, adult white males: effect of increased proportion of men with high school and college education in the labour force between 1950 and 1970[1] on the distribution of those with given education between jobs ranked by income. Number with given education occupied in given grade of jobs, as percentage of all with that education, in 1970, divided by the corresponding percentage in 1950.

Decile of jobs ranked by income	Level of education		
	Elementary	High School	College
Best tenth	0·39	0·61	0·94
2nd best	0·59	0·84	0·96
3rd „	0·46	0·84	1·56
4th „	0·80	0·92	1·03
5th „	0·73	1·02	1·36
6th „	0·81	1·16	1·23
7th „	0·94	1·26	1·04
8th „	1·18	1·32	0·85
9th „	1·31	1·35	1·09
10th „	1·58	0·98	0·80

[1] The recorded change in the education of the U.S. adult white male labour force was

	1949	1969	
	%	%	
Elementary	47	20	
High School	38	51	
College	15	28	
	100	100	(subject to rounding)

Source: Thurow and Lucas (1972), p. 32 and Table 14.

In any case it is no part of the credentialist case to maintain that educational credentials are not generally a reliable indication of capacity; the thrust of the argument is rather that they ought not to be used as the whole indication. If employers use them to screen applicants, some applicants who are in fact well able to do a given job will be rejected because they happen to lack the credentials. Taubman and Wales tested this hypothesis. They calculated the extent to which the particular personal qualities (not including education) recorded for the men in their sample contributed to earnings in each of seven occupational groups—professional, technical, sales, blue-collar, service, white-collar, manager. Applying the coefficients thus obtained to each man's qualities, they found which group he should earn most in, and assigned him to it. They then compared this hypothetical distribution with the actual. In the hypothetical they found few men, whatever their level of education, in the blue-collar, service, and white-collar groups. But in the actual distribution 'a substantial frac-ton (39 per cent) of high school graduates, a smaller fraction (17 per cent) of the some college group, and only 4 per cent of the BA holders enter these occupations. Since the discrepancy between the expected and actual distributions is directly related to education we conclude that education itself is being used as a screening device to prevent those with low educational attainment from entering the high-paying occupations' (1973, p. 46). This means also that those who get into the higher-paid occupations because their educational attainments are higher would not necessarily have lacked the capability to follow those occupations if the further education had not been 'invested in them'.

It is from the possibility of such investment that human capital theory sets out. From our discussion of it here we must conclude that the analogy between educating a human being and building a machine is defective. The role of education in the formation of productive capacity seems rather to be like that of water in the growth of a plant. That growth depends on many factors—warmth, light, nutrients, as well as water. A plant whose growth is fostered by these other factors cannot grow unless it can take up more water. There is no question, similarly, but that doctors and engineers cannot be qualified without courses of training, and it is quite possible that general education provides a similar condition of development for other forms of proficiency. But when the amounts of the growth-fostering factors are fixed, we cannot get more growth beyond a certain point by pouring on more and more water. Similarly it seems that spending more on education, beyond a certain point, will not of itself increase earning power.

7.8. Entry into employment

The differences that we have seen between classes in parents' attitudes towards education and in the educational attainments of their children naturally extend into the children's entry into employment.

A main link is the age of leaving school. The range of occupations open to those who leave earlier is narrowed through their lacking the educational attainments that are prerequisite for entry to many occupations. One reason for early leaving is the pressure of economic need on the family, requiring the children to start earning as soon as possible. The study of British National Servicemen called up in 1956–8 found that in each socio-economic class the proportion who had left school at the minimum age of 15 rose uniformly with the size of family (Ministry of Education 1960, p. 129). In their study of U.S. Census data, Duncan, Featherman, and Duncan (1968, Table 9.1.1) find that, other things being equal, the bigger a young person's family, the lower was the socio-economic status of his first job.

But many children leave school at an early age even where they are not under economic pressure to begin to earn and even in schools where it is customary to stay on longer. The British National Serviceman who had left schools of that type at the age of 15 gave as their main reasons, other than 'money short at home', that a particular job was available, and that they 'saw no point in staying at school longer', or were 'fed up with school' (Ministry of Education

1960, p. 135). To many young people, especially among the children of manual workers, continued schooling is not only uncongenial in itself but purposeless, because it is not seen as leading to any clearly envisaged goal.

The adolescent's capacity to envisage the goal of a career has been found to depend greatly on parents' attitudes. Among manual workers these attitudes have been found to be sometimes negative: the child is given no guidance. Carter (1966, p. 50), in a study of school leavers in an English industrial city in 1959, found that 'at the core of the working class are the families who accept, more or less, many of the standards upheld in the wider society—as reflected in the law and by the school—but who are easy-going and inclined to take life as it comes'. These parents have few ideas about choice of jobs. 'The main thing is for the kids to be happy', but they do not consider in any systematic way how this can be achieved. There are many other manual workers' families in which the children are encouraged to get on, and the parents do discuss the choice of jobs; but here there are still limitations of knowledge. The range of jobs considered is that within the personal knowledge of the parents, and though they may be aware that a child is capable of moving up the educational ladder, they do not have a clear enough picture in their minds of the occupations to which this gives access, for them to instil aspirations towards them. Remarking on the extent to which the applicants for admission to the university of Novosibirsk came from homes of the intelligentsia, Liss (1973, p. 281) remarks apologetically, 'It must be emphasized that there is no social exclusiveness in the formation of occupational inclinations of youth under socialism.. . . But the very fact of belonging to a certain social stratum, the greater familiarity with the kind of employment typical for its members, and the greater opportunity for assimilating its mode of behaviour, create the conditions for developing the kind of occupational orientation which is more typical for this stratum.'

It is a purpose of vocational guidance in the schools and, in the U.K., of the Youth Employment Service, to provide young people with wider information about possible jobs and careers. Generally it seems that such information helps young people to make their way in directions in which they are already tending, rather than bring about a change of direction by presenting some attractive prospect not known before. Part of the difficulty arises when the choice of occupation coincides with the crisis of self-identity in adolescence (Hill 1969, p. 34; Maizels 1970, pp. 318–19). Associated with this is the main limitation, that young people do not see themselves in parts that they have not grown up to regard as naturally theirs. It is the influence of the home that predominates—the occupations of parents, relatives, friends, and neighbours; and, when the parents (especially the mother) do give guidance, the occupations they commend.

A Russian study (cited in Yanowich & Dodge 1969) has shown the same division as has been noted in the West between the careers envisaged for their children by parents who are manual workers and those who are more highly educated. Among the parents of secondary school graduates at Nizhnii Tagil in

1964, about 60 per cent of the intelligentsia but less than 40 per cent of the manual workers preferred medicine, education, and science as occupations for their children, whereas a greater proportion of the manual workers than of the intelligentsia preferred industry and transport.

Another Russian study (Titma 1973) has shown how the relative importance attached by graduates of Estonian secondary schools in 1966 to various characteristics of jobs varied according to the socio-economic level of their parents. 'It seems evident that the intelligentsia exercise a significantly greater influence on the transmission of occupational values to their children. This influence is of an individual nature, and it is particularly conspicuous with respect to [the values 'material remuneration' and 'recognition by people in one's immediate social environment'], an area where official social policy conducted through formal channels is negatively oriented or is absent altogether. Moreover, children of the intelligentsia are less susceptible to the influence of formal channels (schools, mass media, etc.) (p. 224). It was thought to be in part because the children of agricultural and unskilled manual workers are given less guidance at home that they set much more store than did the others on the officially inculcated value, 'usefulness to the national economy'.'

But manual workers may give powerful guidance to their children to enable them to escape afflictions that beset the parents' own lives. The son of a Welsh miner remembers how in the hard days between the wars his parents urged him to get on at school so that he could escape from the pits to a white-collar job; another son, this time of an unemployed London worker, remembers how his father resisted his going on to the university rather than leave school to make sure of a safe job as an accountant. The children of manual workers have been found to show less appetite for risk than do middle-class children (Hyman 1967, Table 7), and it is natural that those who have known what it is to live under the threat of destitution should set a higher value on a modest security than on a chance of making a lot of money linked with a chance of losing all. It is natural also that the children of manual workers should set more store than middle-class children do by the pay that different occupations offer, relatively to the interest of the work and the congeniality of the conditions in which it is done (Hill 1965, p. 283; Hyman 1967, p. 490). Generally, manual workers who are concerned for their children's advancement look towards the occupations that they judge most promising among those that are known to them and that are readily accessible. In so far as they do this, they instil in their children the expectation that they too will follow manual occupations.

Children so influenced will leave school early even though they have the ability needed for higher education. In the cohort of children born in England and Wales in 1946, it was found that among the boys who by ability were alike in being at the borderline of entry to grammar school, 48 per cent of the upper-middle-class boys wanted to enter a profession, and 28 per cent of the lower-middle-class, but only 17 per cent of the upper-working-class and 7 per cent of the lower-working-class. If this cohort was typical of its generation, more than half of the working-class boys in the top third of measured ability would remain in working-class occupations (Douglas, Ross, & Simpson 1968, pp. 99–100). Of the British National Servicemen who were the sons of manual workers and were placed in the highest of the six grades of ability, nearly two-thirds had left school at 15 or 16 (Ministry of Education 1960, pp. 118–19).

At a time of great increase in the numbers proceeding to secondary and tertiary education, the experience of those who have already done this will influence the choice of course by their successors. Initially it may well have been generally expected that those who obtain, for example, a university degree will also obtain the kind of job and pay commonly enjoyed hitherto by university graduates. An increased number of graduates can be absorbed in employment only in so far (in the absence of a coincidental extension of demand) as the relative pay of the occupations formerly filled by graduates falls, and as graduates enter posts formerly 'beneath them' in the occupational scale. But the fall in relative pay has been strenuously resisted—in Sweden, university graduates have their own union, which called a strike of all its members in the endeavour to uphold their relativities. For more than one reason such endeavours are unlikely to be wholly successful, but they delay the adjustment of pay and the absorption of young graduates. The spread of graduates into occupations formerly filled by those with only secondary education is part of the raising of educational qualifications throughout the economy and in time it will come to be regarded as natural, but meanwhile the entrants are apt to feel disappointed: society seems to have broken its contract with them, and in acquiring their qualifications they seem to have been wasting their time. Some of the young people who might have followed them will be put off. The deterrent influence will be heightened by the sight of graduate unemployment.

Some of those who go from school to employment in their teens have made a definite choice of job, or have a particular opening if not career in view. But for many the finding of a first job is a haphazard affair. In their study of manual workers in New Haven, Connecticut, in 1946–47, Reynolds and Shister (1949) found that the great majority of them had found their first jobs simply by applying at a firm that happened to have been mentioned to them by a relative or acquaintance, or by being introduced to a firm by someone working there already. Some had gone back for full-time employment to a firm for which they had already worked part-time during the school holidays. The great majority, again, took the first job they found without comparing it with other jobs. Partly this was induced by the sense, surviving at that time from the 1930s, that jobs were hard to get. But half of those interviewed said that neither they nor their parents had had any definite occupational plans while they were at school, so that they had few standards of comparison; some were chiefly anxious to get out of school; and others simply took it for granted that they would go into the level of job their family expected them to take.

Informal methods—suggestions by relatives and friends, or calling at firms to see if there was a job going—were still predominant among a national sample of young men in the U.S. in 1966, despite the availability of employment agencies in the school and in the community (Miljus, Parnes, Schmidt, & Spitz

1968). The effectiveness of these agencies in placement, as distinct from counselling and providing information, has been limited by the willingness of applicants to use them, and the users have tended to be of two minority types—those who knew just what they wanted and went to the agency to find out where jobs of that description were available; and those who lacked the connections, energy, or attractiveness to employers through which jobs are found informally (e.g. Maizels 1970, in a study of teenagers in the London borough of Willesden in 1965). There has been a vicious circle here, in that employers have not notified jobs to the agencies when they have not expected the agencies to have suitable applicants on their books.

These various disabilities that beset manual workers' children in occupational choice and job-finding have combined to present a sad picture of the small chances they have, in comparison with middle-class children, of advancing themselves. Thus three American sociologists, reflecting on a study of wage-earners in Oakland, California, in 1949–50, observed (Lipset, Bendix, & Malm 1955, p. 231):

If an individual comes from a working-class family, he will typically receive little education or vocational advice; his job plans for the future will be vague while he attends school; and when he leaves school he is likely to take the first available job he can find. Unfavourable economic circumstances, lack of education, absence of personal 'contacts', lack of planning, and failure to explore fully the available job opportunities which characterize the working-class family are handed down from generation to generation. The same cumulation of factors which in the working-class case adds up to mounting disadvantages, works to the advantage of a child coming from a well-to-do family.

That verdict would need to be qualified today by the extension of education, of vocational counselling, and, in the U.K. at least, by the liaison effected between parents, school, and employers in the Youth Employment Service. The implication of social immobility seems in any case to have gone beyond what we know of the upward mobility of the children of manual workers.

That this is as great as it is despite the obstacles we have listed can be accounted for in great part by the possibilities of an advancement after the first job has been found. These possibilities are realized in some measure by job changing: the high rate of turnover of young workers marks a movement that may seem as random as that into first jobs, but that serves to widen the young worker's knowledge of the possibilities of employment, and to help him find the kind of work that suits him. Often too the movement is in fact towards more skilled work. In her study of job-changing in Battersea and Dagenham (industrial districts, one in the centre and one on the outskirts of London), Jefferys (1954) found that only between a quarter and a third of the skilled men had entered their trade on leaving school, and remained in it throughout: a half or more of them had started in semi-skilled or unskilled work. The first jobs of some of them had been as tea boys or messenger boys; often they had moved up to skilled work from machine operating or craftsman's mate, or, to a lesser extent, from heavy labouring. A study of the U.S. programmes designed to provide more education and training and better job placement for those who fell short of their potential on their first entry into work found that about a third of entrants to employment stood in need of such a 'second chance' in the 1960s. The remainder owed much to progress after their first entry. 'The school to work transition process of the American manpower system provides reasonable preparation for employment to less than half of those who traverse it. However, with native ability and employer "make do", probably two-thirds end up with a reasonably satisfactory working career.. . .' (Mangum 1968.)

'Employer "make do"' comprises on-the-job training. Some entrants are attracted to first jobs by the prospects these offer of being trained; others not consciously seeking training are likely to find themselves drawn into courses formal or informal. An important form of on-the-job training is simply the gathering of experience by doing a job, and working alongside others who have been on the job longer. Surveying U.S. and Canadian studies of how skill is acquired, Doeringer and Piore (1971, p. 18) find that 'by far the largest proportion of blue-collar job skills is acquired on the job'. In white-collar jobs educational attainment appears to count for more, but this may be only the attainment of trainability in managerial and professional skills, or a means of selecting the trainable. 'On-the-job training then provides either the large proportion of skills actually utilized in the performance of work or is a prerequisite for the successful utilization of formal education.' Mincer (1962) estimated the total investment in on-the-job training in the U.S.A. on the assumption that the greater part of the costs of such training are charged to the trainee through a reduction in his pay below what a similar person not receiving training would be paid. After allowance for part of the costs not so charged but borne, at least during the period of training, by the employer, Mincer concluded that 'it is probably correct to say that, in the male half of the world, on-the-job training—measured in dollar costs—is as important as formal schooling' (p. 63.)

On-the-job training is thus an important offset to the bias, constraints, and randomness that vitiate the entry into employment of many children of manual workers. This appears by difference where access to on-the-job training is restricted: we saw in Chapter 4 how women and blacks alike have suffered from such restriction—that the earnings of blacks are lower than those of whites with the same educational attainment has been attributed to the blacks having less access to jobs that carry the prospect of advancement by learning and experience. The extent to which forms of planned training were provided for school leavers aged 15–17 in Great Britain in a recent year is shown by Table 7.13. More than half of the boys went into jobs offering some form of planned training, and not a few of those who went into clerical jobs will additionally have received training there. But among those who left school at 15, and who will have been mostly the sons of manual workers, nearly 40 per cent entered jobs without provision for training. Nearly 60 per cent of the girls went into clerical jobs, and the likelihood that training was in fact provided in some

Table 7.13
Training for Entrants to Employment

Great Britain, 1973: proportions of school leavers at ages 15, 16, 17 entering each of five classes of employment, classified by provision of training.

	Age at entry					
	Boys			Girls		
	15	16	17	15	16	17
	%	%	%	%	%	%
Apprenticeship or learnership to skilled occupation (including pre-apprenticeship training in employment)	39·3	52·7	31·8	5·7	4·8	4·0
Employment leading to recognized professional qualifications	0·7	1·7	5·6	1·0	3·2	6·3
Employment with planned training, apart from induction training, not covered above	15·3	13·6	17·1	11·4	11·8	11·3
Subtotal, all courses with planned training	55·3	68·0	54·5	18·1	19·8	21·6
Clerical employment	5·3	10·5	23·8	48·6	58·5	61·1
Other employment	39·3	21·6	21·7	33·3	21·8	17·3
	100·0	100·0	100·0	100·0	100·0	100·0
Number of entrants, '000s	15·0	96·9	28·6	10·5	69·4	27·2

Source: Dept. of Employment Gazette (H.M.S.O., London), 82, 5, May 1974, p. 393.

of these forms an offset to the relatively small proportion—only a fifth—who entered employments recorded as providing planned training. But here appears again the disability of women, that employers are unwilling to invest in the training of workers whom they expect to leave employment before long; together with the other disability, that traditionally much skilled work is 'not women's work'. Among all these school leavers, boys and girls together, the proportion who entered non-clerical jobs that provided no planned training was about 23 per cent; among those who left school at 15 it was a third or more. The inverse proportions mark the extent of on-the-job training, though we do not know how far this was effective in enabling entrants whose start was unequal to their potential to develop it subsequently, and find their way into occupations suited to them.

7.9. Review and discussion

(a) An initial question was why the numbers moving in intergenerational mobility vary inversely with the social distance moved. The answer at which we have arrived is that, whether or not there are social barriers or gradients, a large part is played by the association between the parents' social class and the capability developed by their children. We have reached this conclusion by the following steps:

(*a*.1) Extensive studies of the relation between occupational level, as conventionally ordered or as ranked by average earnings, and the I.Q.s of the adults occupied have shown a close positive relation between the two—the higher the level of an occupation in the socio-economic scale, the higher the average I.Q. of those working in it; though this ordering of the averages goes with a wide dispersion of I.Q.s, at least on the upper side of the mean, within each occupation, and so with much overlap between occupations.

(*a*.2) Studies of the correlations between I.Q.s of relatives, between those of identical twins brought up in different homes, and between those of foster-children, their foster-parents, and their natural parents have indicated that a genetic element plays a significant part in the differentiation of I.Q. They have also indicated that genotype I.Q. may be inherited in the same way as some physical characteristics.

(*a*.3) Putting together (*a*.1) and (*a*.2), we conclude that though the genotype I.Q.s of the children of parents in a given class of occupations will be spread over a normal distribution, the average I.Q. of the children will be highly correlated with that of their parents. This remains significant even though, if mating is not completely assortative, the average I.Q. of the children of parents in each class will be nearer the mean than that of their parents. The average I.Q.s of the children of parents in given occupational classes will thus tend to be ranked in the same order as those classes.

(*a*.4) The I.Q. scores of school children and adults will be differentiated by their upbringing in the home and their schooling. Capability in an occupation also depends on qualities of personality which I.Q. does not measure and which are not necessarily correlated with I.Q. The development of both intelligence and personality depend greatly on upbringing during the first five years of life. Here again there is a differentiation by class. Studies of the upbringing of little children in 'middle-class' and 'working-class' families in the U.K. and the U.S.A. have shown a systematic difference of style, that of the 'middle-class' providing more stimulus to the child's interests and activities, and inculcating more self-reliance.

(*a*.5) The conjunction of these genetic and environmental factors in the formation of the child's potential and in its development leads us to expect a high correlation between the occupational level of the parents and the capability of the children. So far as capability is indicated by I.Q., this expectation is borne out by inquiries in the U.K. and the U.S.A.

(*b*) The outcome of this train of reasoning from the evidence is thus that much of the concentration of the children of a given class of families upon entry into occupations of their parents' class and adjacent classes must be put down to the high correlation between the parents' occupational level and the capability which is imparted to the children genetically and by upbringing in their early years. If most of the entrants to the top class of occupations are the children of parents in the top class and the one below, that is because most of the young people with the required capability are the children of parents in those classes. Most, but not all: we have seen also that some intergenerational mobility takes its rise in every class.

(c) We have seen also that in each occupation there is a substantial number of persons with I.Q. well above the average for that occupation and often above the threshold of much higher occupational levels. We do not know whether these are persons in whom, whatever level they were born into, traits of personality offset I.Q. so as to keep them where they are; or whether they were born into or below their present level, but have been prevented from rising by lack of opportunity or by 'class barriers'. Lack of opportunity may take the form of the parents' inability to see that the child gets a sufficiently good and lengthy course of education; or lack of knowledge of possible occupations and how to get into them; or being tied to a particular locality. 'Class barriers' would take the form of an unwillingness of those already in an occupation, or employing members of it, to accept and admit those who have grown up in a different life-style, whatever their present capability.

(d) To what was noted in the previous chapter concerning downward mobility we can now add the probability that an important source of downward moves is the presence of lower genotype I.Q.s within the normal distribution of the I.Q.s of the children of parents at the occupational levels in which the higher I.Q.s predominate. Another source will lie in the mishandling of early upbringing. The extent of downward mobility from the higher parental levels casts doubt on the belief that those children born into the higher levels who remain in or rise above them do so mainly because of the advantages their parents are able to procure for them. But it remains true that most of those who move down do not go far: they will settle in a higher occupation than they are likely to have attained if, with equal endowment, they had started from a home at a lower level.

(e) We have just been citing the evidence for a link between mobility and I.Q., but we have also seen (p. 233) that 'more than half of the boys of high ability from working class homes [in England & Wales] are unlikely to move out of the social class into which they were born'. One evident reason for this is that where the income of the family is low, and especially where the children are numerous, there are fewer resources to maintain them through extended years of education. In Western countries of late the force of this constraint has been reduced by the rise of the standard of living and the extension of educational opportunity. But differences in the style of upbringing in the home continue to operate to differentiate upward mobility by class. There is much evidence from the U.K. and the U.S.A. that this style has differed between 'middle-class' and 'working-class' in a way that makes the middle-class children more likely to develop the aptitudes, interests, and habits of mind that will enable them to profit by education; they are also more likely to have been made to feel that their parents want them to do well at school, and that ways of advancement in life are open to them if they do so. These differences do much to explain why the approach to equality of educational opportunity in the social democracies has not done more to equalize the probabilities of being well educated for children of given genotype I.Q. born into families of different class.

(*f*) A further factor, it may be held, lies in the greater ability of the parents of higher income to buy education for their children. This contention seems to be strongly supported by the finding in the U.K. that a high proportion of the men in the high-paid occupations came from the 'public schools', that is, private schools with high fees. An alternative interpretation of this finding would be that these men came from families of the class whose children have a high average genotype I.Q. and are brought up in a way that develops their educability, the type of school they were sent to forming part of the life-style of their families but not of itself giving them additional earning power. This raises the general question of how far earning power is increased by education of any kind. A systematic relation has been observed between extent of education and subsequent earnings—the more years of schooling, the higher in general the earnings in later life. This relation would be intelligible if education itself conferred earning power. Evidently particular forms of training—a doctor's, for instance—are a necessary condition for entry to certain occupations. The cost of such training can then be regarded as an investment on which the return is the excess of the student's subsequent earnings over what he could have earned otherwise. This view can be broadened to cover all forms of education. The cost of a young person's education and training can thus be regarded as closely analogous to investment in the building of a machine, and as building 'human capital'.

But our study of this view led to largely negative conclusions. The question we have had to put to the statistical evidence is not whether there is a correlation between years of schooling and earnings in later life, but whether, when the factors such as I.Q. and socio-economic class are held constant, an extension of education is reliably associated with an increment of earnings. We concluded that education was a necessary condition for acquiring the capacity to earn, but that providing more of it beyond a certain point would not increase that capacity. It was a road and not a bus.

(*g*) It follows that measures to provide greater 'equality of educational opportunity', which not long ago were of very great value, can be extended in contemporary social democracies with only limited effect. There are still some points at which lack of means denies children access to the further education by which their mind and motivation equip them to profit; in particular in the U.K. there is a lack of support between the legal school-leaving age and entry to the university. But the best hope of improvement lies in developing the capacity and the will to make use of existing opportunities. That development depends largely on the interaction between parent and child in the early years of life. The spread of pre-school playgroups, as providing stimulus to the children but even more as involving the mothers and increasing their ability to help their children develop, may seem a small affair to those whose aims extend to a new order of society, but offers a real prospect of reducing class differences in educational attainment.

(*h*) Throughout our discussion those differences have been seen to depend on a mixture of economic and cultural factors—on limitation of means and amenities in the lower-income families, and on differences of outlook, habits of thought and speech, and aspiration. The same factors affect the entry into employment. The need for immediate earnings combines with restricted knowledge and confined aspiration to differentiate occupational choice by class more than need be were the differentiation of the entrants' capability the only determinant.

8

Differences of Individual Earnings Within an Occupation

8.1. The extent of the variance of earnings within particular occupations

Hitherto we have been concerned only with the differences between one occupation and another in prevailing rates of pay. These rates we have taken to be representative of the occupations in which they prevail, one rate for each occupation. The procedure is justified in that there are wide differences between average earnings occupation by occupation, and the ranking of occupations by these earnings generally agrees with the ranking of the persons in those occupations by status and class, in the stratification of society. It has been a major interest of ours to examine the significance of that agreement. But now we must go on to take account of the extent of the variance of the earnings of persons within the same occupation.

This is generally large. In the public service, it is true, if we define occupation by grade in the formal scale, though there may be provision for increments according to length of service within the grade, the range is usually not wider than the distance between the mid points of two adjacent grades. But elsewhere we commonly find so wide a range within each occupation that the higher earnings in an occupation of lower average earnings are above the lower earnings in an occupation of much higher average. Whereas hitherto we have implicitly been looking on the pay structure as if it were a cliff face in which the strata, each representing an occupation, lay horizontally, we have to see the strata now as tilted, so that the upper part of one will be higher above the beach than the lower part of another that lies above it. This is illustrated for some occupations in Great Britain in 1973 in Fig. 8.1.

The fanning-out of the curves in this Figure shows that the variance of earnings is greater in the higher-paid occupations because earnings extend farther upwards above the median in these occupations than in the others, while below the median there is much less difference. At the bottom decile earnings in the highest-paid occupations are about double those in the lowest, whereas at the top decile the ratio is about five to one. In our simile of the cliff, the upper strata slope up more steeply than the lower. This is the inverted counterpart of what we found for the distribution within occupations of the scores in tests of mental ability. Figure 7.1.1 showed the variance of these scores as greater in the occupations of *lower* average scores; and this is so because in these occupations the scores extend farther *downwards*, while at the top end of the ranges there is much less difference.

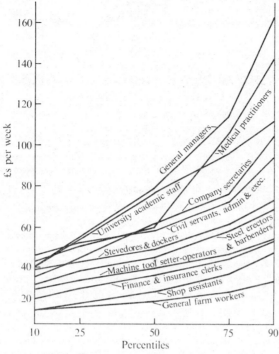

Fig. 8.1. Distribution of earnings within occupations.

Quartiles and median, with lowest and highest deciles, of earnings of full-time adult men in each of eleven occupations in Great Britain in a week of April 1973. *Source*: Dept. of Employment (1974), Table 86.

There is no reason to believe that such variance of earnings as we have instanced in Great Britain is peculiar to that country. Table 8.1 compares one measure of dispersion—the range between the upper and the lower quartiles, divided by the median—for a number of occupations whose titles in the U.S. Census of Population and the G.B. *New Earnings Survey* are similar. The U.S. figures are of income for the whole year, even though not all of it was worked, and they include all employed persons, women as well as men, and juveniles as well as adults. The British figures are of the earnings in one week of those who worked the full week, and are only for adult males. Though the effect of these differences will be damped somewhat by our taking only the quartiles and not the extremes, we are not surprised to find that the U.S. earnings are more widely dispersed than the British in every occupation save the compositors'. Further factors that contribute to this are likely to be the vastly greater area of the U.S.A., with its greater regional differences; and the wider coverage and greater centralization of collective bargaining in Great Britain. This last source of difference will have contributed to the markedly greater variance of manual wage-earnings in the U.S.A. than in Great Britain. Generally the dispersion is wider the higher are average earnings in Great Britain, but not in the U.S.A.,

Table 8.1

Dispersion of Earnings Within an Occupation in U.S.A. and G.B.

A measure of dispersion, $(Q3 - Q1) \div Q2$, calculated for earnings in each of 15 occupations in the U.S.A., 1959, and G.B., 1973.

U.S.A.: annual income (in 5% samples) of all workers who worked during the year, including those who did not work a full year.

G.B.: earnings of full-time adult males in a week of April 1973.

Q3: first or highest quartile
Q2: middle quartile or median
Q1: third or lowest quartile

U.S.A. Occupational title	$\dfrac{Q3 - Q1}{Q2}$		G.B. Occupational title
1. Managers and officials, manufacturing	0·77	0·43	Production and works managers, works foremen
2. Managers and officials, wholesale trade	0·77	0·49	Managers, wholesale distribution
3. Engineers, mechanical	0·46	0·37	Engineers, mechanical
4. Engineers, civil	0·48	0·47	Engineers—civil, structural, municipal
5. College presidents, professors, instructors (n.e.s.)	0·65	0·53	University academic staff
6. Authors, editors, and reporters	0·60	0·51	Writers, journalists
7. Compositors and typesetters	0·46	0·51	Compositors
8. Electricians	0·43	0·35	Electricians—installation and maintenance—plant etc.
9. Blacksmiths, forgemen, and hammermen	0·49	0·36	Smiths, forgemen
10. Locomotive engineers	0·36	0·33	Railway engine drivers, motormen
11. Plumbers and pipe fitters	0·54	0·34	Plumbers, pipe fitters
12. Carpenters	0·76	0·41	Carpenters and joiners—building and maintenance
13. Longshoremen and stevedores	0·67	0·38	Stevedores and dockers
14. Sailors and deck hands	0·73	0·32	Deck and engineroom hands (seagoing), boatmen etc.
15. Cooks, excl. private households	0·82	0·42	Chefs/cooks

Sources: H. P. Miller (1966), Appx. C, Table C.3; Dept. of Employment (1974), Table 86.

where managers' incomes, it is true, are widely dispersed, but so also are those of some manual workers.

From Fig. 8.1 we can form an impression of the extent of the variance within particular occupations, relatively to the difference in average earnings between one occupation and another. The survey from which it is drawn (Dept. of Employment 1974, Table 86) shows that among the manual occupations the range of the median earnings of adult men, from stevedores and dockers down to kitchen porters, was 2·3 to 1. If within each occupation we pass over the extremes of individual earnings, and take only the ratio of the highest decile to the lowest (the interdecile ratio), very generally we find a ratio which also was over 2 to 1: for manual occupations as a whole it was nearly 2·2. In the clerical occupations it was much the same. In the professional and managerial occupations it was bigger: the professions showed ratios of 2·3, 2·7, and 2·8 according as they were mainly associated with technology, education, and administration; for managers below the top the ratio was 2·6, and for the top (general) managers it was over 4·0. The range of median earnings was also bigger in this field: the highest and lowest median earnings cited happen both to be those of managers, and the range from the top managers down to the hotel, catering, and pub managers was 2·6 to 1. Thus, alike in manual occupations and in the professional and managerial, the range of individual earnings *within* occupations was about as big as the range of average earnings *between* the highest- and lowest-paid occupations.

Another way of bringing out the extent of the variance of earnings generally found within any one occupation is to compare it with the variances found when we group the same persons not by occupation but by industry or region. The British survey of earnings already cited provides particulars of the distribution of the earnings of all full-time adult men in 11 regions: the interdecile ratios run from 2·7 in Greater London down to 2·2 in the Midlands. These are higher than some of the ratios found in particular occupations, but not than all—out of the 18 groups of occupations in the survey, 10 had ratios of 2·2 or more. We can also compare the ratios within occupations with those within industries, though here we have data only for manual workers. Among the 27 branches of industry distinguished in the survey, the ratios ranged from 1·8 in gas, electricity, and water to 2·4 in insurance, banking, and finance; more than half the ratios lay between 1·9 and 2·1. Equally among the groups of manual occupations, the ratios within occupations ranged from 1·9 to 2·2.

There was thus little difference in the proportionate spread of individual earnings within groups, whether these groups were formed by bringing together those who worked in the same kind of occupation or, whatever their occupation, in the same region or the same industry. This does not mean that the grouping by occupation has no special significance: we must not forget how much more the *average* earnings in groups differ from one another when the groups are occupational than when they are regional or industrial. But it does mean that when we are concerned with the variance of individual earnings as we are here, we see differences of occupation as only one contributor to that variance among many. Lydall (1968, pp. 103–5) concluded from the data of the U.S. Census of Population 1960 that 'not more than 25 per cent of the total variance of earnings is attributable to the variance between occupations'. Using a different method, and data for 1949, Jencks (1972, c. 6, n. 12) estimated the corresponding percentage as 24. 'The range of earnings within an occupation', he also said, 'is about 85 per cent of the range for the nation as a whole.'

Let us now consider in turn the factors that set up the variance of individual earnings within given occupations, and that make the variance of the earnings of all employees so much greater than it would be if its only source were the difference between the earnings (supposed uniform) in one occupation and another.

8.2. Short-period fluctuations of earnings

The earnings of some employees fluctuate from week to week, or year to year, about a normal level that remains unchanged, or (in recent times) is raised at intervals by a given amount. The effect of these fluctuations is to increase the variance of individual earnings. Evidently if a number of employees who all had the same earnings as one another and the same earnings from week to week began to experience weekly fluctuations, the distribution of their earnings in any one week would now show some variance, even though the earnings of each and all over the year remained the same. Similarly if we begin with a distribution of unequal but steady earnings, and then suppose these earnings to fluctuate from week to week: the variance of the distribution of weekly earnings will be raised. In the same way again, if earnings generally rise from one period to the next, the variance at any one time will be higher if individual rises are some more and some less than the average.

The earnings of the same persons in successive years in Great Britain have been found to change in very different proportions.

Thatcher (1971) studied a random sample of all male employees who had worked for at least 48 weeks in each of two successive financial years, 1963–64 and 1964–65. He worked throughout with the logarithms of earnings. A first finding was that the year-to-year changes differed considerably from one man to another: the correlation between each man's earnings in the two years was below 0·80 for most age-groups except the oldest, whose earnings fluctuated least. Thatcher also found that the process of fluctuation took a particular form. When he observed the relation between the divergence of each man's earnings from the average of all earnings in the second year, and the corresponding divergence in the first year, he found that the second year's divergence was generally smaller than the first year's—that is, those whose earnings diverged from the mean whether upwards or downwards in the first year had earnings in the second year that were nearer that year's mean. This was an instance of 'regression towards the mean'. It was more marked for the younger than for the older men.

A further study analysed a matched sample of nearly 80,000 men and women whose earnings in a week of April were reported in the *New Earnings Survey* in both 1970 and 1971 (Dept. of Employment 1973). The upper part of Fig. 8.2 shows the changes that were found on the average of each of four groups, men and women being each divided into manual and non-manual. The average earnings in each group rose, by 10·3 and 12·9 per cent respectively for the manual and non-manual men, and 15·8 and 14·2 per cent for the manual and non-manual women. That the women's earnings rose more than the men's probably owes something to the pressure exerted at the time towards 'equal pay for equal work'. But at given earnings the men's rises were bigger than the

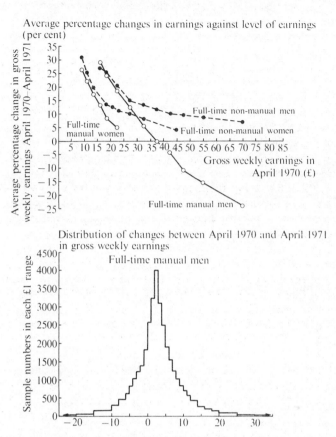

Average percentage changes in earnings against level of earnings (per cent)

Distribution of changes between April 1970 and April 1971 in gross weekly earnings

Fig. 8.2. Changes between April 1970 and April 1971 in earnings of a matched sample of British employees. *Source: Dept. of Employment Gazette* (H.M.S.O., London), 81, 4, Apr. 1973, p. 339.

women's, and the average rises of the men were lower only because their earnings extended into higher levels where percentage rises were smaller.

This tendency of the percentage rise to be smaller, the higher the earnings of the earlier year, is a remarkable finding. It is shown consistently by all four groups. Two processes probably underlie it. First, although in the manual groups some of the lower earnings are associated with higher age, in all groups many low earnings are those of young people, who change jobs more often with a view to earning more, and are more often given rises as they gain experience in the same job. Second, the process is one of 'regression towards the mean', and this comes about here as individuals whose earnings in the earlier week were exceptionally high or low in comparison with their own usual level of earnings revert towards that level. The process is specially marked for the manual men, among whom indeed those with higher earnings at the earlier date actually earned less, and those with the highest earnings as much as 25 per cent less, at the later date.

This shows the extent to which the earnings of many manual workers fluctuate from week to week. All in the sample, it must be remembered, worked a full week. It was found that little difference was made to the pattern of change according as the earnings in both weeks did or did not include overtime. But within given hours there can be big differences in the opportunities those who are paid by results enjoy to add to their earnings, or in the use they make of a given opportunity. Some of the changes in earnings will also be due to changes of job, not always towards higher earnings.

The lower part of Fig. 8.2 presents another striking finding: for the manual men the absolute changes in earnings were symmetrically distributed, in a leptokurtic distribution, i.e. one highly peaked, with long tails. But the corresponding distributions for non-manual men and for both groups of women, though also highly peaked, were not symmetrical, the longer tail extending through the smaller absolute rises.

We began by noting that the dispersion of the earnings of any group of employees would be increased if the earnings were subject to short-period fluctuations, and the data provided by the Department of Employment enable us to calculate the extent of the increase, using a formula due to Thatcher (private communication).[1] We find that the interdecile ratio for manual males, which was actually 2.19 in 1970, would have been 1·91 in the absence of short-period fluctuations.

The contribution of short-run fluctuations in earnings to the variance of earnings has also been studied in the U.S., and has been found to be 'comparable in size' there with the contribution of the association between the earnings of employees and their ages (Mincer 1970, p. 21). This association is the next factor to be examined here.

---

[1] If, following Friedman (1957), we put

$$y = u + v \tag{1}$$

where y is the log of the earnings of an individual in a particular period, v is a transient component, and u is the 'permanent income', and similarly in a subsequent period we put

$$y' = u + v' \tag{2}$$

then if the periods are far enough apart for v' to be independent of v, the regression of y' on y will be linear, and the correlation between y' and y in a group of earners will be given by the ratio of the variance of u to that of y:

$$r_{y'y} = \frac{\text{var}(u)}{\text{var}(y)} \tag{3}$$

If H and L are the highest and lowest deciles of the observed distribution of earnings, and H' and L' are the corresponding deciles of the distribution after the transient components have been removed, then

$$\log\left(\frac{H'}{L'}\right) = r_{y'y}^{\frac{1}{2}} \cdot \log\left(\frac{H}{L}\right) \tag{4}$$

8.3. The variation of earnings with age

The earnings of individual employees usually vary with their age: up to a certain age earnings rise, and then they level out, or fall off. But within this common pattern the particular shape of the age–earnings curve varies greatly from one group of occupations to another. This is illustrated by Fig. 8.3, which gives the curves for a number of groups (taking men and women together) in France in 1966, and Fig. 8.4, which divides the employees covered by the British *New Earnings Survey* of 1974 according as they were manual or non-manual, and men or women.

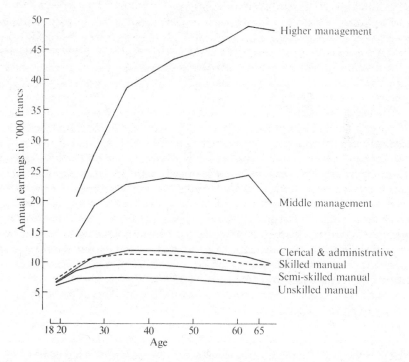

Fig. 8.3. Annual earnings of French employees at different ages.

France, 1966: average annual earnings of six categories of employed persons, both male and female, in successive age-brackets. *Source*: Blanchemanche (1968), Table IX.

In considering these curves we must bear in mind that the data for them were gathered from returns of the earnings of the persons who were in each age-bracket at a given date. That is to say, they are cross-sections: they show us, for example, what persons in certain occupations who were in their 30s at the time were earning, compared with what was being earned by those in the same occupations who were in their 40s at the same time. This comparison is not a sure guide to how those who are now in their 30s will fare as they go on to reach their own 40s ten years later. The difficulty is not just that during

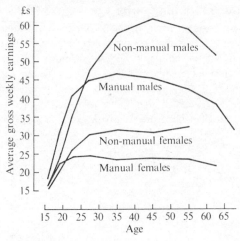

Fig. 8.4. Age–earnings profiles.

G.B., April 1974: average gross weekly earnings in different age-brackets of 4 groups of employees. *Source*: *New Earnings Survey* 1974, *Dept. of Employment Gazette* (H.M.S.O., London), 82, 11, Nov. 1974, pp. 1003–4.

those ten years there will be changes in the general level of earnings. If we abstract from these changes, there remains the difficulty that the cohorts, the one containing those who were in their 30s at the time of the inquiry and the other those who were in their 40s, differ because they are made up of persons who were born in different decades. Those who are older and younger today grew up when the circumstances of home and school are likely to have been different, and sometimes very different—contrast, for instance, the lot of British children born in 1935 and subject to evacuation, interruption of schooling, and absence of the father during the Second World War, with that of children born ten years later. Generally in the present century those born later will have had the opportunity of better schooling, and in the last fifty years will generally have been raised in homes with progressively higher standards of living. Similarly the circumstances in which the persons of one cohort found their first jobs and experienced their early years of employment are likely to have differed substantially in the fluctuation of economic conditions between one cohort and the next, and widely and generally in the course of economic development between cohorts separated by 30 or 40 years.

The extent of possible divergence in recent years in the U.K. is shown by Fig. 8.5. Here we see three cohorts, made up of those aged 20, 30, and 40 in 1963, and follow them through 1973; we also have cross-sections of their earnings in 1963, 1968, and 1973. During these years there was an inflationary rise in money earnings, which has been deflated by a price index, to leave us with real earnings. These too rose, so that the successive cross-sections lie one above the other; but not by equal distances throughout their course. We notice, for instance, that the rise between the ages 30 and 40 is bigger in 1973 than in 1963:

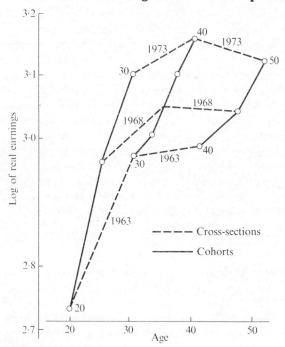

Fig. 8.5. Cross-sections and cohorts.

U.K., 1963–73: annual earnings of sample of 687 persons who paid not less than 48 N.I. contributions in each of 1963, 1966, 1970, and 1973, made up of cohorts aged 20, 30, and 40 in 1963. *Source*: P. E. Hart, 'A cohort analysis of changes in the distribution of incomes, United Kingdom, 1963–73', *University of Reading Discussion Papers in Economics*, Series A, No. 74, Aug. 1975. Data from U.K. Dept. of Health and Social Security.

this appears because the cohort aged 30 in 1963 advanced more than would have been expected from the 1963 cross-section after taking account of the general rise in real earnings through the ensuing years. Cross-sections have the advantage of bringing out the changes associated specifically with differences in age, as distinct from the changes people experience in the course of time as part of the general experience of the economy. But they still do not eliminate the effect of differences, other than age, between the cohorts of which they have made a snapshot.

We have to bear in mind also that whether we are looking at cross-sections or at cohorts, the persons in a given group of occupations may be differently distributed between them at different ages. For women there is this further consideration, that those at work in their 20s will include married women who will shortly withdraw from paid employment in order to raise a family, and those at work in their 40s some who have returned to paid employment after having done this, so that those at work in the intervening years of age will contain an exceptionally high proportion of unmarried women.

With these considerations in mind we can examine the salient features of the age—earnings curves of Figs. 8.3 and 8.4. One striking feature in both countries is the contrast between the ages at which the manual occupations (together in France with the clerical) and the others reached their highest earnings. In France the manual workers in their later 20s had earnings only a very little less than the earnings of those in their 30s, and then as we move into higher ages the curves show a gentle but progressive decline. The clericals differ only in that the rise through the younger ages is more marked, to a maximum in the 30s. In the two levels of French management, on the other hand, it was those aged 61–5 who were earning the most; this maximum was not much above what middle management had reached in its 40s, but the earnings of higher management rose steeply throughout. In Great Britain, again, among the women the highest earnings were for those aged between 25 and 30 for the manual, but over 30 for the non-manual. Among males the corresponding ages were the 30s for the manual and the 40s for the non-manual. How can we account for this earlier peaking of manual earnings?

The possibility of advancing to higher pay by length of service might be regarded as one of the traditional privileges of the white-collared, coming down from the time when their attainments were scarcer than they are now. It has also been held that the earnings of the white-collared continue to rise at a time of life when those of manual workers have reached and passed their peak, because it is in the nature of white-collar employment to give scope for learning by experience, to an extent not generally found in manual employments. Certainly the value of some clerical and of many administrative employees to their firm or organization increases with their experience of its work. This warrants a rise for the competent employee simply by virtue of his length of service; and because the experienced employee is much more useful than a newcomer of equal ability, employers gain by giving him an inducement to stay on. For many manual workers the scope for 'on-the-job learning' after the initial period of training does not extend so far. Yet the contrast between non-manual and manual in this respect is far from complete. There are not a few clerical jobs in which, once a routine is learned, further experience will not add much to efficiency; and on the other hand there are not a few manual jobs that call for decision-taking and problem-solving, and in which experience builds up proficiency accordingly.

It is probable therefore that the major reason for the differences lies in another feature of employment, in which the contrast is more complete. White-collar employments, namely, are commonly organized in superimposed levels of authority, oversight, and responsibility; the higher levels are more highly paid, and they are generally filled by promotion from grades below, whether within the organization concerned or in another one from which someone moves 'to improve his position'. There is no counterpart to this arrangement among manual employments. Its effect is to make pay rise with age. For suppose a new organization were set up in which the staff were arranged in five grades, and all grades were filled at the outset by persons of the same age: then in the course of time casual vacancies would arise in the higher grades, and be filled by those who had already served some time in the grades below, so that eventually the higher the grade, the greater generally would be the length of service and the age of those who had reached it.

But we have to account not only for the placing of the highest earnings in Figs. 8.3 and 8.4, but also for the course of the curves subsequently. In all the French manual groups and the clerical, and in the British manual women, we see a plateau sloping very gently downwards through the higher ages. This might well be explained by the extent to which the manual worker's earnings, after his initial training, depend on his physical energies: as these decline with advancing years, and as the need for household income decreases when children grow up, he will make less use of voluntary overtime and of opportunities to earn bonus on output. There is a plateau too, but with a lift instead of a drop at the end, in the curves for middle management in France and non-manual women in Great Britain: we may see here the predominance of those in white-collar occupations who after making their way up to a certain grade in their 30s do not achieve further advancement, or must wait for it until they have acquired considerable seniority. The sustained rise of the curve for higher management in France may show that here by contrast we have a type capable of achieving progressive advancement; and this may owe something, as we shall see, to initial educational qualifications. What is hard to account for is the sharp downward movement of the curve for the British non-manual males in their 50s and 60s, and perhaps likewise the extent of the downward movement of the other curve for British males, the manual. Some part of the explanation is likely to lie in the distinction between cohorts and cross-sections: the men who were in their 50s and 60s in 1974 will have grown up in the hard years of 1910–39, and may in any case have been less educated than younger men, and less trained than they in developing techniques.

In the last paragraph we raised the possibility of the shape of the age–earnings curve being affected by educational qualifications. In fact it has been found widely that the rise of the earnings of those with further education, though it begins comparatively late, is then steep and persistent, so that the earnings diverge progressively from those of the less qualified. Empirical evidence in the U.S.A., Mincer reports (1970, p. 14), 'does show that earnings of the more educated peak later, grow faster in dollar terms at given years of age as well as at given years of labour force experience, grow also relatively faster (in logarithms) at given ages, but no faster at given years of experience'. In his study of the salaries of higher management in France, Roustang (1971) found that the age-gradient was much steeper for those who held a diploma than for the others: a given proportionate rise in age was associated with a rise in earnings about 1·4 times as great for the holders of diploma, but only about 0·8 times for the others. In England and Wales a similar divergence appears in Fig. 8.6, which presents cross-section data of the earnings in 1966–67 of a 1 per cent sample of the economically active people who recorded their educational qualifications in the British 10 per cent sample census of population in 1966 (Morris & Ziderman 1971).

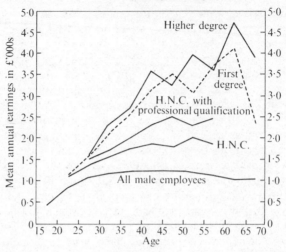

Fig. 8.6. Age-earnings profiles for different educational qualifications.

England and Wales, 1966–67: mean annual earnings in given age-brackets of men with four levels of educational qualification, and of all male employees. H.N.C.: Higher National Certificate (in technology). H.N.C. with professional qualification: H.N.C. with endorsements obtained by subsequent part-time study and qualifying the holder for membership of a major professional institution. *Source*: Morris & Ziderman (1971), p. xxii.

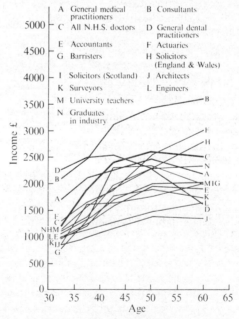

Fig. 8.7. Age-earnings profiles in various professions.

U.K., 1965–66: median annual earnings reported in response to questionnaire issued by Royal Commission on Doctors' and Dentists' Remuneration 1957–60. *Source*: Royal Commission (1960). p. 31.

In Sec. 6.4 we raised the question whether this relative rise marked a greater capability that further education had built in, or was a characteristic of the 'career paths' to which educational qualifications gave access. The latter possibility is supported by the finding that the age–earnings curves for occupations all of which require professional training can be very different. This is illustrated by Fig. 8.7. The divergences here are less easily explained by differences in the capability built in by education, than by differences in the nature of the occupation—it is not hard, for instance, to account in this way for the contrast between the curves for barristers and for solicitors (England and Wales), or between those for consultants and for dentists.

But just as the variance of the average earnings in occupations increases with the age of those who work in them, so does the variance of individual earnings within each occupation. Fig. 8.8 illustrates this for British chemists and engineers. This may arise in part from what is nominally one profession like engineering containing career paths that are fairly distinct from the outset. But the major reason is probably that most professions contain different levels of responsibility, and advancement to higher levels depends in great part on personal qualities. This is a consideration that we shall develop in the next section.

The divergence of earnings as age rises affects the significance of the difference between the higher- and lower-paid occupations in two opposite ways. On the one hand those who follow the lower-paid occupations are denied the prospect of betterment and the incentive to achieve advancement that is afforded to the higher-paid, and to that extent the distance between the two levels of occupation is greater than appears from their pay alone. On the other hand, those who receive the higher salaries are with few exceptions at least in their 40s, and mostly in their 50s and 60s, and their earlier earnings were a good deal lower: whereas the pay of manual workers varies much less with age. It follows that the difference in lifetime earnings between, say, top managers and the manual workers in their employ is much less than the difference between the earnings attaching to their posts. An estimate prepared by the Confederation of British Industry (Royal Commission 1976a, p. 230) takes the annual earnings before tax of a fitter as £2,860 in 1974–75; at the same time the salary of a senior manager aged 62 was put at £10,000 before tax, or $3\frac{1}{2}$ times the fitter's earnings. But the total incomes received in the course of their working lives and retirement through the age of 72 (assuming both to have an occupational as well as a national pension) were related only as $2\frac{1}{2}$ to 1. Thus part of the inequality of individual earnings at any one time arises from the variation of earnings with age in particular occupations.

8.4. Differences in individual performance

Wherever workers are on piece-rates or any form of 'payment by results', differences in the outputs credited to them individually result in differences of earnings. The outputs differ because one worker's skill, energy, or motivation exceed another's, but also because the opportunities to earn, or the interruptions of earnings, are variously distributed over the workers in one shop at a

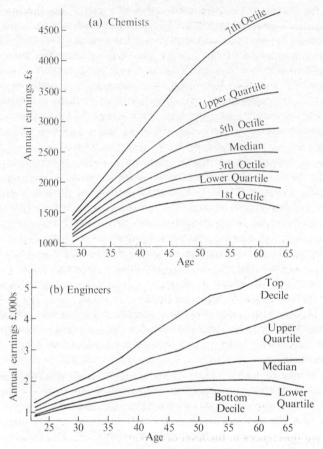

Fig. 8.8. Variance of professional earnings by age.

Fig. 8.8a. U.K., 1962: annual earnings of qualified members of the Royal Institute of Chemistry. *Source*: Creedy (1974).

Fig. 8.8b. U.K., 1965–66: annual earnings of engineers with a university degree or diploma in technology, being members of institutions affiliated to the Council of Engineering Institutions. *Source*: Ministry of Technology (1967), Table 13.

given time, and often for any one worker between one time and another—we have seen that this is a cause of short-period fluctuations in earnings. Workers not paid by results may still be differentiated by the amounts of bonus they earn, for example for good time keeping, or economy of materials; or by discretionary awards of 'merit money'.

The above differences can arise even when workers are all engaged on precisely the same task; but differences in personal capability among those engaged in the same occupation are often associated with wide differences in the tasks performed. Though the titles of occupations are exceedingly numerous, they seldom provide a subdivision of tasks so fine that there is no room for further differentiation. This is recognized by the very name of 'job evaluation'—not 'occupation evaluation'—and the need to begin by drawing up a detailed description of each actual job. Nailing up rough shuttering in which concrete will be poured, and building hardwood fittings into a showroom, are both carpenter's work, but will be given very different job descriptions. In the Chinese wage structure of the 1950s the differentials between the eight grades were all a sixth of the pay in the lower grade, and any one occupation often extended across a number of grades: thus 'machine tool operator', extending over Grades 3 to 8, included jobs so different that the wage-rate of the highest paid was more than twice that of the lowest (Howe 1973, p. 71). In occupations that have no material product great pains have been taken to distinguish and define different levels of difficulty, discretion, complexity, and responsibility. A survey, for instance, of British engineers, all of whom were members of a professional institution, invited the respondents to specify their own level of responsibility by locating it within a framework made up of four elements each containing six levels (Ministry of Technology 1967). The four elements were Duties; Recommendations, decisions and commitments; Supervision received; Leadership, authority and/or supervision exercised. The six levels of Recommendations etc. run, for instance, from A, 'Routine decisions with ample precedent or with clearly defined procedures as guidance', up to F, 'Makes responsible decisions on all matters including large expenditure and/or implementation of major programmes subject only to overall policy and financial control'.

A survey of the salaries in U.S. professional and technical occupations (U.S. Dept. of Labor 1969) distinguished and defined a number of levels in each occupation, in much the same way as has just been described for the British engineers. Fig. 8.9 shows how the variance of earnings in each occupation arose not only from differences in the level of responsibility but also from individual differences at each level: average earnings rose with the level of responsibility, but so also did the range of earnings. The first finding is of a familiar kind—it is a general experience that workers command higher pay in proportion as they are qualified by ability and experience to meet more exacting job requirements. But why should the earnings of the abler and more experienced workers be spread over a much wider range than those of others?

The reason may be that jobs with a high threshold of qualifications are generally also of their nature jobs in which differences of personal quality make more difference to the product than they do in jobs that can be performed by less qualified persons. We have already remarked (Sec. 4.7) how a given difference in the personal quality of two managers, for instance, will make more difference to the product, the larger the scale of the operations of which they are in charge. This 'scale of operations effect' can be seen as a form of the 'job sensitivity' analysed by Reder (1969, p. 221). A job is insensitive 'if there is but a negligible marginal product to a higher degree of any aptitude beyond that commonly possessed by persons filling such jobs. Bank teller is a good example

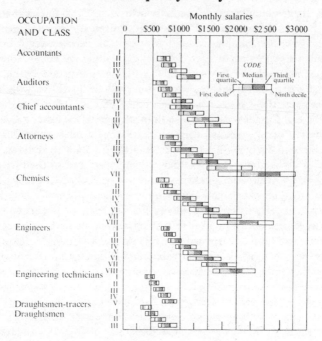

Fig. 8.9. Variance of individual earnings within occupations.

U.S.A., June 1968: interdecile range and quartiles of monthly salaries at each level of difficulty and responsibility distinguished within each of a number of professional and technical occupations. *Source*: U.S. Dept. of Labor (1969a), Chart 2.

of a job having low sensitivity.' Conversely, a sensitive job is one in which the product is raised substantially by aptitude greater than that required to do the job adequately. There can be jobs with a high threshold of qualifications but without sensitivity in this sense—the airline pilot may be a case in point. There are also occupations where the same title covers what are really a number of distinct jobs distinguished by skill. But it is not mainly technical skill that differentiates the grades that are recognized formally or informally in such occupations as those in Fig. 8.9. What generally differentiates these grades, apart from length of experience, seems to be that the higher grades call for more initiative, judgement, decision-taking, and ability to carry conviction with other people and win their co-operation. These are qualities of personality. It seems to be in the nature of work that performance generally depends more on these qualities in jobs with higher thresholds of qualification than it does in those with lower thresholds.

8.5. Differences within local labour markets
The wide variation of earnings among people in the same occupation persists even when the people concerned are limited to those in one locality. 'In all oc-

cupational wage surveys,' the U.S. Bureau of Labor Statistics reports, 'varying degrees of intraoccupational wage dispersion are found, no matter how narrowly the job or area is defined. The highest paid workers often exceed by 100 per cent or more the rate paid other workers in the same occupation, industry division, and area.' (U.S. Dept. of Labor 1969, p. 92.) A number of studies of the local labor market besides those of the Bureau of Labor Statistics itself bear that finding out, in France (Daubigny, Fizaine, & Silvestre, 1971; Daubigny 1971), Great Britain (Robinson 1970; Mackay et al., 1971), and the U.S.A. (Reynolds & Shister 1949; Slichter 1950; Lester 1952; Douty 1961; Buckley 1969; Rees & Schultz 1970).

Much in the differences that these studies reveal is only the manifestation in particular localities of the sources of the spread of earnings within an occupation that are considered in other sections of this chapter. It is these sources that must account for most of the spread of earnings within an occupation in one and the same firm. But the local surveys have also brought to notice a distinct source of variation in the differences that remain, after allowance for difference in personal quality and job content, between workers in the same occupation but different firms, even closely adjacent firms.

These differences are possible where there is an internal labour market (Sec. 4.7 above; Doeringer & Piore 1971). Evidently the more an employee looks for advancement within his present firm rather than by way of change of firm, the more possible it is for his present pay to differ from what is being paid for closely similar work elsewhere. Even where he does not expect advancement, he may judge the adequacy of his present pay more by internal than by external comparisons. The extent to which internal differentials may determine pay is shown in the U.S.A. by the tendency of the rates for jobs that are common to a number of industries, whether unskilled like the janitor's or skilled like the maintenance electrician's, to earn more in the industries of higher average earnings, though there is no reason to suppose their work is more exacting there (Slichter 1950). But this tendency affects the skilled and the unskilled in various degrees: Kanninen (1953) found that the ratio of the maintenance electrician's pay to the janitor's varied, over twenty industries, from 1·28 to 1·89, and this was on taking the median of the widely varying ratios firm by firm in each industry. Something depended on whether the electrician's rate formed part of the internal structure or was negotiated separately by a craft union.

Union organization may also affect the extent to which the internal pay structure is insulated. That structure is a reality, explicitly provided for, in many British firms, but the employees concerned are well informed through their unions of what is being paid elsewhere, and exert effective pressure to ensure that, job for job, they do not fall short. So it is that Brown and Sisson (1975, pp. 27–8) have found that in the engineering firms of Coventry and the newspaper houses of Fleet Street 'fair comparison' does the job of the market; in the Coventry firms the dispersion of average standard earnings in six skilled occupations was less than in any of eight semi-skilled and unskilled occupations.

Neither in these Coventry firms nor in the Fleet Street printing houses 'does in-plant promotion or seniority play an important part and in neither does hiring primarily take place on the lower rungs, at least for manual occupations'. How, then, can the internal pay structure be a matter of concern within them, as it certainly is? The answer is that the trade unions make it so, and we have seen that the effect is to reduce, not protect or create, differences between firms in the pay for the same work. Lydall (1968, pp. 172–3) has remarked that the impact of unionization is often to be understood in this way. 'Where there are weak trade unions,' he says, 'there are usually considerable market imperfections, which the growth of trade unions tends to sweep away. Thus, a once-for-all strengthening of trade unions may appear to have a large effect, although it is really only a means of bringing the market closer to its underlying equilibrium position.'

But where trade unionism is less effective there is more possibility of divergence. For a number of reasons a firm may be able to attract and retain labour although it is paying less for given work than other firms in the same locality. Many employees have for their own part little definite information about what is being paid elsewhere, or doubt whether high rates of pay that are quoted may not be offset by poor working conditions, harder driving, or insecurity. Even where rates of turnover are high, it is only a minority that moves at short intervals, and most employees remain and expect to remain with the firm for years together. To the extent that there is any threat of redundancy, employees who have acquired seniority in their present firm will not readily leave it to become 'last in first out' in another. Sometimes a particular firm offers a more convenient form of employment than is available elsewhere, by reason of the hours of work, or simply its location: especially for the lower-paid the cost of travel is a strong deterrent to taking a job at a distance. The radius of travel is a specially limiting factor for married women, both because of the time that may be claimed by their children in the mornings and evenings, and because they are tied to their husband's place of residence. These constraints of locality may be reinforced by more positive ties with a particular place of work and those who work in it: in small firms especially there may be a sociability that keeps 'the regulars' together. Where the employer is in daily personal contact with the workers, the sense of community may include him or her.

Where in these various ways the employees of a firm become reluctant to leave it, or would in any case be hard put to it to find another job that suited them so well, the employer has a margin of discretion. He may adopt a deliberate policy of paying high or low, and this has been held to be associated with the attraction of a high or low quality of labour, or the maintenance of a brisk or relaxed pace of work, so that the employers' labour costs do not differ as much as the workers' pay. But in his survey of a U.S. labour market Lester (1952) found that, the two or three highest- or lowest-paying firms apart, there was little correlation between the rate of pay and the quality of the workforce or the pace of work. Once established, an association between a particular employer and a relatively high or low rate of pay is likely to maintain itself:

what was instituted as an act of policy, or was shaped by the circumstances of a particular time, becomes traditional and may be accepted as part of the natural order of things.

The differences that come about in these ways between the earnings of a given occupation in different firms may be random, or explicable only as a matter of history. But there is one form of difference that is systematic: in the U.K. and the U.S.A. at least we find that earnings are generally higher in the larger firms than the smaller. The average weekly earnings of male manual workers in U.K. manufacturing industries in October 1958 were analysed by size of employing firm (Ministry of Labour 1959). Very generally the bigger the firm the higher were the average earnings, which in the biggest firms often exceeded those in the smallest by 15 per cent. Out of 112 industries, in all but 8 the firms with less than 100 manual workers showed lower average earnings than those with 100 or more. Analysing data of wages per man-hour provided by the U.S. Bureau of Labor Statistics for 1954, and using a classification by size with the smallest class having 10–19 employees and the largest 1,000 and over, Lester (1967) found that in manufacturing industries other than textiles and clothing the average wages in the biggest firms typically exceeded those in the smallest by 25 to 30 per cent. In both countries garment-making forms an exception, no doubt because of the presence of small high-quality and specialized workshops over against large factories producing garments for sale 'off the peg'.

Various reasons can be suggested to show why the bigger firms have to pay more highly, or are able to. They may have to, because they must needs draw their workers in from greater distances. A firm will generally have a limited number of potential employees resident so near to it that they can work for it at less cost of time and money in travel than for any alternative employer; but as it expands it will have to attract those who live farther away. In their study of the Chicago labour market in 1963 Rees and Shultz (1970, pp. 169–74) found that individual earnings were generally higher the longer the individual's journey to work, in ten out of the twelve occupations they studied; though they remind us that 'commuters can also be compensated for their time by savings in the cost of housing and the nonpecuniary income associated with preferred residential locations'. With the exception of a few instances of the 'company town', big firms are found in big cities or conurbations, which make extended recruitment possible by the density of their housing and by their provision of public transport. At the end of the nineteenth-century the increased difficulty of the journey to work as the radius of recruitment lengthened was checking the growth of British firms, until the difficulty was reduced by the coming of the electric tram and the motor bus (Phelps Brown 1959, pp. 10, 11). The employee meanwhile began to acquire his own means of transport, bicycle, motor bicycle, and car. These developments have allowed firms to expand on their existing sites, or to set up plants on sites that were suitable in other respects though not in a built-up district. They have also given the employee a greater choice of employer: where local transport is difficult a firm may be a near monopsonist of labour resident near it, but as improved transport lengthens the radius of recruitment of firms generally, they must compete with one another for labour.

On two counts, then, the larger firm is likely to have to pay more for given labour: despite improvements in transport it must still compensate its marginal employees for a longer journey to work, and these employees must be attracted and retained when other firms are equally accessible to them. These are also reasons why pay in a given industry is generally higher in big towns than small. But the causality also runs in some measure the other way: there being independent reasons for pay being higher in the bigger towns, the need of big firms to locate in them is a further reason for their having to pay more. To this it may be added that in countries where unionization is partial, big firms are more likely to be unionized than small.

The big firms not only have to pay more but are able to: indeed they would not have become big unless they could. Their ability lies in 'the economies of scale'.

8.6. Differences of region and of unionization

In discussing local labour markets we noted the possible effect on the general level of pay in a city of the city's size. It is a matter of common observation that pay tends to be higher in cities. In the U.S.A. it has been found fairly generally that the bigger the city, the higher the general level of pay. Kanninen (1962) found that much of this association could be explained by most of the big cities being in the regions where pay was generally higher in any case. But in a later study Fuchs (1967) found that the remaining differences of pay were positively linked with size of city even within a given region.

Several reasons can be advanced for this finding. We have already noted the possibility that by enabling firms to gather a big labour force in one place cities allow them to achieve economies of scale in production. There are also economies of scale in distribution in densely populated areas. These considerations agree with and help to explain the findings that differences in the cost of living among the major U.S. cities are small compared with those in pay (Lamale & Stotz 1960), so that the differences between those cities in pay in dollars mostly mark similar differences in real earnings. It has been suggested also that the cities have had an expanding demand for labour, so that competition between employers for a periodically insufficient supply of labour has raised pay and served to draw labour in from other places. Certainly this explanation has been offered for the relative height of wages in the English towns of the eighteenth century. 'In the towns, burials usually exceeded baptisms. Yet the towns grew. They must have refreshed themselves with people from the countryside; and, since the belief that large numbers were driven off the land is no longer tenable, the migrants must have been attracted to the urban centres.' (Ashton 1955, p. 15.) Even in later years when in healthier cities it was the baptisms that exceeded the burials, economic growth can still have been fast enough to maintain a periodically excess demand for labour. Associated with this is the possibility that the migrants were selected for ability and enterprise. Fuchs controlled for certain indicators of personal quality, viz. colour, sex, age, and education, but thinks that these may well not have captured those differences in personal quality due to 'better quality schooling, more on-the-job training, selective in-migration to the big cities of more ambitious and hard working persons' (p. 26b). This factor would contribute to the explanation of why real earnings increase with the size of city, if, as seems possible, the bigger the city the more selective it is towards the qualifications and energies of the migrants into it.

It is also possible to regard the relations between cities and other areas as closely analogous to those between more and less developed economies. In the more developed economies prices, taking manufactured products and services together, have been higher, and the bigger real incomes have been mediated by money incomes that have been higher still. This has been compatible with, has perhaps been a necessary condition of, the maintenance of the balance of payments between the two types of economy, at a fixed rate of monetary exchange.

A city is a concentrated type of region. When we turn to regions in their usual, wider sense we find that there were great differences in the past in the pay of a given occupation in the regions of one country, and that these differences have diminished substantially in recent years. Those in Great Britain in the eighteenth century were recorded by Adam Smith (1776, Bk. I, c. 8). 'Eighteen pence a day', he said, 'may be reckoned the common price of labour in London and its neighbourhood. At a few miles distance it falls to fourteen and fifteen-pence. Tenpence may be reckoned its price in Edinburgh and its neighbourhood. At a few miles distance it falls to eightpence, the usual price of common labour through the greater part of the low country of Scotland. . . .' But by 1906 the labourer's pay in London and the Home Counties, instead of being about double that in the lowlands of Scotland, had come to exceed it by only some 16 per cent (Hunt 1973, p. 70). None the less, big differences remained: the carpenter who was getting $10\frac{1}{2}d.$ an hour in London was getting only $5d.$ in Taunton, less than 150 miles away (p. 68). These were extremes, but the South-west of England as a whole was still 20 per cent below the London level. In Germany the average hourly earnings of masons in the Eastern region were 25 per cent below those in the highest-paying region, the North-west, in 1865, and 27 per cent below them in 1905. In the regions adjoining the North-west they were lower in 1905 by 14 per cent in the South-west and 16 per cent in the Central region (Bry 1960, Table 26). In France before 1914 the reported rates of pay in the Paris region were often 50 per cent above those in the provinces. In the U.S.A. the regional variation of farm wages has been seen as a pattern of concentric circles 'with South Carolina at the focus and the main axis of increase toward the Northwest, with highest farm wages in Washington state'; this pattern has changed little since the Civil War (W.D. Weatherford as cited by Leiserson 1966, p. 43). Table 8.2 shows a somewhat similar pattern in manufacturing earnings, which have been lowest in the South and higher, in ascending order, in the North-east, the Middle West, and the Far West. The

The Inequality of Pay

Table 8.2

Regional Differences in Wage Rates in U.S.A.

U.S.A., all occupations in manufacturing: medians of regional relatives of occupational wage rates, with the North-eastern rate in each occupation = 100, for three other regions at four dates, from 1907 through 1945–46.

	Median of relatives to North-east = 100		
	South	*Middle West*	*Far West*
1907	86	100	130
1919	87	97	115
1931–32	74	97	113
1945–46	85	101	115

Source: Bloch (1948).

differential to which the greatest attention has been devoted in the U.S.A. is that between the South and the rest of the country, or between South and North, and this changed little from end to end through the first half of this century (Bloch 1948).

Studies of this differential have brought out one feature that may well be common in regional differences—in different occupations they appear in very different degree. This is illustrated by Fig. 8.10. Here we have data for average earnings industry by industry, and the occupational mix in a given industry may not be the same in the South as elsewhere; but in so far as particular oc-

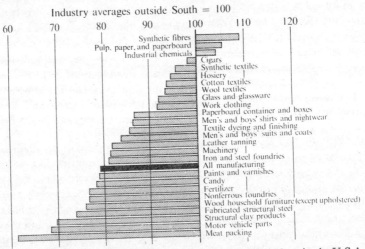

Fig. 8.10. Inter-regional differences of earnings in different industries in U.S.A.

U.S.A., 1962–66: straight-time average hourly earnings in given industry in the South, as percentage of those earnings in that industry on the average of the rest of the country. *Source:* Douty (1968), drawing on Bureau of Labor Statistics, U.S. Dept. of Labor, *Industry Wage Surveys*, various dates 1962–66.

cupations predominate in this or that industry, Fig. 8.10 indicates how widely the Southern differential has varied from one such occupation to another.

The explanation of regional differentials may take two forms, which are related in the same way as the statements 'The glass is half full' and 'The glass is half empty'. Regions are distinct not because they occupy different areas on the map but, economically, because there is both interpenetration and insulation between them. To the extent that it observes the interpenetration, our explanation will rely on the theory of international trade; but it may also observe the insulation, and treat different regions as separate economies, each able to go its own way.

We have approached the first form already in our discussion of cities, in which we likened the relations between city and countryside to those between countries at different stages of development. Regional differences in pay in money generally mark substantial if not equal differences in real earnings. Hunt has shown, for instance, that in Great Britain in the twenty or thirty years down to 1914 'prices of commodities were similar throughout the country. Rent varied more than any other item of expenditure and was the main cause of regional variation in the cost of living; food prices varied but to a smaller extent. These differentials introduce some modifications into the wage pattern . . . but none of any significance' (1973, p. 104). We are dealing, therefore, with wide differences in real earnings, and unless there were also wide inter-regional differences in the division of the product between pay and profits, which we have no reason to believe, we must be dealing with wide differences in productivity. These in turn we must ascribe to all the factors that bear upon the economic development of any area. But now we must bring in the constraints and pressures that arise from the relations between one area and another. The monetary expression of the real earnings in a given region would depend upon its trading relations with the rest of the country, when its currency was maintained at a fixed rate of exchange with that of the rest, and any surplus or deficit in its balance of payments would result in an increase or a drawing down of its stock of currency by an equal amount. Money wages are affected also by the need to maintain another balance, if enough labour is potentially mobile for a widening of an inter-regional differential to result in a reduction of the labour force of the lower-paying region.

But we envisage the region as such only because there is far from complete mobility of resources, even in the long run, between it and the rest of the country. In the second form of explanation of regional differentials we regard each region as something of an enclave, in which economic events may take their course, within a wide margin of tolerance, independently of what is going on in neighbouring regions. The extent of isolation imposed by great distances and difficult communications will account for such differences as those of nearly 2 to 1 in real earnings that appear to have existed between the provinces of China in the 1950s (Howe 1973, Table 35). Or it may be that the relative rates of pay set by the forces of an earlier period persist after those forces have receded. Thus in the U.S.A. the gradient of pay from east to west still follows the

historical direction of the advancement of 'the frontier' across the con-
tinent—'the frontier', which must offer high pay to draw labour out to it, just as in
the U.S.S.R. rates in Siberia are deliberately set high today.

The two-sided explanation we have suggested makes a number of observations intelligible. Table 8.3 provides some indication of regional differentials
in Great Britain in 1886 and some eighty years later, in 1967. The comparison
of the two years is very rough, because for 1886 we have rates of pay in two occupations in the one industry of building, whereas in 1967 we have actual earnings in a given week of men manual workers in all industries within the scope
of the inquiry—mainly manufacturing, construction, public utilities, and public
administration; there are some marked differences, moreover, in the boundaries

Table 8.3
Regional Differences in Wages in G.B., 1886 and 1967

1886: Carpenters' and labourers' wages for a 9-hour day, in regions as delimited by Hunt (1973),
pp. 8–9, as relatives to average for all G.B.

1967: Average weekly earnings of full-time men manual workers, in all industries covered by the
6-monthly inquiry by the Dept. of Employment and Productivity in April 1967, in regions as
defined by the Dept., the averages being standardized by weighting earnings by industry in each
region by the distribution of men manual workers between industries in the whole economy.

Region	1886 Carpenters	Labourers	Region	1967 Standardized regional averages
London and Home Counties	117	117	London and South-east	104·7
Midlands	113	115	Midlands	101·0
Northumberland and Durham	111	105	North	97·4
Cumberland and Westmoreland	94	100		
Lancs, Cheshire, W. Riding Yorks.	106	115	North-west	98·3
Lincs, Rutland, E and N Riding Yorks.	98	110	Yorkshire and Humberside	95·8
South Wales	100	93	Wales	96·0
South Scotland	100	88		
Central Scotland	97	105	Scotland	96·7
Northern Scotland	86	93		
Rural South-east	97	88	East and South	100·2
South-west	78	88	South-west	94·3
G.B. average	100	100	U.K. average (including N. Ireland)	99·3[1]

[1] Less than 100, because the regional averages obtained by standardization compose a national average
that is lower than the original.

Sources: 1886, Hunt (1973), Table 1.6; 1967, Dept. of Employment and Productivity (1969).

of the regions in the two years. But there is evidence enough here to show that by 1886 the range between regions had become far narrower than it had been in Adam Smith's day, and in particular the gradient no longer ran steadily downwards from London to the Lowlands of Scotland: the impact of the Industrial Revolution had fallen meanwhile on the North and North-west of England and on Scotland south of the Highlands, and raised wages there relatively to London and the South-east. But the data for 1967 show how since 1920 what has been called the Second Industrial Revolution has reversed this emphasis, and raised London, the East, and South again, while the regions of earlier development have been relatively and sometimes absolutely depressed. Evidently much of the regional differences in pay can be accounted for by the course of economic development in each region.

But what also appears in Table 8.3 is the reduction between 1886 and 1967 in the range of those differences. Some part, at least, of this must be attributed to institutional rather than market forces. The extension of trade unionism and industry-wide wage administration through the First World War, and the effective pressure of trade unions especially during the years of full employment since 1945, have reduced the original jumble of district rates to uniformity by bringing the lower rates up, until today the 'London allowance' is often the only remaining regional differential. But this holds only of rates: the range of 10 per cent that Table 8.3 shows as remaining between regional earnings in 1967 marks the continued assertion of differences in regional development against the intentions of institutional regulation.

Regional averages such as we have just been considering may well contain a diversity in particular industries or occupations such as Fig. 8.10 showed in the U.S.A., and we have to ask how we can account for this too. It implies that the inter-industrial wage structure in the South of the U.S.A. is very different from that in the rest of the country. Such a state of affairs is possible in so far as the relative availability of different types of labour differs in the two regions: in particular we know that unskilled labour has been more plentiful in the South. The theory of comparative costs suggest how the relative development of different industries in the two regions will have been moulded accordingly. But another effect has been a great migration of that labour to the rest of the country. That this has not done more to bring the two wage structures into line may be ascribed to the inertia of those structures, the hold of custom, and the endeavour of those concerned to maintain their relativities. In this tendency of structures brought about by the conditions of yesterday to perpetuate themselves in the changed conditions of today, and to do this in different regions despite increased interpenetration, we come back to the form of explanation that emphasizes the wide limits of tolerance within which regions remain free to go their own way.

We have seen how trade unionism worked towards uniformity between regions in Great Britain, but where unionization is partial it can be a source of differentiation. In the U.S.A. some sectors of a given industry may be unionized while others are not, and these sectors commonly lie in different regions, or are distinguished as are the big cities and the smaller towns within one region. The statistician can analyse the comparative data thus provided so as to separate the effect of unionism in differentiating the wages of workers in the same occupation or industry. Since the classical study of Gregg Lewis (1963) found that unionism had generally raised members' wage rates by some 10 to 15 per cent above those of comparable non-unionists, a number of studies (surveyed by Ashenfelter & Johnson 1972) have used more recently available data to control for associated differences of personal quality, and have arrived at considerably bigger estimates of the impact of the union, ranging between 16

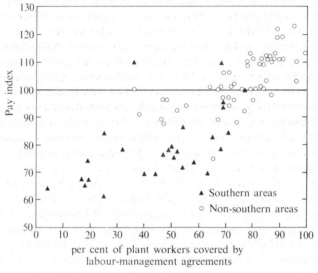

Fig. 8.11. Effect of differences in unionization.

U.S.A., 1960–61: 80 Standard Metropolitan Statistical Areas together with Boise, Idaho, and Burlington, Vermont: in each area, regression of index showing pay of unskilled plant workers as relative to national average of pay of such workers, on percentage of plant workers in that area covered by labour–management agreements. *Source*: Kanninen (1962).

to over 30 per cent, and in one instance over 50 per cent. Figure 8.11 shows the association between the degree of unionization and the relative pay of unskilled plant workers in 82 areas within the U.S.A. in 1960–61. This association is positive and very clearly marked; no less apparent is the extent to which the degree of unionization varies from one area to another. Conceivably some areas might arrive at higher pay independently of unionization, for which the higher pay would then provide a necessary condition: but though no doubt there is some reciprocity of influences here, there seems no reason to doubt that the degree of unionization makes its own contribution to differences in pay between areas. Figure 8.11 shows, however, that this contribution is far less marked within the South than in the rest of the U.S.A.

8.7. Review and discussion

(a) The basic interest of the present inquiry is in the question why different kinds of work are paid at different rates. In the present chapter we have been asking how it comes about that those engaged in the same kind of work achieve different earnings. The two questions are not distinct, and our answer to the second throws some light on the first.

Part of that answer has been that, with the same work and a common rate of pay for it, individuals will often still earn different amounts. They do so because output fluctuates in the short run, or because when people are paid by results some people fairly consistently achieve higher outputs than others. When we add that in many occupations, especially those with a high threshold of education, earnings vary with age, we introduce a consideration that links the rate of pay with the nature of the work. For in these occupations the nature of the job generally changes with the age of the worker, becoming increasingly complex and responsible, and more highly paid, as the worker gains experience. We have seen, moreover, that the higher in these ways the grade of the work, the greater the range of individual earnings in it, because what duties are in practice undertaken by a person at these levels often depends on his distinctive personal capacity and energy. So differences in pay within the same occupation merge with differences of occupation, albeit under the same occupational title. This apart, the differences of earnings of this first group arise from differences between persons rather than between tasks.

But the present chapter has also brought to notice some instances of the same work being paid at different rates even when the same kind of person does it. We have seen that this is so between cities of different size, and between different regions. We can regard this as analogous to the familiar differences between countries, the economic relations between different localities within any one country differing in pervasiveness rather than in kind from those between one country and another. An insulation of another type accounts for work of much the same kind being paid differently in neigbouring firms: after we have made allowances for some compensatory elements of amenity or disadvantage in those firms, differences of earnings remain that are explicable only by obstacles to movement even between adjacent firms, ties that bind a substantial part of each firm's labour force to it, and the absence of trade unionism.

To quote 'a rate of pay' for a given occupation is therefore generally to strike some sort of average of a variety of rates. We have also seen that the title of the occupation may cover a variety of tasks and operations, to which different rates of pay would continue to attach even in a market that allowed only one rate for each distinct kind of work.

(b) Thus as we now go on to examine the distribution of individual earnings, we have to take account of many more causes of difference than occupation alone. We have seen the effects of differences between one person and another doing the same work; between the rates at which the same work is paid in various places and firms; and between the tasks comprised under any one occupational title. It is tempting, then, to discard the concept of occupation altogether. Earlier we took the analogy of the strata revealed in a cliff, stacked one above the other in the usual socio-economic stratification of occupations, and we had to recognize that the strata are tilted quite steeply, so that jobs in the upper part of a lower stratum may be more highly paid than those in the lower part of a higher stratum. Has not the time come now, we might say, to cease to bother about the distinguishing marks of the strata, and see the cliff face instead as honeycombed with a myriad particular jobs, distinct in themselves, and to be grouped, if grouped they need be, simply by the level of earnings they provide? But this would be going too far. It would be to neglect both the relative ease or difficulty of movement between one job and another, and the difference of the paths by which various jobs are reached. A young accountant, a maintenance electrician and a long-distance truck driver may be earning the same: is it more helpful to group them together on that account, or to consider separately the professions entered by examination, the skilled manual occupations entered by apprenticeship, and the manual occupations that are open but subject to trade test?

(c) None the less, the sources of diversity that we have seen here are extensive enough to account for a significant part of the variance of individual earnings, even among employees as a whole, including those who are less affected than manual workers. We must bear this in mind as we go on to consider how we can account for the form of the distribution of individual earnings, and what factors contribute to their variance.

9
The Distribution of
Individual Earnings

9.1. The form of the distribution of individual earnings

When we consider distributions of earnings we may be interested in the extent of the dispersion as that is evidenced by some of their properties, such as the standard deviation, or the decile ratio—that is, the ratio of the highest decile to the lowest. Such measures may be used to compare the inequality of earnings between one country and another, or between two periods in the same country. But here our interest is in the *form* of the distribution, irrespective of dispersion: is the form normal, for instance, or lognormal, or Paretan,[1] or does the distribution take one of those forms over part of the range of earnings and another over another part? We are interested in this question because of the inferences that can be drawn from the forms of the distribution, concerning the processes by which the forms are generated, that is, by which individuals come by their earnings.

The achievement of Lydall (1968) in bringing together distributions of earnings of comparable coverage from more than thirty countries affords a remarkable conspectus. The comparable coverage, which he calls his Standard Distribution, is that of the earnings in money, before tax, of full-time adult male employees in all occupations and industries except farming. The Standard Distributions prove to be sufficiently alike in form for a typical distribution to be defined. This distribution is humped, that is, unimodal, and has a long upper

[1] Actual distributions of earnings may approximate to a number of forms, each of which can be fully specified only by an algebraic formula; but the three forms mentioned in the text are among those most often considered, and we can envisage their characteristic profiles. In one form of graph, the profiles appear when we measure earnings along the horizontal scale, and the number of persons having each given amount of earnings on the vertical scale.

If the distribution is *normal*, the profile formed in this way will be bell-shaped, and symmetrical about the mean.

Alternatively, we may take the logarithm of earnings, and assign equal distances on the horizontal scale to equal differences of the logarithms. This implies that we are regarding equal proportionate differences in earnings, and not as before equal absolute differences, as equivalent to one another. If when we do this a profile of the same form as the normal appears, the distribution is said to be *lognormal*. If we took the original data that yield a lognormal distribution, and plotted them with the same horizontal scale as for a normal distribution, we should find a skewed profile—the mode or hump would be to the left of the mean, and there would be a long tail extending to the right through the higher amounts of earnings. See Fig. 9.1.

To envisage the *Paretan form*, we should enter on the vertical scale not the number of persons having a given amount of earnings, but the number whose earnings are equal to or greater than that amount; and on *both* scales we should enter the logarithms of the original data. If the Paretan formula fits, the profile will then be a straight line. See Fig. 9.2.

tail. The central part, 'from perhaps the 10th to the 80th percentile from the top', is closer to a lognormal than a normal distribution. But even if we take the logs of earnings, the distribution has thicker or longer tails than lognormality allows; the upper tail, moreover, covering about the top 20 per cent of earners, is fitted closely by Pareto's formula (pp. 37, 66–7, 238–9).

An example of such a distribution from more recent data, the earnings of male manual workers in Great Britain in 1973, appears on both a natural and a semi-logarithmic scale in Fig. 9.1: the distribution is evidently more nearly

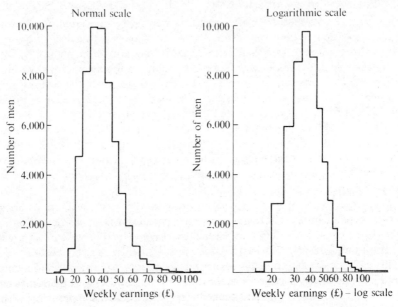

Fig. 9.1. Distribution of wage-earnings on natural and logarithmic scales.

Gross weekly earnings of full-time male manual employees aged 21 and over, whose pay for the survey pay-period in April 1973 was not affected by absence. *Source*: Dept. of Employment (1974), Table 82. Figures taken here from Royal Commission (1975a), Figs. C.1, C.2, pp. 179–81.

lognormal than normal, but it departs from lognormality at the higher levels of earnings. Here, it seems, the Paretan formula obtains: Fig. 9.2 shows how closely the linear relation it implies holds for the top quarter of British employment incomes in recent years, but not for the rest.

Censuses of the earnings of most of the civilian labour force in the U.S.S.R. have been stated by Russian statisticians to compose distributions that closely approximate the lognormal (Chapman 1975). There is no mention here of the Paretan upper tail; it seems not to appear in the Soviet-type distributions (Lydall 1968, p. 66), though Pryor (1972, p. 644 n. 10) wonders whether this may not be due to the Soviet data excluding the bonuses that are given to the higher-paid.

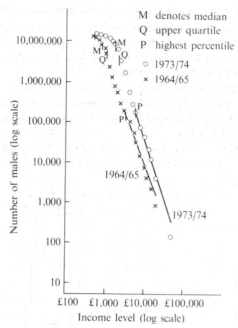

Fig. 9.2. Paretan tail of earnings distribution in U.K.

Number of males in the U.K. with total employment income above specified levels, 1964–65 and 1973–74, with fitted Paretan lines. 1964–65 $\alpha = 2\cdot55$, 1973–74 $\alpha = 2\cdot95$. *Source*: Royal Commission (1967), Fig. E2, p. 167.

The wide manifestation of the lognormal form or lognormal–Paretan hybrid is striking, and highly suggestive of some basic processes being at work that are common to a number of different economies. But these forms appear only when we bring together into one distribution persons of many different types: more homogeneous groups show a variety of forms. Thus Thatcher (1976), examining the earnings of all employees in Great Britain as those are reported in the *New Earnings Survey*, has pointed out that the over-all distribution, which is of the hybrid form, is made up of the distributions of the earnings of different types of employee, and these are of various forms. The earnings of manual men are lognormal, and have been so (with no change, either, in dispersion) since the first Wage Census in 1886. The earnings of non-manual men are skewed, with a Paretan tail (Thatcher 1968). Those of manual women are lognormal (Thatcher 1968). The over-all distribution also comprises non-manual women, juveniles, and part-time workers, each group with its own distribution.

The question then arises whether the form of the over-all distribution is a form in its own right, presenting tendencies operative throughout its coverage, or arises simply as an aggregation of dissimilar parts. Edgeworth and Bowley (1902), indeed, showed how what we have just treated as one of the component distributions, the earnings of manual males, could itself be decomposed into two normal distributions. Putting these two together gave a better fit to the aggregate data than did a normal curve: that is, we can see now, it approximated to a lognormal curve. Their results, said Edgeworth and Bowley, 'would be expected if the group of wage-earners dealt with was in the main

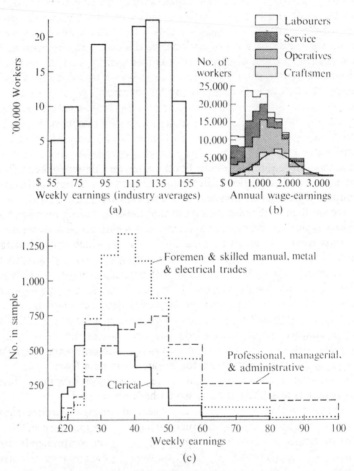

Fig. 9.3. Distribution of earnings of groups of employees.

(a) *Production Workers in U.S. Manufacturing, 1966,* distributed by their average weekly earnings in 119 industries. Number per $10 interval. *Source:* U.S. Dept. of Labor, Bureau of Labor Statistics, *Employment and Earnings Statistics for the United States 1909–67* (Bulletin 1312–5, 1967, Washington, D.C.).

(b) *Manual Workers in Minneapolis and St. Paul, 1938–39.* Annual wage income. Number per $250 interval. *Source:* taken here from Staehle (1943).

(c) *Employees in Great Britain, 1973.* Distribution of gross weekly earnings of full-time adult men whose pay in the survey period in April 1973 was not affected by absence. Number per £2 interval. *Source:* Dept. of Employment (1974), Table 82: professional, managerial, and administrative, sum of II, IV, and V; clerical, VII; foremen and skilled manual, metal and electrical trades, XIV.

composed of two groups: one, about two-thirds of the whole, with an average wage of 22s. 3d., that of unskilled, or partly skilled, or unspecialized labour; the rest with an average wage of 29s. 6d., that of skilled labour; while in addition to these there was an intermediate detachment not belonging strictly to either group' (p. 353). Later Bowley went farther. 'A medley of curves massed together', he said (1933, pp. 360–1), 'gives a normal appearance even in apparently unfavourable circumstances. If normality is found in the wages of a large and heterogeneous community, this may not be because careers are open to all, the earnings are proportional to aptitude, but because the numerous obstacles to freedom of opportunity and bargaining and the levelling of wages within occupations make the kind of complex which results in normality from a number of abnormal factors'. Figure 9.3 illustrates the very various forms that may be taken by the distributions of the earnings of component groups. The groups in Minneapolis and St. Paul, and in Great Britain, are by occupation, and are all unimodal, but those in U.S. manufacturing are by industry, and here there are at least two modes. All three of the groups of employees in Great Britain are skewed with a long upper tail, but the figure for Minneapolis and St. Paul shows how a skewed distribution with a long upper tail may be built up from component groups of different size that are not themselves markedly skewed.

Are we then to dismiss the notion that the distribution of individual earnings takes a typical, widely manifest form, from whose properties we should be able to draw some inferences concerning the way in which individual earnings are determined? The preceding discussion suggests that we need to distinguish between two sorts of group, which we may call composite and homogeneous. The composite group—such as all employees in an economy—brings together persons who are really in different communities or markets, although they are in the same country: they form non-competing groups, even though intergenerational mobility upwards and downwards means that they are not separate castes. The members of a homogeneous group are interchangeable, in the sense not that a carpenter, for instance, can do a fitter's job, but that a lad who became a carpenter might quite likely have become a fitter instead, whereas it is less likely that he would have become a lawyer. The distribution of earnings within one of these homogeneous groups therefore shows the impact of variations of personal qualities and of circumstance within a relatively narrow range, whereas the composite distribution comprehends the full range. This would appear most clearly if we conceived of an economy in which the earnings in each occupation were standardized: there would remain the question of how the labour force was distributed over different occupations. It is basically this question that concerns us here. An aggregate may be subject to constraints that do not apply to its components severally. When we find, following Lydall, that the composite distributions of earnings take similar forms in a large number of countries, we must attribute this to common tendencies in the distribution of the labour force as a whole over job opportunities at all levels. We wish to see what we can infer about those tendencies from the forms of the distributions. Let us now consider how the lognormal form may be generated.

9.2. Processes by which distributions are formed

We know ways in which distributions of various forms can be simulated, and it seems probable that the forces generating any distribution of like form in the real world will be acting in similar ways. These ways therefore provide a framework or template for the impact of the forces that we have reason to believe act upon personal earnings, and for the combination of their impacts.

We know first that a normal distribution can be developed as the cumulation of a large number of events, in each of which there is the same chance of a given absolute amount being added to a sum that is being built up, and which are independent of one another. An example of such an event would be the tossing of coins, with a head being taken as scoring 1, a tail 0; whether in a given toss the coin came down heads or tails would not be influenced by the results of previous tosses. Suppose we tossed a coin in sequences of 10 tosses. The first toss might yield a head or a tail: either of these results might be followed by a head or a tail in the second toss; and so on. At the extremes, one head might follow another throughout the 10 tosses, giving a score of 10, or we might have nothing but tails all the way through, with a score of 0: the range of possible scores would be 0, 1, 2, 3 ... 9, 10. If we repeated the sequence of 10 tosses a great many times, we should find each of the above scores appearing with a certain frequency. Intuitively we should expect scores of 0 and 10 to be very infrequent, and should look for the highest frequencies in the middle, around the score of 5. The actual frequencies to be expected can be worked out as a binomial expansion: the outcome bears out our intuition, for the frequencies of the various scores prove to form a symmetrical distribution with mode and mean together in the middle—an approximation to the normal curve.

The process that underlies the algebra can be visualized with the aid of the Pearson–Galton analogue apparatus (Yule & Kendall 1946, 10.13) that is sketched in Fig. 9.4. A shallow glass-fronted case contains rows of wedges which fill the space between the back and the glass so that any shot fed through the funnel at the top must drop on the wedges and be deflected by them to one side or the other as it finds its way down. Suppose a single shot dropped so as to fall on wedge 1: if the wedge deflects it to the left let us take this as corresponding to a coin coming down tails, and if to the right as corresponding to its coming down heads. The shot then drops on to wedge 2 or wedge 3, at each of which it may again be deflected in either direction; and so on. Corresponding to the sequence of 10 tossings there will be 10 rows of wedges. It will be seen that in the third row the middle wedge will receive a shot that has fallen on either of the two wedges above: when it reaches that wedge it will have been deflected once to the left and once to the right, which represents a score so far of one tail, one head. Similarly in the rows below: all the wedges except the two at the end are placed so as to receive shots that can reach it by a number of paths, but all such paths represent the same score.

Suppose now that we take a grain of sand to do what has been done by the shot, and pour a quantity of sand into the funnel. Each grain as it goes down takes one of the paths that a shot might have taken, and each path, it will be

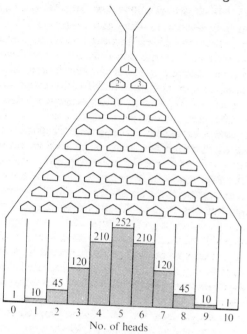

Fig. 9.4. The generation of a normal distribution.

Analogue apparatus of Pearson–Galton type, showing the frequencies of 0, 1, 2 ... 10 heads in repeated sequences each of 10 tosses of a coin. The number at the top of each column at the base indicates the relative amount of sand that will arrive in the given pen, and gives the expected frequency of the number of heads corresponding to the given pen in a total of $2^{10} = 1,024$ sequences.

remembered, represents what happens in a sequence of 10 tosses, so the way in which the sand as a whole reaches the bottom will represent the outcome of repeating the sequence a very great number of times. At the bottom of Fig. 9.4 we see 11 pens corresponding to the 11 possible scores 0–10; the heights of the columns of sand finishing up in each pen are proportional to the frequencies with which the several scores will occur. We thus see one way at least in which a normal distribution (or more strictly, a 'stepped' approximation to it) can be generated.

We must now notice some of the assumptions that have been built into the apparatus, and consider the effect of varying them.

One assumption is that in each event we score 1 (a head) or 0 (a tail). Alternatively there might be events which added, or subtracted, other amounts to the score: the event might decide, for instance, whether the score was raised by 10 units or by 3, or whether it was raised by 1 unit or lowered by 1 unit. In the example of Fig. 9.4, we could regard displacement to the left as reducing the score by an amount proportional to the length of the displacement, and displacement to the right similarly as raising the score. Another alternative is that the score should be raised or lowered not by absolute amounts but by a given percentage of the score up to that point. Here again the question arises whether the percentage should be the same throughout—for example, all events either raise or lower the score, cumulated up to the given event, by 5 per cent; or should vary as between raising and lowering, or as between different parts of the system. In the example of Fig. 9.4 what we are now calling in question is the breadth of the wedges, and whether they should be symmetrical, displacing equal distances to either side, or with a longer slope on one side of the apex than the other.

One important possibility here is that already mentioned—that in each event the score up to that point is either raised or lowered by the same percentage. This means that in an apparatus of the Fig. 9.4 type, in which we have adopted the convention that the score rises from left to right, the wedges must be wider the further they are to the right, as is shown in Fig. 9.5. It was an analogue of this kind that was built by the Dutch botanist Kapteyn (Aitchison & Brown

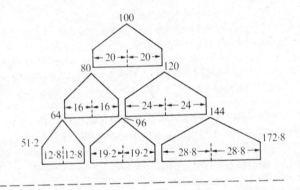

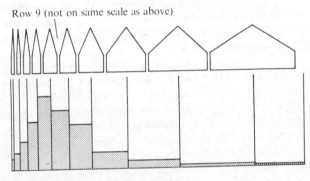

Row 9 (not on same scale as above)

Fig. 9.5. The generation of a skew distribution.

Elements of the Kapteyn analogue apparatus. Top 3 rows, initial value of 100, with equal probability of displacement by ± 20 per cent of value attained at each subsequent stage: with wedges proportionate to value attained at apex, as measured by distance of apex from a left-hand margin. Row 9 (from Aitchison & Brown (1957), plate facing p. 23), bottom row of analogue constructed on the above principle, with sand in pens below showing resultant skew distribution.

1957, pp. 22–4), to demonstrate what has been called 'the law of proportional effect'—if the forces determining the outcome of the event affect the score in a given proportion and not by contributing a given absolute amount, the result will be a distribution that is skewed in natural numbers and approximately normal in the logarithm of the score.

There remains another assumption to be examined: that the apex of each wedge is rightly placed in the middle of the channel through which the sand falls on it, so that any one grain is equally likely to be deflected to the one side as the other. Evidently if we are dealing with different sorts of event at the different stages the likelihoods could be different too. But even if all the events were of the same kind, there could still be different likelihoods if the result of a given stage was influenced by that at the stage before. We assumed, when we were tossing a coin, that each toss was independent: what had happened in the immediately preceding tosses had no more effect on the next one than if they had taken place a hundred years ago. But in such a sequence as the accumulation of profit in successive transactions, it may well be that a successful outcome at one stage, by adding to the dealer's resources and reputation, makes a successful outcome more likely at the next stage. In our analogue this would be represented by separating the stream of sand dropping from the right flank of a wedge from the stream dropping from the left flank of its neighbour on the right: the first of these streams would be made up of grains that had just experienced a successful outcome, and the wedge on which it fell would accordingly be sited with its apex to the left of its centre, so that more than half the stream fell on the right flank of the wedge and experienced a further success. Similarly the apex of the wedge receiving the grains that had just experienced a reverse would be set to the right of the centre of the descending stream. (This splitting of the streams that are each made up of two confluents in Fig. 9.4 or Fig. 9.5 would mean that the number of wedges in each stage was twice that in the preceding stage, so that in our 10-stage apparatus there would be 2^9 or 512 wedges in the bottom row.) We can see at once that if a positive correlation betweeen the results of successive events predominated in the real world, the resultant distribution would be U-shaped, with the highest frequencies at the extremes: for a grain that happened to be deflected in either direction at the outset would have more than an even chance of being further deflected in the same direction at the next stage, and so on—we should have built in a centrifugal tendency. There can be very few actual distributions of earnings that are U-shaped, but we shall see that this does not preclude the possibility of some positive correlation between the results of successive stages being present among other tendencies in the generation of distributions resembling those of the real world.

We shall now apply our analogue to that world: we shall take the successive stages of the analogue—the rows of wedges—to represent the successive stages of early life through which a person accumulates his ability to earn. The preceding discussion has shown us some possible variations of the analogue that we must keep in mind as we proceed. These are chiefly:

(a) Instead of all events affecting the score by the same absolute amounts, they may affect it by the same proportionate amounts. In that case the wedge will be wider, the farther they are to the right.

(b) Instead of the result of each event being independent of the preceding results, these may exert an influence on what ensues. In particular we shall take up the possibility that 'success breeds success' and vice versa: formally, that there is a positive correlation between successive results. In that case the confluent streams falling from two adjacent flanks must now be separated, and the apex of the wedge that each separated stream falls on must be set to the right or the left of its centre.

The possibilities that the two flanks of a wedge might be of unequal lengths, and that, whatever the form of the wedges, they might be of different sizes in the different rows, may well have their counterparts in the real world, but we shall not try to find a place for them in the argument that follows.

This argument begins with a discussion of 'ability to work', which we shall be taking as the counterpart in the real world of what we have called the score in our analogue.

9.3. An index of ability to work

We are to treat ability to work (ATW) as capable of representation by an index such that the actual earnings of individual employees will generally be found to stand in a fairly systematic relation to the indexes of their ATWs. A counterpart to the formation of such an index may be found in the now widely accepted procedure known as job evaluation. This procedure relies on a systematic relation between actual average earnings job by job and the index it forms of job requirements. These requirements set out what any person who is to do the job must be able to do, and not the personal attributes that enable him to do it: job evaluation therefore provides a counterpart to the formation of an index of ATW, and not an instance of it. But the counterpart is close. Some requirements of the job can be translated directly into personal attributes—a given level of responsibility, for instance, calls for the capacity to bear such responsibility. Other requirements imply reliance on some objective achievement of a person, such as a certificate of education, or the completion of a certain number of years of experience in the job, as warranty that the person has acquired certain attributes.

The first step in job evaluation is to arrange what experience suggests as the requirements of the jobs in question under a number of heads, such as mental and physical ability, training and experience, the capability of bearing responsibility, or tolerance of arduous working conditions. Under each of these heads a number of requirements may be distinguished: responsibility, for instance, may be for the performance of subordinates, or for the care of equipment, or the conservation of materials.

The extent to which each requirement is present in each job is then assessed. One way of doing this is to use a 5-point scale. Where the requirement is present to the greatest extent apparent within the range of jobs surveyed, 5 points are awarded; where to the least extent, 1 point. An average extent is marked by 3 points; 2 and 4 points are assigned to extents that are judged below or above average without running to extremes. These assessments are necessarily subjective, in the sense that if two assessors differ, there is no measuring-rod that will oblige them to agree on an assessment; but there is little disagreement in practice between evaluators who are familiar with the jobs surveyed, and so much as there is can usually be removed by discussion in which various jobs are compared in respect of the requirement in question.

The next step raises more difficulty: the requirements must be weighted according to the extent that each contributes to the building-up of the rates of pay that the jobs studied generally command. Usually, for instance, the requirement of a given extent of training and experience will be found to be associated with higher pay than that of an equal extent of physical ability: in that case whatever points are awarded job by job for training and experience must be multiplied by a higher factor than that applied to the points for physical ability, if the totals of points for the various jobs are to bear a systematic relation to the actual rates of pay for those jobs. But how are the weighting factors to be determined? In practice they are chosen according to what experience suggests as representative and application shows to produce intelligible results. Such reflection and adjustment may be regarded as a rough and ready form of statistical analysis. Suppose we were concerned with the contribution to the growth of plants made by temperature, water supply, light, and nutrients in the soil: raising a number of plants with various measured inputs of these contributors, and measuring also the resultant growths, we should have the data for calculating the regression of growth on the inputs. From this regression we could calculate for any set of inputs a kind of composite index, showing the amount of growth that would result from them; and the regression coefficients would embody weighting factors marking the extent to which each kind of input is found to contribute to growth. It is the same with the weighting factors in job evaluation: they express the extent to which each kind of job requirement is found—albeit only on an intuitive analysis of experience—to contribute to the pay that jobs command.

This reference to actual pay would involve the procedure in circularity if the purpose of job evaluation were to obtain from non-monetary measures of job requirements an indication of the pay that given jobs should properly command. But this is not its purpose, which is rather to find a means of finding what pay for a given job is consistent with the way in which the community is setting rates of pay on jobs generally at the relevant time. If this process of pay-setting changes because, it might be (if we allow the effectiveness of market forces), of a shift in the demand for the ability to meet certain requirements, or in the supply of that ability, or both, then the form of job evaluation must change. Suppose, for instance, that a widening of educational opportunity increases the supply of the ability to meet the job requirement 'to have completed a secondary education'. Unless this happens to be matched by an extension of the demand for that ability, it will result in a fall in the pay that jobs requiring a secondary education command relatively, it may well be, to the pay for jobs requiring heavy muscular exertion or the ability to bear rough working conditions. Correspondingly the weighting factor for education must be reduced. The verdict of the market has changed, and job evaluation must change likewise, for its purpose is to provide a systematic account of the processes by which pay is set, and not to supersede them.

There remains the last step in job evaluation—the step by which 'points are turned into pence'. The average pay prevailing for each job is plotted against the total of points for the job, and a systematic relation is looked for in the resultant scatter. In the simplest case this could be a straight line, or perhaps more often one straight line fitting one part of the scatter and another, with a different slope, the other part; but where a wide range of jobs is covered the regression may prove to be curvilinear, or best approximated by a sequence of steps. Whatever the form of the regression, it provides a formula by which for any total number of points the rate of pay can be calculated that a job with that total will command if its pay is determined in the same way as is that of the other jobs surveyed.

It will be seen that this last step may serve to reduce the effect of errors in the choice of weighting factors. Suppose, for instance, that there were only two job requirements—let us call them brain and brawn. Suppose further that it was brawn that was given the bigger weight, so that navvying jobs came out with higher totals of points than the professions. If in fact the navvying jobs were paid less, the regression of pay on points would slope downwards, the jobs with higher points carrying lower pay; but if the fit were good, that is, if the relation were systematic, the corresponding formula would still enable a consistent rate of pay to be calculated for any job from its total points.

The regression also throws light on the significance of the total of points as a composite index of the ability of the components of a job to attract pay. Evidently the index is not merely ordinal, arranging jobs in a ranking order that could be as fully indicated by assigning to each a letter of the alphabet: for the extent of the differences between the indexes for two jobs gives us further information. But on the other hand the index is not cardinal—the ratio of one index number to another is arbitrary, in the sense that the index could retain all its properties if subjected to a linear transformation. Perhaps we may take the analogy of the thermometer: measurements, in degrees Centigrade and degrees Fahrenheit serve the same purposes; in neither scale does it make sense to say that a temperature of 60° is twice one of 30°.

This account of job evaluation will serve to show how a composite index of ATW can be formed in principle. We can begin by listing the personal attributes that everyday experience suggests attract pay, in the sense that the more a person has of any of them, the higher in general his pay will be. Such attributes will be, among others, mental and physical ability; education, training, and experience; co-operativeness; enterprise; ability to bear responsibility; drive, determination, and persistence. But there will also be accidental or intrinsic attributes, such as having a skill that happens to be in particular demand, or having the manners and bearing imparted by a certain type of social background when these facilitate access to particular employments. Comparing one person with another, we then judge the extent to which a given attribute is present in each person, using for this, it may be, the 5-point scale. There comes then the choice of weighting factors, and we note, on the analogy of job evaluation, how this involves implicit reference to the way in which the community is actually setting a valuation in terms of pay upon this or that attribute. Applying the weighting factors to the points allotted to a given person in respect of each attribute, we obtain a total of points for him or her and this is his or her ATW index. It remains for us to 'turn points into pence'—to find what relationships obtain between the index of the amalgam of attributes making up persons' ATWs and the actual pay that they are generally able to command. In many settings these relationships may be seen as established by the index of ATW (calculated albeit only intuitively) assigning persons to grades, and differentials then being assigned to the grades.

It may be asked why we should find the relationship between points and pence in two stages when we might go to it directly. In the above procedure we look for and rely on it first when we weight different personal attributes according to the relative extent to which the community is willing to pay for each; and being then able to calculate a total of points for each person, we go on to ask how much the community is willing to pay for this or that total. But when we trace the extent to which the community is willing to pay for each attribute, why should we not express that extent in pence from the first? Just as calculating the regression of plant growth on the various contributory factors would give us coefficients showing how much difference, in grammes, a unit difference in the input of each factor will make to the weight of the plant, so we could calculate the regression of rates of pay on the various personal attributes that make up the ability to work, and obtain coefficients showing how much difference, in £s per week, a unit difference in each attribute would make in the pay. For any person of known attributes we could then calculate the rate of pay he or she would command according to the practice of the community concerned at the time. A counterpart is to be found in one method of job evaluation—the factor-comparison method—that does effectively proceed in this way, albeit by trial and error and not by running a regression (Benge, Burk, & Hay 1941). But the procedure we have proposed seems preferable, for two linked reasons. One is that we can measure the attributes only by way of an index that provides a rank order together with significant intervals in that order, and it seems more in keeping therefore to measure the amalgam of attributes in a person by an index of the same kind, rather than by a cardinal measure in the form of money. We see such an index of the amalgam as serving to assign persons to grades, to which the community then assigns differentials. That this corresponds more closely to practice than does a summing of monetary values assigned to attributes severally is the second reason for preferring to proceed by two steps.

The present argument, then, is meant in the first place to show how the various attributes on which the pay that any person can get depends can be reduced conceptually to a single figure, namely a particular value of a composite index. We can then give numerical form—that namely of a change in the index—to the impact of the various forces that go to shape a person's ability to work, from conception onwards. In the next section we shall construct a framework for the operation of those forces at successive stages of a person's development. We shall not go into the particular ways in which his experience at each stage affects his ATW so as to bring it about that the index at the end of the stage not only differs in value from what it was at the beginning, but is differently composed: we shall simply consider how the value of the index may be raised or lowered at each stage relatively to the average. But this simplification will enable us to illustrate the way in which the cumulation of changes in the index stage by stage can generate particular forms of the distribution of ATW. In doing this we shall be contributing to a second and wider purpose of the present argument, which is to draw from the form of the distribution of earnings inferences that may help answer our basic question of how pay is determined. But to do this we must establish a link between the distributions of ATW and of earnings. Section 9.5 accordingly will ask how we can envisage the assignment of rates of pay to the persons whose qualities and qualifications are summed up in this or that particular value of the index of ATW.

9.4. The generation of the distribution of ability to work by factors impinging in successive stages of personal development

In setting out the conclusions he had drawn from the great international survey of the distribution of earnings on which we have already placed so much reliance, Lydall (1968, pp. 133–6) showed how a skewed distribution of the ability to earn would intelligibly be generated by the influences bearing on the entrant to employment at successive stages of his or her development. Even if the genetically determined potential is normally distributed, the upbringing of children in the home, the kind of schooling they receive, the courses of preparation open to them, and their access to different sorts of employment, are all differentiated by the class of the parents so that favourable influences tend to be linked with and compounded by favourable, and unfavourable by unfavourable, with the familiar consequence of an approach to lognormality. In a masterly account of 'The Inheritance of Inequalities', Meade (1973) has displayed the network of 'biological, demographic, social and economic factors' that impinge upon the child through his or her parentage, upbringing, education, and entry into work. This network includes much more than the factors that bear directly on the development of the ability to earn: it also displays the transmission of property and examines the effects of assortative and random mating, of the size of family and the practices of bequest, so as to chart the interplay of the factors that decide whether a society will move through successive generations towards greater or less equality of 'fortune' in the widest sense.

We can see these accounts as bringing together those links between the socio-economic level of the parents and that achieved by the child that have been noticed in the course of the preceding discussion:

1. Genetic endowment
2. Upbringing in the home
3. Education and training
4. Access and entry to occupations
5. Early work experience or 'on-the-job training'.

In Chapter 7 we saw how the fate and experience of children and young persons at each of these stages in effect differentiate their ATWs. Here we shall provide some numerical examples of the ways in which they may generate particular forms of distribution of ATW.

We shall do this by applying the analogue described in Sec. 9.2, the five stages corresponding to five successive events. The tossing of a coin serves, at least initially, as a type of these events, for we shall assume to begin with that at each stage the child or young person has an equal chance of coming under two sorts of influence on his development, which we shall take to be simply 'below average' or 'above average'. At birth, for example, the child is genetically endowed with a certain potential of physique, intellect, and temperament: we shall assume that a composite index of this endowment can be formed, with 100 as the average for the whole population, and we shall take it that each baby has an equal chance of being either below average, at 95 or 90, or above average, at 105 or 110. The simplification is heroic: even if the use of a single index for a variety of attributes is permissible, we still ought to consider the full distribution of the index, and follow the subsequent courses of those who start in each part of it. But the simplification has at least this justification, that if the distribution is normal or approximately so, then about half the population will be on one side of the mean and about half on the other.

The index of genetic endowment constitutes the initial stock which will be reduced or increased in the four later stages to form in the end an index of ATW. In providing a numerical expression for what happens at these stages we shall at first use the same simplification as at the first stage, and this in two ways: we shall not analyse the change in the composition of the index, but simply consider the effect of a person's experience at a given stage on the value of his composite index; and we shall assume that everyone has an equal chance of a below-average or above-average experience at that stage. At the stage of upbringing in the home, for example, we shall take it that those whose genetic endowment was below-average, and started them off with an index of say 90, will half of them be brought up in homes that are below average in the help they give to a child's development, and half in homes that are above average in this respect; and similarly for those who were started with an index of 110. Later we shall introduce the possibility that those with an above-average genetic endowment, for instance, are more likely to have an above-average upbringing, and conversely; but in the first instance we assume that a person's chance of being below or above-average at any stage is unaffected by his experience at a preceding stage. We shall also take it that the indexes of those whose experiences are below average or above average will be respectively lowered or raised to the same extent. It may seem strange to say that a person's ability to work is actually lowered by, for instance, below-average education, when he will certainly be more employable after even poor schooling than after none at all; but our index measures not the absolute amount of a person's ability to work but the relation of that ability to the average. The question then is, in what way is the effect of an above-average or below-average experience at any stage to be expressed in numbers?

The first possibility is that the index is lowered or raised by equal absolute amounts. Figure 9.6 shows some possible outcomes. The chart at the top displays the 32 paths on which a person may travel through the five stages, his index of ATW being lowered or raised at each stage: the chart indicates a lowering by a move to the left (from the point of view of the reader) and conversely, but no significance attaches here to the breadth of displacement on paper. On the assumption that those reaching each fork in a path will be equally divided between the two branches, it follows that the numbers reaching the 32 terminals will be equal, so that out of a population of 100,000 the number arriving at each terminal will be 3,125. But the net extent to which the index of ATW has been raised or lowered by the completion of the fifth stage is of course not the same for all paths: the table in Fig. 9.6 shows the six possible outcomes on our assumption that the index is lowered or raised by the same absolute amount at every fork. Since the number who reach each terminal is the same, the relative frequencies of the different values of the index will be the same as the relative numbers of terminals severally yielding the six outcomes. These numbers are shown in the right-hand column of the table in Fig. 9.6, and illustrated in the adjacent histogram, on the assumption that $a = \pm 5$ in stages 2–5.

The two other histograms show the consequences of varying the assumption that the absolute change a is the same throughout. The first results from the assumption that a is 10 index points in the first stage—in effect, that half the population have an index of 90 at birth and half have one of 110; but throughout the rest of the system a remains 5 as in the previous example. This is to assume that people's ATWs are more differentiated genetically than by the influences that play upon them at any one later stage. The second of the lower histograms shows the effect of adding to the above system the assumption that a is also 10 at the third stage—education and training.

These distributions are all symmetrical, and it is in the nature of the system that they should be so, though with different assumptions about the value of a at the various stages we could obtain distributions that are not unimodal.

The justification of developing examples such as these that are simplified to the point of artificiality is that they provide a framework within which the interplay of more realistic assumptions can also be exemplified. One of these is that when the factors playing on the index at a certain stage make for a rise or fall, the amount of the change will be proportionate to the current value of the index, and not the same amount whether the index affected is high or low. Figure 9.7 gives

SEQUENTIAL PATHS

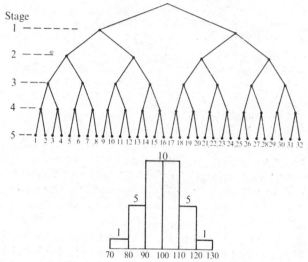

Initial value of index = 100; $a = 5$ throughout. Relative frequency of values of index at stage 5.

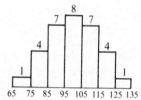

Initial value of index = 100; $a = 10$ at stage 1; and 5 in stages 2–5. Relative frequency of values of index at stage 5.

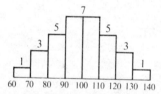

Initial value of index = 100; $a = 10$ at stages 1, 3; and 5 at stages 2, 4, 5. Relative frequency of values of index at stage 5.

Fig. 9.6. A type of 5-stage generation of distributions of ATW.

Distributions of ATW obtained on the assumption that in each of 5 stages of a person's development his ATW is equally likely to be raised or lowered by a given absolute amount.

If the numbers are evenly divided at each fork, the same number, viz. 2^{-5} times the initial number, will arrive at each terminal.

The values of the index at stage 5, when index is changed by $\pm a$ at each stage, will be:

Change from initial value	Terminals	Rel. Fqcy.
$-5a$	1	1
$-3a$	2, 3, 5, 9, 17	5
$-a$	4, 6, 7, 10, 11, 13, 18, 19, 21, 25	10
$+a$	8, 12, 14, 15, 20, 22, 23, 26, 27, 29	10
$+3a$	16, 24, 28, 30, 31	5
$+5a$	32	1
		32

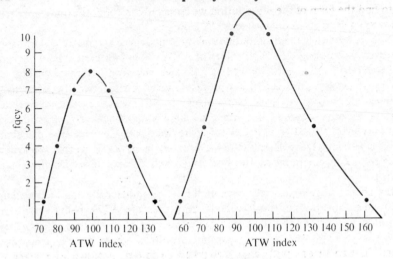

Index values at first stage, 90 or 110

At each subsequent stage, multiplication by 0·95 or 1·05		At each subsequent stage, multiplication by 0·90 or 1·10	
ATW Value	Fqcy.	ATW value	Fqcy.
73	1	59	1
81	4	72	5
90	7	88	10
99	8	108	10
109	7	132	5
121	4	161	1
134	1		32
	32		

Fig. 9.7. Generation of distribution of ATW when value of index is changed proportionally stage by stage.

two examples of the effect of this assumption. In both, we begin in stage 1 with indexes of 90 or 110, but in each subsequent stage the indexes of those who go to the left are multiplied by 0·95 in the first example, and 0·90 in the second, while those who go to the right are multiplied by 1·05 and 1·10 respectively. As before, the number of persons reaching any fork is divided equally between the two roads that branch from it, so the number reaching each of the 32 terminals will be the same, and to find the form of the distribution we have only to count the number of terminals at which a given final value ATW emerges.

It will be seen that the distributions are now no longer symmetrical, but have tails extending through the high values of ATW. How this comes about we can see if we consider the path followed by a person who acquires one of the higher ATWs. On such a path there is a preponderance of rises, and the later rises follow earlier ones: they would be no bigger on this account if all rises were of the same absolute amount, but when rises are proportional any rise will add more absolutely to ATW if it follows a previous one. Conversely, a fall that follows a previous fall will deduct less absolutely from ATW, so that the lower values of ATW emerging at the final stage will be less distanced from one another.

This effect is strengthened when we bring in additionally the assumption already mentioned, that the likelihood of a person's ATW being raised or lowered at a given stage varies with his experience at the preceding stage. It seems likely that those whose parents transmit to them an above-average genetic constitution will also generally—though not without exceptions—provide them with an above-average upbringing. It seems even more likely that those who have enjoyed an above-average upbringing in the home will have more than an even chance of an above-average gain from their schooling; and so on in the later stages. Unfortunately the converse also seems to hold—that those whose experience has been below average at any stage will have more than an even chance of a below-average experience at the next stage. This correlation will be given effect in our model if we give up the assumption that the number reaching any fork will be divided by it equally, and assume instead that of those reaching if after taking the left-hand branch at the previous fork, more than half will take the left-hand branch at this one; and similarly for those who reach it by way of a right-hand branch. Figure 9.8 shows the effect of assuming that after the first stage, in which the numbers are still divided equally at birth, at each fork 70 per cent will take the same branch as at the previous stage, and only 30 per cent having approached by a right-hand branch will now take the left-hand one, or conversely.

By itself this positive correlation between the changes at successive stages would throw the persons experiencing it outwards, towards either extreme: for any person taking a turn towards higher values at one stage will be more likely to move farther in the same direction at the next, and conversely. The outcome would be a U-shaped distribution, very different from the form of actual distributions of earnings. But here this tendency is combined with and splayed by the proportional form of the changes. We have seen that this form already ensures that the higher emergent ATWs will be dispersed more widely, the lower ones compressed: this effect is now compounded by a rise in the relative numbers following the paths leading to the terminals in either wing.

The outcome is the skewed unimodal distribution with a long upper tail, that is shown in the upper part of Fig. 9.8. The lower part indicates that the dis-

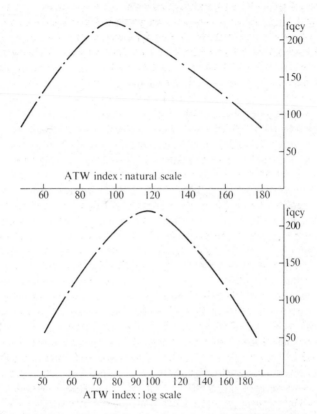

ATW index values at first stage 90 or 110. At each subsequent stage, multiplication by 0·9 or 1·1. At stages 2–5, for 70 per cent of persons multiplication is by same factor as at preceding stage, for 30 per cent by the other factor.

ATW value	Fqcy.
59	120
72	169
88	211
108	211
132	169
161	120
	1000

Fig. 9.8. Generation of distribution of ATW when value of index is changed proportionally stage by stage, and changes at successive stages are positively correlated.

tribution—at least so much of it as our calculations account for—is approximately lognormal.

We have thus shown how the cumulation of proportional changes, together with a positive correlation between the directions of successive changes, can generate a distribution of a type that has much but not everything in common with the distribution of earnings widely found in practice. The lognormal distribution is usually seen as generated by the cumulation of a very large number of random and small proportional changes: here we have come near generating one by a small number of quite big proportional changes, when successive changes are positively correlated with one another.

That a distribution having much in common with the actual world emerges on these assumptions is far from showing that they are indispensable or that they represent the determinants of actual distributions of earnings. Distributions of the actual form have in fact been derived on assumptions that find no place for any particular determinants of a person's earnings, and only see them as moving in a 'random walk' or Markov chain from one value to another, with a given probability at each step of making a move of given size and direction. Champernowne (1953), for instance, considered the distribution that would emerge on the principal assumption that the probability of a person's earnings moving in the course of time from one class to another, when the class intervals were in geometric progression, depended only on the proportionate distance moved and not on the starting-point. From this he himself derived Pareto distributions. Aitchison and Brown (1957, 11.3) found that his formula could be adapted to yield a longnormal distribution. The simplified (two-parameter) version of his formula has been found to give a Pareto tail together with a close fit also to the main body of the distribution of earnings in the U.K. (Thatcher 1968; Royal Commission 1976a, Appx. E). A lognormal distribution will be generated simply by a long succession of random proportionate changes, but the variance of the distribution will go on rising as that of incomes does not: Kalecki (1945) met this difficulty by assuming that the higher the income, the smaller would be the proportionate changes to which it would be subject, and Rutherford (1955) met it by the observation that though the variance of the incomes of each cohort of persons increases as time goes on, those persons die or retire and their place is taken by another cohort starting with a lower variance.

But while the possibility of generating distributions of forms approximating those of actual earnings on assumptions very different from those we have taken here warns us against seeing our assumptions as validated by their outcome, we can claim for them that in however simple a form they do represent the working of factors whose actual effect on the ability to work can hardly be disputed. These are the factors that Lydall found to be 'the main influences determining the shape of the Standard Distribution' of earnings, namely 'genetic inheritance, family class background, formal education and training, age (representing changes in experience and ability during adult years), and the hierarchic structure of organizations' (1968, p. 202).

But we must remember that though we have been comparing the form of the distribution we have generated with that of distributions of earnings, the variable in our distribution is not earnings but an index of ATW. It remains for us therefore to consider how rates of pay get set on different values of this index.

9.5. The link between ATW and pay

In the present section we take up the question of how a monetary valuation gets set upon the package of various attributes, present to various extents, that make up a person's ATW. In doing this we are attempting something more than restating in a complex form our initial question of why some occupations earn more than others. It might seem that in describing the package of attributes making up ATW we were only detailing the qualifications that make one person employable as a carpenter, another as an accountant, and so on. If that were so, to ask how a rate of pay gets attached to a particular value of the index would really be only to pose in a more complicated form the initial and basic question, why carpenters, accountants, and the rest earn what they do. But the concept of the index should be more helpful than that. Whereas we might begin by looking at the carpenter's and the accountant's jobs simply as two heterogeneous articles of commerce, each with its price, like cotton and copper, the index treats the qualities and qualifications that make persons employable in those jobs as commensurable. They are so in the sense that persons employable in quite different jobs may be found to have equal ability to work, or one of them to have more ability to work than another—we are not left with irreducible qualitative differences, as with cotton and copper. Instead we set the ability to work of different persons in a common scale, which not only ranks them but provides us with information about the extent of the differences between them.

Our doing this can be justified if we can give reason to believe that a systematic relation will exist between ability to work as our composite index measures it and actual earnings. The purpose of the pressent section is therefore to offer an account of the way in which those who hire labour judge what it is worth to pay for the work of persons whose employability is summed up in given values of the ATW index.

This account will proceed on the assumption that relative rates of pay tend to be adjusted by a process that is dependent on the valuations set by consumers and employers on the services of employees of various ability. This is not the only assumption on which we might proceed: in Chapter 1 we saw that an intelligible account can be given of the workings of an economy in which rates of pay were fixed by custom, convention, or power, and did not respond to the interplay of supply and demand. But the assumption that relative rates of pay tend to be adjusted by this interplay, in which an essential part is played by valuations of the services employees are capable of rendering, is necessary to the completion of the present model, whose purpose is to show how a distribution of earnings may be generated whose form resembles that of actual distributions.

In some cases valuation may be made directly by the final consumer, as when a householder considers what it is worth his while to pay for the services of a gardener—if a knowledgeable and experienced man is asking more than an odd-job man, is he worth it? But more often the employer is an intermediary between the consumer and the worker: he sets a valuation on the worker's services according as he judges them to contribute to output as that is valued by the consumer. This requires the employer to separate the contributions of different factors of production, attributing to each a marginal value product. How this can be done has been indicated by Marshall (1890, V, VI, 1 and 2). What seems unrealistic as an account of the explicit ground of business decisions can be upheld as displaying what must be their implicit ground (Phelps Brown 1962, c. V).

Whether the valuation is done by consumer or employer, it may take either of two forms. It may be performed by a bidding process, as when employers raise pay by competing for scarce labour. Alternatively the rate of pay may be fixed, by the employee himself, a collective agreement, or a governmental regulation, and then in the first instance the valuation can only decide how much labour shall be employed; but according as these decisions result in more or fewer vacancies than there are applicants, they will exert pressure towards raising or lowering the relative rate of pay as time goes on.

Let us then consider how a potential user of a person's services can set a valuation upon them. He seems likely to set about this in much the same way as we have supposed the ATW index to be constructed. Clearly such a calculation is not generally explicit, but it is of a kind that all of us do in practice make, for we often have to and do decide whether some piece of equipment that is in effect a package of advantages and drawbacks is worth the price asked for it. A dwelling house, for instance, can be regarded as a package of factors, such as the amenity of the site and neighbourhood, the quality of the architecture, the soundness of the structure, the convenience of the fittings, and so on. Comparing one house with another, the potential purchaser can grade each of these factors, and somehow he must weight them too, for he does in practice decide whether the house as a whole is worth a certain amount to him, and whether or not it offers better value for the money than some other house; and this reduction of many factors to a single figure does imply the ability to combine them according to their importance. This is so none the less when the process is intuitive, even unconscious. Similarly with labour: the package of factors bound up in one person can be reduced to a single figure, for the purpose of comparing one person with another, by the judgement of the potential user.

In practice this single figure is likely to be a sum of money: the potential user will go straight to what seems the appropriate rate of pay, because he can refer to what is being paid all around him for persons of comparable capabilities. But to use this reference as an explanation of how rates of pay get attached to particular capabilities would be to argue in a circle. The link between ATW and relative pay must be established independently.

It may be found in a consensus concerning the extent of difference in pay that should be associated with a unit difference of ATW. Such a unit difference may be provided by the *minimum sensibile*—the amount of difference in the composite index that is just sufficient to set one person unmistakably above or below another. Persons can then be arranged in a ranking order where each is separated from his neighbours by a unit interval. Corresponding to this array will be an array of pay, in which also the rates of pay are set at intervals that are in some way equal—but in what way? It has been suggested by some consultants with experience of working out wage and salary scales that people generally feel that unit differences in ATW should be associated with equal *percentage* differences in pay. Certainly there is evidence for the attachment of employees at many levels to the percentage form of their differentials. We have already suggested (Sec. 4.3) the analogy of the Weber–Fechner law, according to which what may be regarded as unit differences of sensation, because they are just sufficient for a clear judgement of greater or less to be made, are associated with equal percentage differences of the stimulus.[1] But the attachment to the percentage conception of differentials is not universal, and it could well be that different forms of differential were felt appropriate in different parts of the same hierarchy. What is essential to the present view of the link between differences of ATW and relative pay is only that there should be generally entertained a conception of a unit interval, or difference of grade, in ATW, and that over against a ranking of persons at such unit intervals there should be a scale of relative pay, with given pay differentials matching unit differences in ATW.

That the size of the difference in earnings associated with a unit difference in ATW might vary with the level of ATW was the implicit assumption of Moore's pioneering analysis of the distribution of earnings (1911, c. 4). He took 'industrial ability—general sagacity and energy' to be normally distributed, but was able to derive from the normal distribution a curve that fitted closely a highly skewed distribution of wages in Massachusetts manufactures, by dividing the wage distribution into a lower and an upper half, and fitting to each the corresponding half of the normal distribution. The lower half he took to cover the unskilled workers, the upper the skilled. A difference of one standard deviation in the index of 'industrial ability' was found to correspond to a lesser difference in the wage in the lower half than in the upper.

In Secs. 4.7 and 8.4 we have referred to the 'scale of operations effect' (Mayer 1960; Reder 1969, pp. 219–20), and this provides an alternative account of the link between ability and relative pay. On his assumption that abler persons will mostly be employed in posts of bigger through-put, Mayer has shown that a given difference in ability will be associated with differences in earnings proportionate to the level of pay as we go up the scale of ability and earnings; and a normal distribution of ability will go with a lognormal distribution of earnings. This finding applies wherever and for whatever reason the unit interval of ATW is associated with proportionate differences of pay. If the distribution of ATWs were normal, to affix proportional differences in pay to unit differences in ATW would be in effect to substitute a logarithmic for a natural scale in the base line of the distribution. Where the distribution of individual ATWs was already skewed, as in the later examples of the preceding section,

---

[1] J. Pen (1971 VI, 2) has pointed out that the possibility of a connection between the Weber–Fechner law and the lognormal form of distribution goes back to Galton in 1879, and was applied to the distribution of personal income by J. van der Wijk in his *Inkomens- en vermogensverdaling* in 1939.

the affixing of proportional differentials of pay would make the distribution of individual earnings even more skewed.

This discussion of the effect of applying proportional differences in pay to unit differences of grade provides a convenient approach to Pareto's formula and the closeness of its fit to the upper tails of many distributions of earnings. The formula may be written

$$\frac{N_{i+1}}{N_o} = \left(\frac{Y_i}{Y_{i+1}}\right)^a$$

where i and $i + 1$ denote two grades, and N_i is the number of persons whose pay is equal to or greater than Y_i. Suppose we have a structure of grades in which each grade is paid 10 per cent more than the one below, and the constant a is $2 \cdot 5$, which is about its value in Great Britain in the 1960s (Royal Commission 1976, Appx. E): then Pareto's formula will fit the resultant distribution if the number of persons in a given grade falls by about 21 per cent as we move from each grade to the one next above. Thus the formula goes beyond the general tendency of proportional differentials to produce a positively skewed distribution, by imposing a special condition on the change in the number of persons from grade to grade: in the special case of pay differentials being proportional and the same throughout, the formula requires that the number of persons in each grade shall likewise be a constant proportion of that in the grade below. Simon (1957) and Lydall (1959) independently pointed out that this case would be realized in a hierarchy or pyramid of management in which the pay of adjacent grades differed by the same percentage throughout, and the number of persons in any grade bore a constant ratio to that in the grade below, as it would do, Lydall suggested, if the persons in the superior grade were the supervisors of those in the grade below, and each supervisor had the same number of subordinates. But such a structure is likely to be numerically very different from the case we have taken here, in which there are as many as 79 persons in each superior grade to every 100 in the grade next below. If a is $2 \cdot 5$, then for each grade to be made up of supervisors each in charge of, say, four persons in the grade below would require the intergrade differential in pay to be as much as 74 per cent. Alternatively, if the pay differential were kept down to 20 per cent, a will have to be $7 \cdot 6$, which is far above the values found in practice.

But there is no reason to reject the notion of a fairly steady proportionate reduction in numbers as we go up the higher grades in the organizations of a country as a whole. Within some organizations there may be a hierarchy in the strict sense of the term, with most of the persons in a given grade being each the superior authority to whom four or five persons in the grade below report; in other organizations, such as public administration, there may be many persons in a given grade who do not stand in this direct relation to persons in the grade below, but the numbers per grade still decrease in fairly steady if much lower proportion as we go up the structure. If at the same time the percentage differentials between the pay of adjacent grades tend to be much the same throughout, then a Pareto distribution will be formed. That these conditions obtain fairly generally in the region of the higher salaries is not implausible by the test of common knowledge, and provides the most probable explanation of a remarkable fact of statistical observation.

At the conclusion of our discussion of the link between ATW and pay, we may express the hope that it has shown how the concept of ATW avoids a perplexity that has been the subject of some discussion in the past. On the assumption that the distribution of ability is normal, the problem has been to account for the skewed form of the distribution of the payments made for that ability (Staehle 1943). The belief that ability is distributed normally seems to rest almost wholly on the distribution of marks in examinations and the scores in intelligence tests, but the form of any such distribution depends on the construction of the test, and the normal form is observed in practice only because the tests have been constructed and adjusted so as to yield it (Mayer 1960, Appx.). The normal form also depends on the arbitrary assumption that the average scores of persons aged n, n+1, n+2 . . . years mark unit differences in ability (Lydall 1968, p. 77). Mandelbrot (1962, p. 61, n.6) cites evidence for his finding that 'the distributions of uncorrected psychological scores are usually very skew and with long tails in one direction'. In any case, our index of ATW differs radically from scores in intelligence tests. It is not confined to a particular kind of ability: the inheritance with which it begins is one of physique and temperament as well as of cognitive ability, and this initial stock is then seen as being modified and developed through successive stages of upbringing, schooling, and training, so as to embody a variety of general and particular proficiencies and limitations. At the outset a normal distribution is assumed to this extent, that the numbers below and above average are taken to be equal; but thereafter the process of modification and development is taken to be one that inherently leads to a skew distribution. We have therefore no reason to find the skewed distribution of earnings paradoxical.

9.6. The influence of particular factors upon individual earnings

In the preceding sections we have assumed that particular factors, such as genetic endowment, upbringing in the home, education, and experience on the job, affect the ability to work and thereby the achieved earnings themselves. We have now to ask how far this assumption is justified by analysis of the observed association between measurable factors and individual earnings, and how much information that analysis gives us about the extent of the influence of this or that factor.

The analysis proceeds by way of multiple correlation, which is intended to measure the extent to which knowledge of the factors bearing upon a particular individual enables us to predict his earnings, and provides us at the same time, in the form of the partial coefficient attaching to each factor, with estimates of the extent to which a given change in the factor will affect the earnings of the individual concerned, when the other factors are held constant. The regression equation may also contain joint terms, intended to bring out the extent to which the effect taken by a given amount of one factor may depend on the amount of another that is present at the time. So far the analysis proceeds on the assumption that the influence of each factor, or linked pair of factors, follows a single path to the earnings that form the dependent variable; but another form of the analysis introduces the possibility of indirect as well as direct influences. A good home, for instance, may be expected to raise earnings both by its direct effect on the personality of the child, and by the concern of the parents to get the child a good education: its effects must therefore be sought both along one path running directly to earnings and along another that leads in the first place to education. The analysis designed to measure the influence following each such path is known as path analysis; it involves a recursive system of equations. An account of it will be found in Duncan (1966); see also Atkinson (1975, pp. 92–7).

We noticed a number of multiple regressions when we discussed the effect of education on earnings, in Sec. 7.7 on human capital theory. Many others in the same field are included in the survey by Psacharopoulos (1975). We would mention also, apart from the studies to be noticed later in the present section, those by Adams (1958), Hill (1959), and Morgan (1962). These inquiries have used three sorts of statistical evidence: through the U.S. Census of Population particulars have been collected of the earnings, age, and length of schooling of large samples of adults; certain household surveys have collected such particulars in more detail; and, in the U.S., two large and specially informative samples, to be described below, have become available through the administration of the armed forces.

The methods and findings of these inquiries call for certain observations of general application.

(1) If a given independent variable such as extent of education proves to be closely associated with individual earnings, we cannot simply take the relation to be a causal one, and infer that providing people with more education will raise their subsequent earnings. For it may be that the independent variable really figures only as a surrogate for another that is not included elsewhere in the equation but is the real causal factor. 'Extent of education', for instance, may be only a surrogate for 'socio-economic level of the person's parents': in that case providing persons of unchanged socio-economic background with more education may by no means have the effect on their subsequent earnings that the coefficient of 'extent of education' seems to imply. Or it might be the other way about. Thus Perrucci and Perrucci (1970), in studies of the subsequent advancement of graduates in engineering, found that a close association between social background and advancement, found in an initial study, disappeared in a later study which introduced educational attainment and grades as independent variables. They concluded that in this case at least social background 'exerts a direct influence on such intervening variables as educational attainment and grades, which in turn exert a direct influence on' advancement.

(2) The factors explicitly entered in these regressions account in all for only a small part of the variance of individual earnings. We may take examples among the regressions containing a relatively large number of factors. Blau and

Duncan (1967), taking father's education and occupation, and son's education and first job, found (p. 403) that these particulars of origins accounted for somewhat less than half the variance of 'occupational achievement'. A rather similar outcome was reached by de Wolff and van Slijpe (1973), taking I.Q., social class of parents, and level of education. Surveying a number of analyses of the NBER-TH sample to be described below, Taubman (1976, n. 4) reports that 'we never explain more than 45 per cent of the variance in earnings'. This proportion may be taken as the general maximum: in some inquiries the proportion has been much lower. In the analyses of the NBER-TH sample reported by Taubman and Wales (1974, c. 4), although the explanatory variables comprised ability (indexes of four facets), background characteristics, state of health, marital status, and father's education, 'the fraction of explained variance . . . is only about 10 per cent'. Jencks's path analysis leads him to conclude (1972, p. 226) that 'neither family background, cognitive skill, educational attainment, nor occupational status explain much of the variance in men's incomes. Indeed, when we compare men who are identical in all these respects, we find only 12 to 15 per cent less inequality than among random individuals.' This kind of finding has been general.

One particular reason for it is that the variance of earnings, especially the earnings of manual workers, commonly contains substantial elements of the kind described in Chapter 8, and no independent variable corresponds to these in the regressions. 'In the United Kingdom', Lydall reports (1976, p. 27), '. . . the variance of weekly earnings of all full-time male employees appears to contain a transitory component equal to about 16 per cent of the total, but for manual workers separately the corresponding figure is more than 30 per cent.' Another substantial part of the variance is linked with age, or length of work experience, and will not be accounted for unless age enters as an independent variable. But another and major reason for so large a part of the variance of the earnings of employees as a whole remaining 'unexplained' in these regressions may well be that the independent variables do not include the character traits that common observation suggests as being closely linked with economic advancement. Lydall (ibid., p. 27) has summarized these traits as the D-factor, 'where D stands for drive, dynamism, doggedness, or determination'; we might add enterprise, willingness to take risks, and ability to work with other people. In addition, the earnings of any one person are likely to be affected, temporary fluctuations quite apart, by a variety of circumstances that are beyond the ability of any person to foresee or control, and whose impacts are usually comprehended under the title of luck.

The importance of the factors of personality and luck would explain why the proportion of the variance of earnings that can be accounted for in a multiple regression runs much higher when the data are aggregated. Tinbergen (1976) notes that while not more than half the variance of *individual* earnings can generally be accounted for, the regression he reports accounts for more than four-fifths of the variance of the average earnings of *groups* of workers—he takes 7 classes of age and 6 of years of schooling, making 42 groups in all, and uses only age and years of schooling as independent variables. We can understand this if the factors bearing on individual earnings but not represented in the regressions are of a kind to cancel each other out when individuals are grouped, and this does seem likely: personalities can be weak as well as strong, and luck bad as well as good. The factors that are represented, however, are not of this dual nature, and so their explanatory power increases when the effect of the dual-natured factors is removed by self-cancellation. There is a further possible explanation for the higher correlations found for grouped data, though it relates to a statistical pitfall rather than to the substantial issue of how earnings are determined. This pitfall is, that the very act of grouping may introduce a side-relation: in forming a group of those with many years of schooling, for instance, we may be bringing together workers from the more advanced regions of the economy, in which regions earnings of workers of all kinds are also relatively high.

(3) It is a limitation of these inquiries that they have to use observational, not experimental data, and the explanatory variables, recorded as they occur, are highly correlated with one another. In an inquiry designed to measure the separable contribution of different factors to plant growth, it will be possible to arrange for plants to be kept in warm air some with a big and some with a small supply of water, and similarly with those kept in cool air; but in the inquiries with which we are concerned here it is as if we could observe only cases of warm air going with a more or less ample supply of water, and cool air going with a more or less stinted water supply. Some cases there will be of divergence—children of high I.Q., for instance, who leave school early; but more generally high or low values of the explanatory variables will be observed together. It is questionable whether such divergences as there are within this prevailing correlation will be sufficient to enable the effect of different factors to be separated and measured with confidence.

This limitation also appears in the form of the possibility that the effect assigned by the procedure to one variable really belongs to it only in conjunction with others which are correlated with it and for which it appears as a surrogate. We have noticed this already in our discussion of 'human capital' and the return assignable to investment in education (Sec. 7.7). A large number of studies which attempt to separate the proportion of differences between individual earnings that is due to level of schooling from that due to ability, together in some studies with one or more other factors, are reported by Psacharopoulos (1975, Table 3.9): the great majority agree in putting the proportion due to level of schooling at from 0·65 to 0·90. But if predominantly the number of years of schooling is correlated with at least a threshold of ability, the variation of ability at a given level of schooling, on which variation the measured effect of ability depends, will be small compared with the variation of ability between one level of schooling and another, which variation will not enter into the argument because it will not appear separately from the differences of level. That so much effect has been assigned to schooling may well be due only to level of schooling being a portmanteau for a number of other

factors that make no appearance in their own right: style of upbringing, parental resources and concern, and the student's own motivation, energy, persistence, and aim. When Weisbrod and Karpoff (1968) studied the effect of
differences in ability among graduates of colleges of average quality, and
measured ability by 'class rank in college', they found that only being in the top
10 per cent made a substantial difference to the rate at which earnings rose in
subsequent employment; but is it possible to separate the differences in ability
that help a student to get into the top 10 per cent from differences in energy,
stamina, competitiveness, and ambition?[1]

(4) Linked with the above limitation is the consideration that the influence
of the explanatory variables is not generally exerted in the form of a continuous
quantitative variation. In the studies led by Taubman and reported below this
has been recognized by entering mental ability, for instance, in the form not of
a continuous index but of five grades, each with an assigned value, as with a
dummy variable. But more generally the regression equations are cast in a form
that assumes continuous variation of the explanatory variable and of its effect,
and this will not generally correspond to the actual interplay of forces. The contribution of education, for instance, to the development of a young person may
be likened to that of water to the growth of a plant. If the impulse to grow is
there, and the other requirements of growth are present, then a certain intake of
water is a necessary condition of growth, and within certain limits the greater
the supply of water the greater will be the growth; but it is not the case that in
all circumstances a variation in the supply of water will cause a variation in
growth, and if the plant is not genetically programmed for growth beyond a
certain point, more water will have no effect. Similarly the explanatory
variables generally introduced in studies of the determination of earnings are
necessary conditions in the sense that the animating principle, the D–factor,
must be able to take up certain amounts of them if a person is to develop; but only in
certain circumstances and within certain limits will providing less or more of any
one of them decrease or increase development.

These observations call for caution in interpreting the results of regression
analyses, but by no means preclude the possibility of obtaining valid and instructive information from such analyses when a large number of possibly explanatory
variables are recorded for a large sample of diverse persons. Such are the unusually
rich materials known as the NBER–TH sample. These materials originated in the
test scores and the particulars of schooling, interests, and experience recorded for
the men who in 1943 volunteered for training as aircrew in the U.S. Army Air
Corps. To be admitted to the battery of 17 tests they had had to have obtained
scores in the top half of a general ability test, so they were of above average intelligence. In 1955 Thorndike and Hagen (1959) obtained particulars of the

---

[1] It has been argued by Gintis (1971) that the real link between education and subsequent earnings lies not in the cognitive achievements towards which education is formally directed, but in
the traits of personality that it inculcates in practice—he mentions especially subordinacy; discipline; the supremacy of cognitive over affective modes of response (this being a particular
requirement of bureaucracy); and motivation by external reward.

experience since the war of some 10,000 of these men who were now civilians, with their present occupations and earnings. Further and up-to-date particulars were obtained in 1969/1970 and in 1972 from some 4–5,000 of those who had responded in 1955. These returns, together with the particulars recorded for those concerned in 1943, were analysed by Taubman and Wales (1974) and Taubman (1975, 1976).

Some of the principal findings as reported by Taubman (1976) were as follows. The level of education was found to have a substantial positive effect on the earnings, even in a regression which took account of many other explanatory variables for which in their absence education might be suspected of being a surrogate. The effect of ability, especially of mathematical ability, was also substantial, this again after taking account of a number of facets of socio-economic status to which some of the apparent effects of ability might be imputed if those facets did not figure explicitly in the equations. But the effects both of the level of education and of ability were small in comparison with those due in the aggregate to socio-economic status and to personality and temperament. It is a special interest of these studies that they introduce a number of indicators of these generally unrepresented factors. Socio-economic status, for instance, is indicated by father's education and occupation, and by a 'biography variable' made up of various particulars reported by the candidate in 1943 of the income of his family and his own schooling, activities, and interests. But the indicators also include the mother's education, and the wife's and even her father's education, which proved to have a positive relation with the respondents' earnings—perhaps because those who married into families of high socio-economic status had the advantage of the family connection, or were of the ambitious type whose drive would in any case have brought them high earnings, and might also have made them attractive to the daughters of high-status parents. To have attended a private school was associated wtih higher earnings, but the association was reduced when the figure of the respondents' business assets was introduced, and this suggests that the private school may not have taken effect as a form of education but have served only as an indicator of family resources. Among the indicators of personality and temperament, religion was prominent: among the high school graduates, Jews earned from 33 to 40 per cent more than Catholics, and Protestants from 3 to 9 per cent less. Other indicators of personality were obtained from the answers to the question, 'Indicate how you spent your time while growing up'—those who had engaged more in part-time jobs earned more in later life, those who had given more time to chores at home earned less. In discussing this last finding Taubman refers to the view of the sociologist R. Merton that insistence on chores is a lower-middle-class trait, and tends to produce compliant rather than enterprising personalities.

Here, as in the separation of the effect of being self-employed, and attitudes towards so being as compared with being salaried, we come on the D-factor. It is a remarkable feature of these inquiries that they introduce a number of indicators of personality, as also of the family setting that helps to form it; and they show how much effect personality and socio-economic background take in comparison with the usually more prominent factors of education and ability. But it is also remarkable that despite this breadth of coverage so much of the variance of earnings remains unaccounted for. Is this because important personal qualities remain unrepresented by the indicators cited, or is it that a great part is played by a variety of circumstances and happenings that can only be comprehended under the title of luck?

A second exceptionally informative material has also been explored and analysed by Taubman (1976a, 1976b). This is the NAS–NRC sample of twins. It proved possible to identify in the address list maintained by the U.S. Veterans Administration some 16,000 pairs of male twins born in 1917–27 whose names had been obtained from the registers of births in forty-two of the fifty-six states, and appeared in the address list because both of each pair had served in the armed forces during the Second World War. The sample was originally drawn for purposes of medical research but was made available to Taubman, who obtained replies to a mailed inquiry, concerning among other things earnings in 1973, from some 2,468 pairs. Among these it was possible to identify 1,019 pairs as identical (monozygotic, MZ), and 907 as fraternal (dizygotic, DZ), by their answers to the question 'As children, were you and your twin alike as "two peas in a pod" or of only ordinary resemblance?' A check of identification by such answers against more exact tests has shown it to be correct in 95 per cent of the cases.

The special value of this material lies in the opportunity it offers of separating the effects of genetic endowment and early environment from those of factors such as schooling which have been suspected of borrowing much of their statistical plumage—if people with more education earn more, is that not in part because they were abler people to start with, and came from better homes? One of the uses that Taubman has made of it in this way rests on comparison of the regressions of earnings on various independent variables, *within* pairs of each sort of twin, and *between* pairs. If we can take it that the two sorts of twin shared a common environment in equal measure during their early years, then in regressions *within* pairs, whether MZ or DZ, we shall have standardized for environment. In regressions *within* MZ pairs we shall have standardized for the genetic factor. Regressions *between* pairs, whether MZ or DZ, show the effects of differences both environmental and genetic. Comparison of the coefficients obtained in MZ *within* and DZ *within* enables us to estimate the effect of genetic difference when environment is held constant. Comparison of the two kinds of *within* regressions with the two kinds of *between* indicates the effect of genetic and environmental differences combined, and provides a measure of the bias imported into regressions that do not hold the genetic factor constant as the MZ *within* regressions do, or the environment constant as both MZ and DZ *within* regressions do. In particular, Taubman finds a substantial upward bias in the coefficients that have been estimated for education, which has been credited with much of the effect that it can now be shown really comes from genetic and environmental factors. 'Education', he concludes, 'has relatively little influence on earnings. Except for people who obtain a Ph.D,

M.D. or LL.B. each additional year of schooling adds no more than 6 per cent and probably as little as 4 per cent to annual earnings even though the difference in earnings by education level is usually largest when people are between 40 and 50'—as the men in the sample were between 46 and 56 in 1973. Correspondingly, the findings bring out the importance of the genetic endowment, and the even greater importance of the family background and early upbringing.

9.7. Review and discussion

(a) We have been developing a model to show how the distributions of earnings of the commonly observed form can conceivably be generated. The first part of the model generates a distribution of ability to work, ATW. The materials of this part are matters of everyday knowledge—that each person starts life with a certain genetic endowment, which is then modified positively or negatively in the successive stages of his or her development, in the home, at school, and in the opening years at work. These materials are made to operate within the model by the assumption that over the whole population certain probabilities govern the distribution of persons, first between above-average and below-average genetic endowments, and at each subsequent stage between experiences that enhance or impair ATW. Given the distribution of ATW, money values may be set upon particular values of the ATW index by the hirers of labour deciding how much it is worth their while to pay to the bearer of a given index value, or whether or not it is worth their while to employ him or her at the rate of pay that he or she stands out for or that is externally imposed. Alternatively, if a firm takes rates of pay as given, its customers in effect decide how many shall be employed at those rates, by their decisions to buy or not to buy the product at a price that must cover the cost of production, which will be higher if the pay is higher: the relation between the number for whom there are jobs at the given rate of pay and the number of applicants at that rate may then take effect as time goes on to raise or lower the relative rate. We saw some reasons to believe that it was in the nature of the process of valuation to turn a normal distribution of ATW into a skewed distribution of earnings, or if, as is more likely, the distribution of ATW is already skewed, to make that of earnings still more skewed.

The influence of the factors that were taken to act on ATW in the successive stages of a person's development has been confirmed by the multiple correlations that trace the dependence of adult earnings on these factors so far as they have been recorded quantitatively. But such factors account for less than half the variance of earnings. Everyday knowledge leads us to ascribe the remainder to the other sources of variance discussed in Chapter 8, together with the incidence of particular circumstances and happenings that may be termed luck; and traits of personality, including those of the D-factor. These traits have their place within our scheme of development of ATW through successive stages, for they begin with a genetic endowment, and this endowment is enhanced or impaired, and new traits are instilled, by upbringing in the home and by schooling. These processes play an essential part in the development of ATW: if they do not appear in the regressions, that is only because we lack measures of the factors concerned—such as the way in which a child is treated by its parents.

(b) The model that we have formed and tested in these ways not only shows us one way in which distributions of earnings of the actual form may be generated, but also suggests a reason why that form remains as stable as it does over time. An analogy from genetics—the form of the distribution of an endowment such as height—may help us here. With a given gene pool, and abstracting from some possibilities of change such as mutations, the form of the distribution of height will remain the same, generation after generation, basically because on the assumption of random mating each allele affecting height will be combined with each other such allele in proportions given by the relative numbers of those alleles in the pool. It is these proportions that govern the form of the distribution, and as long as the relative numbers of the relevant alleles in the pool remain unchanged, the form of the distribution will also be stable. If we introduce some degree of assortative mating, the form of the distribution will be changed but not its stability. In the generation of the distribution of ATW, the counterpart to the alleles that tend to raise or lower height will be the factors that we have taken to raise or lower ATW in the successive stages of development. These factors will be present in a given society in certain relative numbers—so many good homes, so many bad, and so forth. If initially we assume no correlation between the experiences of a person in successive stages—this corresponds to the assumption of random mating—then over the whole population the effect of any one factor will be combined with the effects of others in proportons given by the relative extents of the several factors in the society. So long, then, as those relative extents remain unchanged, the form of the distribution of ATW will remain stable. If, as we did in building our model, we introduce correlation between the representative person's experiences in the successive stages—this being the equivalent of assortative mating—again we shall change the form of the resultant distribution but not its stability. The analogy may serve to bring out the essential condition of stability, even though there is one respect in which it does not hold, namely that whereas a person's genetic endowment of height depends on the alleles brought together by two parents, the development of ATW depends on the combination of a number of factors—if we condense these into one composite factor operating at each stage, our model still embodies five stages, and this in our analogy is as if it took five parents to beget one child.

(c) It remains for us to consider the way in which a person in whom a given ATW has been developed gets value for it, so to speak, in paid employment. He does so, of course, by finding a job. In Chapter 8 we saw how, if the occupational structure is likened to the strata exposed in a cliff, the strata are so tilted that jobs at the same level of pay occur in several strata: though the difference of strata remains significant, we can also see the face of the cliff as a honeycomb with a myriad cells, each representing a job with certain requirements and certain pay. We could conceive of an economy in which each person was able to find and enter the cell that paid the highest out of all those whose requirements his ATW enabled him to meet. This need not be an economy of equal opportunity, for all manner of privilege or handicap might have gone to form the distribution of ATWs: but that distribution being given, there would be a sufficient variety of job opportunities to enable workers generally to find jobs that fitted them. We might therefore call the economy one of sufficient access within the market, each person having access to a number of jobs such that, whatever his ATW, he could find a job that would pay him as much as any job would do among those that his ATW would enable him to perform. In such an economy the distribution of earnings would be determined by that of ATWs. We shall go on to notice evidence indicating that in the actual Western economies access is less than sufficient in this sense; but in Chapter 6 we have also noticed the extent of intergenerational occupational mobility, both upward and downward in those economies—we can have no doubt that a process of finding jobs that fit ATW is going on in them actively.

(d) It is here that we may find the explanation of the remarkable stability in the form of the distribution of the earnings of British male manual workers, from 1886 to the present day, that appears in Table 9.1. In this span of nearly seventy years there have been big changes in the distribution of manual workers between different occupations, industries, and regions, and in the relative pay of different grades and groups: yet not only has the form of the distribution of earnings been lognormal throughout, but the dispersion has varied little at any time, and in 1974 was almost exactly what it had been in 1886. This stability is too sustained to be dismissed as coincidence. It is intelligible if we assume, in our simile of the cliff, that as particular strata deepen or contract in the course of time, or even change their place in the stacking order, the face of

Table 9.1
Distribution of Earnings of Male Manual Workers in Great Britain from 1886

Earnings of full-time male manual employees as reported in censuses of earnings at dates from 1886 to 1974.

	Median earnings	Lowest decile	Lower quartile	Upper quartile	Highest decile
	£ per week	as per cent of median			
1886	1·2	68·6	82·8	121·7	143·1
1906	1·5	66·5	79·5	126·7	156·8
1938	3·4	67·7	82·1	118·5	139·9
1960	14·2	70·6	82·6	121·7	145·2
1968	22·4	67·3	81·0	122·3	147·8
1974	41·8	68·6	82·2	121·0	144·1

Source: Royal Commission (1975a), Table 22.

the cliff still forms a honeycomb of close-packed cells, so that a worker will generally be able to fit himself into the cell that offers him as good terms as any for his ATW. This is more likely to obtain if, as was the case in Great Britain at this time, large numbers of workers are concentrated in industrial conurbations in which a number of different employments are within the worker's range of daily travel; and if the group of workers is comparatively homogeneous and does not extend over a wide range of ATW. In such a setting we can expect individual earnings to respond to individual ATW and motivation or need for earnings: and if the distribution of these individual attributes is stable over time, so also will be that of earnings.

The requirements of the setting may be amplified by the conditions set out by Marshall (1890) for the equalization of efficiency-earnings. His concept of the personal efficiency of the worker is virtually ours of ATW, and the conditions that enable efficiency-earnings to be equalized will be those that enable each ATW to obtain commensurate earnings.

The tendency then of economic freedom and enterprise [he said (Bk. VI, iii, 2)] (or, in more common phrase, of competition), to cause everyone's earnings to find their own level, is a tendency to equality of efficiency-earnings in the same district. This tendency will be the stronger, the greater is the mobility of labour, the less strictly specialized it is, the more keenly parents are on the look-out for the most advantageous occupations for their children, the more rapidly they are able to adapt themselves to changes in economic conditions, and lastly the slower and the less violent these changes are.

This explanation of the stability of the distribution of individual earnings may seem audacious, and hard to reconcile with the heart-breaking difficulties that often beset the worker in his search for a job in a year of heavy unemployment, or with the big differences commonly found in what is paid for similar work by firms in the same locality. But these facts are consistent with the presence of effective choice of job by young entrants, and voluntary job-changing, including occupational and regional mobility, on a sufficient scale to characterize the aggregate by a fairly close adjustment between the earnings afforded by a job and the ATW and motivation or need of the job-holder.

The explanation might even be carried one stage further. We know that differentials between occupations and regions in the earnings of British manual workers have contracted considerably since 1914. If then the dispersion of earnings has not contracted, we must infer that the dispersion of earnings *within* occupations and regions has increased. Why should it have done so? We might suggest that the distribution of ATW, being so to speak denied some of its counterpart or outlet in the differentials between occupations, has found a compensating counterpart for itself by increasing differentials within occupations and regions. Individual differences in overtime and in earnings under systems of payment by results will have played their part in this.

(e) At the same time we know that the adjustment between ATW and earnings is in many cases far from close. That there can be systematic divergences between them has been shown by studies of low wages. Generally it has been found that low wages go to persons of poor education and disadvantageous social background. Considering three industries referred to it as having relatively many low-paid workers, the (British) National Board for Prices and Incomes observed in its report on problems of low pay (1971, para. 99) that a common factor in these industries was that 'they offer a high proportion of relatively undemanding jobs in terms of skill, and the pay which is afforded tends to attract those who are at a greater disadvantage than most in competing in the labour market. Workers in these industries were not very interested in actively seeking better work.' But it has also been generally agreed that the low pay of these workers is not simply a match to their low ATW and motivation. Some types of worker evidently have less opportunity than others to get value for given ATWs: the return to a given level of education has been found in a number of countries to be lower for women than for men, and in the U.S.A. to be lower for ethnic minorities than for whites. The industries with many low-paid employees are generally low-paying at all levels of skill. 'Enterprises in these industries are often small and are lacking in managerial resources; employment is predominantly dead-end and there is little opportunity for on-the-job training; work is often seasonal or unstable; turnover rates and job vacancies tend to be above average; and they are least likely to be organised by trade unions' (Doeringer 1974, p. 9). A study of low wages in the U.S.A. found that pay varies with personal characteristics but that when these are held constant it also varies with the employing industry (Wachtel & Betsey 1972).

Evidence such as this shows that no implication of harmony or exact adjustment can be read into the explanation we have put forward of the form of the earnings distribution. But we spoke only of 'a fairly close adjustment': for the distribution to take a certain common form and retain it over time it is necessary not that each worker should have found the job in which he gets the fullest possible value for his ATW, but that the degree of maladjustment should remain stable.

(*f*) Before we leave the simile of the cliff face honeycombed with cells we must note that it can only serve provisionally, because it takes the structure of job opportunities and of pay to be given independently of the number of applicants. It also abstracts from the effects on the job structure of changes in technique and in the choices made by the final buyer. Though the simile does justice to the situation of any one applicant at any one time, it does not take account of the changes in the job structure that come about in the course of time through the interplay of the supply of and demand for labour in particular employments.

10

Conclusions Concerning the
Sources and the Malleability
of the Inequality of Pay

10.1. The sources of the inequality of pay

Where we cannot experiment, the account we give of a body of materials in order to make them intelligible is apt to depend on the paradigm we bring to them. The economist can give a coherent and persuasive explanation of the inequality of pay; but so also can the sociologist, and it will be a quite different one. This is not merely a matter of clinicians trained in different specialisms being each alert to certain indications and less observant of others, though it is partly that: much more it is a matter of a previously developed system of concepts and mechanisms being filled out with so much as fits it in the materials, so as to shape a consistent and self-contained account of them.

The remedy for this importation of doctrine is partly to use the comparative method, partly to examine the evidence in detail. The comparative method enables us, for example, when we think we may have found cause and effect in one country, to check our thinking by seeing whether some other country shows the same effect without the supposed cause, or the same cause without the supposed effect. Examining the evidence in detail also provides a check on our thinking, because it obliges us to descend from the level of generality and abstraction, at which different lines of explanation may seem equally plausible, to particular circumstances and events, in whose nature it is to demand a closer fit of explanations.

For these reasons the inquiry we have now completed has ranged widely but also has examined much detail. It has led to the following conclusions concerning the sources of the inequality of pay.

(1) We must distinguish between the factors affecting the pay structure *before* the market and those affecting it *within* the market. The numbers of workers potentially available to meet the requirements of particular jobs, and the terms on which they will be so available, are influenced, before the market, by the structure and culture of each society. These matters are considered in paras. (2)–(4) below. Within the market, relative pay is largely determined by the forces of supply and demand: the case for this is set out in para. (5). But even here other forces intervene in the zones of indeterminacy that the imperfection of the market leaves in the interplay of supply and demand; they also intervene in enclaves that are partially insulated from that interplay. Particular relativities may be affected by the intervention of combinations and

governments. These matters are considered in paras (6)–(8). The sources of the variance of individual earnings are summarized in para. (9).

(2) The *socio-economic class* of the parents is associated with the child's prospects of earning in the following ways:

(*a*) Differences of socio-economic class are associated with differences of average I.Q. The study of twins shows that a substantial component of I.Q. as indicated by performance in tests is transmitted genetically. The higher the socio-economic class and average I.Q. of the parents, therefore, the higher on the average is the I.Q. of the children; but at each level the children's I.Q.s are normally distributed about their average.

(*b*) The development of the child's cognitive ability depends substantially on how he is treated by his parents in his pre-school years. Studies in the U.K. and the U.S.A have found a difference in the prevailing styles of this treatment in the homes of manual and of non-manual workers: some features of the former inhibit mental development, which some features of the latter stimulate and support.

(*c*) Non-manual parents generally make more effort to secure good schooling for their children and take more interest in their progress at school.

(*d*) Parents with higher incomes are able to pay for private schooling when good schooling is not available locally. But it does not appear that the power to purchase education confers additional ability to earn on a child regardless of his endowment of ability and personality. A child's capacity to profit by education is largely determined by genetic endowment and upbringing in the home by the time he enters school. Where that capacity is well developed, better and longer education will increase earning power up to a point; but it is not possible in all circumstances to 'invest in education' as one might invest in a machine.

(*e*) Parents with higher incomes are better able to support their children through extended courses of general education and professional training.

(*f*) The social contacts of non-manual parents will acquaint their children with careers that are beyond the purview of many children of manual workers. These contacts may also ease the children's entry into employment.

(3) It is as a result of the above factors that most of the supply of labour to jobs at a given socio-economic level is provided by the children of parents themselves at that level and at the immediately adjacent levels. In all Western societies the short-range intergenerational mobility between occupations, together with a certain amount of mobility over longer ranges, makes up a substantial movement, both upwards and downwards. This may be seen as the outcome of the distribution of I.Q. and traits of personality among the children of parents at each level. But, at least by the criterion of I.Q., the mobility is far from sufficient to bring each person into the highest occupation whose threshold requirement of I.Q. he can pass: that threshold rises systematically with the socio-economic level of the occupation, but many persons are found with I.Q.s much above all but the highest thresholds. We do not know how far this is due to the high I.Q.s being linked in these cases with traits of personality

that hold people back, and how far to lack of opportunity, positive obstacles to movement, and immobilization by circumstance.

(4) Access to employment may be restricted by prevailing attitudes. In particular, the attitudes that assign inferior status to certain ethnic minorities, or to women, have denied them access to occupations for which, had they had the prospect of employment, many of them would have been able to qualify.

(5) Given the above conditions of the availability of persons qualified to meet the requirements of different occupations, the relative rates of pay that given levels of qualification command are determined for the most part by the market forces of supply and demand.

It is true that the relative rates of pay for particular occupations may be rigid downwards; but if an excess of the supply of over the demand for persons qualified for a certain occupation does not result in a reduction of the relative pay for that occupation itself, some persons at the given level of qualification must find employment in lower-paid occupations to which they were formerly superior, so that the average pay of persons at that level of qualification is reduced.

It is also true that attitudes towards status intervene, as does the power of combination, to prevent rates of pay moving as they must do if they are to balance the supply of and demand for persons in particular employments; but such intervention does not appear to decide the differentials between the average pay of the main levels of qualification.

These differentials depend ultimately on what consumers think it worth their while to pay for different kinds of work, and on the number of persons able and willing to do each kind of work at a given rate of pay. Consumers are willing to pay more for skilled work than for unskilled, just as—given the amounts available—they are willing to pay more for a yard of silk than for a yard of cotton. The amounts available depend on the costs of supplying them, and on physical scarcities of component elements. It is thus not inherent in the *nature* of skilled work that it should command higher pay than unskilled—if a greater amount of it becomes available, relative to unskilled, then unless there is a coincidental extension of demand its relative pay will fall, though it is just as skilled as before. But generally in practice the acquisition of skill requires application to study, and years of apprenticeship and other ways of gaining experience, and it may call too for an initial potential that is possessed by relatively few persons. Certain occupations, moreover, and certain posts within an occupation such as those of added responsibility, have aspects sufficiently deterent to enough persons otherwise able to perform in them, to prevent their all being filled unless they carry additional pay. Consumers, then, are not only *willing* to pay more for skilled than unskilled work, they generally *have* to pay more for it in so far as the supply is restricted by physical scarcity, and the need to compensate the additional effort or strain imposed by some applications of it.

The conclusion that so far as the main proportions of the pay structure are determined within the market they are determined by supply and demand is supported by the following observations:

(a) The very generality of the pay structure and rank order of types of oc-cupation is better explained by the play of market forces than by that of custom, convention, status, or power. To ascribe a common outcome to these latter factors we must be able to show that they are alike in their operation in economies whose social and political structures and philosophies are very different—in the Western economies, the Soviet-type economies, and China and Cuba. This seems less probable than that wherever transactions go on between persons who do not meet and know one another but deal 'at arm's length', the prices set upon products and services will have to be such as to in-duce the buyer to buy and the producer to produce.

(b) In the Soviet-type economies, the planners seek (subject to political pressures) to arrive at differentials that will be 'correct' because they encourage entrants to acquire needed qualifications, bring about the desired allocation of labour between different occupations, industries, and regions, and stimulate performance in posts of responsibility. Relative pay fulfils these functions because it is adjusted to the forces of a labour market in which workers are free to choose and change jobs.

(c) In the Western economies the earnings of the self-employed clearly de-pend on market forces. It seems improbable that the earnings of those working as employees in the same occupations depend on quite other forces.

(d) The two main changes in differentials in the course of time are more readily explained by shifts in supply and demand than by changes in conven-tion, status, class, or power. The rise in the differential for skilled over un-skilled manual labour in the early stages of the industrial revolution in the West and under Stalin in Russia may be ascribed to an extension of demand; the subsequent decline in that differential in both instances may be ascribed to the subsequently increased supply of skilled labour. The decline in the pay of the lower clerical grades relatively to that of manual workers that has come about in the present century in the Western economies, and has been given effect in the pay structure of the Soviet-type economies, may be ascribed in great part to the extension of the supply of persons qualified for such work by their schooling: that it has not gone farther, despite the magnitude of the extension of supply, may be ascribed in part to the extension at the same time of the demand for clerical and administrative services.

(e) The form of the distribution of individual earnings, strikingly similar in many countries, and in some instances known to have changed little over time, can be accounted for by the generation of individual abilities to work by the cumulation from birth onwards of the influences set out in (2) above, and by the setting of monetary values upon those abilities to work according ultimately to the consumer's willingness to pay for them. It is hard to see what explanation of the form of the distribution could be built out of convention, status, class, and power as determinants.

(f) The economic explanation of the formation of individual earnings is sup-ported by our knowledge of the extent of intergenerational occupational mobility, both upwards and downwards, in the Western economies.

(g) What we know of the surviving hunter-gatherers indicates that man is not by origin *homo hierarchicus*, with a genetically transmitted propensity to evaluate by ranking. The higher status attaching to greater earnings or wealth appears to be consequent upon the emergence of such differentiation in the neolithic revolution, and not prior to it in time or etiology. Similarly the notion that an occupation is entitled to earnings adequate to maintain a certain station in life appears to arise from the *de facto* link between occupations and certain levels of earnings and expenditure, and not to be an independent and originating cause of the earnings being what they are.

(h) Pay and status do not always go together. Their rank orders sometimes differ. They can be associated negatively, lower status being compensated by higher pay and conversely.

(6) None the less, *status* is an active force in pay determination within the zone of indeterminacy left by the operation of market forces, and especially in enclaves such as the higher levels of administration and management, on which those forces bear only indirectly. It also animates the claims pressed in collective bargaining. It operates in a number of ways:

(a) It seems likely that status was attributed to particular occupations originally according to the degree of esteem felt for the qualifications they required, qualifications that also decided how much the market would pay for the work they performed, so that status and pay, though the outcome of separate processes of evaluation, had a common base and went together. They also went together because the life-style associated with high or low pay became itself the object of deference or derogation. But the contingent association between status and relative pay once having been formed in these two ways, it came to be seen as a necessary and direct relation: people generally find a request to rank occupations in order of social standing readily intelligible, and it has become widely accepted as only 'right and proper' that an occupation of high status should have high pay. This belief operates to resist the market forces where these tend to narrow differentials, and to help shape pay structures in so far as these are discretionary.

(b) The same belief is reinforced by the view of many employees themselves that their relative pay is the measure of the esteem in which they are held by their employers or—and more especially—by the community. They press for the maintenance of their differentials because they see them as essential to their self-respect and to their standing with their neighbours.

(c) However a relativity may have been established in the first place, when it has persisted for some time it becomes customary; and custom, though not inviolable in time of upheaval as in war, has its sanctity, which may maintain a relativity through much swaying to and fro of the balance of supply and demand. Some of the differences between countries in the ranking order by pay of different occupations, and of the relative pay of higher management, may be ascribed to the relativities arrived at in the particular circumstances of some past period in each country having become traditional, or to differences in the status accorded to different occupations in the cultures of the various countries.

(*d*) What has been said in the last three paragraphs about status applies also to station in life. When once a *de facto* association between an occupation and the station in life, or level of consumption, generally afforded by the earnings in it becomes accepted as inherent in the nature of the occupation, and is made sacrosanct by custom, it becomes an independent force tending to uphold differentials. It does this the more, because those following one of the higher-paid occupations are apt to feel that the efficient performance of their duties as well as their standing in the community depend on their being able to maintain a high level of consumption. Conversely, a modest standard of living is seen as appropriate and sufficient for those whose work is unskilled.

(*e*) The last consideration is the more important because there is an asymmetry in the working of demand and supply. An extension of the demand for a particular type of labour will generally raise its relative pay, whereas a contraction of demand is not nearly so likely to bring its relative pay down in the short run. A contraction of the supply of a particular type of labour will commonly result in employers bidding up its relative pay. Custom, and not only the self-interest but the self-respect of those in post, create the elbow-joint or ratchet effect that stops the pay falling; it is not broken down by the competition for jobs of those who would be willing to take them at less than the going rate, partly because of the sense that undercutting is anti-social, partly because potential workers simply do not put themselves forward where no vacancies appear. It is therefore possible that in a number of occupations the relative pay exceeds the supply price of the present number of workers in that occupation. But we have seen that this is consistent with a fall in the relative pay attained on the average by persons with the level of qualification having the supply price in question, for some of these must now find employment in lower paid jobs. As rates of pay rise generally in the course of time, moreover, the rise will tend to be smaller where applicants for any vacancy at the going rate are plentiful.

(*f*) The demand for labour operates largely through the intermediacy of employers, who have to assess the contribution made to production by this and that type of employee when many types are employed together and in conjunction with various forms of capital. These assessments are often matters of a judgement which is liable to be influenced by traditional and conventional views about what particular types of employees are worth, and these views in turn are bound up with the status that the society assigns to those types. Thus employers may agree spontaneously in being unwilling to pay members of ethnic minorities or women as much for given work as they would pay for the same work were it done by a white person or a man. But in so far as these conventional views make costs of production higher than they need be, competition is liable to break through them.

(7) Relative pay may be affected at particular points by the bargaining or monopoly *power* of trade unions. The elbow joint or ratchet effect shows the

propensity even of unorganized workers to unite in resistance to cuts. Where, as in the U.S.A., trade unions embrace only part of the labour force, they are estimated to raise the pay of their members as a whole relatively to that of non-members. A trade union that is sheltered from the direct or indirect competition of other labour will generally be able to push up the relative pay of its members without causing many of them to lose their jobs, albeit entrants may be restricted. Some groups may have gained and maintained a higher differential in this way. But other unions will be vigilant to defend the differential as they see it from their side, and the general effect of trade unions on relativities is probably to conserve them against market forces making for change. There is evidence, however, that unionism as a whole has raised the pay of the unskilled manual worker relatively to that of the skilled.

(8) Governments, and sometimes trade union confederations, have intervened of set *policy* to change relativities, either implicitly, by imposing minimum rates, or explicitly, in an endeavour to help the lower-paid. Such intervention has encountered that vigilance of others to defend their differentials which was mentioned above: rates of pay in the neighbourhood of those raised by regulation have themselves been raised after a time so as to restore former relativities, or when negotiations at the national level have raised the rates of the unskilled nearer to the craftsman's, his differential has been restored by wage drift.

(9) The variance of individual earnings as measured at any one time contains short-term fluctuations, and differences of earnings associated with differences of age in any one job, which do not enter into life-time earnings. The variance of individual life-time earnings is the outcome partly of the factors that bring about a certain distribution of personal ability to work, partly of the extent to which persons of given ability to work are able to find jobs that pay for that ability as fully as possible. Any one person's ability to work is compounded of his genetic endowment of cognitive ability and traits of personality; his upbringing in the home; his schooling; and his experience, and training on the job, in the early years of his working life. Pay in the array of jobs whose threshold requirements a given person can satisfy is diversified by reason of regional differences, the imperfections of the local market, the prosperity or depression of particular firms or industries, and the impact of bargaining power or administrative policy at particular points. What earnings are actually achieved by a man of given qualifications faced with a given array of job opportunities depend in part on his possession of the D-factor of drive etc., but in large part also, it seems, on luck.

10.2. The possibilities of reducing the inequality of pay
Most people accept the need for some inequality of pay, and indeed regard the differentiation implicit in the socialist principle of 'payment according to the quantity and quality of the work' as only fair. But granted that there is to be differentiation the question is, how much? There are many who think that society would be more just, and people would be more co-operative, if the

highest earnings before tax were never more than say five times those of the median manual worker. In the light of our study of the sources of the inequality of pay, what prospect can we see of reducing the present inequality, and on what conditions?

If we look first to intervention *within* the market, we must distinguish between the main proportions of the pay structure that we have found to be set by the interplay of supply and demand, and the particular rates that have been affected by attachment to status, or by custom or power.

In the first of those areas the pressing-down of rates of pay would raise all the familiar difficulties of price control. If certain types of labour are to be available at rates of pay lower than enterprises and consumers have been willing to pay for them hitherto, how are they to be allocated between would-be users, and how are these to be prevented from covertly bidding the effective remuneration up again? If again the rewards offered for acquiring certain qualifications are reduced, will as many people as before be willing to acquire them? It is not in doubt that some people would continue to persevere through years of study and training and sit stiff examinations, in order to become doctors, or lawyers, or engineers, out of their interest in the preparatory studies, and the prospect of independent or absorbing or socially useful work: the question is whether enough would do it. Pay has to induce the marginal entrant to make the effort. We do not know how many who make it now would not do so if it would bring them no more income than they could get without it, but it seems likely that there would be a shortfall. One condition for a reduction in the relative pay of the professions would therefore be an increased subsidization of training. If this went as far as meeting all the costs of training formerly falling on the student, and additionally paying him as much as he could be earning if he had gone into paid employment meanwhile, there would still remain the 'psychic costs', the effort and self-control required: if a further allowance had to be made to compensate this, or if various privileges and perquisites had to be provided, this would be going some way towards restoring the cut in salary. A similar problem of incentive arises where the higher pay is reached on the higher rungs of a ladder of promotion, and the prospect of gaining it serves to stimulate the energies of those on the way up. Again it will be pointed out that there are powerful motives other than money for seeking to achieve promotion and hold high office; but again the question is whether these motives will be strong enough, in conjunction with a reduced monetary incentive, to compensate the psychic costs of endeavour in a sufficient number of aspirants, and the burden—as many would feel it—of heavier responsibility.

These problems do not arise where attachment to status, or custom, or bargaining power, has set relative pay higher than it need be to attract the number of qualified persons for whom there are jobs at that rate of pay. But these cases cannot be identified readily, for though there may be many persons who would qualify for entry to the employment concerned if they saw a sufficient prospect of a job in it, they see little prospect of one, and so no queue of applicants appears.

But it may be said that there is no need to ask hypothetical questions, when progressive income tax throughout the Western economies has shown the possibility of a general reduction of differentials in earnings after tax, without evident detrimental effect, however loud the outcry of the taxpayer, on the progress of the countries concerned. In the U.K., the ratio of the earnings of a high grade of manager to those of the median manual worker is 8:1 before direct tax but 4½:1 after tax. The inference might be that expectations adapt themselves: what would have been an inadequate incentive if it had stood alone comes to be regarded as adequate—or at least as the most one can expect—when the reduction has been general and sustained. And, it may be said, so it might be if a general reduction were carried still farther.

This argument calls for two comments. One is that a reduction of salaries by taxation leaves the salary as the price of a factor of production intact, whereas a reduction of the salary itself raises the difficulty already referred to, of rationing the demand for and allocating a factor that is available at a price lower than enterprises are prepared to pay for it. The other comment is that for expectations and judgements of adequacy to be adjusted, it is necessary for the reductions to be carried out on the same scale in most of the countries within the purview of the inhabitants of any one of them: so that there will be no country to serve as a referent for invidious comparison. But more than this: the sense that higher qualifications should be more highly paid may not be merely conventional, but rest upon a categorical judgement of fairness that goes deep in human nature. The exceptional character of the circumstances in which the Kibbutzim have been able to separate income from qualifications emphasizes the generality of the conviction that the two should be linked; and we have seen the strain set up even in the Kibbutzim in so far as qualifications have become more differentiated. One can conceive of a society in which an intensive religious-political indoctrination from the earliest years of life onwards made people willing to work and work hard, as some devoted servants of the community have always worked, with scant regard to material reward. But it seems doubtful whether such a society could ever be very large: only in groups small enough for each member to identify himself with the whole will those who contribute more to the product be generally willing to take no more out of it than those do who contribute less. Such altruism is natural within a close-knit family, but not as between those who deal with one another 'at arm's length'. Even China and Cuba, where intensive efforts have been made to inculcate a collectivist morale, have retained a wage structure explicitly differentiated according to productivity.

When we turn to the formation of the labour force *before* the market we find more constructive possibilities. It has been one of our conclusions that the principal cause of the high relative earnings of some professional and managerial occupations is the scarcity of persons with the required training, mental ability, and force of character. Enabling more people of that kind to come forward would reduce the inequality of pay as a by-product of increasing society's resources of manpower and making it possible for some people to realize their potential for personal development more fully. That such an unfulfilled potential exists is indicated by the studies of the distribution of I.Q. by occupation, reported in Sec. 7.1: though people of low I.Q. do not get into the more demanding occupations, not a few people of high I.Q. are found in the less demanding. I.Q. is a partial indication of potential, and some of the high I.Q.s in the less demanding occupations will have been kept there because they are not supported by such personal qualities as the D-factor, or are offset by traits that actually inhibit advancement. But we also have reason to believe that some people who by genetic endowment were fully capable of advancement are denied it by their upbringing.

This may be so because their families lacked the resources to maintain them during adolescent years of continued schooling and training. The provision of free state education and, as in the U.K., of grants for the maintenance of students in teritiary education, does not relieve the poorer families of the strain of maintaining children in secondary education, or remove the attraction to the young people themselves of the immediate gain of money to spend if they leave school and take a job. This is one reason why many young people with high I.Q.s leave school at or soon after the minimum age. But at the standards of living now attained by manual workers in Western societies, the most powerful inhibitory factor lies in the upbringing of the child in the home, and the attitude towards learning and advancement that is instilled in him there. Many parents who have themselves gained little from education tend to perpetuate deprivation by failing to foster, or actually repressing, the growth of intellectual curiosity, activities, and self-confidence in their own children; and these children enter school without having been encouraged to make good use of the opportunities it offers for learning, or motivated to use education as an avenue of advancement.

Here are two restrictions on the supply of trained ability that policy can try to remove. The pressure on family resources in the years of adolescence would be reduced, in the U.K. at least, by the provision of more adequate maintenance grants for those continuing in education between the ages of school leaving and university entry. It has been proposed (Blaug 1972, pp. 296–7) that part at least of the great cost of such grants could be recouped by substituting loans for the outright grants now made to students in the universities. The other restriction goes much deeper: how can we change a culture, how influence the way in which mothers and fathers talk to, occupy, discipline and encourage their children in their first five years? The development of playgroups can serve a threefold purpose here: by enlarging the interests and activities of the children; by bringing mothers together for mutual support and discussion of their problems; and by diffusing among fathers and mothers generally knowledge of all that has been discovered in recent years about the deep-going and lasting effect of formative influences in the first five years of life.

An increase in the numbers of persons coming forward with the training and personality required for the higher-paid occupations will make in the long run for both a higher national product and a reduced inequality of pay, but in the shorter run it will raise problems of adjustment. In so far as those already working in the higher-paid occupations exert an effective pressure to maintain their relative pay, they will to that extent preclude an increase in the available number of jobs of that kind, and the overspill of potential entrants will have to find jobs at lower levels of qualification and pay. At the extreme there is the outcome typified in a developing country as 'bus conductors with Ph.Ds', but the more likely outcome is that described by Thurow and Lucas (1972; see Table 7.12 above), in which an array of applicants ranked by level of qualification is seen as set over against an array of jobs ranked by pay, and if more applicants appear with the highest level of qualifications, those in excess of the number of jobs at the corresponding level of pay take the jobs at the level of pay next below, jobs that would otherwise have been filled by applicants with lower qualifications, who now themselves go in lower down still, and so on. But this is only the effect in the short run. Studies of the relation between the availability of educated ability and the structures of organizations have indicated that these structures are flexible, and adapt themselves to changes in the relative supplies of different sorts of qualification: we may expect, then, not that the increased number of qualified entrants will be absorbed by a general expansion of the existing higher-paid occupations, but that there will be changes in the relative sizes of those occupations, and very likely a development of new ones. At the same time, despite the concern of organized employees to maintain their relativities, the increased availability of labour at the higher levels, and its necessary counterpart in a reduction of availability at other levels, are likely to carry further the effect they have already taken, and differentiate the general movements of pay by degrees so as to reduce its inequality.

Such appear to be the constructive ways to that end. We have found that the main cause of the inequality of pay is the inequality of abilities to work. There are great difficulties in the way of breaking the link between pay and ability, and prescribing equal pay for unequal work. The best way to reduce the inequality of the effect is to reduce that of the cause.

References

Acton Society Trust (1956). *Management Succession—the Recruitment, Selection, Training and Promotion of Managers* (London).

Adam, J. (1972). 'Wage Differentials in Czechoslovakia', *Industrial Relations*, 11, 2, May 1972, 157–71.

Adams, F. G. (1958). 'The size of individual incomes: socio-economic variables and chance variation', *Review of Economics and Statistics*, 40, 4, Nov. 1958, 390–8.

Aitchison, J. & Brown J. A. C. (1957). *The Lognormal Distribution* (Cambridge U.P.).

Anderson, C. A., Brown, J. C. & Bowman, M. J. (1952). 'Intelligence and occupational mobility', *Journal of Political Economy*, 60, 3, June 1952, 218–39.

Arrow, K. J. (1972). 'Models of job discrimination', c. 2 in A. H. Pascal (ed.), *Racial Discrimination in Economic Life* (Lexington, Mass.).

Ashenfelter, O. (1970). 'Changes in labour market discrimination over time', *Journal of Human Resources*, 5, 4, Fall 1970, 403–30.

—— (1972). 'Racial discrimination and trade unionism', *Journal of Political Economy*, 72, 3, May–June 1972, 435–64.

—— & Johnson, G. E. (1972). 'Unionism, relative wages, and labor quality in U.S. manufacturing industries', *International Economic Review*, 13, 3, Oct. 1972, 488–508.

Ashton, T. S. (1955). *An Economic History of England: the 18th century* (London).

Atkinson, A. B. (1975). *The Economics of Inequality* (Oxford).

Badenhoop, L. E. (1958). 'Effects of the \$1 minimum wage in seven areas', *Monthly Labor Review*, 81, 7, July 1958, 737–43.

Baker, J. R. (1974). *Race* (Oxford).

Becker, G. S. (1962). 'Investment in human capital: a theoretical analysis', *Journal of Political Economy*, 70, 5, Pt. 2, Supplement, Oct. 1962, 9–49.

—— (1964). *Human Capital: a Theoretical and Empirical Analysis, with special reference to Education* (National Bureau of Economic Research, N.Y.).

—— (1971). *The Economics of Discrimination*, 2nd edn. (Chicago).

Bell, Philip W. (1951). 'Cyclical variations and trend in occupational wage differentials in American industry since 1914', *Review of Economics and Statistics*, 33, 4, Nov. 1951, 329–37.

Benge, E. J., Burk, S. L. H. & Hay, E. N. (1941). *Manual of Job Evaluation* (N.Y.).

Bergmann, B. R. (1971). 'The effect on white incomes of discrimination in employment', *Journal of Political Economy*, 71, 2, Mar.–Apr. 1971, 294–313.

—— & Lyle, J. R. (1971). 'The occupational standing of negroes by areas and industries', *Journal of Human Resources*, 6, 4, Fall 1971, 411–33.

Bergson, Abram (1964). *The Economics of Soviet Planning* (Yale U.P.).

Bernardo, R. M. (1971). *The Theory of Moral Incentives in Cuba* (Univ. of Alabama).

Berndt, R. M. (1972). 'The Walmadjeri and Gugadja', c. 5 of M. G. Bicchieri, *Hunters and Gatherers Today* (N.Y.).

Bernstein, B. (1961). 'Social Class and linguistic development: a theory of social learning', in Part IV of A. H. Halsey, J. Floud, & C. A. Anderson, *Education, Economy and Society* (London).

—— & Henderson, D. (1969). 'Social class differences in the relevance of language to socialization', *Sociology*, 3, 1, Jan. 1969, 1–20.

Bertaux, D. (1970). 'L'hérédité sociale en France', *Économie et Statistique*, 9, Feb. 1970, 37–47.

Bićanić, R. (1963). *Economic Policy in Socialist Yugoslavia* (Cambridge U.P.).

Bicchieri, M. G. (1972). *Hunters and Gatherers Today* (N.Y.).

Bienefeld, M. A. (1972). *Working Hours in British Industry* (London).

Birren, J. E. (1954). 'Age changes in mental abilities', *Journal of Business*, 27, 2, Part 1, Apr. 1954, 156–63.

Blain, A. N. J. (1972). *Pilots and Management: Industrial Relations in the U.K. Airlines* (London).

Blanchemanche, M. (1968). 'Les salaires dans l'industrie, le commerce et les services en 1966', *Études et Conjoncture*, 23, 7, July 1968, 1–45.

Blau, P. M. & Duncan O. D. (1967). *The American Occupational Structure* (N.Y.).

Blaug, M. (1972). *An Introduction to the Economics of Education* (London, first published 1970; Penguin 1972).

——, Peston, M. H. & Ziderman, A. (1967). *The Utilization of Educated Manpower in Industry* (London).

Blinder, A. S. (1973). 'Wage discrimination: reduced form and structural estimates', *Journal of Human Resources*, 8, 4, Fall 1973, 436–55.

Bloch, J. W. (1948). 'Regional wage differentials, 1907–46', *Monthly Labor Review*, 71, 4, Apr. 1948, 371–7.

Bloom, B. S. (1964). *Stability and Change in Human Characteristics* (N.Y.).

Blum, F. H. (1947). 'Marginalism and economic policy: a comment', *American Economic Review*, 37, Sept. 1947, 645–52.

Board of Inland Revenue, (1975). *Inland Revenue Statistics 1975* (H.M.S.O., London).

Bowles, S. & Nelson, V. I. (1974). 'The "inheritance of I.Q." and the intergenerational reproduction of economic inequality', *Review of Economics and Statistics*, 56, 1, Feb. 1974. 39–51.

Bowley, A. L. (1933). 'The action of economic forces in producing frequency distributions of income, prices and other phenomena: a suggestion for study', *Econometrica*, 1, 4, Oct. 1933, 358–82.

—— (1937). *Wages and Income in the United Kingdom since 1860* (Cambridge U.P.).

B.P.P. (British Parliamentary Papers) (1948). *Report of the (Spens) Inter-Departmental Committee on the Remuneration of General Dental Practitioners* (Cmd. 7402, May 1948, H.M.S.O., London).

Bronfenbrenner, U. (1958). 'Socialization and social class through time and space', in E. E. Maccoby, T. M. Newcomb, & E. L. Hartley (eds.), *Readings in Social Psychology* (3rd edn. 1958, N.Y.), 400–25; reprinted in R. Bendix & S. M. Lipset (eds.), *Class Status and Power* (2nd edn. 1967, London), 362–77.

Brown, W. & Sisson, K. (1975). 'The use of comparisons in workplace wage determination', *British Journal of Industrial Relations*, 13, 1, Mar. 1975, 23–53.

Bruner, J. S. (1970). *Poverty and Childhood* (Merrill-Palmer Institute, Detroit), reprinted in J. S. Bruner, *The Relevance of Education* (Penguin Education, London 1974).

Brus, W. (1974). 'Income distribution and economic reforms in Poland', *Il politico* (University of Pavia), 39, 1, 5–28.

Bry, G. (1960). *Wages in Germany 1871–1945* (National Bureau of Economic Research, N.Y., and Princeton U.P.).

Buckley, J. E. (1969). 'Intra-occupational wage dispersion in metropolitan areas 1967–68', *Monthly Labor Review*, 93 (9), Sept. 1969, 24–9.

Burns, R. K. (1954). 'The comparative economic position of manual and white-collar employees', *Journal of Business*, 27, 4, Oct. 1954, 257–67.

Burt, C. (1943). 'Ability and income', *British Journal of Educational Psychology*. 13, 83–98.

—— (1959). 'Class differences in general intelligence, III', *British Journal of Statistical Psychology*, 12, 1, May 1959, 15–33.

Burt, C., Spielman, W. & Gaw, F. (1926). *A study in Vocational Guidance* (Industrial Fatigue Research Board, London, Report No. 33).

Butcher, H. J. (1968). *Human Intelligence: its nature and assessment* (London).

Byrns R. & Henmon, V. A. C. (1936). 'Parental occupation and mental ability', *Journal of Educational Psychology*, 27, 284–91.

Cairnes, J. E. (1874). *Some Leading Principles of Political Economy Newly Expounded* (London).

Carol, A. & Parry S. (1968). 'The economic rationale of occupational choice', Reprinted with permission from *The Industrial and Labor Relations Review*, 21, 2, Jan. 1968, 183–96. Copyright © 1968 by Cornell University, all rights reserved.

Carter, C. O. (1970). *Human Heredity* (Penguin, revised edn.; 1st edn. 1962).

—— (1976). 'The genetic basis of inequality', pp. 98–119 in Atkinson, A. B. (ed.) *The Personal Distribution of Incomes* (London).

Carter, M. (1966). *Into Work* (Pelican, London).

Chalmers, Sir George (1801). *An Estimate of the Comparative Strength of Great Britain* (London).

Champernowne, D. G. (1953). 'A model of income distribution', *Economic Journal*, 63, 250, June 1953, 318–51.

—— (1973). *The Distribution of Income between Persons* (Cambridge U.P.).

Chapman, Janet (1970). *Wage Variation in Soviet Industry: the Impact of the 1956–60 Wage Reform* (Rand Corporation, Santa Monica, Calif.).

—— (1975). 'Soviet wages under socialism', in A. Abouchar (ed.), *The Price Mechanism in the Socialist Economy* (Duke U.P.).

Clark, Colin (1937). *National Income and Outlay* (London).

Clark, D. G. (1966). *The Industrial Manager, his background and career pattern* (London).

Clastres, P. (1972) 'The Guayaki', c. 4 of M. G. Bicchieri (ed.), *Hunters and Gatherers Today* (N.Y.).

Clay, H. (1929). *The Problems of Industrial Relations* (London).

Clements, R. V. (1958). *Managers: a Study of their Careers in Industry* (London).

Coleman, J. S. *et al.* (1966). *Equality of Educational Opportunity* (U.S. Dept. of Health, Education and Welfare, Office of Education, National Center for Educational Statistics, Washington, D. C.).

Copeman, G. H. (1955). *Leaders of British Industry* (London).

Creedy, J. (1974). 'Earnings in chemistry: past and present', *Chemistry in Britain*, 10, 2, Feb. 1974, 50–3.

Crookes, T. G. & French, J. G. (1961). 'Intelligence and wastage of student mental nurses', *Occupational Psychology*, 35, 3, July 1961, 149–54.

Dahrendorf, R. (1959). *Class and class conflict in industrial society* (London).

Damas, D. (1972). 'The Copper Eskimo', c. 1 of M. G. Bicchieri (ed.), *Hunters and Gatherers Today* (N.Y.).

Daubigny, J. P. (1969). 'Actualité du système "Parodi" dans les comportements salariaux des entreprises', *Revue Économique*, 20, 3, May 1969, 497–514.

—— (1971). 'Les disparités des salaires internes à la firme', *Revue Économique*, 22, 3, May 1971, 370–94.

—— Fizaine, F. & Silvestre, J. J. (1971). 'Les différences de salaires entre enterprises', *Revue Économique*, 22, 2, Mar. 1971, 214–46.

—— & Silvestre, J. J. (1972). *Comparaison de hiérarchie des salaires entre l'Allemagne et la France* (Laboratoire d'économie et de sociologie du travail, Faculté de Droit et des Sciences Économiques, Aix-en-Provence).

Davie, R., Butler, N. & Goldstein, H. (1972). *From Birth to Seven: The Second Report of the National Child Development Study (1958 Cohort)* (London).

Dept. of Employment (1973). 'Low pay and changes in earnings', *Dept. of Employment Gazette*, Apr. 1973, 335–48.

—— (1974). *New Earnings Survey 1973* (H.M.S.O., London).

Dept. of Employment and Productivity (1969). 'Effect of regional employment structures on average earnings', *Employment and Productivity Gazette*, 77, 3, Mar. 1969, 232–4.

Dewey, D. (1952). 'Negro employment in Southern industry', *Journal of Political Economy*, 60, 4, Aug. 1952, 279–93.

Doeringer, P. B. (1974). 'Low pay, labour market dualism and industrial relations sytems', in *Wage Determination: papers presented at an international conference, Paris, 3–6 July 1973* (O.E.C.D., Paris 1974).

—— & Piore, M. J. (1971). *Internal Labor Markets and Manpower Analysis* (Lexington, Mass.).

Dore, R. (1973). *British factory—Japanese factory: the origins of national diversity in industrial relations* (London).

Douglas, J. W. B. (1964). *The Home and the School* (London; Panther Paperback 1967).

—— Ross, J. M. & Simpson, H. R. (1968). *All our Future* (London).

Douty, H. M. (1953). 'Union impact on wage structures', *Proceedings of the Sixth Annual Meeting, Industrial Relations Research Association, Dec. 28–30, 1953*, 61–76.

—— (1960). 'Some effects of the $1.00 Minimum Wage in the United States', *Economica*, 27, 106, May 1960, 137–47.

—— (1961). 'Sources of occupational wage and salary rate dispersion within labor markets', *Industrial and Labor Relations Review*, 15, 1, Oct. 1961, 67–74.

—— (1968). 'Wage differentials: forces and counterforces', *Monthly Labour Review*, 91, 3, Mar. 1968, 74–81.

Dumont, L. (1970). *'Homo Hierarchicus', the Caste System and its Implications* (London).

Duncan, B. (1967). 'Education and social background'', *American Journal of Sociology*, 72, 4, Jan. 1967, 363–72.

Duncan, O. D. (1961). 'A socioeconomic index for all occupations', and 'Properties and characteristics of the socioeconomic index', cs. VI and VII of A. J. Reiss (ed.), *Occupations and Social Status* (Glencoe, Ill.).

—— (1966). 'Path analysis: sociological examples', *American Journal of Sociology*, 72, July 1966, 1–16.

—— (1968). 'Inheritance of poverty or inheritance of race?', in D. P. Moynihan (ed.), *On Understanding Poverty* (N.Y.), 85–110.

—— Featherman, D. L. & Duncan B. (1968). *Socioeconomic Background and Occupational Achievement: Extensions of a Basic Model* (U.S. Dept. of Health, Education and Welfare. Project No. 5-0074 (EO-191), Final Report. Washington, D.C.).

Edgeworth, F. Y. & Bowley, A. L. (1902). 'Methods of representing statistics of wages and other groups not fulfilling the Normal Law of Error', *Journal of Royal Statistical Society*, 65, Pt. II, June 1902, 325–354.

Edwards, A. M. (1938). *A Social Economic Grouping of the Gainful Workers of the U.S.* (Bureau of the Census, Washington, D.C.).

Engen, T. (1971). c. 3, 'Psychophysics', in R. S. Woodworth & H. Schlosberg (L. A. Riggs & J. W. Kling, eds.), *Experimental Psychology*, 3rd edn. (N.Y.).

Erickson, C. (1959). *British Industrialists. Steel and Hosiery 1850–1950* (Cambridge U.P.).

Fallers, Lloyd A. (1964). 'Social stratification and economic processes in Africa,' in M. J. Herskovitz & M. Harwitz (eds), *Economic Transition in Africa* (Evanston, Northwestern U.P.), 113–30; reprinted in R. Bendix & S. M. Lipset (eds.), *Class, Status, and Power* (2nd. edn. 1967, London), 141–9.

Fein, R. (1967). 'An economic and social profile of the Negro American', in Talcott Parsons & K. B. Clark (eds), *The Negro American* (Boston, Mass), 102–133.

Fischlowitz, E. (1959). 'Manpower problems in Brazil', *International Labour Review*, 79, 4, Apr. 1959, 398–417.

Fisher, A. G. B. (1932). 'Education and relative wage rates', *International Labour Review*, 25, 6, June 1932, 742–764.

Fishlow, A. (1972). 'Brazilian size distribution of income', *American Economic Review, Papers & Proceedings*, 62, 2, May 1972, 391–402.

Flanagan, R. J. (1973). 'Racial wage discrimination and employment segregation', *Journal of Human Resources*, 8, 4, Fall 1973, 456–71.

Fogarty, M. P. (1961). *The Just Wage* (London).

Fox, A. (1973). 'Industrial relations: a social critique of pluralist ideology', in J. Child (ed.), *Man and Organization* (London), 185–233.

Fox, T. & Miller, S. M. (1966). 'Intra-country variations: occupational stratification and mobility', in R. Bendix and S. M. Lipset (eds.), *Class, Status and Power* (2nd edn. 1967, London), 571–81.

Fraser, E. (1959). *Home Environment and the School* (London).

Frayn, M. (1974). *Constructions* (London).

Friedman, M. (1957). *A Theory of the Consumption Function* (National Bureau of Economic Research N.Y.).

—— & Kuznets, S. (1954). *Income from Independent Professional Practice* (National Bureau of Economic Research, N.Y.).

Fuchs, V. R. (1967). 'Hourly earnings differentials by region and size of city', *Monthly Labor Review*, 90, 1, Jan. 1967, 22–6. This article is an abstract of the same author's *Differentials in hourly earnings by region and city size, 1959* (National Bureau of Economic Research, N.Y., Occasional Paper 101, 1967).

Galenson, W. & Fox, A. (1967). 'Earnings and employment in Eastern Europe, 1957 to 1963', *Quarterly Journal of Economics*, 81, 2, May 1967, 220–40.

Gardner, P. M. (1972). 'The Paliyans', c. 10 of M. G. Bicchieri (ed.), *Hunters and Gatherers Today* (N.Y.).

Gardner Clark M. (1960). 'Comparative wage structures in the steel industry of the Soviet Union and Western countries', Industrial Relations Research Association, *Papers presented at 13th Annual Meeting, 1960*, 266–88.

Gellner, E. (1971) 'The pluralist anti-levellers of Prague', *Archives Européennes de Sociologie*, 12, 2, 312–25: a review article on P. Machonin, *Československá Společnost* (Bratislava 1969).

General Register Office, (1966). *Classification of Occupations* (H.M.S.O., London).

Gibson, J. & Young, M. (1968). 'Social mobility and fertility', in J. E. Meade & A. S. Parkes (eds), *Biological Aspects of Social Problems* (London).

Ginsberg, M. (1929). 'Interchange between social classes', *Economic Journal*, 39, Dec. 1929, 554–65.

Gintis, H. (1971). 'Education, technology and the characteristics of workers' productivity', *American Economic Review, Papers & Proceedings*, 61, 2, May 1971, 266–79.

Girod, R. (1958). 'Évolution comparée du gain annual de manœuvres, d'ouvriers, d'employés et de dirigeants dupuis un siècle environ: le cas de Genéve,' *Schweizerische Zeitschrift für Volkswirtschaft und Statistik*, 94, 2, June 1958, 250–6.

Glass, D. V. & Hall, J. R. (1953). 'Social mobility in Great Britain: a study of inter-generation changes in status', in D. V. Glass (ed.), *Social Mobility in Britain* (London).

Goldthorpe, J. H. (1974). 'Social inequality and social integration in modern Britain', in D. Wedderburn (ed.), *Poverty, Inequality and Class Structure* (Cambridge U.P.), 217–38.

—— & Hope, K. (1972). 'Occupational grading and occupational prestige', in K. Hope (ed.), *The analysis of social mobility: methods and approaches* (Oxford).

—— & —— (1974). *The social gradings of occupations: a new approach and scale* (Oxford).

—— Lockwood, D., Bechhofer, F. & Platt, J. (1969). *The Affluent Worker in the Class Structure* (Cambridge U.P.).

Gordon L. A. & Klopov, E. V. (1973) 'Some problems of the social structure of the Soviet working class', *International Journal of Sociology*, Spring-Summer 1973, 27–46.

Gray, E. M. (1937). *The Weaver's Wage: Earnings and Collective Bargaining in the Lancashire Cotton Weaving Industry* (Manchester).

Gunter, H. (1964). 'Changes in occupational wage differentials', *International Labour Review*, 99, 2, Feb. 1964, 136–55.

Haber, S. (1974). 'The professions and higher education in America: a historical view' c. 7 of M. S. Gordon (ed.), *Higher Education and the Labor Market* (Carnegie Commission on Higher Education, N.Y.).

Hall, J. & Caradog Jones, D. (1950). 'Social grading of occupations', *British Journal of Sociology*, 1, 1, 31–55.

Hall, R. H. (1969). *Occupations and the social structure* (Englewood Cliffs, N.J.).

Halsey, A. H. (1959). 'Class differentiation in general intelligence', *British Journal of Statistical Psychology*, 12, 1, May 1959, 1–4.

Hammermesh, D. S. (1971). 'White-collar unions, blue-collar unions, and wages in manufacturing', *Industrial and Labor Relations Review*, 24, 2, Jan. 1971, 159–70.

Hancock, K. (1969). "The wages of the workers', *Journal of Industrial Relations* (Sydney), 11, 1, Mar. 1969, 17–38.

Hansen, W. Lee (1963). 'Total and private rates of return to investment in schooling', *Journal of Political Economy*, 71, 2, Apr. 1963, 128–40.

Harrell, T. W. & Harrell, M. S. (1945). 'Army General Classification Test scores for civilian occupations', *Educational and Psychological Measurement*, 5, 1945, 231–2; cited in L. E. Tyler, *The Psychology of Human Differences* (1965 N.Y.).

Harris, D. (1975). 'The professional engineer's dilemma over trade union membership', *The Times*, 1 Dec. 1975 (London).

Hatt, P. K. (1950). 'Occupation and social stratification', *American Journal of Sociology*, 55, 6, May 1950, 533–43.

Havighurst, R. J. & Rogers H. H. (1952). *Who should go to College?* (Columbia U.P., N.Y.).

Hazelrigg, L. E. (1974). 'Cross-national comparisons of father-to-son occupational mobility', in J. Lopreato and L. S. Lewis (eds.), *Social Stratification: a Reader* (Harper & Row, N.Y.).

Heer, C. (1930). *Income and Wages in the South* (Univ. of North Carolina Press).

Helm, J. (1972). 'The Dogrib Indians', c. 2 of M. G. Bicchieri (ed.), *Hunters and Gathers Today* (N.Y.).

Hill, G. B. (1965). 'Choice of career by grammer school boys', *Occupational Psychology*, 39, 4, Oct. 1956, 279–87.

Hill, J. M. M. (1969). *The Transition from School to Work* (London).

Hill, T. P. (1959). 'An analysis of the distribution of wages and salaries in Great Britain', *Econometrica*, 27, 3, 355–81.

Himmelweit, H. T. & Whitfield, J. W. (1944). 'Mean intelligence scores of a random sample of occupations,' *British Journal of Industrial Medicine*, 1, 4, 224–6.

Hinde, R. A. (1974). *Biological Bases of Human Social Behaviour* (N.Y. & London).

Hodge, R. W., Siegel, P. M. & Rossi, P. H. (1964). 'Occupational prestige in the United States: 1925–1963', *American Journal of Sociology*. 70, Nov. 1964, 286–302. A fuller version is given in R. Bendix & S. M. Lipset (eds.), *Class, Status and Power*, (2nd edn. 1967, London), 322–34.

——Treiman, D. J. & Rossi, P. H. (1976). 'A comparative study of occupational prestige', in R. Bendix & S. M. Lipset, *Class, Status and Power* (2nd edn.), 309–21.

Hoffmann, Charles (1967). 'Work incentives in Chinese industry and argiculture', in *An Economic Profile of Mainland China* (Joint Economic Committee of the United States Congress, Washington, D.C.).

Howe, Christopher (1973). *Wage Patterns and Wage Policy in Modern China 1919–1972* (Cambridge U.P.).

Hunt, E. H. (1973). *Regional Wage Variations in Britain 1850–1914* (Oxford).

Husèn, T. (1962). 'The influence of schooling upon I.Q.', in A. Anastasi (ed.), *Individual Differences* (N.Y.), 218–25.

Hyman, H. H. (1967). 'The value systems of different classes', in R. Bendix & S. M. Lipset (eds.), *Class, Status and Power*, (2nd edn. 1967, London), 488–99.

I.L.O., (1959). *The Cost of Medical Care* (Geneva).

—— (1962). *Workers' Management in Yugoslavia* (Geneva).

Inkeles, A. (1950). 'Social stratification and mobility in the Soviet Union, 1940–1950', *American Sociological Review*, 15, 4, Aug. 1950, 465–79.

—— & Rossi, P. H. (1956). 'National comparisons of occupational prestige', *American Journal of Sociology*, 61, 4, Jan. 1956, 329–39.

International Metal Workers Federation (1965), *Wages and Working Conditions in the Steel Industries of the Free World* (U.S.A.).

Jackson, B. & Marsden, D. (1962). *Education and the Working Class* (London).

Jefferys, Margot (1954). *Mobility in the Labor Market* (London).

Jencks, C. (1972). *Inequality* (N.Y. 1972; London 1973).

Jensen, A. R. (1969), 'How much can we boost I.Q. and scholastic achievement?', *Harvard Educational Review*, 39, 1, Winter 1969, 1–213.

Johnson, G. E. & Youmans, K. C. (1971). 'Union relative wage effects by age and education', *Industrial and Labor Relations Review*, 24, 2, Jan. 1971, 171–9.

Kalecki, M. (1945). 'On the Gibrat distribution', *Econometrica*, 13, 2, Apr. 1945, 161–70.

Kanninen, T. P. (1953). 'Occupational wage relationships in manufacturing, 1952–53', *Monthly Labor Review*, 76, 11. Nov. 1953, 1171–8.

—— (1962). 'Wage differences among labor markets', *Monthly Labor Review*, 85, 6, June 1962, 614–20.

Keat, P. G. (1960). 'Long-run changes in occupational wage structure, 1900–1956', *Journal of Political Economy*, 68, 6, 584–600.

Kelsall, R. K. (1955). *Higher Civil Servants in Great Britain from 1870 to the Present Day* (London).

Kirsch, L. J. (1972). *Soviet Wages: changes in structure and administration since 1956* (M.I.T., Cambridge, Mass.).

Knowles, K. G. J. C. & Robertson, D. J. (1951). 'Differences between the wages of skilled and unskilled workers, 1880–1950', *Bulletin of the Oxford University Institute of Statistics*, 13, 4, Apr. 1951, 109–27.

Kosters, M. & Welch, F. (1972). 'The effects of minimum wages on the distribution of changes in aggregate employment', *American Economic Review*, 72, 3, June 1972, 323–32.

Krueger, A. O. (1963). 'The economics of discrimination', *Journal of Political Economy*, 71, 5, Oct. 1963, 481–6.

Kuznets, S. (1966). *Modern Economic Growth: Rate, Structure and Spread* (Yale U.P.).

Kýn, O. (1975). 'Czechoslovakia', in H. H. Hohmann, M. C. Kaser, & K. C. Thalheim (eds.), *The New Economic Systems of Eastern Europe* (London).

Lamale, H. H. & Stotz, M. S. (1960). 'The interim city worker's family budget', *Monthly Labor Review*, 83, 8, Aug. 1960, 785–808.

Landes, W. M. (1968). 'The economics of Fair Employment Laws', *Journal of Political Economy*, 76, 4, July–Aug. 1968, 507–52.

Lane, D. (1971). *The End of Inequality? Stratification under State Socialism* (Penguin, London).

Lawrence, E. M. (1931). 'An investigation into the relationship between intelligence and inheritance', *British Journal of Psychology, Monograph Supplement No. 16*.

Layard, P. R. G., Sargan, J. D., Ager, M. E. & Jones, D. J. (1971). *Qualified Manpower and Economic Performance: an interplant study in the electrical engineering industry* (London).

—— & Psacharopoulos, G. (1974). 'The screening hypothesis and the returns to education', *Journal of Political Economy*, 82, 5, 985–98.

Lebergott, S. (1947). 'Wage structures', *Review of Economics and Statistics*, 29, 4, Nov. 1947, 274–85.

Lee, R. B. & Devore, I. (1968). 'Problems in the study of hunters and gatherers', in R. B. Lee & I. Devore (eds.), *Man the Hunter* (Chicago).

Leiserson, M. W. (1966). 'Wage decisions and wage structures in the United States', in E. M. Hugh-Jones (ed.), *Wage-Structure in Theory and Practice* (Amsterdam).

Lenin, V. (1921). 'The Fourth Anniversary of the October Revolution', *Selected Works*, Vol. II, Part 2, p. 601 (Foreign Languages House, Moscow, 1952).

Lerner, S. W., Cable, J. R. & Gupta, S. (1969). *Workshop Wage Determination* (Oxford).

—— & Marquand, J. (1962). 'Workshop bargaining, wage drift and productivity in the British engineering industry', *Manchester School*, 30, 1, Jan. 1962, 15–60.

Lester, R. A. (1952). 'A range theory of wage differentials', *Industrial and Labor Relations Review*, 5, 4, July 1952, 483–501.

—— (1957). 'Economic adjustments to change in wage differentials', c. 8 of G. W. Taylor & F. C. Pierson (eds.), *New Concepts in Wage Determination* (N.Y.).

—— (1967). 'Pay differentials by size of establishment', *Industrial Relations*, 71, Oct. 1967, 57–67.

Lewis, H. Gregg (1963). *Unionism and Relative Wages in the United States* (Univ. of Chicago Press).

Lindbeck, Assar (1975). *Swedish Economic Policy* (London).

Lipset, S. M. & Bendix, R. (1959). *Social Mobility in Industrial Society* (Univ. of California Press & London).

—— —— & Malm, F. T. (1955). 'Job plans and entry into the labour market', *Social Forces*, 33, 3, Mar. 1955, 224–32.

Liss, L. F. (1973). 'The social conditioning of occupational choice', *International Journal of Sociology*, Spring–Summer 1973, 275–88.

Long, C. D. (1960). *Wages and Earnings in the United States 1860–1890*, (National Bureau of Economic Research, N.Y. and Princeton U.P.).

Lowndes, G. A. N. (1937). *The Silent Social Revolution* (London).

Lydall, H. F. (1959). 'The distribution of employment incomes', *Econometrica*, 27, 1, Jan. 1959, 110–15.

—— (1968). *The Structure of Earnings* (Oxford U.P.).

—— (1976). 'Theories of the distribution of earnings', in A. B. Atkinson (ed.), *The Personal Distribution of Incomes* (London), 15–46.

McAuley, Mary (1966). 'Some observations on labour and wages in Czechoslovakia', *Coexistence*, 3, 2, July 1966, 173–88.

McGuire, J. W., Chiu, J. S. Y. & Elbing, A. O. (1962). 'Executive incomes, scales and profits', *American Economic Review*, 52, 4, Sept. 1962, 752–61.

Machonin, P. (1970). 'Social stratification in contemporary Czechoslovakia', *American Journal of Sociology*, 75, 5, Mar. 1970, 725–41.

Mackay D. I. *et al.*, (1971). *Labour Markets under different Employment Conditions* (London).

Maizels, J. (1970). *Adolescent Needs and the Transition from School to Work* (London).

Mandelbrot, B. (1962). 'Paretian distributions and income maximisation', *Quarterly Journal of Economics*, 76, 1, Feb. 1962, 57–85.

Mangum, G. L. (1968). 'Second chance in the transition from school to work', in *The Transition from School to Work* (Industrial Relations Section, Princeton University, U.S.A.), 231–69.

Marris, Robin (1964). *The Economic Theory of 'Managerial' Capitalism* (London).

Marshall, A. (1890). *Principles of Economics* (London).

—— (1892). *Elements of Economics of Industry* (London).

Marshall, R. (1974). 'The economics of racial discrimination: a survey', *Journal of Economic Literature*, 12, 3, Sept. 1974, 849–71.

Martin, F. M. (1953). 'An inquiry into parents' preferences in secondary education', in D. V. Glass (ed.), *Social Mobility in Britain* (London).

Marx, K. (1930). *Capital: a Critique of Political Economy*, trans. from the 4th German edn. by Eden & Cedar Paul (Everyman, London).

Mayer, T. (1960). 'The distribution of ability and earnings', *Review of Economics and Statistics*, 42, 2, May 1960, 189–95.

Meade, J. E. (1973). *The Inheritance of Inequalities: some Biological, Demographic, Social and Economic Factors* (British Academy, Keynes Lecture in Economics, 1973; *Proceedings of the British Academy*, 59, 1973, 355–81. London).

Mehnert, Klaus (1972). *China Today* (London 1972).

Meidner, R. (1974). *Co-ordination and Solidarity. An Approach to Wages Policy* (edited and translated by T. L. Johnston. Stockholm).

Michal, J. M. (1972). 'Size distribution of earnings and income in Czechoslovakia, Hungary and Yugoslavia', paper presented to joint session of the American Economic Association and the Association for Comparative Economic Studies, Toronto, 30 Dec. 1972.

—— (1973). 'Size-distribution of earnings and household incomes in small socialist countries', *Review of Income and Wealth*, 19, 4, Dec. 1973, 407–27.

Miljus, R. C., Parnes, H. S., Schmidt, R. M. & Spitz, R. S. (1968). 'Some correlates of the labour market status of male youth', in *The Transition from School to Work* (Industrial Relations Section, Princeton University, U.S.A.), 47–75.

Mill, J. S. (1848). *Principles of Political Economy*, (1st edn. London).

—— (1852). *Principles of Political Economy*, (3rd edn. London).

Miller, H. P. (1966). *Income Distribution in the United States* (U.S. Bureau of the Census, Washington, D.C.).

Miller, S. M. (1960). 'Comparative social mobility', *Current Sociology*, 9, 1, 1–61.

—— & Reissman, F. (1972). *Social Class and Social Policy* (N.Y.).

Mincer, Jacob (1958). 'Investment in human capital and personal income distribution,' *Journal of Political Economy*, 66, 4, Aug. 1958, 281–302.

—— (1962). 'On-the-job training: costs, returns and some implications', *Journal of Political Economy*, 70, 5, Pt. 2, Supplement, Oct. 1962, S. 50–S. 79.

—— (1970). 'The distribution of labor incomes: a survey with special reference to the human capital approach', *Journal of Economic Literature*, 8, 1, Mar. 1970, 1–26.

Ministry of Education, (1960). *15 to 18: Report of the Central Advisory Council for Education—England, Vol. II (Surveys)* (H.M.S.O., London).

Ministry of Labour, (1922). *Report to the Minister of Labour of the Committee appointed to enquire into the working and effects of the Trade Boards Acts* (Comd. 1645. H.M.S.O., London).

—— (1930). *A Study of the Factors which have operated in the Past and those which are Operating now to Determine the Distribution of Women in Industry* (Cmd. 3508. H.M.S.O., London).

—— (1959). 'Average earnings and hours of men in manufacturing: analysis by size of establishment', *Ministry of Labour Gazette*, 67, 4, Apr. 1959, 125–8.

Ministry of Technology, (1967). *The Survey of Professional Engineers 1966* (H.M.S.O., London).

Mitchell, B. R. & Deane, P. (1962). *Abstract of British Historical Statistics* (Cambridge, England).

Montgomery, G. W. G. (1962). 'Predicting success in engineering', *Occupational Psychology*, 36, 1 & 2, Jan.–Apr. 1962, 59–68.

Moore, H. L. (1911). *Laws of Wages: an Essay in Statistical Economics* (N.Y.).

Moore, T. G. (1971). 'The effect of minimum wages on teenage unemployment rates', *Journal of Political Economy*, 79, 4, July/Aug. 1971, 897–902.

Morecka, Z. (1965). 'Economic expansion and wage structure in a socialist country: a study of Polish experience', *International Labour Review*, 91, 6, June 1965, 461–88.

Morgan, J. (1962). 'The anatomy of income distribution', *Review of Economics and Statistics*, 44, 3, Aug. 1962, 270–83.

—— & David, M. (1963). 'Education and Income', *Quarterly Journal of Economics*, 77, 3, Aug. 1963, 423–37.

Morris, V. & Ziderman, A. (1971). 'The economic return on investment in higher education in England and Wales', *Economic Trends*, May 1971 (H.M.S.O., London).

Muntz, E. E. (1955). 'The decline in wage differentials based on skill in the United States', *International Labour Review*, 71, 6, June 1955, 575–92.

National Board for Prices and Incomes, (1971). *General Problems of Low Pay*, Report No. 169 (H.M.S.O., London, Cmnd. 4648, Apr. 1971).

Newman, H. H., Freeman, F. N. & Holzinger, K. J. (1937). *Twins: a Study of Heredity and Environment* (Chicago).

Newson, J. & E. (1963). *Infant Care in an Urban Community* (London).

Nisbet, J. (1961). 'Family environment and intelligence', in A. H. Halsey, J. Floud, & C. A. Anderson (eds.), *Education, Economy, and Society* (London).

N.O.R.C. (National Opinion Research Centre), (1947). 'Jobs and Occupations: a popular evaluation', *Opinion News*, 9, 1, Sept. 1947, 3–13; reprinted in R. Bendix & S. M. Lipset (eds.), *Class, Status and Power* (1954), 411–26.

Nove, A. (1966). 'Wages in the Soviet Union: a comment on recently published statistics', *British Journal of Industrial Relations*, 4, 2, July 1966, 212–21.

Ober, H. (1948). 'Occupational Wage Differentials, 1907–1947', *Monthly Labor Review*, 67, 8, Aug. 1948, 127–34.

O'Boyle, E. J. (1969). 'Job tenure: how it relates to race and age', *Monthly Labor Review*, 92, 9, Sept. 1969, 16–23.

O.E.C.D., (1965). *Wages and Labour Mobility: a study of the relation between changes in wage differentials and the pattern of employment* (Organization for Economic Co-operation and Development, Paris).

Office of Population Censuses and Surveys, (1970). *Classification of Occupations 1970* (H.M.S.O., London).

O'Herlihy, C. St. J. (1969). *Measuring minimum wage effects in the United States* (I.L.O., Geneva).

Oxnam D. W. (1950). 'The relation of unskilled to skilled wage rates in Australia', *Economic Record*, 26, 50, June 1950, 112–18.

Ozanne, R. (1962). 'A century of occupational differentials in manufacturing', *Review of Economics and Statistics*, 44, 3, Aug. 1962, 292–9.

—— (1968). *Wages in Practice and Theory: McCormick and International Harvester 1860–1960* (Univ. Of Wisconsin).

Palekar, S. A. (1962). *Problems of wage policy for economic development* (London).

Parsons, Talcott (1954). *Essays in Sociological Theory*, revised edn. (N.Y. & London).

Pascal, A. H. & Rapping, L. A. (1972). 'The economics of racial discrimination in organized baseball', c. 4. of A. H. Pascal (ed.). *Racial Discrimination in Economic Life* (Lexington, Mass.).

Peitchinis, S. G. (1965). *The Economics of Labour: Employment and Wages in Canada* (Toronto).

Pen, J. (1971). *Income Distribution* (London).

PEP, (Political and Economic Planning) (1974). *Reshaping Britain: a programme of economic and social reform* (London).

Perlman, R. (1969). *Labour Theory* (N.Y.).

Perrucci, C. C. & Perrucci, R. (1970). 'Social origins, educational contexts, and career mobility', *American Sociological Review*, 35, 3, June 1970, 451–63.

Peterson, J. M. (1957). 'Employment effects of minimum wages, 1938–50', *Journal of Political Economy*, 65, 5, Oct. 1957, 412–30.

Phelps, E. S. (1972). 'The statistical theory of racism and sexism', *American Economic Review*, 62, 4, Sept. 1972, 659–61.

Phelps Brown, E. H. (1949). 'Equal pay for equal work', *Economic Journal*, 59, 235, Sept. 1949, 384–98.

—— (1959). *The Growth of British Industrial Relations* (London).

—— (1962). *The Economics of Labor* (Yale U.P.).

—— & Browne, M. H. (1968). *A Century of Pay* (London).

—— & Hopkins, S. V. (1955). 'Seven centuries of building wages', *Economica*, 22, 87, Aug. 1955, 195–206.

—— & —— (1956). 'Seven centuries of the prices of consumables, compared with builders' wage-rates', *Economica*, 23, 92, Nov. 1956, 296–314.

—— & —— (1959). 'Builders' wage rates, prices and population: some further evidence', *Economica*, 26, 101, Feb. 1959, 18–38.

Piore, M. J. (1972). 'Fragments of a "sociological" theory of wages', *Industrial Relations Research Association, Proceedings of the 25th Anniversary Meeting*, Dec. 1972, 286–95.

Polanyi, G. & Wood, J. B. (1974). *How much inequality?* (Institute of Economic Affairs, London).

Praderie, M. & Passagez, M. (1966). 'La mobilité professionnelle en France entre 1959 et 1964', *Études et Conjoncture*, 21, 10, Oct. 1966, 1–163.

—— Salais, R. & Passagez, M. (1967). 'Une enquête sur la formation et la qualification des Français', *Études et Conjoncture*, 22, 2, Feb. 1967, 3–109.

Prais, S. J. (1955). 'Measuring social mobility', *Journal of the Royal Statistical Society (A)*, 118, Pt. I. 56–66.

Pryor, F. L. (1972). 'The distribution of non-agricultural labor incomes in communist and capitalist nations', *Slavic Review*, 31, 3, Sept. 1972, 639–50.

Psacharopoulos, G. (1975). *Earnings and Education in O.E.C.D. Countries* (O.E.C.D., Paris).

Rabkin, L. Y. & Spiro, M. E. (1970). 'Postscript: the Kibbutz in 1970', in M. E. Spiro, *Kibbutz*,

Venture in Utopia (new edn., N.Y.).

Rathbone, E. (1917). 'The remuneration of women's services', *Economic Journal*, 27, 105, Mar. 1917, 55–68.

Reder, M. W. (1955). 'The theory of occupational wage differentials', *American Economic Review*, 45, 5, Dec. 1955, 833–52.

—— (1968). 'The size distribution of earnings,' in J. Marchal & B. Ducros (eds.), *The Distribution of National Income* (London & N.Y.), 583–610.

—— (1969). 'A partial survey of the theory of income size distribution', in Lee Soltow (ed.), *Six Papers on the Size Distribution of Wealth and Income* (N.Y.), 205–53.

Rees, A. & Shultz, G. P. (1970). *Workers and Wages in an Urban Labor Market* (Univ. of Chicago Press).

Reiss, A. J. (with O. D. Duncan, P. K. Hatt, & C. C. North), (1961). *Occupations and Social Status* (N.Y.).

Reynolds, L. G. & Shister, J. (1949). *Job Horizons* (New York).

—— & Taft, C. H. (1956). *The Evolution of Wage Structure* (Yale U.P.).

Ricardo, D. (1817). *Principles of Political Economy and Taxation* (London).

Richman, B. M. (1969). *Industrial Society in Communist China* (N.Y.).

Rilett, J. W. (1975). letter to *The Times* (London), 24 Jan. 1975.

Rishøj, T. (1971). 'Metropolitan social mobility, 1850–1950: the case of Copenhagen', *Quality and Quantity*, 5, 1, June 1971, 131–41.

Robinson, D. (ed.) (1970). *Local Labour Markets and Wage Structures* (London).

Robinson, W. P. & Rackstraw, S. J. (1967). 'Variations in mothers' answers to children's questions, as a function of social class, verbal intelligence test scores and sex', *Sociology*, 1, 3, Sept. 1967, 259–76.

Rogoff, N. (1953). *Recent Trends in Occupational Mobility* (Glencoe, Ill.).

Rosen, S. (1970). 'Unionism and the occupational wage structure in the United States', *International Economic Review*, 11, 2, June 1970, 269–86.

Roustang, G. (1971). 'La formation des salaires des cadres', and 'Évolution du salaire des cadres supérieurs en fonction de l'âge', *Revue Économique*, 22, 2, Mar. 247–70, and 3, May, 395–429, 1971.

Routh, Guy (1954). 'Civil service pay, 1875 to 1950', *Economica*, 21, 83, Aug. 1954, 201–23.

—— (1965). *Occupation and Pay in Great Britain 1906–60* (Cambridge U.P.).

Rowe, J. W. F. (1928). *Wages in Practice and Theory* (London).

Royal Commission on the Distribution of Income and Wealth (1975a). *Report No. 1: Initial Report on the Standing Reference* (Cmnd. 6171, H.M.S.O., London).

—— (1975b). *Report No 2: Income from Companies and its Distribution* (Cmnd. 6172, H.M.S.O. London).

—— (1976a). *Report No. 3: Higher Incomes from Employment* (Cmnd. 6383, H.M.S.O., London).

—— (1976b). *Report No. 4: Second Report on the Standing Reference* (Cmnd. 6626, H.M.S.O. London).

Royal Commission on Doctors' and Dentists' Remuneration 1957–60 (1960). *Report* (Cmnd. 939, H.M.S.O., London).

Royal Commission on Equal Pay 1944–46 (1946). *Report* (Cmnd. 6937, H.M.S.O., London).

Rutherford, R. S. G. (1965). 'Income distribution: a new model', *Econometrica*, 23, 3, July 1955, 277–94.

Rutkevich, M. N. & Filippov, F. R. (1973). 'Social sources of recruitment of the intelligentsia', *International Journal of Sociology*, Spring-Summer 1973, 241–74.

Sadler, P. (1970). 'Sociological aspects of skill', *British Journal of Industrial Relations*, 8, 1, Mar. 1970, 22–31.

Samuels, N. (1957). 'Effects of the $1 minimum wage in seven industries', *Monthly Labor Review*, 80, 3, Mar. 1957, 322–8; 80, 4, Apr. 1957, 441–6.

Sanborn, H. (1964). 'Pay differences between men and women', *Industrial and Labor Relations Review*, 17, 4, July 1964.

Sarapata, A. & Wesolowski, W. (1961). 'The evaluation of occupations by Warsaw inhabitants',

American Journal of Sociology, 66, 6, May 1961, 581–91.

Sawhill, I. V. (1973). 'The economics of discrimination against women: some new findings', *Journal of Human Resources*, 8, 3, Summer 1973, 383–96.

Schultz, T. W. (1961). 'Investment in human capital', *American Economic Review*, 51, Mar. 1961, 1–17.

Scitovsky, T. (1966). 'An international comparison of the trend of professional earnings', *American Economic Review*, 66, 1, Mar. 1966, 25–42. 'Les tendances des revenus des professions libérales: une comparaison internationale', *Analyse et Prévision*, 1, 3, Mar. 1966, 177–206.

Scott, W. H., Banks, J. A., Halsey, A. H. & Lupton, T. (1956). *Technical change and industrial relations* (Liverpool).

Segal, Lord (1956). Speech in the House of Lords, 3 Feb. 1965, Parly. Debates, 5th series, CCLXII, pp. 1198–1203; letter in *The Times*, London, 12 Feb. 1965.

Sellier, F., Maurice, M., Silvestre, J.–J. (1972). *La Hiérarchie d'encadrement dans l'entreprise: recherche d'un effet sociétal*. Projet de recherche. Laboratoire d'Économie et de Sociologie du Travail, Faculté de Droit et des Sciences Économiques, Aix-en-Provence.

Shkaratan, O. I. (1973a). 'Sources of social differentiation of the working class in Soviet society', *International Journal of Sociology*, Spring–Summer 1973, 10–26.

—— (1973b). 'Social groups in the working class of a developed socialist society', *International Journal of Sociology*, Spring–Summer 1973, 63–105.

—— (1973c). 'Social ties and social mobility', *International Journal of Sociology*, Spring-Summer 1973, 289–319.

Shkurko, A. S. (1964). 'The industrial wage system in the U.S.S.R.', *International Labour Review*, 90, Oct. 1964, 352–64.

Šik, Ota (1967). *Plan and Market under Socialism* (N.Y.).

Silberbauer, G. G. (1972). 'The G/Wi Bushmen', c. 7 of M. G. Bicchieri (ed.), *Hunters and Gatherers Today* (N.Y.).

Silvestre, J-J. (1971). 'La dynamique des salaires nominaux en France', *Revue Économique*, 22, 3, May 1971, 430–49.

—— (1974). 'Industrial wage differentials: a two-country comparison", *International Labour Review*, 110, 6, Dec. 1974, 495–514.

Simon, H. A. (1957). 'The compensation of executives', *Sociometry*, 20, 32–5.

Skodak, M. & Skeels, H. M. (1949). 'A final follow-up study of one hundred adopted children', *Journal of Genetic Psychology*, 75, 85–125.

Slichter, S. H. (1950). 'Notes on the structure of wages', *Review of Economics and Statistics*, 32, 1, Feb. 1950, 80–91.

Smith, Adam (1776). *The Wealth of Nations* (London).

Smith, J. H. (1943). 'Work output capacity of women employed in agriculture', *Welsh Journal of Agriculture*, 17 June 1943, 51–8.

Spiro, M. E. (1970). *Kibbutz, Venture in Utopia* (new edn. N.Y.).

Stacey, B. G. (1968). 'Inter-generation occupational mobility in Britain', *Occupational Psychology*, 42, 1, Jan. 1968, 33–48.

Staehle, H. (1943). 'Ability, wages and income', *Review of Economics and Statistics*, 25, 1, Feb. 1943, 77–87.

Stafford, F. P. (1968). 'Concentration and labor earnings: a comment', *American Economic Review*, 58, 1, Mar. 1968, 174–81.

Stevens, S. S. (1961). 'To honor Fechner and repeal his law', *Science*, 133, 3446, 13 Jan. 1961, 80–6.

Steward, U. H. (1968). 'Causal factors and processes in the evolution of pre-farming societies', in R. B. Lee & I. Devore (eds.), *Man the Hunter* (Chicago).

Stieber, J. (1959). *The steel industry wage structure* (Harvard U.P.).

Strmiska, Z. & Vavakova, B. (1972). 'La stratification sociale de la société socialiste', *Revue française de Sociologie*, 13, 2, Apr–June 1972, 213–57.

Sussman, Z. (1973). 'The determination of wages for unskilled labor in the advanced sector of the dual economy of mandatory Palestine', *Economic Development and Cultural Change*, 22, 1, Oct. 1973, 95–113.

Suttles, W. (1968). 'Coping with abundance: subsistence on the North-west Coast', in R. B. Lee & I. Devore (eds), *Man the Hunter* (Chicago).

Svalastoga, K. (1959). *Prestige, Class and Mobility* (Copenhagen).

Taira, K. (1966). 'Wage differentials in developing countries: a survey of findings', *International Labour Review*, 93, 3, Mar. 1966, 281–301.

Tannenbaum, A. S., Kavcic, B., Rosner, M., Vianello, M. & Wieser, G. *Hierarchy in Organizations* (San Francisco).

Taubman, P. (1975). *Sources of Inequality in Earnings* (Amsterdam).

—— (1976). 'Personal characteristics and the distribution of earnings', in A. B. Atkinson (ed.), *The Personal Distribution of Incomes* (London), 193–213.

——(1976a). 'Earnings, education, genetics, and environment', *Journal of Human Resources*, 11, 4, Fall 1976, 447–61.

—— (1976b). 'The determinants of earnings: genetics, family, and other environments; a study of male white twins', *American Economic Review*, 66, 5, Dec. 1976, 858–70.

—— & Wales, T. J. (1973). 'Higher Education, mental ability, and screening', *Journal of Political Economy*, 81, 1, Jan.–Feb. 1973, 28–55.

—— & —— (1974). *Higher Education and Earnings* (Carnegie Commission on Higher Education, N.Y.).

Taussig, F. W. (1929). *Principles of Economics*, 3rd edn. (N.Y.).

Tawney, R. H. (1938). *Equality*, 3rd edn. (London).

Taylor, D. P. (1968). 'Discrimination and occupational wage differences in the market for unskilled labour', *Industrial and Labor Relations Review*, 21, 3, Apr. 1968, 375–90.

Tersmeden, C. R. (1972). 'Sweden: unofficial strikes', in Guy Spitaels (ed.), *La Crise des relations industrielles en Europe* (College of Europe, Bruges).

Thatcher, A. R. (1968). 'The distribution of earnings of employees in Great Britain', *Journal of the Royal Statistical Society*, (A), 131, 133–80.

—— (1971). 'Year to year variations in the earnings of individuals', *Journal of the Royal Statistical Society* (A), 134, Pt. 3, 374–382.

—— (1976). 'The New Earnings Survey and the distribution of earnings', in A. B. Atkinson (ed.), *The Personal Distribution of Incomes* (London), 227–59.

Thorndike, R. & Hagen, E. (1959). *Ten Thousand Careers (N.Y.)*.

Thorndike, R. L. (1973). *Reading Comprehension Education in Fifteen Countries* (International Association for the Evaluation of Educational Achievement, N.Y., London, & Stockholm).

Thurow, L. C. & Lucas, R. E. B. (1972). *The American Distribution of Income: a Structural Problem* (Joint Economic Committee, U.S. Congress. Washington, D.C.).

Tinbergen, J. (1976). 'Personal characteristics and income', in A. B. Atkinson (ed.), *The Personal Distribution of Incomes* (London).

Tiryakian, E. A. (1962). 'The prestige evaluation of occupations in an underdeveloped country: the Philippines', *American Journal of Sociology*, 67, Mar. 1962, 561–5.

Titma, M. Kh. (1973). 'The influence of social origins on the occupational values of graduating secondary school students', *International Journal of Sociology*, Spring–Summer 1973, 187–226.

Tough, Joan (1973). *Focus on Meaning: talking to some purpose with young children* (London).

Troyat, H. (1970). *Tolstoy* (Pelicans Biographies, London).

Tuck, R. H. (1954). *An Essay on the Economic Theory of Rank* (Oxford).

Tuddenham, R. D. (1948). 'Soldier intelligence in World Wars I and II', *American Psychologist*, 3, 54–6; cited in A. Anastasi, *Differential Psychology* (3rd edn. N.Y. 1958), 210–11.

Turnbull, C. M. (1968). 'The importance of flux in two hunting societies', in R. B. Lee & I. Devore (eds.), *Man the Hunter* (Chicago).

Turnbull P. & Williams, G. (1974). 'Sex differentials in teachers' pay', *Journal of the Royal Statistical Society* (A), 137, 2, 245–58.

Turner, H. A. (1952). 'Trade unions, differentials and the levelling of wages', *Manchester School*, 20, 3, Sept. 1952, 227–82.

—— (1962). 'Wage policy and economic development', *Manchester Statistical Society*, 12 Dec. 1962.

—— (1965). *Wage Trends, Wage Policies, and Collective Bargaining: the Problems for Underdeveloped Countries* (University of Cambridge, Dept. of Applied Economics, Occasional Paper 6).

Tyler, L. E. (1965). *The Psychology of Human Differences*, 3rd edn. (N.Y.).

U.N., E.C.E. (1967). *Incomes in Post-War Europe: Economic Survey of Europe in 1965*, Part 2 (Geneva).

U.S. Bureau of the Census, (1969). *Current Population Reports, Consumer Income* (Washington, D.C.).

——(1970). 'Annual mean income, lifetime income and educational attainment of men in the United States, for selected years 1956 to 1968', *Current Population Reports*, Series P. 60, No. 74 (Washington, D.C.).

U.S. Dept. of Health, Education and Welfare, (1971). *Intellectual Development of Children by Demographic and Socioeconomic Factors*. Data from National Health Survey, Series 11, no. 110, Dec. 1971 (Washington, D.C.).

U.S. Dept. of Labor (Wage Hours and Public Contracts Division) (1959). *Report Submitted to the Congress in accordance with the requirements of Sec. 4(d) of the Fair Labor Standards Act, 31 Jan. 1959* (Washington, D.C.).

—— (1965). *Dictionary of Occupational Titles*, Vol. I (Washington, D.C.).

—— (Wage Hours and Public Contracts Division) (1966). *Minimum Wages and Maximum Hours under the Fair Labor Standards Act—an evaluation and appraisal* (Report to the 89th Congress by the Secretary of Labor, Jan. 1966. Washington, D.C.).

—— (1969). *Wages and Related Benefits, Part II: Metropolitan Areas, United States and Regional Summaries, 1967–68* (Bureau of Labor Statistics, Bulletin No. 1575–87. Washington, D.C.).

—— (1969a). *National Survey of Professional, Administrative, Technical and Clerical Pay, June 1968* (Bureau of Labor Statistics, Bulletin No. 1617, Jan. 1969. Washington, D.C.).

U.S. Federal Reserve System, Board of Governors, (1957). *Consumer Installment Credit* (Washington, D.C.).

U.S. Govt. (1943). *Sixteenth Census of the United States: 1940. Population, Occupation Statistics for the United States, 1870–1940* (U.S. Govt. Printing Office, Washington, D.C.).

Vernon, P. E. (1947). 'The variation of intelligence with occupation, age and locality', *British Journal of Psychology (Statistical Section)*, I, Oct. 1947, 52–63.

—— (1949). 'Occupational norms for the 20-minute Progressive Matrices test', *Occupational Psychology*, 23, 1, Jan. 1949, 58–9.

—— (1950). The Structure of Human Abilities (London).

—— (1960). *Intelligence and Attainment Tests* (London).

Vincent, D. F. (1952). 'The linear relationship between age and score of adults in intelligence tests', *Occupational Psychology*, 26, 4, Oct. 1952, 243–9.

Vodzinskaia, V. V. (1973). 'Orientations towards occupations', *International Journal of Sociology*, Spring-Summer 1973, 153–86.

Wachtel, H. M. & Betsey, C. (1972). 'Employment at low wages', *Review of Economics and Statistics*, 54, 2, May 1972, 121–9.

War Cabinet Committee on Women in Industry (1919). *Report*, B.P.P. Cmd. 135; with Appendices: Summaries of Evidence &c. Cmd. 167 (H.M.S.O., London).

Warner, W. Lloyd & Low, J. O. (1947). *The social system of the modern factory* (Yale U.P.).

Webb, S. & B. (1926). *Industrial Democracy* (London; first published 1897).

Weber, Max (1968). *Economy and Society*, ed. by G. Roth and C. Wittich (N.Y.).

Wedderburn, D. & Craig, C. (1974). 'Relative deprivation in work', in D. Wedderburn (ed.), *Poverty, Inequality and Class Structure* (Cambridge U.P.), 141–64.

Weisbrod, B. A. & Karpoff, P. (1968). 'Monetary returns to college education, student ability, and college quality', *Review of Economics and Statistics*, 50, 4, Nov. 1968, 491–7.

Weiss, L. (1966). 'Concentration and labor earnings', *American Economic Review*, 56, 1, Mar. 1966, 96–117.

—— (1968). 'Concentration and labor earnings—a reply', *American Economic Review*, 58, 1, Mar. 1968, 181–4.

Weisskoff, F. B. (1972). ' "Women's Place" in the Labor Market', *American Economic Review* (Papers & Proceedings), 72, 2, May 1972, 161–6.

Wesolowski, W. (1967). 'Les notions de strate et de classe dans la société socialiste,', *Sociologie du Travail*, 9, 144–64.

Whyte, M. K. (1973). 'Bureaucracy and modernization in China: the Maoist critique', *American Sociological Review*, 38, 2, Apr. 1973, 149–63.

Wilkinson, B. W. (1966). 'Present values of life-time earnings in different occupations', *Journal of Political Economy*, 74, 6, Dec. 1966, 556–72.

Wise, D. A. (1973). *Academic Achievement and Job Performance: Earnings and Promotions*, Paper P. 37, Ford Foundation Program for Research in University Administration, University of California.

Witteveen, H. J. (1960). 'Het systeem van loonvorming,' Preadviezen voor de Jaarvergadering van de Vereniging voor Staathuishoudkunde (Papers for the Annual Meeting of the Netherlands Economic Society).

Wohlstetter, A. & Coleman, S. (1972). 'Race differences in income', c. 1 of A. H. Pascal (ed.), *Racial Discrimination in Economic Life* (Lexington, Mass.).

Wolff, P. de & Slipje, A. R. D. van (1973). 'The relation between income, intelligence, education and social background', *European Economic Review*, 4, 235–64.

Wolfle, D. & Smith, V. G. (1956). 'The occupational value of education for superior high-school graduates', *Journal of Higher Education*, 27, Apr. 1956, 201–14.

Woodworth, R. S. (1941). *Heredity and Environment* (N.Y.: Social Science Research Bulletin 47).

—— & Schlosberg, H. (1954). *Experimental Psychology* (N.Y. & London).

Wootton, B. (1946). Appendix IX to Minutes of Evidence taken before the Royal Commission on Equal Pay (H.M.S.O., London).

—— (1955). *The social foundations of wage policy* (London).

Yanowich, M. & Dodge, N. T. (1969). 'The social evaluation of occupations in the Soviet Union', *Slavic Review*, 28, 4, Dec. 1969, 619–43.

Yule, G. U. & Kendall, M. G. (1946). *An Introduction to the Theory of Statistics* (London).

General Index

Aberdeen, 221
Ability, rent of, 15
Ability to work
  index of, 294–8
  formation and distribution of, 298–305, 318, 328
    link with pay, 306–10, 317–21
Aborigines, Australian, 125
Achievement, tests of, 215–16
Affinity, index of, 181–93
Africa
  countries of, 60, 70, 88
  hunter-gatherers in, 124–5
Age–earnings profiles, 30, 149, 263–9
Agricultural Wages Act, 119
Airlines, 129
Alleles, 228
Amalgamated Society of Engineers, 72
Amenity of occupations, differential, 13, 16, 30–1
Argentine, 63
Artisans, 1, 4
Asian countries, 60
Aspirations, of white and non-white children, 161, 166
ATC (administrative, technical, & clerical) 5, 33, 42, 50, 60, 102
ATW, see Ability to work
Augsburg, 69
Australia
  aborigines, 125
  arbitration, effect on differentials, 77
  evidence cited from, 36, 59, 60, 63, 73–4
  mobility, intergenerational, into upper non-manuals, 202–3
  sorting factor in, 197

Bakers, and status, 128–9
Bargaining power, see Trade Unions
Barristers, status of, 119–22
Baseball, professional players, 166
Battersea (London), 249
Belgium, evidence cited from, 59, 63, 64, 65
Binet, measures of mental ability, 215–16
Black Death, 68
Blacks, discrimination against, 160–74
Bombay, 88
Brahmins, 88
Brazil, 70–1
Building
  craftsman's and labourer's rates
    since 1300, 6, 68–9, 134
  industry, relative pay in
    changes in G.B., 90–1
    in different countries, 64
Bulgaria, 64

Canada
  distribution of national income, 4
  evidence cited from, 35–6, 38, 64, 73–4
  lifetime earnings in, 239–40
  North-West, 124
  status, ranking by in, 105
Capital
  owners of, in Ricardo, 3
  technical advances economizing, 4
Caribbean countries, 70
Caste, 80, 117, 123
Catholics, 315
Census of Population, social classes in, 185
Central framework agreement, Swedish, 96–7
Charisma, 111
Chicago, 74, 76, 173, 275
China
  incentives in, 51–4, 330
  managers, relative pay in, 66
  wage structure, 51–4, 271, 325
Chinese, in S.E. Asia, 160
Cities, size of, associated with level of pay, 276–7
Civil servants
  relative pay, in different countries, 36–8, 66
    changes over time, 81–3
  social origins of, 206
  test scores of, 211
Class, social
  barriers, 253
  and education of children, 232–6
  and intergenerational mobility, 181–207
  and mental ability and education of members, 208–55
  in neolithic revolution, 127
  of parents, and children's I.Q., 223–9, 252, 323
    effects on child's prospects
      summarized, 323
  and pay structure, 20–1
  and status, 111
  and style of child upbringing, 220–3, 252–4
  Weber's definition of, 185
Clerical workers
  persistence of differential, 66
  proportion of in working population, 5
  relative pay in British civil service, 81–2
Cliff, analogy of, 256–84, 318–21
Coalmining
  constraints on pay, 8
  pay in different countries, 64–5
  pay in G.B. compared with other industries, 90–2
Cognitive ability, see I.Q.
Cohesion, index of, 184
Collective bargaining, see Trade Unions
Colonies, American mainland, professions in, 119

Compositors
  changes in relative wages of, in G.B., 90–2
  and status, 128
Confederation of British Industry, 269
Congo, Belgian, 105
Construction, *see* Building
Convention
  and managerial salaries, 131–2
  and women's wages, 154–5
Copenhagen, 199
Corn Production Act, 119
Cottagers, 1
Coventry, 76–98, 273–4
Craftsmen—*see also* Building
  in 1688, 1
  status of, 116
Credentialism, 179, 242–5
Critique of the Gotha Programme, 43
Cuba, pay scales and incentives, 54, 66, 325, 330
Cultural Revolution in China, 53
Current Population Survey, 189, 190
Custom, effect of on differentials, 6, 87, 134–6, 141,
    142, 326–7, 329
Cycle, business, 75
Czechoslovakia
  incentives in, 44, 137
  pay structure in, 41–2, 46–8
  wage equalization in, 135
  women, employment of, in, 48

D-factor, 312, 315–16
Dagenham (England), 249
Daughters, 191–2
Deference, 8–9, 18, 114, 117
Demand, *see* Market forces
Demarcation, of 'women's work', 150–1
  of white and Negro jobs, 163–6
Denmark, evidence cited from, 32, 38, 64, 84, 194
Discrimination, 144, 145–80
Disequilibrating rates of pay, 13
Distribution, statistical, forms of, 285
  of individual earnings, 285–321
  ways in which formed, 290–4
Distance, social, 140, 207
Dividends, 5
Division of labour, 112, 126
Dogrib, 124, 125
Dual labour market, 130

Earnings, individual
  differences of, within occupations, 256–84
  fluctuations of, 260–2, 328
  form of distribution of, 285–321
East Africa, 122
Education—*see also* Training
  and age–earnings profiles, 267–9
  of blacks in U.S.A., 161
  class differences in
    extent of, 232–6, 331
    use made of, 229–32, 331
  cost of, in U.S.A., 163
  effects of,
    on ability to work, 299–305
    on professional salaries, 37

distinguished from those of ability, 313–14,
    316–17
  extension of, effects, 4–5, 80, 86
  as investment, 236–45, 254
  in relation to social class and mental ability, 20,
    184, 186, 208–55
  as source of status, 111, 114
Edwards occupational index, 116–17, 211
Egalitarianism
  in Czechoslovakia, 135–9
  heresy in U.S.S.R., 43, 45
  among hunter-gatherers, 124–6
  in Kibbutzim, 55
  in relation to socialism, 3, 6
Egypt, 127
Elbow-joint effect, 327–8
Élite, mobility into and out of, 199–206
Employment, agencies, 249–50
  entry into, 245–51
Engineering
  differentials in, changes of, in U.K., 72
  pay structures compared in
    Leningrad and G.B., 40
    Soviet-type economies and G.B., 41
Engineers, professional status of, 129
England, South of, differentials in, 6, 68–9
England & Wales—*see also* Great Britain, United
    Kingdom
  affinity, indexes of, in, 187–8
  age–earnings profiles in, 149, 267–9
  children in,
    cohort b. 1946, 221, 223, 225, 232, 233, 247
    number in family, 223
    test scores, 225
  family line, length of stay in status category, 189
  intergenerational occupational mobility in, 189,
    194
  ranking of occupations in, 106–8
  recruits from, 222
Entry into occupations, restriction of, 13
Environment, effect on I.Q., 218–20
Equal Pay for blacks, 171
  for women, 159
Eskimos, Copper, 125
Esteem, social, 111, 326
  for talents, 143
Exchange theory, in sociology, 18

Factor analysis of mental ability, 212
Fair employment laws, 171
Fair Labor Standards Act, 79, 81, 175
Family
  effect on differential between black and white, 168
  size of, effect on children, 221–2
Farm workers,
  changes in relative wages in G.B., 90–2
  monopsony, subject to, 147
  station in life and wages, 119–21
Firms, variation of wages with size of, 275–6
First World War, effect on differentials, 7, 135
Fitters, changes in relative wages in G.B., 90–1
Fleet Street, 273–4
France
  affinity, indexes of, 192
  age–earnings profiles, 263, 266–7

civil servants, pay of, 66, 81–2
differentials, widening of, 78
education, extent of, by parent's occupation,
    232–4
élite in, 201
evidence cited from, 32, 36, 38, 73–4, 84
local labour markets, 273
management, higher
    salaries of, 132
    social origins of, 203–4
national income, distribution of, 4
salary structures compared with German, 33–4,
    66
sorting factor in, 197
Fringe benefits, 29–30
Full employment, effect on collective bargaining, 7

'g' factor, 212–13
Galton, Francis, 308
General Classification Test, 209–10
Genes, pool, 216, 218
    of endogamous group, 169
Genetic endowment, effect on ability to work,
    229–305
Geneva, 83
Germany, before WW2,
    evidence cited from, 36, 73–4, 84
    regional differences in pay, 277
Germany, Eastern, 41
Germany, West
    evidence cited from, 32–6, 38, 73–4
    mobility, intergenerational, into upper non-
        manuals, 202–3
    national income, distribution of, 4
    salaries
        of chief executives, 132
        structure compared with French, 33–4, 66
Ghana, 105
Goldthorpe–Hope scale, 107–8
Grades, socio-economic, 16
Great Britain—see also England & Wales, United
        Kingdom
    age–earnings profiles in, 264, 266–7
    children, cohort b. 1958, 222, 230–1
    differentials in, 6, 69, 78
    earnings, individual, distribution of, forms of,
        287–9
        within occupations, 256–8
        of male manual workers, 1886–1974, 319
        Pareto constant in, 309
    education, rates of return on, 237
    élite in, 201–2
    local labour markets in, 279–81
    management in,
        salaries of, 132
        social origins of, 204–6
    National Servicemen, 222, 245, 248
    pay structure in, compared with
        Hungary, 39
        Leningrad, in engineering, 40
        Soviet-type economies, 42
        Yugoslavia, 58
    salaries in, relative to wages, 85
    school leavers, training of, 250–1
    wages, relative, in different industries, 90

white-collar occupations in, 5
    salary structure of, 60
Growth, economic, 9
Guayaki, 125
Guilds, 122
G/Wi bushmen, 124

Hexameters, Latin, example of, 143
Histadrut, 54, 55, 96
Home Counties, (England), 277
Hours of work, 30–1
Housing, effect of on children, 221–3
Human capital, 4, 236–45, 254
Hungary,
    evidence cited from, 42, 46, 64
    pay structure compared with G.B., 39
    sorting factor in, 197
Hunter-gatherers, 124–7, 141, 326

Iceland, 37
Ik, 125
Immobility between regions, 14
Incentives
    in China and Cuba, 51–4, 330
    in Czechoslovakia, 137
    in Kibbutzim, 55–6, 330
    in Soviet-type economies, 44, 325
    and supply of trained labour, 329
Income tax, 330
Incomes policy, effect of
    on collective bargaining, 7–8
    on differentials in the Netherlands, 92–3
India
    civil servants, relative pay of, 37–8
    education, rate of return on, 328
    ranking order of occupations by status, 105
Indianapolis, 199
Indians, N.W. American coast, 126
Indonesia, 105
Intelligentsia, Estonian, occupational values of
        children of, 247
International Labour Organization, 36
I.Q.
    age, decline of score with, 210–11
    Binet measure, 215–16
    children's, association with parents' class, 223–9,
        252
    education, association with
        extent of, 241
    environment, effect of, on, 218–20
    genotype, 9, 214–20, 227, 252–3
    intergenerational regression and dispersion, 228
    midparental, 227
    occupations
        ranking of average in, 208–14, 252, 323–4, 331
        thresholds of, 213–14, 240–53
    and school-leaving, 313
    T tests, 225
    of women, 148
Ireland, skill differential in, 63
Israel
    civil servants, relative pay of, 37
    education, rate of return on, 238
    egalitarianism in, 54–6

Italy
élite in, 200
pay structure, 32–3
skill differential, 63

Japan
dual labour market in, 130
mobility, intergenerational, into upper non-manuals, 201–2
status, inquiry into, 104–5
Jews, 315
jnd (just noticeable difference), 109
Job attributes, 113–14
Job Evaluation, 65, 109, 132, 294–8
factor-comparison method, 297
Just Wage, 121

Kalahari, 124
Kapteyn, 292
Kazan, 193
Kibbutzim, 55–6, 65, 66, 127, 143, 330
filling posts of responsibility in, 136–7
Kiruna, 98
Kumel' skii, 43

Labourers
in 1688, 1
in Ricardo, 3
Labour markets, local, 272–6
factors *before* and *within*, 322–4
Landowners
in 1688, 1
in Ricardo, 3
in contemporary U.K., 5
Language, class differences in, 320
Latin-American countries, 60, 70
Latvia, 36
Lawyers, in 1688, 1
Lenin, 44
Leningrad, 40, 42, 103, 104, 114
Life assurance policies, 5
Life chances, 181
Life-style
in Czechoslovakia, 138–40
occupations, linked with, 116, 141, 206
and station in life, 118
and status, 142, 326
in Weber, 111
Lifetime earnings, 30, 234–5, 328
Liu Shao-Chi, 53
L.O. (Sweden), policy of solidarity, 96–7
Lognormal form of distribution, 285–94
London, 259–277
allowance, 281
Low wages, 321
Luck, and individual earnings, 312, 316, 328

McCormick (International Harvester), wages in, 74–6
Managers
in airlines, as seen by pilots, 129
salaries
of chief executives, 132
Marris's theory of, 131–2
in matched pairs of French and German firms, 33

as ratio to product per head, 36
social origins of,
in France, 203–4
in Great Britain, 204–6
Manchester, 205, 242
Manual workers
margin for skill among, 63, 68–81
rank order of wages by occupation, 61–2
Mao, 52, 53, 140
Market forces
and changes in differentials, 98–100
demand, working of, 329–30
economist's view of, 10–17
and pay structure, 66–7, 100
supply of labour
restrictions on, 331
adjustments to extension of, 331–2
supply price, 329–30
as ultimate source of differences in pay, 141–2, 144, 324–6
and women's wages, 158
Markov chain, 305
Marxism
'bourgeois equity', 119
classes as seen in, 20, 66
common stuff of labour, 3
principle of pay under socialism, 3, 43
Massachusetts, 308
Mbuti, 125
Medical practitioners
earnings of, 38, 46
relative earnings in U.S.A., 83–4
status of, 119, 122, 128
Mental ability
'g' factor in, 212–13
in relation to social class and education, 208–55
tests of, *see* I.Q., General Classification Test, Progressive Matrices Test, Stanford–Binet
Merchants, in 1688, 1
Merton, R., 315
Mexico, 127
Michigan Survey of Consumer Finances, 94
Midlands (England), 259
Migration
into cities, 277
between U.S. regions, 281
Mikoyan, 50
Minimum, social, 120
Minimum sensible, 108, 307
Minimum wage
in Brazil, 70–1, 81
effects of raising, 81, 174–7, 178
Fair Labor Standards Act, 79, 81, 175
Minneapolis, 289
Minorities, discrimination against, 160–74
Mobility, intergenerational, 181–207, 233, 253, 323–4, 326
Monopsony, and discrimination, 146, 152
Moscow, 232

NAS–NRC sample, 316–17
National Child Development Study, 222, 229–31
National Health Service, 59, 119, 128
National Servicemen (G.B.), 222, 245, 248
National War Labor Board, 79

NBER-TH sample, 312, 314–15
Negroes, 79
Neolithic revolution, 127–41
Netherlands
  élite in, 201–2
  evidence cited from, 36, 38, 63
  incomes, variance of, 6
  intergenerational occupational mobility in, 194
  pay structure, effects of incomes policy, 92–3
New Earnings Survey, 40, 41, 42, 57, 58, 60, 91,
    101–3, 107, 110, 257, 260, 263, 264, 287
New Haven, Connecticut, 248
New York, 63, 70, 222
New Zealand
  differentials in, 36, 60, 63
  miners' earnings in, 64
  ranking order of occupations by status, 105
Nizhnii Tagil, 246
Non-completing groups, 16, 186
Normal distribution, 285
  generation of, 290–92
Norway, evidence cited from, 32, 38, 84
Nottingham, 220
Novosibirsk, 246

Oakland, California, 249
Orientation, occupational, of young people, 246, 323

Pakistan, civil servants in, relative pay of, 37–8
  craftmen's rates, 64
Paliyans, 125
Paraguay, 125
Parents, middle class and working class, and child
    upbringing, 229–32
Pareto distribution, 285–7, 305
  tail, 40, 133, 286–7, 305, 309–10
Paris, 277
Parodi scale, 35, 78
Path analysis, 311–12
Payment by results, 269–70
Pearson–Galton analogue apparatus, 290–2
Pensioners
  receipt of dividends by, 5
Pension schemes, 5
Peru, 127
Physicians, *see* Medical practitioners
Piece-work, 49, 50, 269–70
Pilots, airline, and status, 129
Playgroups, 254–5, 331
Poland
  differentials in, attitude towards, 65
  miners, earnings of, 64
  pay structure in, 36, 41, 42, 46, 51
  ranking order of occupations by status, 104–5
Portugal, 36
Power
  bargaining, 327–8, *and see* Trade Unions
  defined, 21
Prestige, 105, 111, 114
Professions
  age–earnings profiles in, 268–9
  earnings, relative, 59, 84
  in 18th century, 119
  formation of associations in U.S.A., 122
  and status, 128–9

Progressive matrices test, 209–10
Property income, 4, 5
Proportional effect, law of, 293
Protestants, 315
Puerto Rico, 194, 200, 203

Reading, achievement related to children's homes,
    232
Regions, differences of pay in, 277–81
Regression towards the mean, 227–8, 252
Responsibility, levels of, 271
Rolland, Romain, 117

San Francisco, 63
Scale of operations effect, 132, 271–2
Scarcity, as source of status, 143
Schooling, *see* Education
School leaving, age of, 245–6
Schoolmen, 121
Scotland
  children's test scores, 225
  evidence cited from, 210
  relative pay in, 277, 281
Scottish Mental Survey, 221
Segregation in employment
  of blacks, 163–6, 170
  of women, 152, 158
Self-employment, 4, 5
Sensitivity of jobs, 271–72
Shares in companies, 5
Siberia, 44, 280
Socialism
  and egalitarianism, 3, 6
  evolutionary and revolutionary, 3
  orientation of young people under, 246
  principle of pay under, 3, 43
  selection for higher education under, 232–3
  status under, 112
Socio-economic groups, 118
  see also Class, Status
Sorting factor, 195–6
South American countries, 60, 70
South Carolina, 277
Soviet-type economies
  differentials in, 67, 105, 325
  managers' salaries in, 133
  pay structure in, 38–51, 325
  power in, 21
  principle of pay in, 3, 325
Spain, evidence cited from, 36, 60, 64
Stalin, J., 44, 325
Standing, social, 18, 104, 115, 116
  see also Status
Stanford–Binet tests, 212
Station in life
  as basis of assigned income, 118–22, 141, 327
  rights attaching to, 18
  see also Status
Status
  as basis of pay in modern societies, 128–33
  categories of, Hall & Caradog Jones, 186
  and conventional valuation, 155
  and discrimination, 147–8, 153, 173, 177–80
  and job segregation, 165
  nature of, 111–18

Status (*continued*)
  occupational, Duncan's scale of, 224
  offsetting pay, 136–7, 141
  parents', and children's earnings, 315
  and pay differentials, 107–11
  and pay structure, 141–4, 326–7, 329
  ranking occupations by, 104–7
  and scarcity, 143
  under socialism, 112
  and station in life, 120
  stratification by, differing from ranking by pay, 137–41, 141, 326
  symbols of, 133
  of white-collared, 87–8
  and women's pay, 158
Steel plants
  differentials in U.S.S.R. and the West, 45
  job evaluation in, 132
Stockholm, 36, 63
Stratification
  as a human propensity, 122–8
  technocratic, 140
Style of life, *see* Life-style
Subsistence, 120
Sumer, 127
Supply, *see* Market Forces
Surgeons, status of, 119, 122
Sweden
  central framework agreement, 96–7
  élite in, 201
  evidence cited from, 38, 63, 64, 84
  graduates' relativities, 248
  solidarity policy, 96–7
Switzerland
  distribution of national income, 4
  evidence cited from, 38, 63, 64, 65

T tests, 225
Tatar Republic, 103, 104
Taunton, 277
de Tocqueville, 37
Tolowa, 126
Tolstoy, 117
Trade Boards, 153, 154, 175
Trades Union Congress, 150, 151
Trade unions
  and blacks, policy towards, 170
  British, effects of down to 1890, 7
  expansion of, in U.K. and U.S.A., 77
  in France and Germany, contrasted, 35
  and market imperfections, 273–4
  occupational differentials, effects on,
    in British engineering, 72–3
    of industrial unions in U.S.A., 77
  policy, 96–8, 99, 328
  pay structure, effects on reviewed, 327–8
  and regional differences, 281
  union/non-union differences of wages, 94, 281–82, 327–8
Training—*see also* Education
  ability to work, effect on, 299–305
  and class differences, 184, 186
  costs of, 15, 163, 329
  increase of, 4
  on the job, 250–1, 299

Troilus and Cressida, 123
Turkey, 104, 122
Twins, analysis of characteristics of, 215–20
  in NAS–NRC sample, 316–17

Ulysses, 123
United Kingdom—*see also* England & Wales, Great Britain
  civil service, pay structure of, 82
  evidence cited from, 32, 36, 38, 59, 64, 66, 71, 73–4, 84, 224, 238, 252, 254, 264–5, 275
  national income, distribution of, 4
  Navy and Army, test scores of entrants, 208–11
  professions in, in 18th century, 119
  real income in, 9
United States of America
  affinity, indexes of, 191
  Army Air Force, test scores in, 208–11, 218
  blacks, discrimination against, in, 160–74
  Census of Population, 257, 259, 311
  élite in, 201–2
  evidence cited from, 32–3, 35–6, 38, 59, 63, 64, 66, 71, 73–4, 84, 215, 218–19, 220, 222, 224, 237, 238, 239–40, 242, 244, 252, 253, 257–8, 267, 271–2, 273
  local labour markets in, 274–6
  mobility, intergenerational, in, 194, 197
  national income, distribution, of, 4
  occupations ranked
    by status, 104–5, 107
    by income and years of schooling, 190
  population growth in South and North, 70
  regional differences
    of earnings, 278–80
    in unionization, 281–2
  salaries in,
    of chief executives, 132
    relative to wages, 85
    structure of, 60
  trade unions in,
    extension of membership, 77
    wages, effect of on, 94–6
  worklife, expectancy of, in, 157
Upbringing of children
  ability to work, effect of on, 299–305, 323
  classes, difference between in, 220–3, 252–4
  style of, 8–9
U.S.S.R.
  intergenerational occupational mobility in, 192–3, 207
  pay structure in, 38–46, 49–51, 52, 64, 103–4
  regional differentiation of pay, 44, 280
  women, as compositors, 151
  working class in, structure of, 139–40

Valencia, 69
Value, labour theory of, 3
Victoria, Australia, 59
Vocational guidance, 246

Wage Census, 287
Wallace, Governor, 166
Warsaw, 106
Wealth, total net, of persons, 5
Weber–Fechner law, 109–10, 308

Western economies, pay structure in, 3, 31–8
White-collar occupations
  age–earnings profiles of, 266–7
  demand for, extension of, 86–7
  as proportion of labour force, 5
  salaries of,
    structures in G.B. and U.S.A., 59
    relative to wages of manual workers, 81–9
  in Soviet-type economies, 42, 46, 48, 65
  upbringing of children of, 220
  valuation of work in, 8
Willesden (London), 249
Wisconsin, 223–4

Women
  age–earnings profiles of, 264–7
  discrimination against, 148–60
  intergenerational occupational mobility of, 190–2
Working population, occupational distribution, 5
Worklife expectancy, of men and women, 157
Works Council, in Germany, 35
World Wars, effects on differentials, 77

Youth Employment Service, 246, 249
Yugoslavia
  evidence cited from, 36, 64
  pay structure, 56–8, 67

Index of Authors

Acton Society Trust, 204
Adam, J., 46–9
Adams, F. G., 241, 311
Ager, M. E., 24
Aitchison, J., 292–3, 305
Anderson, C. A., 211, 229
Arrow, K. J., 147, 170, 171, 172
Ashenfelter, O., 170, 282
Ashton, T. S., 69, 276
Atkinson, A. B., 311

Badenhoop, L. E., 176, 177
Baker, J. R., 216
Bechhofer, F., 139
Becker, G. S., 147, 170, 236, 241, 242
Bell, Phillip W., 76
Bendix, R., 222, 249
Benge, E. J., 297
Bergmann, B. R., 162, 166
Bergson, Abram, 44
Bernardo, R. M., 52, 54
Berndt, R. M., 125
Bernstein, B., 221
Bertaux, D., 202, 204
Betsey, C., 321
Bićanić, R., 56, 58
Bicchieri, M. G., 124
Bienefeld, M. A., 30
Birren, J. E., 211
Blain, A. N. J., 129
Blanchemanche, M., 263
Blau, P. M., 189, 190, 199, 200, 202, 222, 231, 311–12
Blaug, M., 238, 241, 242, 331
Blinder, A. S., 150, 164, 165, 167, 168
Bloch, J. W., 278
Bloom, B. S., 220
Blum, F. H., 176
Board of Inland Revenue, 6
Bowles, S., 229
Bowley, A. L., 85, 91, 287–8, 289
Bowman, M. J., 211, 229
B.P.P., 119
Bronfenbrenner, U., 220, 229
Brown, J. A. C., 292–3, 305
Brown, J. C., 211, 229
Brown, W., 76, 273
Browne, M. H., 4
Bruner, J. S., 221
Brus, W., 21, 65
Bry, G., 277
Buckley, J. E., 273
Burk, S. L. H., 297
Burns, R. K., 85, 86
Burt, C., 127, 214

Butcher, H. J., 211, 218
Butler, N., 222, 230, 231
Byrns, R., 223

Cable, J. R., 128
Cairnes, J. E., 16
Caradog Jones, D., 186
Carol, A., 240
Carter, C. O., 227
Carter, M., 246
Chalmers, Sir George, 1
Champernowne, D. G., 20, 305
Chapman, Janet, 38, 39, 43–6, 286
Chiu, J. S. Y., 132
Clack, J. R., 120
Clark, Colin, 1, 2
Clark, D. G., 205
Clastres, P., 125
Clay, H., 6
Clements, R. V., 205, 242
Coleman, J. S., 161
Coleman, S., 162, 163, 167, 168
Copeman, G. H., 205
Craig, C., 30
Creedy, J., 270
Crookes, T. G., 213

Dahrendorf, R., 181
Damas, D., 125
Daubigny, J. P., 33, 35, 78, 273
David, M., 241
Davie, R., 222, 230, 231
Deane, P., 91
Dept. of Employment, 107, 108, 257, 260, 262, 286, 288
Dept. of Employment and Productivity, 280
Devore, I., 124
Dewey, D., 165, 170
Dodge, N. T., 246
Doeringer, P. B., 34, 130, 134, 250, 273, 321
Dore, R., 130
Douglas, J. W. B., 221, 223, 225, 231, 232, 233, 248
Douty, H. M., 70, 77, 81, 96, 273, 278
Dumont, L., 123
Duncan, B., 164, 168, 223, 231, 245
Duncan, O. D., 114, 164, 165, 167, 168, 189, 190, 199, 200, 202, 222, 223, 224, 231, 245, 311, 311–12

Edgeworth, F. Y., 287–88
Edwards, A. M., 116–17, 211
Elbing, A. O., 132
Engen, T., 109
Erickson, C., 205

Fallers, Lloyd, A., 122
Faulds, G. A., 210
Featherman, D. L., 164, 168, 223, 245
Fein, R., 166
Fillipov, F. R., 232
Fischlowitz, E., 70
Fisher, A. G. B., 36
Fishlow, A., 71
Fizaine, F., 273
Flanagan, R. J., 172
Fogarty, M. P., 121
Fox, A. (U.K.), 22
Fox, A. (U.S.A.), 51
Fox, T., 201
Fraser, E., 221
Frayn, M., 122
Freeman, F. N., 215
French, J. G., 213
Friedman, M., 84, 262
Fuchs, V. R., 276–7

Galenson, W., 51
Gardner, P. M., 125
Gardner Clark M., 39, 44, 45
Gaw, F., 214
Gellner, E., 47
General Register Office, 185
Gibson, J., 228
Ginsberg, M., 199
Gintis, H., 314
Girod, R., 83
Glass, D. V., 186, 187, 188, 199
Goldstein, H., 222, 230, 231
Goldthorpe, J. H., 21, 22, 104, 106, 107, 108, 113, 114, 139
Gordon, L. A., 139
Gray, E. M., 156
Gunter, H., 70
Gupta, S., 128

Haber, S., 119, 122
Hagen, E., 314
Hall, J., 186, 187, 188, 199
Hall, R. H., 131
Halsey, A. H., 217–18
Hammermesh, D. S., 95
Hancock, K., 78
Hansen, W. Lee, 237
Harrell, M. S. & T. W., 208, 209, 210
Harris, D., 129
Hart, P. E., 265
Hatt, P. K., 115
Havighurst, R. J., 233
Hay, E. N., 297
Hazelrigg, L. E., 197, 198, 202
Heer, C., 70
Helm, J., 125
Henderson, D., 221
Henmon, V. A. C., 223
Hill, G. B., 247
Hill, J. M. M., 246
Hill, T. P., 311
Himmelweit, H. T., 208, 209
Hinde, R. A., 126
Hodge, R. W., 105, 112, 114

Hoffmann, Charles, 53
Holzinger, K. J., 215
Hope, K., 104, 106, 107, 108, 113, 114
Hopkins, S. V., 6, 68, 69, 91
Howe, Christopher, 53, 271, 279
Hunt, E. H., 277, 279, 280
Husèn, T., 241
Hyman, H. H., 233, 247

I.L.O., 56
Inkeles, A., 105, 192
International Metal Workers Federation, 70

Jackson, B., 230, 231, 233
Jefferys, Margot, 249
Jencks, C., 161, 259, 312
Jensen, A. R., 169, 217
Johnson, G. E., 95, 282
Jones, D. J., 24

Kalecki, M., 305
Kanninen, T. P., 273, 276, 282
Karpoff, P., 242, 314
Keat, P. G., 79, 83
Kelsall, R. K., 206
Kendall, M. G., 290
King, Gregory, 1, 2
Kirsch, L. J., 38, 50, 51
Klopov, E. V., 139
Knowles, K. G. J. C., 76
Kosters, M., 175, 176
Krueger, A. O., 169
Kuznets, S., 4, 84
Kýn, O., 47

Lamale, H. H., 276
Landes, W. M., 171
Lane, D., 39
Lawrence, E. M., 218
Layard, P. R. G., 24, 242, 243
Lebergott, S., 64
Lee, R. B., 124
Leiserson, M. W., 277
Lenin, V., 44
Lerner, S. W., 128, 155
Lester, R. A., 174, 273, 274, 275
Lewis, H. Gregg, 94, 282
Lindbeck, Assar, 31
Lipset, S. M., 222, 249
Liss, L. F., 246
Lockwood, D., 139
Long, C. D., 71
Low, J. O., 116
Lowndes, G. A. N., 39
Lucas, R. E. B., 242, 243, 244, 332
Lydall, H. F., 132, 133, 259, 274, 285, 286, 289, 298, 305, 309, 310, 312
Lyle, J. R., 166

McAuley, Mary, 135
Macgregor, D. H., 154
McGuire, J. W., 132
Machonin, P., 47, 138–9
Mackay, D. I., 273
Maizels, J., 246

Malm, F. T., 249
Mandelbrot, B., 310
Mangum, G. L., 250
Marquand, J., 155
Marris, Robin, 131
Marsden, D., 231, 233
Marshall, Alfred, 7, 14, 17, 147, 307, 320
Marshall, R., 165
Martin, F. M., 233
Marx, K., 3, 119
Maurice, M., 34
Mayer, T., 132, 308, 310
Meade, J. E., 298
Mehnert, Klaus, 53, 156
Meidner, R., 97, 98
Merton, R., 315
Michal, J. M., 42, 43, 46
Miljus, R. C., 248
Mill, J. S., 16, 66, 80, 86, 87, 92, 128, 151
Miller, H. P., 258
Miller, S. M., 193, 194, 200, 201, 242
Mincer, Jacob, 163, 236, 241, 250, 262, 267
Ministry of Education, 222, 245
Ministry of Labour, 175, 275
Ministry of Technology, 270, 271
Mitchell, B. R., 91
Montgomery, G. W. G., 214
Moore, H. L., 308
Moore, T. G., 176
Morecka, Z., 51
Morgan, J., 241, 311
Morris, V., 237, 267–8
Muntz, E. E., 79

National Board for Prices & Incomes, 81, 321
Nelson, V. I., 229
Newman, H. H., 215
Newson, J. & E., 220
Nisbet, J. 221
N.O.R.C., 113–14
Nove, A., 41, 49

Ober, H., 75, 79
O'Boyle, E. J., 158
O.E.C.D., 64
Office of Population Censuses and Surveys, 28, 106, 108
O'Herlihy, C. St. J., 175
Oxnam, D. W., 78
Ozanne, R., 71, 74–6

Palekar, S. A., 88, 128
Parnes, H. S., 248
Parry, S., 240
Parsons, Talcott, 19, 123
Pascal, A. H., 166
Passagez, M., 190, 192, 204, 234
Peitchinis, S. G., 73
Pen, J., 6, 19, 308
PEP, 8
Perlman, R., 79–80
Perrucci, C. C. & Perrucci, R., 311
Peterson, J. M., 175
Phelps, E. S., 157
Phelps Brown, E. H., 4, 68, 69, 91, 153, 275, 307

Piore, M. J., 34, 130, 134, 250, 273
Platt, J., 139
Polanyi, G., 151
Praderie, M., 190, 192, 204, 234
Prais, S. J., 188, 189
Pryor, F. L., 286
Psacharopoulos, G., 84, 243, 311, 313

Rabkin, L. Y., 55
Rackstraw, S. J., 221
Rapping, L. A., 166
Rathbone, E., 158
Raven, C., 210
Reder, M. W., 75, 120, 132, 179, 271, 308
Rees, A., 273, 275
Reiss, A. J., 107, 115
Reissmann, F., 242
Reynolds, L. G., 80, 248, 273
Ricardo, D., 3
Richman, B. M., 52
Rilett, J. W., 141
Rishøj, T., 199
Robertson, D. J., 76
Robinson, D., 273
Robinson, W. P., 221
Rogers, H. H., 233
Rogoff, N., 199
Rosen, S., 95
Ross, Sir David, 153
Ross, J. M., 231, 233, 248
Rossi, P. H., 105, 112, 114
Roustang, G., 267
Routh, Guy, 5, 78, 82, 83, 85
Rowe, J. W. F., 72, 134, 135
Royal Commission on the Distribution of Income and Wealth, 5, 6, 31, 36, 269, 286, 287, 305, 309, 319
Royal Commission on Doctors' and Dentists' Remuneration, 59, 268
Royal Commission on Equal Pay, 150, 153, 156, 157
Rutherford, R. S. G., 305
Rutkevich, M. N., 232

Sadler, P., 128
Salais, R., 190, 192, 204, 234
Samuels, N., 176, 177
Sanborn, H., 152, 156
Sarapata, A., 105, 106
Sargan, J. D., 24
Sawhill, I. V., 152, 157
Schlosberg, H., 109
Schmidt, R. M., 248
Schultz, G. P., 273, 275
Schultz, T. W., 236
Scitovsky, T., 36, 38, 82–3
Scott, W. H., 205
Segal, Lord, 128
Sellier, F., 34
Shakespeare, W., 123
Shatil, J. E., 56
Shister, J., 248, 273
Shkaratan, O. I., 103, 104, 112, 193, 232
Shkurko, A. S., 50
Silberbauer, G. G., 124
Šik, Ota, 44

Silvestre, J.-J., 33, 34, 75, 273
Simon, H. A., 132, 309
Simpson, H. R., 231, 233, 248
Sisson, K., 76, 273
Skeels, H. M., 218
Skodak, M., 218
Slichter, S. H., 273
Slipje, A. R. D. van, 312
Smith, Adam, 1, 70, 118, 119, 136, 143, 235, 239, 277
Smith, J. H., 155
Smith, V. G., 241
Spielman, W., 214
Spiro, M. E., 55, 56
Spitz, R. S., 248
Stacey, B. G., 204, 205
Staehle, H., 288, 310
Stafford, F. P., 95
Stevens, S. S., 109
Steward, U. H., 124
Stieber, J., 132
Stotz, M. S., 276
Strmiska, Z., 105, 137, 140
Sussman, Z., 54, 55
Suttles, W., 126
Svalastoga, K., 107, 199

Taft, C. H., 80
Taira, K., 70
Tannenbaum, A. S., 55, 58, 137
Taubman, P., 241, 242, 244, 312, 315, 316
Taussig, F. W., 16
Tawney, R. H., 3
Taylor, D. P., 173
Tersmeden, C. R., 98
Thatcher, A. R., 260, 262, 287, 305
Thorndike, R., 314
Thorndike, R. L., 232, 314
Thurow, L. C., 242, 243, 244, 332
Tinbergen, J., 312
Tiryakian, E. A., 107
Titma, M. Kh., 247
Tocqueville, A. de, 37
Tough, Joan, 230
Treiman, D. J., 105, 112, 114
Troyat, H., 117
Tuck, R. H., 132
Tuddenham, R. D., 212
Turnbull, C. M., 125
Turnbull, P., 150, 159

Turner, H. A., 70, 77, 88, 96
Tyler, L. E., 208, 219, 226

U.N., E.C.E., 32, 39, 50
U.S. Bureau of the Census, 234, 235,242
U.S. Dept. of Health, Education and Welfare, 224
U.S. Dept. of Labor, 28, 60, 176, 271–2, 273, 275, 278, 288
U.S. Federal Reserve System, Board of Governors, 238
U.S. Govt., 16th Census, 116

Vavakova, B., 105, 137, 140
Vernon, P. E., 208, 209, 210, 212, 213
Vincent, D. F., 211
Vodzinskaia, V. V., 114

Wachtel, H. M., 321
Wales, T. J., 241, 242, 244, 312, 315
War Cabinet, 150, 153, 156
Warner, W. Lloyd, 116
Webb, S. & B., 120
Weber, Max, 111, 112, 117, 118, 185
Wedderburn, D., 30
Weisbrod, B. A., 242, 314
Weiss, L., 95
Weisskoff, F. B., 152
Welch, F., 175, 176
Wesolowski, W., 105, 106
Whitfield, J. W., 208, 209
Whyte, M. K., 140
Wijk, J. van der, 308
Wilkinson, B. W., 240
Williams, G., 150, 159
Wise, D. A., 241, 242
Witteveen, H. J., 93
Wohlstetter, A., 162, 163, 167, 168
Wolff, P. de, 93, 312
Wolfle, D., 241
Wood, G. H., 91
Wood, J. B., 151
Woodworth, R. S., 109, 219
Wootton, B., 19, 128

Yanowich, M., 246
Youmans, K. C., 95
Young, M., 228
Yule, G. U., 290

Ziderman, A., 237, 267–8